The Tragic and the Ecstatic

The Tragic and the Ecstatic

The Musical Revolution of Wagner's *Tristan and Isolde*

Eric Chafe

UNIVERSITY PRESS

Oxford University Press, Inc., publishes works that further
Oxford University's objective of excellence
in research, scholarship, and education.

Oxford   New York
Auckland   Cape Town   Dar es Salaam   Hong Kong   Karachi
Kuala Lumpur   Madrid   Melbourne   Mexico City   Nairobi
New Delhi   Shanghai   Taipei   Toronto

With offices in
Argentina   Austria   Brazil   Chile   Czech Republic   France   Greece
Guatemala   Hungary   Italy   Japan   Poland   Portugal   Singapore
South Korea   Switzerland   Thailand   Turkey   Ukraine   Vietnam

Copyright © 2005 by Oxford University Press, Inc.

Published by Oxford University Press, Inc.
198 Madison Avenue, New York, New York 10016

www.oup.com

First issued as an Oxford University Press paperback 2008

Oxford is a registered trademark of Oxford University Press

Library of Congress Cataloging-in-Publication Data
Chafe, Eric Thomas, 1946–
The tragic and the ecstatic : the musical revolution of Wagner's *Tristan and Isolde* / Eric Chafe.
p.   cm.
Includes bibliographical references and index.
ISBN 978-0-19-534300-7
1. Wagner, Richard, 1813–1883. Tristan und Isolde. 2. Schopenhauer, Arthur, 1788–1860—
Views on music. 3. Music—Philosophy and aesthetics. I. Title.
ML410.W14C43 2004
782.1—dc22   2004007871

Printed in the United States of America
on acid-free paper

To my friend and colleague Martin Boykan

Acknowledgments

FOR MANY YEARS I have felt the need for a study of *Tristan and Isolde* that would do justice to the influence of Arthur Schopenhauer's philosophy on its musico-dramatic character and design. Many studies have dealt with the influence of Schopenhauer on Wagner in a general way, whereas others have made it their central theme. Some of these studies, most notably in English Bryan Magee's *The Philosophy of Schopenhauer* and his *Wagner and Philosophy,* have greatly illuminated our understanding of the subject from the standpoint of Wagner's biography, his philosophical interests in general, and the poetic text of *Tristan* and the operas that followed it in Wagner's oeuvre. Bridging the gap between those investigations and the composition of the music has proven less tractable, however. I hope with this study to carry the torch further, even to lay a basis for understanding the processes by which extramusical ideas, philosophical and other, became the material of musical designs for Wagner.

I have been helped in this undertaking by many persons. Some have given me concrete assistance in the preparation of the manuscript or acquisition of source material. Among them are Ray Komow, Heather Shaw-Philips, Joseph Morgan, Rachel Cama, Annegret Klaua, Michael Hamad, Rick Beaudoin, Silvio dos Santos, and Katarina Marković-Stokes. A few persons have given selflessly of their valuable time reading drafts of part or all of this book and making suggestions, most of which I have followed: William Youngren, Bonnie Gordon, and Elizabeth Joyce. Mr. Günther Fischer and the staff of the Richard-Wagner Archive in Bayreuth gave every possible assistance to my study of the original sources on the spot and through photocopies. Traate Marshall very kindly read over my translations from Hermann Kurtz's edition of the Gottfried von Strassburg Tristan poem and made suggestions, all of which I followed. And the Brandeis University Mazer Fund for Faculty Research supported this project with grants that enabled me to meet some of the expenses.

I gratefully acknowledge permission from Penguin Books to cite excerpts from A. T. Hatto's magnificent English prose translation of Gottfried von Strassburg's *Tristan*. Schott and Co., London, gave me permission to use a modified version of the 1906 London edition of Karl Klindworth's piano-vocal score of *Tristan* for many of the musical examples (piano-vocal reduction by Karl Klindworth © Schott). I have made corrections and adjustments to Klindworth's score where it seemed necessary, as well as removing obvious pianistic elements. And the Richard Wagner Archive in Bayreuth gave me permission to reproduce the five photographs from Wagner's compositional draft in the appendix. I am grateful to Gertrude Föttinger for her assistance in this regard.

Among those who have helped me out in very substantive ways relating to the content of the book itself, one person stands out, both for his depth of understanding of *Tristan,* Wagner, and music in general, and for the patience and generosity in listening and becoming involved in someone's else's work that very few persons are willing to give. I am speaking of my friend and colleague of more than twenty years, composer Martin Boykan, who shared his profound musical understanding on occasions vastly too numerous even to remember. Marty has taught composition and analysis at Brandeis for well over forty years now; and there are a great many musicians across the country who will know what I am talking about. I have been unusually lucky to have such a resource close at hand, and dedicating this book to him is the best way I can think of to thank him.

Contents

The Tragic and the Ecstatic

Introduction

IF THERE IS ONE SINGLE QUALITY of Wagner's *Tristan und Isolde* that underlies its fascination for musicians, culture historians, and a substantial segment of the opera-loving public from its own time to the present, it is that, more than any other work in the Western musical canon, *Tristan* embodies a vision of human existence in which the tragic and the ecstatic are interwoven, a vision encompassing much that had formerly been the province of religion and that its author now proclaimed the domain of art. That vision drew Wagner to study myth and philosophy, literature and Eastern religion; and it enabled him to recognize qualities in Gottfried von Strassburg's *Tristan und Isolt* that reached across the centuries, bridging the two greatest eras in all of German literature. Once realized in the unique sound world that forms the Tristan style, it communicated itself to all around him, most notably the young Friedrich Nietzsche, and it spread rapidly through Europe and the Western world. By now its influence, direct or indirect, is incalculable.

Wagner's vision is clear from the earliest reference to his plan to compose an opera on *Tristan and Isolde*, a letter to Franz Liszt of December 1854. This letter is also Wagner's first announcement of his discovery of Schopenhauer:

> I have now become exclusively preoccupied with a man who—albeit only in literary form—has entered my lonely life like a gift from heaven. It is *Arthur Schopenhauer,* the greatest philosopher since *Kant,* whose ideas—as he himself puts it—he is the first person to think through to their logical conclusion. . . . His principal idea, the final denial of the will to live, is of terrible seriousness, but it is uniquely redeeming. . . . I have . . . found a sedative which has finally helped me to sleep at night; it is the sincere and heartfelt yearning for death: total unconsciousness, complete annihilation, the end of all dreams—the only redemption!—. . . .
>
> But since I have never in my life enjoyed the true happiness of love, I intend to erect a further monument to this most beautiful of dreams, a monument in which this love will be properly sated from beginning to end: I have planned in my head a *Tristan and*

Isolde, the simplest, but most full-blooded musical conception; with the "black flag" which flutters at the end, I shall then cover myself over, in order—to die.—[1]

A decade later Wagner maintained that he had always viewed Gottfried's Tristan poem (which he had known since the 1840s) as innately tragic, adding, "it was no doubt in part the earnest frame of mind produced by Schopenhauer, now demanding some rapturous expression of its fundamental traits, which gave me the idea for a *Tristan und Isolde.*"[2] Those fundamental traits were ones that Wagner had no trouble extending to Gottfried's Tristan poem: the elevation of desire to the level of an inescapable force, full of metaphysical overtones, a tragic perspective not just on Gottfried's protagonists but on existence generally, and a quasi-religious dissatisfaction with the world offset by longing for redemption. A further connection is evident from Wagner's intention to depict love "properly sated from beginning to end" in the "most full-blooded musical conception." Not only was Gottfried's Tristan a musician, but his very identity as knight and lover was inseparable from music; thus, the fullest and most symbolic consummation of Tristan and Isolde's love, the famous "lovers' cave scene," became, as W. T. H. Jackson argues compellingly, an expression of the inner harmony of music, mirroring Gottfried's conception of ideal love, encompassing joy and sorrow.[3] Its potential resonance with Schopenhauer's view of music as the highest among the arts, "a copy of the Will," could hardly have escaped Wagner. For, although he does not mention Schopenhauer's metaphysics of music in his letter, the third act of *Tristan,* which he described as the "point of departure" for the mood of the whole, and whose striking antitheses are evident in his letter, centers the question of Tristan's identity around music, the "ancient tune" (*alte Weise*) that leads him to a process of self-examination and ultimately self-understanding as vehicle of desire, fated for tragedy. This knowledge enables the process of redemption Wagner describes.

Wagner may have had much of this in mind in 1854. Nevertheless, he did not begin the composition of *Tristan* until nearly three years had passed (fall 1857), during which time he wrote most of the first three operas of the Ring, all the while reading and rereading Schopenhauer incessantly. At some point, struck by the "innate tragedy" of Gottfried's *Tristan,* and "determined to cut away all the inessentials from this central theme," he "jotted down the contents of the three acts in which [he] envisaged concentrating the material when [he] came to work it out at some future date."[4] Eventually, what he called his "secret desire" to set *Tristan* grew more intense, undoubtedly the result of his viewing Gottfried's poem as the vehicle by which to convey the Schopenhauerian frame of mind, with its simultaneously pessimistic and rapturous qualities. By the summer of 1857, it had become irresistible. Wagner broke off composition of the Ring after the second act of *Siegfried* and gave himself over entirely to *Tristan,* which he then composed from prose draft to orchestral full score in less than two years, a record time for him and testimony to the intensity of his early vision.

That vision was, very substantially, a musical one. Whatever Wagner had produced in the way of the dramatic scenario of *Tristan* by March 1857, he nevertheless described *Tristan* at that time as "still only music."[5] No contradiction is involved. Wagner had produced musical sketches for *Tristan* in 1856, if not earlier; and, simultaneously, the musical language of the Ring had evolved to the point where by early 1857 it exhibited many of the traits of the *Tristan* style. This is especially true of the second act of *Siegfried*, the breaking-off point. Wagner's "secret desire" had stolen into the music of the Ring. In addition, Wagner had just produced the essay "On Franz Liszt's Symphonic Poems," in which he first made public his new Schopenhauerian aesthetics, in many respects a turnaround from the Feuerbach-influenced aesthetics that presided over the birth of the Ring. Whereas Wagner's theoretical writings of the late 1840s and early 1850s mark one stage on the road to his mature style, the discovery of Schopenhauer was an equally important one, placing those theories in perspective. *Tristan* was the first work to fully embody the great leap forward, the work in which Wagner felt he had gone "far beyond" his "system" (the above-mentioned writings). In this it not only completed the tendency of Wagner's myth-based poetic texts toward the condition of music itself, a condition manifested in the dominance of inner "psychic" necessity over external, plot-oriented events; it fulfilled Schopenhauer's belief that music was metaphysically prior to the drama, providing the "inside" of any dramatic events with which it might be associated.[6]

By spring 1857, in part under the influence of Schopenhauer, Wagner had imagined a new sound, one uniquely appropriate to *Tristan*, not the Ring. In dramatic terms, the difference is sweeping. Whereas for Siegfried, music is bound up with nature and the heroic (his horn call, the song of the woodbird, and the "forest murmurs"), for Tristan it is the key to the tragic character of existence, the *denial* of nature. In act 3 it emerges as such in the events of the story. With the aid of music, the *alte Weise* that he associates with his early life, its tragic and ecstatic events, Tristan comes to understand the intermingling of desire and tragedy in his life—his fate, embodied in his very name. And, analogous to the deep-rooted significance of the *alte Weise* for Tristan, the discovery of Schopenhauer was for Wagner himself the outcome of a long-standing search for the "depths" of music and the meaning of the philosophical "absolute" (which Wagner associated with music) in a string of authors that preceded his conversion to Schopenhauer. *Tristan* was the fulfillment of that search.

One of the first goals of this book, therefore, is to outline the connection between music and philosophy in Wagner's mind, describing how it led him to Schopenhauer and how, in turn, the discovery of Schopenhauer conditioned his reading of Gottfried von Strassburg's Tristan poem and the design of *Tristan*. In the poetic text of *Tristan*, Wagner translated several of Gottfried's most prominent themes into Schopenhauerian terms, above all the medieval concept of Minne, which took on attributes of Schopenhauer's conception of desire, and the idea of *Liebestod* that flowed from it. Nevertheless, the interaction of Gottfried and Schopenhauer in the composition of *Tristan* was not purely unidirectional. For while composing the love scene of act 2 Wagner announced to Mathilde Wesendonck that he had found a way of expanding or amending Schopenhauer on the basis of his own understanding of the metaphysics of sexual love. And the "amendment," when we examine it closely, turns out to be bound up with Gottfried's Minne, the primary agency in the lovers' progression from desire to transfiguration.

Perhaps the most vivid quality in Wagner's 1854 letter to Liszt is the sense that he perceived tragedy, desire, and religious ecstasy as all of a piece. Love, "this most beautiful of dreams," was to be the subject matter of his new opera, in which it would be "properly sated from beginning to end"; but, at the same time, the love Wagner had in mind was a manifestation of the dream of existence generally, echoing the view put forth from the outset of Schopenhauer's treatise, where we read that "a reality that is . . . an object in itself . . . is the phantom of a dream, and its acceptance is an *ignis fatuus* in philosophy."[7] For both Schopenhauer and Wagner tragedy revealed the deepest truths of existence, especially its fundamental illusoriness: Schopenhauer proclaimed that "at the moment of the tragic catastrophe, we become convinced more clearly than ever that life is a bad dream from which we have to awake," and Wagner identified *Tristan* as his "most tragic subject, since in it nature is hindered in its highest work"—that is, human consciousness.[8] The opposition between tragedy and nature (to be taken up in chapter 7) is an important key to the dramatic structure of *Tristan*. In this light, Wagner's letter reveals that *Tristan* would celebrate physical passion—the dream of love—to the utmost, while at the same time adhering to Schopenhauer's conception of desire as the force behind unfulfilled human striving, dissatisfaction, and tragedy. The black flag, symbol of tragedy in the medieval *Tristan* legend, was equivalent to "total unconsciousness, complete annihilation, the end of all dreams." Tragedy went hand in hand with a deeply pessimistic view of existence; but, at the same time, it admitted the possibility of ecstatic transcendence of the world. Love was the agency of that transcendence.

In this sense *Tristan* embodies a twofold perspective or "twofold truth," centered simultaneously on the physical and the metaphysical, as Carl Dahlhaus has said of Wagner's post-Schopenhauer aesthetics.[9] Love, embodying both the biological species instinct and the search for transcendence, bonds the two aspects of the dream of existence. In the grip of the consciousness of love that follows their drinking the love potion in act 1, Tristan and Isolde celebrate their freedom from conventional morality (the code of chivalry that constituted the moral framework of courtly society in Gottfried's time), reducing it to the level of a dream: in an ecstatic state they sing "Was träumte mir von Tristan's Ehre? Was träumte mir von Isolde's Schmach?" (What did I dream of Tristan's honor? What did I dream of Isolde's shame?). In the second-act love scene, Wagner's equivalent of Gottfried's celebrated "lovers' cave" scene, where Minne rules all, they proclaim that, having internalized the light of the sun, they themselves have become the world ("Barg im Busen uns sich die Sonne . . . selbst dann bin ich die Welt"), after which Brangaene pronounces that they are now under the spell of the dream of love ("Wem der Traum der Liebe lacht").[10] And in the final duet of the scene the lovers associate that dream with the blissful merging of love, night and death, from which they long never to awaken ("vom Erwachens Not befreit . . . übersel'ges Träumen").

After their discovery *in flagrante delecto*, however, the dream of love is broken and the lovers' reawakening to the dream of existence takes on a more deeply pessimistic quality: Tristan describes not merely courtly ideals but the world itself, as embodied in King Mark and his party as mere daylight phantoms, "morning dreams," empty and unreal ("Tagsgespenster! Morgenträume! Täuschend und wüst!"). From that point on, Tristan's longing centers on his search for the end of the dream of existence, a longing in conflict with the presence of desire and the will-to-life within him. The climax comes in act 3, at the central pivot of the act, with Tristan's curse of the love potion, of desire itself, and his own existence as the agency of desire, on completion of which he falls into a state of unconsciousness so deep that Kurvenal takes him for dead. Now that it finally appears that Tristan has attained his end, Kurvenal, speaking virtually to the audience, proclaims Schopenhauer's view of love as "the world's dearest delusion" ("der Welt holdester Wahn"), recalling Wagner's characterization of love as "this most beautiful of dreams." This is the turning point in Tristan's "conversion" to the metaphysical. What follows is his reawakening in a transformed state, with a blissful vision of Isolde that corresponds to what Wagner, echoing Schopenhauer's dream theories, referred to as "clairvoyant dreaming." The dream is now no longer limited to the night as the antithesis of the day. As Wagner described Shakespeare in 1870, Tristan is the clairvoyant who dreams on in waking—that is, who carries his metaphysical intuition from the night of unconsciousness into the daylight, or physical world.[11]

From this point on, events move swiftly toward Tristan's death, which coincides with Isolde's coming to "heal" him, the realization of his vision. The healing, of course, is from life itself; the third and final lovers' meeting is simultaneously Tristan's death, completing the cycle of desire, as the music makes abundantly clear. This is Schopenhauer's tragic catastrophe, Tristan's awakening from the dream of life. In the prose draft of the love scene, Tristan, on hearing Brangaene's warning, had cried: "wer ruft dort zum Erwachen?" (who calls there to awaken?); and Isolde had answered "der Tod!" (death!). Now, after his death, Isolde experiences her own conversion to the metaphysical, hearing rather than seeing Tristan awaken once more ("Horch! Er wacht!") and collapsing unconscious on his dead body. After her revival, now oblivious to the events on stage, the *Liebestod* embodies first her seeing Tristan reawaken to the metaphysical, then her hearing a *Weise* that emanates from him but is inaudible to the others, and finally her succumbing to the waves of metaphysical sound that surround her. The echo of desire at the final cadence projects the union of unconsciousness and transfiguration as "the end of all dreams—the only redemption."

Thus, the dreams of love and existence, at first opposite to one another, are revealed as one. Passing beyond desire to rejection of the will-to-life is the fulfillment of the dream of love, which has become a wholly metaphysical conception. Wagner might well have had all this in mind when he wrote to Liszt in 1854. But it nevertheless took on a more concrete character at the time of his writing the second-act love scene (December 1858), at which time he came to the realization that his thinking on the metaphysics of sexual love differed in important respects from that of Schopenhauer, while remaining within the philosopher's basic ideological framework. In an essay entitled "On the Metaphysics of Sexual Love," Schopenhauer had proclaimed, in a manner that anticipates modern evolutionary biology, the view of love as a delusion (*Wahn*), the product of what he called the species will (*Gattungswille*), whose purpose was solely procreation.[12] Not only was romantic love a deception, cloaking the true meaning of human sexuality, but even sexual love and its raison d'etre, the continuance of the species, were in the service of a still more universal metaphysical principle, that of Will, in the broadest sense. In that context, even the species instinct was a delusion, the agency of the metaphysical Will's need for its own objectification, embodied in the delusion of existence, the world itself. Human brain functions were wired, so to speak, for representation, that is, to create a world of appearances that would satisfy the blind necessity of the metaphysical Will for this objectification. And desire was the motive force behind continuance of the species and the world of representation. The world, therefore, became meaningless in itself, no more than a dream; and romantic love—behind which lay the necessity of the species will—was one of the chief means by which the delusion was perpetuated. This is the meaning behind Kurvenal's pronouncing love "der Welt holdester Wahn." From the purely Schopenhauerian perspective, therefore, the subject matter of *Tristan* is not simply love but the *Wahn* of love, as Tristan cries at one point in the prose draft ("Isolde— ach! Isolde selbst wird mir ein Wahn!").

For many lovers of the work, however, this view of *Tristan* is inadequate or even erroneous, a betrayal of its true meaning. For them, *Tristan* centers on erotic love in all its pain, delight, and yearning for transcendence, and the idea of the denial of the will, so prominent in Schopenhauer and in Wagner's own writings, is merely, as Thomas Mann said, "the moral-intellectual component of Schopenhauer's philoso- phy, which is of little essential significance."[13] To the extent that the work is indebted to Schopenhauer, it mirrors only his doctrine of the will, which is very prominent in the metaphysics of music. In this spirit, some authors, such as Denis de Rougement, have denied the relevance of Schopenhauer to Wagner's work altogether.[14]

This viewpoint fits well with Wagner's early intention that *Tristan* depict love "properly sated from beginning to end" in "the most full-blooded musical concep- tion," but it passes over what he described in the same letter as Schopenhauer's prin- cipal idea. It should make us suspicious, and is, in fact, very difficult to sustain in light of Wagner's countless proclamations of his indebtedness to Schopenhauer and his virtually recasting his aesthetics in a Schopenhauerian mold from at least 1857 on. As we will see, Wagner certainly believed that he had discovered a path to the de- nial of the will through sexual love. I would suggest, therefore, that, perceiving the conflict between the ideal of romantic love with its metaphysical overtones and Schopenhauer's demythologizing of love in terms of desire and the biological in- stinct, he set out to give voice to both in *Tristan*. At an early point in his conception of *Tristan*, Wagner said that it would deal with "love as fearful torment," whereas the Buddhist opera he was simultaneously thinking about, *Die Sieger* (The Victors), would take up love's other side, "supreme redemption." Ultimately, both perspec- tives were embodied in *Tristan*, their dramatic focus being Tristan's curse, relapse, reawakening, and clairvoyant vision in act 3. The double perspective on *Tristan* is, therefore, a vital key to its meaning, in particular to what we sometimes call the *Tris- tan* style, a compound of romantic and antiromantic, tonal and atonal elements, leading to the common perception of the work as simultaneously the last glow of ro- manticism and the dawn of musical modernism.

In order to understand how Wagner could attempt such a dual perspective, we must give attention to what he considered his amendment of Schopenhauer, as cited earlier. In outline it is as follows. While composing the latter part of the second-act love scene, Wagner wrote to Mathilde Wesendonck in his so-called Venice Diary that a new reading of Schopenhauer had "incited [him] to expansion and even . . . amendment of [Schopenhauer's] system." In it, Wagner claimed to have demon- strated a "path to salvation" and "complete pacification of the will" through sexual love. Wagner concluded that sexual love was analogous to the rapturous state of "genial cognition," that is, of artistic inspiration, a state in which, through "enhancement of the intellect of the individual to a cognitive organ of the species," Ideas (in the Platonic sense) might be apprehended. And on that basis Wagner felt that he had proved in love

> a possibility of attaining to that exaltation above the instinct of the individual will where, after complete subjection of this latter, the *species* will (*Gattungs-Wille*) comes to full consciousness of itself; which *upon this height* is necessarily tantamount to complete pacification. [my italics][15]

Wagner meant by this that through sexual love one might attain consciousness of the nature and universality of desire, or Will. This consciousness would lead to transcendence not only of one's own desire—the individual will—but also of the broader conception of desire, or will, that Schopenhauer described in terms of human enslavement to procreation of the species—the will-to-life, or the species will. Transcendence of the Will meant first a state of excitation, stimulating insight into the above-mentioned universality of desire, then a state of quietude or pacification. This dynamic, mimicking that of the sexual act, underlies a considerable number of climactic moments in *Tristan*, all of which anticipate the final pages of the opera. When Wagner says "upon this height," he means that on the highest level (or, in terms of *Tristan*, on the largest scale) this process culminates in what he described in his letter to Liszt as Schopenhauer's "principal idea, the final denial of the will to live," a process that was of "terrible seriousness" but "uniquely redeeming."

In addition to the Venice Diary entry, Wagner began a letter to the philosopher that he neither sent nor finished. It was published posthumously in 1886.[16] At the outset, Wagner cites a passage from Schopenhauer's essay "On the Metaphysics of Sexual Love," in which the philosopher had expressed his failure to comprehend the suicide of lovers "thwarted by external circumstances." Wagner responds by reiterating his claim to have discovered in the "beginnings of sexual love itself" a "path of salvation, to self-knowledge and self-denial of the Will, and that not merely of the Individual will." He then announces his intention to explain the "case adduced by [Schopenhauer]"—that is, the suicide of thwarted lovers—as "an imperfect and lower grade" of that "highest and most perfect instance of the resolution of the Will [*Willensentscheidung*]."

The documents just cited are of primary importance in our determining Wagner's conception of the three-act design of *Tristan*. As we will see, Wagner had a very specific musical analog of how "the beginnings of sexual love" could lead to the path to salvation—that is, he had devised a transformation of the music corresponding to Schopenhauer's conception of desire (the beginning of the opera) that would directly parallel the lovers' progression from desire to transfiguration. This transformation emerges in full at the point of Tristan's conversion in act 3. From Wagner's speaking of grades in the resolution—that is, the pacifying—of the Will, we recognize that the progression of events throughout the three acts of *Tristan* follows the pattern of his amendment. That is, it leads from the lovers' attempted suicide in act 1—the "imperfect and lower grade"—to their transfigurations in act 3: the "highest and most perfect instance of the resolution of the Will." In this progression, the second-act climax mirrors the in-between stage alluded to in Wagner's letter, transcendence of the *individual* will. In the duet "O ew'ge Nacht," Tristan and Isolde proclaim both the loss of their individual identities and a resultant intuition of oneness as the highest rapture of love. Tristan sings "Tristan du, ich Isolde, nicht mehr Tristan" (You Tristan, I Isolde, no more Tristan), and Isolde the counterpart, "du Isolde, Tristan ich, nicht mehr Isolde," following which they sing together "Ohne Nennen, ohne Trennen, neu' Erkennen, neu' Entbrennen; ewig ein-bewußt: heiß erglühter Brust, höchste Liebeslust!" (No more naming, no more separation, new awareness, new ardor, eternally, without end, of one consciousness: burning, glowing breast, highest joy of love). And this climax parallels both the climax of the duet that follows the drinking of the love-death potion in act 1—"du mir einzig bewusst, höchste Liebeslust" (conscious of you alone, the highest joy of love)—and the ending of the *Liebestod*: "ertrinken, versinken,—unbewusst, höchste Lust" (to drown, to sink, unconscious, highest joy). Although in "O ew'ge Nacht" Tristan and Isolde can be said to attain a state of "exaltation above the instinct of the *individual* will," subjection and pacification of the *species* will have to await the events of act 3, which climax in the middle of the act with Tristan's curse of the love potion—that is, of desire, even of love itself—and his own existence as the agency of desire, and culminate in the reappearance and winding down of the B major music of "O ew'ge Nacht" in the *Liebestod*. Not only the "bewusst" / "*ein*bewusst" / "*un*bewusst" parallel but also the change from "*Liebes*lust" to "Lust" at the end of the opera reflect the three stages of Wagner's amendment.

In this, the principal difference from Schopenhauer is that for him neither suicide nor sexual desire had anything to do with pacification of the will, denial of the will-to-life or the "path to salvation." Just the opposite: desire was, of course, affirmation of the will; and so was suicide, because it arose from frustrated desire. The "higher" states of denial and redemption, therefore, could be attained only by neutralizing desire—through self-denial, contemplation, and the overcoming of the will by the intellect. As suicide, death had no metaphysical connotations. For Wagner, however, the lovers' attempted suicide and subsequent consciousness of desire in act 1 comprised a first stage along the way to Schopenhauer's "path to salvation," to be revealed only in act 3. His justification for this view rested on Schopenhauer's maintaining elsewhere that, because of the separation of will and intellect in human consciousness, facing death was the root of the impulse to metaphysics in human beings. Wagner's means of depicting both Schopenhauer's unmetaphysical view of suicide and his view of death as the impulse to metaphysics lies in the relationship of death and desire throughout the act, which climaxes in the drinking of the love-death potion. As we will see in a later chapter, Wagner creates a death motive that dominates the first act, pervading Isolde's state of mind, which is fixated on her plan of suicide through poison, and that mirrors both Schopenhauer's view of death as the impulse to metaphysics and his view of suicide as affirmation of the will-to-life. At the point at which Tristan and Isolde drink the love potion, therefore, Wagner is able to convey by means of easily recognized musical devices the idea that although the lovers' suicide attempt is a deception, arising from desire rather than overcoming desire, it is also, because of the intermingling of death with love's inevitable urge to transcendence, the source of insight into the metaphysical nature of desire. At first, this understanding is close to Schopenhauer's view of the metaphysics of sexual love, which is linked to desire as the fulfillment of the purposes of the species and the Will—the physical cycle of desire, procreation, and death. Within this cycle, however, Wagner perceives the seeds of transcendence of the physical, although this is not manifested in the first act. Ultimately, Wagner's first act becomes the beginning of a metaphysical journey that will move beyond Schopenhauer's conception.

In Wagner's conception through the symbolic joining of love and death in the love potion (as the lovers believe it to be poison and are wholly in a death-centered frame of mind), Tristan and Isolde come to glimpse the deep relationship between love and death that countless poets have articulated (none more than Gottfried von Strassburg) and to which Schopenhauer was very sensitive. Full consciousness of their desire is the outcome. This consciousness is of *individual* desire, symbolized in the lovers' names, their first words on experiencing the full extent of their passion. At the climax of "O ew'ge Nacht," however, their *denial* of names and individual identities affirms Wagner's analogy between the ecstasy of sexual love and the rapturous state in which the artistic genius came to apprehend the nature of the Platonic Ideas. In viewing the latter as "enhancement of the intellect of the individual to cognitive organ of the species," Wagner was articulating a kind of progressive *union* of intellect and will as the source of metaphysical insight, and thereby bonding two aspects of Schopenhauer's thought that were mutually exclusive. Despite his claim that he was keeping basically within Schopenhauer's terms, expanding or extending the philosopher's system, but not breaking with it, Schopenhauer would never have agreed.

Thus, act 1 reveals aspects of Schopenhauer's perspective on desire, death, and suicide, all within the framework of dramatic events derived from Gottfried, whereas the second act marks more overtly the beginning of Wagner's amendment. Already in the prelude to act 2, Wagner introduces the music that will be associated with Isolde's transfiguration in the *Liebestod*, using it to replace the deceptive cadence that usually ends the desire music; and in the love scene he devises a new or "second" death motive to convey the lovers' growing intuition of the bond between desire and death, the fundamental difference from Schopenhauer. That motive might almost be designated the love-death motive: its final climactic appearance is on the phrase "sehnend verlangter *Liebestod*" (longingly hoped-for love-death), to which Liszt very astutely alluded in using the motive to begin his piano arrangement of the *Liebestod*. It is the expression of Wagner's central poetic metaphor, the joining of desire and death under the rubric "night." Wagner's day/night metaphor now pervades the lovers' reinterpretation of their past relationship. The merging of love and longing for death, poeticized as night, leads them to envision the metaphysical noumenon as blissful union beyond death, eternal love, but now without names or individuals. Here Wagner emphasizes the idea of transcendence of the individual will, the word "einbewusst" conveying the merging of individual consciousness into the larger undifferentiated union.

The story of the opera can, of course, be summarized in more usual terms as one centering on individual protagonists—characters—and their interactions—the plot. But, Wagner was very clear about the fact that *Tristan* was solely about inner psychic events; and as his third act reveals, it is only in solitary contemplation of one's inner history and being that self-understanding emerges. In act 3, Tristan, assisted only by Kurvenal (who functions as a sounding board, or proto-psychiatrist), and dominated by his own associative musical memories, is capable for the first time of looking deeply inward, and backward. The inner being he discovers is one who, although fated for desire and death—that is, the cycle of procreation—remains alive, enslaved, as he feels, by the will-to-life, in order to fulfill the purpose of desire. Having been unconscious for an extended period, as the result of Melot's near-fatal wound, Tristan has made contact with something far beyond his own identity: a region of primal forgetting, whose analogy in the waking world is the indescribable and untranslatable "dream of deepest sleep" described by Schopenhauer and adopted by Wagner in his post-Tristan aesthetic writings. Reawakening to the world, however, brings with it a shallower conception of dreams, the "allegorical" dream of existence, dominated as usual by desire. Tristan first succumbs to this vision of reality, imagining Isolde's arrival but unable to "realize" it beyond the return of memories mixed with desire. Only when he submits to the force of a musical embodiment of tragedy, what Schopenhauer described as a "copy of the Will itself," can Tristan comprehend the meaning of his reexperience of desire: that his entire being is composed, as it were, of desires, both ancient and recent, even the desires of his parents, which brought him into being. Through music, Tristan's buried knowledge of his father's dying soon after his conception and his mother's dying after his birth come to light. The *alte Weise* stimulates childhood associations of tragedy, death, and desire that have colored even the later joys and urges that led him inexorably to Isolde. In short, Tristan comes to awareness of the link between his desire for Isolde, and the metaphysical force behind all existence—that is, he experiences consciousness of the delusion of the species Will and its hold on his being. Wagner, of course, poeticizes all this; but its Schopenhauerian pedigree is unmistakable. In fulfillment of his longing for death and release, Tristan curses desire, symbolized by the love potion, and his own existence as "brewer" of the potion, and collapses unconscious again. This point, the center of the act, is the focal point for Wagner's amendment. Kurvenal makes his pronouncement of the Schopenhauerian conception of love as blissful delusion; and a new transformed version of the desire music that began the opera accompanies Tristan's passage from rejection of desire to his clairvoyant vision of Isolde and, above all, his espousal of death—no longer suicide, but abandonment of the will-to-life—as the fulfillment of love. After that, Isolde's *Liebestod* is a poetic confirmation of Tristan's victory over the will, an expression in more sustained musical terms of all that has been accomplished by him at the center of the act. It reiterates the love-death music of act 2, affirming the key of B major with the transfiguration music that Tristan had anticipated, but not completed, in that key after his reawakening; it announces the existence of another musical *Weise* that now Isolde alone can hear—a poeticizing of Schopenhauer's metaphysics of music; and it absorbs an echo of desire into the final cadence, affirming the end of the dreams of love and existence simultaneously.

What I have outlined is the story of *Tristan* told from the perspective of a Schopenhauerian "core" onto which Gottfried's Tristan poem, pared down to three love scenes (as Wagner described it) is grafted, not the reverse. In his *Tristan* poem, Wagner drew on many sources other than Gottfried and Schopenhauer—Novalis, presumably, Calderon, Hermann Kurz's translation of Gottfried's poem, to name only a few. His primary source, however, was within him: the musical language that he had long been developing with the aid of romantic aesthetics and music criticism, but that he had carried beyond the romantic framework in the music that directly preceded the composition of *Tristan* (the already composed parts of the Ring, especially the second act of *Siegfried,* completed earlier that year).

A primary objective of this book, therefore, is to show how the *Tristan* style matches both the Schopenhauerian and the non-Schopenhauerian aspects of the drama, how it realizes Wagner's vision of the union of idea and drama through music. Among the authors who have explored Wagner's indebtedness to Schopenhauer, and generally taken for granted that it is embodied in *Tristan,* there has been remarkably little demonstration of how this is so in terms of the musical language of the work (beyond the inevitable focus on leitmotifs). Even Nietzsche, at the time when he was most addicted to *Tristan* and when he most believed in its Schopenhauerian meaning—that is, in *The Birth of Tragedy*—provides, despite his profound insight into Wagner's musicopoetic intentions, very little in the way of concrete explanation of Wagner's musical language. And other great interpreters of *Tristan* who have attempted such explanations, most notably Ernst Kurth and Alfred Lorenz, have tended toward onesidedness in their seeking a purely musical key, or secret, to that language, altered chords in Kurth's case, closed musical periods in Lorenz's, but without demonstrating how the key in question fulfilled Wagner's musico-poetic needs.

In addition, whereas Wagner criticism has shied away from close musical analysis, preferring to take up biographical, political, or literary issues, musical analysis, and theory have focused solely on small segments of the piece—usually the prelude. Academic musicology, which might be thought to combine these various approaches, has not yet given a satisfactory reading of the work, at least in part because of the very scope of the endeavor. Thus, we have two studies of the sketch material of *Tristan,* that of Robert Bailey, confined to the first act, and that of Ulrich Bartels to the second and third, but neither of which takes up what one might well feel is the most interesting sequence of sketches: the original transition into the duet "O ew'ge Nacht" in the love scene, which contained fourteen extra lines of text that Wagner set to music but deleted from the final version, and the original version of the duet itself, which is likewise very different from the final version.[17] These supremely interesting documents raise questions regarding Wagner's overall poetic intent, especially since in its original form "O ew'ge Nacht" was conceived as the in-between stage described earlier and therefore paralleled the *Liebestod* far less closely than does its final version. Because it was at or very close to the time Wagner was composing these passages that he described his intention to amend Schopenhauer, they take on great importance for our understanding of the work. In fact, they (and a few other deletions and revisions) reveal a more explicit indebtedness to Schopenhauer in the conception of the work than do their final versions. Through them, we recognize that Wagner's celebrated paraphrasing of Schopenhauer at certain points in *Tristan* was undertaken in part to lend a poetic character to concrete philosophical material that was hardly suitable as such for an opera libretto, but that dictated the overall structure of the work.

In this book, I have set myself the task of attempting to reveal the interrelatedness of several different facets of *Tristan* that have mostly been treated separately in the literature. I begin with the romantic background for Wagner's interest in uniting philosophy with music, which long preceded his study of Schopenhauer. Central to this interest is Wagner's fascination with the idea of the metaphysical absolute as set forth in the philosophers of post-Kantian German idealism, particularly Schelling and Hegel, and his associating it with the "deepest recesses" of music as embodied, above all, in the Beethoven Ninth Symphony. This question has been investigated by others, most notably, and brilliantly, by Carl Dahlhaus.[18] Nevertheless, such studies have not been directed explicitly toward the musical language and design of *Tristan*, even though *Tristan* is widely acknowledged as the center of gravity, so to speak, for Wagner's philosophical yearnings. Moreover, neither the writings of the German idealist philosophers nor the related outpourings of the Jena romantics, both of which were of considerable influence directly or indirectly on the conception of *Tristan*, are widely known to English-speaking readers, still less so to those interested in the revolutionary musical language of the work. The path that led Wagner from these authors to Schopenhauer is a fascinating one, with many sidetracks, most notably Wagner's relatively brief infatuation with Feuerbach, but one that is nevertheless consistent and, I hope to demonstrate, highly illuminating of the musico-poetic character of *Tristan*.

In this study musical analysis, both small- and large-scale (harmony, leitmotif explication, periodic, and larger levels of structure), sketch interpretation, literary investigation, Wagner's aesthetics and its philosophical background, especially in Schopenhauer—these and other approaches necessarily rub shoulders fading in and out of the total picture in what, I hope, is a coherent and accurate overview of the work. One of my central premises is that *Tristan* is simultaneously both a culminating and a forward-looking work, "closing the door on romanticism," as Richard Strauss is reported to have said, and opening another door, that which eventually led to the revolution of twentieth-century music, which is no less sweeping than those of modern physics or art. In closing the former door, however, Wagner did not abandon the tenets of romanticism, which, in fact, permeate his compositions and his aesthetic writings. Rather, I would argue, he bracketed them within a perspective that was no longer exclusively the romantic one. Debussy even appears to have felt that Wagner remained solidly within the framework he (Debussy) called "classical" in terms of Wagner's harmony, whereas his own music could "enter and leave by any door," a metaphor not simply for the flexibility and fluidity of Debussy's harmony but also for the rift between the elevated character of Wagner's metaphysical apparatus and its musical analogs and Debussy's own "ground-level" metaphysics, in which transformation, like the Faun's conception of sexuality, is a purely physical event.[19] Regardless of whether or not we consider Debussy's work as an extension of romanticism or the beginning of twentieth-century aesthetics, Wagner's confronts romanticism with something that is entirely different and that is in some sense the equivalent of the Schopenhauerian "wisdom" that Mann felt was missing in *Tristan*.

In endeavoring to demonstrate this last point I will argue that the so-called *Tristan* style is a compound of tonality and atonality, as is its famous signal harmony, the Tristan chord. For the most part the affirmation of tonality within the work corresponds to the romantic perspective, whose supreme embodiment is the *Liebestod*, whereas the tendency toward atonality (exemplified most closely, perhaps, in the music that leads to Tristan's curse and relapse in act 3) mirrors something much closer to Schopenhauer's negative, or pessimistic, wisdom. The two interact continually throughout the work as symbols of the illusion or dream of love and existence versus the tragic reality that lies beneath.

ONE

The Path to Schopenhauer

IN 1854, WHEN WAGNER WROTE to Liszt of his discovery of Schopenhauer, he was certainly no stranger to philosophy. Yet, from the fact that at various times Schelling, Hegel, Feuerbach, and Schopenhauer were recommended to him by one or another of his friends, it seems clear that he did not read extensively or systematically in modern philosophy. By hindsight, however, the sequence of philosophers just mentioned is a meaningful if not a strictly logical or chronological one, covering the second and third of the three most prominent German post-Kantian idealist philosophers—Schelling and Hegel (by Wagner's time Fichte's influence, which was very strong on the early romantics, had waned considerably)—followed by the earliest and most prominent of the next generation, the so-called young Hegelians, Ludwig Feuerbach. In relation to Feuerbach and the direction of German philosophy around the mid-century, however, Schopenhauer, whose work remained in near total obscurity for several decades after its first publication (1818–19), represented a sidetrack, if not a step backward, both chronologically and conceptually. Yet, Wagner's encounter with Schopenhauer brought him closer to his philosophical "roots," so to speak. As he tells us in his autobiography, he "had always felt an inclination to try to fathom the depths of philosophy, rather as [he] had been driven by the mystical influence of Beethoven's Ninth Symphony to plumb the deepest recesses of music."[1] That inclination went as far back as his student days in Leipzig. More important for us, however, than the specific philosophers he encountered before the two who influenced him most—Feuerbach and Schopenhauer—is the question of what exactly Wagner was looking to get from his philosophical studies. His object was not to master the discipline of philosophy per se; for, as he continues, "none of the Leipzig professors had been able to hold my attention with their lectures on basic philosophy and logic." Schelling's *System of Transcendental Idealism* had proven frustrating, after which, as he says, "I had scratched my head in vain to make anything of it, and had always gone back to my Ninth Symphony." In the case of Hegel,

16

however, Wagner gives us an important clue to what it was that drew him to philosophy: "The more incomprehensible I found many of the most sweeping and speculative sentences of this tremendously famous intellect, . . . the more I felt impelled to get to the bottom of what was termed 'the absolute' and everything connected with it."

In this light, it seems fitting that, as Carl Dahlhaus has pointed out, Wagner himself coined the term "absolute music" in an 1846 set of program notes for the Beethoven Ninth Symphony.[2] And, thanks to Dahlhaus's study, it is well known that Wagner's aesthetics were deeply grounded in the writings of those romantic authors who viewed instrumental music as a metaphor for the metaphysical absolute—principally, Wackenroder, Tieck, and Hoffmann. None of those authors, however, can be considered a philosopher; they did not use the word "absolute" at all in the philosophical or musical sense, although had they done so it would have been fully in keeping with what Dahlhaus calls their "metaphysical excesses," centered on a vision of music as the element of life that most reached into the sphere of the ineffable. Although the poetic character of their writings on music undoubtedly spoke more directly to Wagner than the abstract, often opaque tone of the idealist philosophers, it may well have been a desire to go beyond what Walter Benjamin calls "the striving on the part of the romantic aestheticians after a resplendent but ultimately non-committal knowledge of an absolute" that sent him to systematic philosophy.[3]

The concept of the absolute was, in the main, the property of the philosophers of the post-Kantian idealist movement, what is sometimes called "absolute idealism," Fichte, Schelling, and Hegel, for whom the absolute represented the highest principle of philosophy. But at no earlier time in history were philosophers and artists as closely interrelated as in the era of German Idealism and early Romanticism, especially among the writers and philosophers of the Jena circle around 1800. Schiller studied Kant closely (a fact that Wagner was later to imply paralleled his own relationship to Schopenhauer), whereas Novalis and Friedrich Schlegel immersed themselves in Fichte; Hölderlin was an astute critic of Fichte; and Friedrich Schlegel produced a *Transcendentalphilosophie* of his own.[4] Those romantic writers who used the term "absolute" in the philosophical sense—principally, Novalis, Friedrich Schlegel, and Schleiermacher—not only bridged between romanticism and post-Kantian idealist philosophy but also did much to create the situation that music, because of its nonrepresentational character, became increasingly the model for meaning in the arts in general. If, for them, philosophy yielded ground to poetry in its capacity to convey a sense of the absolute, poetry in turn tended toward music for just the same reason. Not only was music emancipated from language, it became for several of the romantic authors the standard by which the true meaning of language was measured, the ideal toward which language strove.[5] Novalis, who spoke often of the mutual conditioning and interpenetration of philosophy and poetry, used the expression "schöne (absolute) poësie" to convey a sense of what in the case of music he called "wahre Musik" or "eigentliche Musik," namely sonatas, symphonies, fugues, variations, and the like.[6] And, as Friedrich Schlegel put it, music itself, although without determinate meaning, exhibited a "tendency towards philosophy," and should therefore be regarded "less as a representational art than as a philosophical language," lying "higher than mere art."[7] Likewise Schleiermacher raised questions concerning the "absoluteness" of the various arts, including music, whereas his writings on hermeneutics, as is well known, gave a very prominent place to the "musicality" of language.[8] Long before Wagner the process that Oskar Walzel calls "the aestheti-cizing of philosophy" was a *fait accompli.*[9] And for some, at least, music, increasingly viewed as the most characteristic (or romantic) art of the modern age, began un-mistakably to take the lead.

It was, in fact, the first two philosophers to whom Wagner refers, Schelling and Hegel, who most used the term "absolute" to signify the highest principle of philos-ophy and who assigned a central role to art as one of the means (in Schelling's case the *chief* means) by which the absolute manifests itself in finite reality. Although both philosophers were intimately connected to the romantic movement (Schelling, Hegel, and Hölderlin were friends from their student days; in Jena Schelling had close contact with Novalis and the Schlegels as well), Schelling was by far the closest of the idealist philosophers to romanticism, the one whose work both influenced and was itself conditioned by romanticism, and the one who—in the work for which he is still best known, the *System of Transcendental Idealism* (1800)—most nearly echoed the vision of art that was shared, in various less systematic ways, by the romantics. In the sixth and last section of his treatise, Schelling proclaims that it is only in art and artistic intuition that we "first resolve the entire problem of tran-scendental philosophy (that of explaining the congruence between subjective and objective)," for, "in art the philosopher finds revealed objectively that which grounds his entire system, namely, the absolute itself, or absolute identity [of freedom and necessity, the ideal and real, conscious and unconscious, subject and object, etc.]."[10] From the contradiction of conscious and unconscious the artistic urge, which strikes at the "ultimate" in the artist, "the root of his whole being," is set in motion: "It is as if, in the exceptional man . . . that unalterable identity, on which all existence is founded, had laid aside the veil wherewith it shrouds itself in others." Artistic cre-ation proceeds from the subjective freedom of conscious activity to the objective un-conscious necessity that characterizes the finished work, pacifying our "endless striving," and resolving "the final and uttermost contradiction within us."[11] As in it-self the absolute transcends all oppositions, for Schelling the unconscious in art has priority over the conscious, itself functioning as "a kind of absolute," its workings re-maining "hidden and forever enigmatic."[12] Through its agency arises the element of *poetry* in art, through which the artist involuntarily imparts "unfathomable depth" to his work, "and which neither he nor anyone else is wholly able to penetrate."

Art, therefore, is the primary organ of the revelation of the absolute, as it "ever and again continues to speak to us of what philosophy cannot depict in external form, namely the unconscious element in acting and producing, and its original identity with the conscious." Thus, art for Schelling was the informing of the ideal into the real, the infinite into the finite:

This unknown, however, whereby the objective and the conscious activities are here brought into unexpected harmony, is none other than that absolute which contains the common ground of the preestablished harmony between the conscious and the un-conscious. Hence, if this absolute is reflected from out of the product [that is, the work of art], it will appear to the intelligence as something lying above the latter, and which, in contrast to freedom, brings an element of the unintended to that which was begun with consciousness and intention.[13]

Although Wagner admitted to frustration in his study of Schelling, there are distinct affinities between Schelling's metaphysics of art and certain of Wagner's writings, both before and after his discovery of Schopenhauer. Above all, Schelling was the philosopher who was most responsible for introducing the teleologies of nature and history into idealism as the counterpart of the subjectivity of the self-positing "absolute" ego of Fichte's *Wissenschaftslehre*. Thus, although Schelling's starting point remained very much in tune with Fichte, the activity of the "I" nevertheless had a prior history in the unconscious processes of nature that culminated in human consciousness. Although philosophical reasoning turned back to reflect on the entire process, only in art could it be truly revealed in the union of unconscious and conscious productivity. The combination of transcendental idealism and nature philosophy in Schelling pointed the way to Hegel's *Phenomenology of Spirit* and the book that Wagner read, *The Philosophy of History*. For Wagner, it lay at the basis of the teleology of the Ring and much of the theory that led to it.

It was not Schelling, however, but Hegel who exerted the greatest influence on aesthetics during this period (and later), and this despite the fact that Hegel did not assign art the same elevated position as Schelling did. For Hegel, as for Schelling, religion, art, and philosophy constituted the means by which the absolute, or the union of the finite and infinite, real and ideal, could be represented. But, whereas Schelling views art as the organ of philosophical representation, giving greatest weight to intuitive and unconscious processes as keys to artistic meaning, and valuing the irrational as counterpoise to philosophy's rational processes, Hegel sees pure conceptual understanding (absolute understanding) as the highest goal, possible only through philosophy. For Hegel, the absolute is not the starting point, but the end point; true teleology has absolute understanding—the absolute Idea—as its goal, achieved through the development of spirit (*Geist*) in human history. Hegel is certainly indebted to Schelling's metaphysical view of art as revelatory of the absolute but, for him, the sequence of art, religion, philosophy is an ascending one, moving from the sensuous to the imagistic to the conceptual, as art itself ascends through the stages of its history from the symbolical through the classical to the romantic.[14] Hegel's famous disparagement of Schelling's absolute as the "night in which all cows are black" refers to the fact that Schelling took the absolute as a given starting point ("absolute identity" or "nondifference"), without sufficient grounding in the concrete realities of existence, whereas for Hegel the teleology that Schelling had outlined for nature permeated, as the ascent of "Spirit," all of human existence. Despite his proclaiming the "end of art" in his own time, Hegel certainly did not disparage art. Just the reverse; his linking it with the absolute unmistakably draws art within the highest stages of the ascent of Spirit, enabling it to "sacrifice its own exclusively 'aesthetic' form to open out upon a fuller religious configuration."[15] In the introduction to his *Lectures on Fine Art*, Hegel makes clear that "art stands on one and the same ground with religion . . . and philosophy. . . . Owing to the sameness of content the three realms of absolute spirit differ only in the *forms* in which they bring home to consciousness their object, the Absolute." In art, the Absolute, or the "Idea," became the "ideal" manifestation of the union of concept and reality, providing a crucial element of concreteness that was lacking in Fichte: "for Hegel the Absolute entails an emergence from within experience itself of its own ultimate dimensions."[16] Because art is rooted in experience, it can be considered the (sensuous) beginning of this emergence.

As this study will indicate, Wagner's indebtedness to Schopenhauer was enormous and nearly all-consuming. Yet, without wishing to deny that fact, we must recognize that much of Wagner's understanding of art and music also derives, directly or indirectly, from other sources, among which Hegel is far more prominent than is generally supposed. Wagner's relatively brief enthusiasm for Ludwig Feuerbach in the 1840s and early 1850s had the immediate effect that in several writings of that time he adopted Feuerbach's rejection of the Hegelian absolute in all its various forms, transferring them to music and viewing them largely in pejorative terms. Later, after reading Schopenhauer, Wagner, sensing that Schopenhauer's "Will" was a form of absolute, dropped the pejorative usages, while picking up on Schopenhauer's rabid denunciations of Hegel (Schopenhauer also rejected Fichte, Schelling, and the term "absolute"). Wagner certainly believed the tone of *Tristan* to be Schopenhauerian. But, at the same time, he draws elements of his earlier philosophical study within his overall Schopenhauerian perspective. In his absorption with Schopenhauer, Wagner was hardly aware of this lack of purity. Nevertheless, it is of considerable significance for Wagner's music, which hardly fits at all with the kind of music Schopenhauer considered parallel to his own ideas (largely Rossini and Bellini).

The close interaction of philosophy and art that characterizes the period we have been discussing is the broad background for Wagner's achievement in *Tristan*. In comparing his urge to fathom the depths of philosophy with the "mystical influence" of the Beethoven Ninth Symphony, Wagner tacitly acknowledges that his philosophical interests had, in fact, been awakened and formed in large part not only by the writings of those romantic authors who viewed instrumental music as a metaphor for the metaphysical absolute—principally, Tieck, Wackenroder, and Hoffmann—but by the critical reception of Beethoven, especially the Ninth Symphony.[17] Because of its unprecedented introduction of the human voice in the finale, the Ninth Symphony embodied a "philosophical" idea that Wagner made into the core of his music aesthetics: the relationship of absolute music and "word" (taking "word" in its broadest sense as the symbol of everything in music that reaches, or seems to reach, into the realm of verbal-conceptual ideas). That question remained with Wagner throughout his entire creative life, receiving its fullest and most interesting treatment in his most extensive Schopenhauerian statement on the meaning of music—the 1870 Beethoven essay.

Deeply impressed by the romantic writings on music, Wagner emulated them in the early 1840s in a string of Hoffmannesque essays and stories that, taken together, constitute his first sustained venture into music aesthetics. Although they hardly qualify as philosophy, these writings address fundamental questions in aesthetics, especially the nature and limits of musical representation. And in several respects they reveal the patterns of thought mentioned earlier, those that bridge to Wagner's Schopenhauerian aesthetics. A few comparisons with Schopenhauer make this clear. Thus, in the best known of Wagner's stories, "A Happy Evening" (1841), two music-loving friends attempt to describe how both Mozart's and Beethoven's symphonies evoke the "sense of something higher beyond this earth" (*Ahnung des Höheren, Überirdischen*).[18] This leads them to articulate essentially the same view of music's ideal expressive character as that set forth by Schopenhauer in both volumes of *The World as Will and Representation*. Wagner puts it thus:

> What music expresses is eternal, infinite and ideal. It speaks not of the passion, love and longing of this or that individual in this or that situation, but of passion, love and longing in themselves, and furthermore in all the infinite variety of motivations which arise from the exclusive nature of music and which are strange to, and beyond the expression of, every other form of language.[19]

And Schopenhauer says,

> Therefore music does not express this or that particular and definite pleasure, this or that affliction, pain, sorrow, horror, gaiety, merriment, or peace of mind, but joy, pain, sorrow, horror, gaiety, merriment, peace of mind *themselves*, to a certain extent in the abstract, their essential nature, without any accessories, and so also without the motives for them.[20]

This remark directly follows Schopenhauer's discussion of analogies between music and the "movement of the will," a passage in which he speaks of the kinds of musical devices that are central to the language of *Tristan*: delayed resolution of dissonance and avoidance of tonal closure as the counterpart of unfulfilled desire, sudden modulation to a distant key as a simile of death, minor-key adagios as the expression of suffering, and the like. At the same time, Schopenhauer and Wagner condemn tone-painting and program music, as it emphasizes the aspect of music that is bound up with its worldly (or, as Schopenhauer puts it, "phenomenal") rather than ideal nature. Thus, Wagner contrasts the elevated sphere of the composer of higher instrumental music—the "immeasurable realm of the unearthly"—with that of music that remains bound to "worldly appearances."

> One is dragging the musician down from his lofty position when one demands that he suit his inspiration to the appearances of everyday life. And the instrumental composer would be betraying his mission and exposing his weaknesses were he to attempt to transfer the limited proportions of worldly appearances into the sphere of his own art.[21]

Likewise, in Schopenhauer's view,

> [music] never assimilates the material, and therefore, when it accompanies even the most ludicrous and extravagant farces of comic opera, it still preserves its essential beauty, purity and sublimity; and its fusion with those incidents cannot drag it down from its height to which everything ludicrous is really foreign.[22]

In similar fashion, Schopenhauer and Wagner make comparable statements regarding such diverse topics as the relationship of rhythm and harmony, the self-contained character of Rossini's melodies, and even the nature of Beethoven's music, especially its seeming to invite programmatic interpretation.[23] At this time there was, of course, no influence of Schopenhauer on Wagner. That there are close parallels with Schopenhauer's metaphysics of music is because, as Carl Dahlhaus points out, Schopenhauer, "had himself received the romantic aesthetic. . . . The outlines of [his] aesthetic are nothing other than the romantic metaphysics of absolute music philosophically interpreted in the context of a metaphysics of the 'will'."[24]

On Beethoven, Schopenhauer says: "we certainly have an inclination to realize it [a Beethoven symphony] while we listen, to clothe it in the imagination with flesh and bone, and to see in it all the different scenes of life and nature. On the whole, however, this does not promote an understanding or enjoyment of it, but rather gives it a strange and arbitrary addition. It is therefore better to interpret it purely and in its immediacy." In "A Happy Evening," one of the musician friends describes this dualism as the capacity of Beethoven's music to create the impression that it was composed according to a certain preconceived "philosophical idea" (*nach einer gewissen philosophischen Idee*), in contrast to the immediacy of Mozart's purely musical inspirations.[25] And elsewhere in the story the other friend speaks of how Beethoven's conception of the symphony, although derived from Mozart's, went further in its active striving to "grasp the infinite." In this view, Beethoven expanded the form of the symphony by discarding the proportions of the traditional periodic structure of Mozart's works. The result was that "since he knew how to impart a philosophical consistency (*philosophische Konsequenz*) to those daring flights of his, . . . Beethoven created a completely new genre on the basis of the Mozart Symphony."[26]

Although Wagner does not define either the "philosophische Konsequenz" or the "new genre," he makes clear that Beethoven's music, in creating the impression that it was composed according to a "certain philosophical idea," did not descend to the purely descriptive level of program music but retained its ideal character.[27] Music might derive from inner sources or from life experiences, even from external sources, but the feelings associated with any such sources are transmuted into music before the act of composition; they, therefore, remain hidden and mysterious. The "new genre," therefore, is not the symphonic poem, and the "philosophische Konsequenz" (or "philosophische Idee") is not the same as a program.[28] Because much of "A Happy Evening" is occupied with rejecting program music, it is clear that for Wagner such a "philosophical idea"—even when suggesting preplanned, quasi-narrative formal designs—deals with extramusical content only in a general, abstract, or universal manner; in this respect, it does not conflict with the notion of "pure" (or "absolute") music any more than do Schopenhauer's afore-mentioned analogies.

"A Happy Evening" provides us with several of the principal themes of Wagner's "romantic" aesthetics, the most significant being the sense that although the musical impulse may involve close parallels with the world of (extramusical) ideas, such parallels, suggesting conscious activity, are secondary to the purely musical ones, in both the act of composition and the listening experience. The idea of the absolute in music is, as we have found with Schelling, bound up with the priority of "necessary," unconscious, and therefore unfathomable, processes over conscious, "free" motivations (or in Wagner's terms intuitions over conceptions). Although Wagner's use of the word "philosophical" is very loose indeed in "A Happy Evening," it probably reflects the impact that early romantic writers, such as Schlegel, had on music criticism. Behind it lies a way of thinking about music that was shared by all the romantic writers on music and that will come into sharper focus in Wagner's post-Schopenhauer writings, beginning with the 1857 essay on Liszt's symphonic poems and culminating in the 1870 essay on Beethoven—namely, the division of music into inner/outer and depth/surface qualities. The latter qualities are already very pronounced in Wackenroder and E. T. A. Hoffmann, from which they carry over into Wagner's early writings, where they are associated primarily with music's capacity to mirror the dualism of unconscious and conscious processes, the latter aspiring to the condition of "word" and philosophy. In his later writings, Wagner gives the dualism much more of a philosophical twist, associating music's inner and outer aspects, respectively, with its metaphysical origin and its form (or its "appearance" in the world)—in Schopenhauerian terms, will and representation.[29]

By the time of "A Happy Evening" German music criticism, thanks largely to the inspiration of Hoffmann's writings, had reached a very high level, in luminaries such as Weber, A. B. Marx, and Schumann. The "metaphysical excesses" of Wackenroder and Tieck are no longer the center of such criticism; Schumann's dislike of the word "romantic" can probably be understood as his response to such excesses. Nevertheless, the subjective or romantic tradition certainly persisted, and in some cases the attempt to ground it in philosophy produced interesting results that form a clear background for Wagner's aesthetic writings. Robert Wolfgang Griepenkerl, for example, in his novel *Das Musikfest oder die Beethovener* (1838, with an 1841 edition that adds a quasi-philosophical preface), describes passages from the Beethoven Eroica and Ninth Symphonies in such terms. Thus, the famous thirty-six measures of syncopated chords from the Eroica first movement development section (mm. 244–79) are followed by "the tremendous breakthrough of the basses, in order to attain the heavenly spheres of E minor and A minor, and then the theme once again in bright, victorious C" (mm. 280–307). With the word "breakthrough" (*Durchbruch*), Griepenkerl is alluding to what, in his preface, he refers to as the "breakthrough" that has been completed in the events of recent history and that have caused him to refer glowingly to the thirty-six measures of the "Eroica" as "ein Stück neunzehntes Jahrhundert."[30] For Griepenkerl Beethoven's instrumental music inaugurated a new era characterized by the reciprocal relationship of historical process and individual achievement, as symbolized in the French Revolution and Napoleon. Griepenkerl's new age is one in which the individual Spirit understands itself as a moment in the stream of universal *Substanz*, finding thereby its highest expression of true worth, and bringing the "totality" and the "Idea" to consciousness and to awareness. Griepenkerl is clear about the fact that his own time, in contrast to earlier epochs, is powered by such an "Idea": "into the consciousness of the people steps the reciprocal relationship of the universal Spirit and the individual Spirit, the latter no longer feeling isolated and confined, but instead reflecting itself self-consciously as part in the stream of the great totality. 'Wherever we look the individual Spirit directs and moves itself towards the majesty and nobility of the general Spirit. . . . Everyone feels it for himself:' What a time! What a great age we live in! . . . Great is any era in which the Idea breaks through into life!'"

Griepenkerl, clearly, has encountered Hegel's *Philosophy of History*, from which he summarizes the history of the "Spirit" in earlier eras, culminating the entire process, as Hegel does, in the Christian era, in which the "concrete Idea," manifested in the union of the divine and the human, came into existence. Philosophy, despite its skepticism, gave this achievement a rebirth through thought in his time. Likewise art, whose purpose is that of an "eternal hymn in praise of the Idea," received its "eternal law" from the hand of philosophy, the law that it obeyed for centuries unconsciously; and that law was none other than that of the universe itself, the union of spirit and nature, ideal and real. Thus, from its source, "the highest spheres of the Absolute," the Idea was realized through history as the Ideal in art.[31] Griepenkerl alters Hegel's sequence of art, religion, and philosophy to that of religion, philosophy, art (and he ultimately also places music at the apex of art as well, disagreeing elsewhere in the book with "the philosopher Hegel, who only valued music that was linked to poetry"), but he follows Hegel in emphasizing that the content of art is the same as that of "its two sisters."

Thus, for Griepenkerl, the "Idea" pushes through into life, a process mirrored in Beethoven's instrumental music, with its many striking contrasts and its capacity to mirror the panorama of the world and the conflicts underlying great historical events. Beethoven was the first to raise "die eigentliche Musik"—that is, instrumental music—"to such a height of independence that one could be in no doubt concerning the true colors of his intentions." In his quest for the "Idea" (which Griepenkerl links with the sublime, which is more characteristic of music than of the other arts), Beethoven disregarded the play with conventional forms that characterized an earlier age enslaved by the "Kunstabsolutismus des Individuums." His symphonies— "nine fearful moving forces of thunderous time," impel all the "concealed, wild driving forces of the century. With the dizzying convergence of all wheels from all sides upon one point, the trifling activity ("nichtige Treiben") of the world collapses, in the face of a sun-smiling Idea from the heights of heaven."[32]

In Griepenkerl's jumbled hyperbole, we may well discern an echo of Wackenroder, who in one of his stories (to be taken up below) describes the roaring "wheel of time" and its eventual cessation in terms of frenzied worldly activity and its transcendence through love and music. The story prefigures Schopenhauer's descriptions of saints and mystics who attain a state of metaphysical understanding that enables them to abandon the will-to-life in all its forms; Wagner describes Beethoven in the same terms in his 1870 essay on the composer. What we encounter in Griepenkerl to a striking degree is the extent to which the "religion of art," spawned by the early romantics, had spread, in the first half of the nineteenth century, even beyond Hoffmann's none too discrete (or discreet) boundaries, and its association with philosophy.

In all this we perceive that Griepenkerl has read his Hegel and draws it, with the appropriate modifications, into the service of grounding his Hoffmannesque effusions on the ideal nature of music. In his discussions, whether general or of specific pieces, ideas of the kind described above are seldom far away. And in describing actual performances, Griepenkerl usually attempts to indicate how they reveal the uniting of the ideal and the real that for him was their goal. The most interesting such description is of the long improvisation of the character who most represents what Griepenkerl presents as true understanding of Beethoven, the organist Pfeiffer (among whose posthumous papers, Griepenkerl tells us, the document used as the 1841 preface to the novel was found). The improvisation itself is a form of "Liebestod" for Pfeiffer, whose love for Cäcilie remains unfulfilled and who is found dead at the organ console at the end of his solo, having ended with open fifths derived from the beginning of the Ninth Symphony (discussed earlier in the novel as a symbol of creation from and return to the void). Passages of diminished sevenths, extended pedal points, and deceptive cadences (*Trugschluss auf Trugschluss*) rub shoulders with a fugue and various reminiscences of the Ninth Symphony. In the absence of musical examples and a concrete sense of structure, the description makes little sense. Its climax, nevertheless, is revealing, in that Pfeiffer returns to evoke the passage from the Eroica described earlier as the "Durchbruch." Now, in response to the cry "Sacrilege" (*Kirchenfrevel*) from some of the hearers, Griepenkerl launches into a paean to the "religion of art," describing Pfeiffer's ascent from the physical to the sphere of the Spirit and the "absolute Idea."

> He had completely forgotten the sacred instrument beneath his hands, forgotten the sacred place. Elevated into the sphere of the Spirit, where religion is not understood as in the confines of the individual, but beyond that, where religion reveals itself as the highest manifestation of the absolute Idea itself in the appearances of world history— having attained this, the player stepped out of the forms of one-sided church music and sought from the sum total of all appearances, in keeping with their contradictions, to call forth the Idea more overpoweringly and convincingly. A characteristic of art, whose final attainment, religion, lies in the highest meaning of the Word. Thus future eras will not bring forth oratorios in the usual sense; undoubtedly, however, oratorios in the newer sense: that is, *speaking* monuments of great human conditions, in which, finally, the world-historical consequences of the Christ-son will emerge, not the prevalent disgustingly preferred scenes of blood and martyrdom. For every art, even painting, those conditions are over.[33]

Thus, art passes from the sensuous to the religious, paralleling what Hegel called "the leap that is made into the supersensible when the sequences of the sensible are broken off."[34]

Highflown as this kind of writing is, the way of thinking that underlies it lasted, nevertheless, throughout much of the century, from the time of Friedrich Schlegel's pronouncing longing for the infinite as the "essence of philosophy" to Wagner's attempt to realize Tristan and Isolde's search for what he calls the "Durchbruch" into the sphere of eternal love in the *Tristan* prelude, and Gustav Mahler's building the designs of his earlier symphonies around his own notion of the "Durchbruch." It remains closely bound up with what composers and writers felt that Beethoven had achieved.[35]

Griepenkerl's reference to speaking oratorios of the future extends the capacity of music to represent the "absolute Idea" to vocal as well as instrumental forms. In raising the question of absolute music (Griepenkerl, like Novalis, uses the expression "die eigentliche Musik" repeatedly) versus "word" he is not only providing Wagner with what I have called the core of his aesthetics but also reflecting back on what was a major concern for Hoffmann as well, expressed by him in the essay "The Poet and the Composer" (1813), which, as is well known, was of direct influence on Wagner in another of his stories from the early 1840s, "A Pilgrimage to Beethoven" (1840).[36] "The Poet and the Composer" mirrors, paradoxically, the hope of the idealist philosophers that conceptual understanding might be capable of grasping the Absolute, as well as the romantics' denial that it could ever do so. This question is played out in terms of the relationship of words and music in opera. After introducing the same kind of characterization of instrumental music that had permeated his famous essay "Beethoven's Instrumental Music" (1810), Hoffmann has his principal character, the composer "Ludwig," articulate the impossibility of setting any libretto that is not conceived simultaneously with the music, and therefore the product of the composer himself. That Mozart achieved such success with his libretti was the result of his ability to choose texts that genuinely suited the music. Otherwise, the only possibility is "romantic" opera, in which the poet penetrates the "essential nature of music," drawing on the "sublime language" and "indescribable effect of instrumental music. . . to come to grips with the world of phenomena." Through the "magical power of poetic truth . . . a romantic dimension reveals itself before our eyes in which language is raised to a higher power, or rather (since it is part of that distant realm of music) takes the form of song . . . for the secret of words and sounds is one and the same, unveiling to both [poets and musicians] the ultimate sublimity."[37]

In "A Pilgrimage to Beethoven," Wagner adopts several of Hoffmann's ideas, putting them directly into Beethoven's mouth. Prominent among these is rejection of operatic set pieces, a restriction for both librettist and composer. Hoffmann makes this point several times in his story, complaining of the demand for "trios, quartets, finales, etc.," the conventional forms that drag the musical inspiration down from its exalted state; and Wagner, in his story, has Beethoven, discussing his concessions to the public in *Fidelio,* describe the true nature of music drama as possessing "none of your arias, duets, trios, and all the stuff they patch up opera with today. What I should set in their place no singer would sing, and no audience listen to." In this and other writings of the time, Wagner is voicing his negative stance toward excessive periodicity, which he viewed as fundamentally external in nature and hence an obstacle to artistic truth. Wagner was occupied at the time with the first of his "romantic" operas of the 1840s, *The Flying Dutchman,* the work in which, as he later revealed, he first turned from historical to mythological subject matter in his quest for the "inner psychic motives" that would replace the external dramatic causality of earlier operas, and in which he claimed to learn how to create poetic texts that mirrored the freedom and flexibility of symphonic music, rather than the traditional operatic forms.[38] The uniting of instrumental and vocal comes to signify, as Beethoven explains to "R" in Wagner's story, the union of the "wild, unfettered elemental feelings, represented by the instruments" with the "clear and definite emotion of the human heart, as represented by the voice," thereby lending the voice the freedom of instrumental music, and uniting the qualities associated with absolute music with the sphere of concrete human feeling.[39]

The question of transition versus periodicity and its impact on the musical language of *Tristan* will be taken up at various points in this book. For Wagner, it represented a central issue in the possibility of opera's aspiring to the condition of absolute music. Ultimately, the principle Wagner called "the art of transition," which he traced back to his next opera, *Tannhäuser,* but that reached its apex in the second-act love scene of *Tristan,* would elevate transition to a position of priority over periodicity. The *Tristan* love scene embodies this in the lovers' progression from life to longing for death and transcendence. Wagner viewed the principle in Schopenhauerian terms; but the musical techniques through which he achieved it have far less to do with Schopenhauer than with Hegel, whose work, in its constant mediating quality (the dialectic), articulates the very dynamic quality of the Absolute that Wagner's remarks on transition emphasize. Not only the desire music but also the "Tristan chord" itself embody this mediating quality. The character of transcendence in *Tristan*, bound up musically with the potentially cadential "transfiguration music" that climaxes the end of the opera (the *Liebestod*), is, like Hegel's conception of the Absolute, concerned with dialectical motion and teleology. What is really Schopenhauerian is Wagner's making the point that the fulfillment of transcendental ecstasy is one with abandonment to nothingness and unconsciousness. Thus, the many appearances of the transfiguration music in acts 2 and 3 are all incomplete and adjusted so as to dissolve in further motion—transition—until the last and greatest (the climax of the *Liebestod*) completes the long-awaited cadence, replacing transition with closure. None of Wagner's dominant pedals—and there are many in *Tristan*—ever attains anything comparable to the new events they usher in in Beethoven and the romantics; instead, the greatest insight is into what Wagner called "the nothingness of the world," of which Isolde's abandonment to unconsciousness is the final expression.

As a central musical principle, transition is much less suited to Schopenhauer than to Hegel, whose writings fully embody this all-pervading aspect of nineteenth-century thought.[40] In this light, we may note that Hegel's belief in the "rise of thought beyond the world of sense, its passage from the finite to the infinite" was articulated in response to its opposite: Kant's "rejection of all theoretical proofs of the existence of God . . . as a syllogizing, i.e., a transition."[41] In *Tristan*, the passage from the finite to the infinite is not one of *thought*, as it was for Hegel, but of feeling, intuition, and ultimately unconsciousness. But it is certainly possible to argue that the phrases of the desire music (the first seventeen measures of the prelude), and the unfolding of the prelude as a whole, exhibits striking features of the pattern of thesis, antithesis, synthesis. In this view, the motion toward the climax of the prelude is a mediated or dialectical, transitional one, the basic difference from Hegel being that, instead of progressing onward toward the "Absolute," it obeys Schopenhauer and cycles back to the beginning.

These ideas may be latent in romantic thinking, but they were not present in Wagner's mind in the 1840s. Nevertheless, when Wagner finally coins the term "absolute music," in the 1846 set of program notes for the Beethoven Ninth Symphony mentioned earlier, there is certainly an element of the quasi-Hegelian language he picked up, perhaps, from Griepenkerl. Wagner cites excerpts from Goethe at several points in order to help convey a sense of the work's "artistic design" (*künstlerischen Anordnungen*), but disclaims any implication that the Goethe passages could lead to an "absolute understanding" (*zu einem absoluten Verständnisse*) of Beethoven's work, for such understanding comes from "a personal inner intuition" (*aus einer eigenen innerer Anschauung*).[42] Nevertheless, although "the essence of higher instrumental music consists in speaking in tones what is unspeakable in words," Wagner makes clear that the Goethe passages are capable of conveying in sublime fashion the "higher human moods" (*höheren menschlichen Seelenstimmungen*) that underlie Beethoven's "purely musical creation." Thus, music possesses qualities that lend themselves to poeticized verbal description and conceptual understanding—the "artistic designs" of individual works and the "human" moods they express—as well as ones that lie beyond and remain the province of "absolute understanding," linked with intuition.

The idea that music has inner and outer dimensions—the former representing its true essence—permeates the writings of Wackenroder and Tieck, especially the essay "The characteristic inner nature of music and the religious doctrine [Seelenlehre] of present-day instrumental music," where it is closely associated with the metaphor of depth and surface, expressed with the imagery of unfulfilled desire attempting to struggle from its watery depths in search of redemption. Hoffmann, too, used it extensively in writings such as his famous essay on Beethoven's Fifth Symphony.[43] And, in addition to including passages from Goethe in his notes for the Ninth Symphony, Wagner at one point cites Ludwig Tieck's characterization of the content of symphonic music as "insatiate desire" arising from the "deepest ground" (tiefsten Grund), an "unspeakable longing that nowhere finds fulfillment," that "seeking rescue, sinks deeper and deeper" into the depths.[44] Wagner associates the passage with Beethoven's conception of the "nature" (Wesen) of instrumental music in the first three movements of the Ninth Symphony, which for Wagner exemplify music's "infinite, indefinite expression," that is, its transcendence of all verbal-conceptual descriptions. The "shriek of horror" at the beginning of the finale, however, takes on another, more definite, "speaking" character, the instrumental recitative "almost breaking the bounds of absolute music," and the subsequent passing from indefinite (instrumental) to definite (vocal) utterance serving as a metaphor for the progression from chaos to light.[45]

If we view this passage not in Kantian terms—that is, not in terms of an unbreachable split between concept and intuition, appearance and essence—but in terms of the Hegelian telos of absolute Idea, toward which the motion of Spirit is directed, or, in the expression Wagner uses, toward "absolute understanding," then what Wagner would later describe as the all-important "artistic deed" within the Beethoven Ninth Symphony, the event that caused him to describe the work as the "last symphony," is the climax of the idea of the philosophische Konsequenz mentioned in "A Happy Evening." And the Beethoven symphony represents a "new genre" because of the composer's capacity to "write the world history of music" on his works, to embody both the ideal (or purely musical) and the human spheres as two coexisting aspects of its expressive nature.[46] Wagner's reference to desire sinking "deeper and deeper into the depths" recalls the ubiquitous ocean/land metaphor of Opera and Drama, which underlies the opening scenes of Das Rheingold and the setting of the first act of Tristan. It also underlies, of course, the poetic idea behind the Tristan prelude, which, as Wagner described it in his 1859 notes for the version with concert ending, bears a remarkable resemblance to the excerpt he cited from Tieck (Wackenroder) in 1846, and in addition associates the idea of a Durchbruch with the lovers' search for transcendence. After his discovery of Schopenhauer, these oppositions all revolve around the dualism of the metaphysical and the phenomenal, usually expressed in terms of surface versus depth or inner versus outer motivations. The emergence of human consciousness and "word" from the inexpressible depths of music and feeling does not, therefore, mean that the absolute has somehow been demoted but, rather, that it extends beyond instrumental music to include the definite human emotions as well. Friedrich Schlegel's characterization of philosophy as "becoming" or "incomplete," centering on longing for the infinite, opened the way for a dynamic interpretation of the Absolute, which is the way Hegel viewed it. Wagner characterizes musical form in the same way, initially as becoming, and ultimately as the principle of transition.[47] The progression from unconsciousness to consciousness also dictated the character of several climactic ending points in the Ring, as well as that of the ending of the first act of *Tristan,* where the lovers' desire comes to the light of day as the ocean voyage gives way to the arrival at land. It remained a beacon that guided Wagner's life's work, even after the reading of Schopenhauer inspired him to depict its extinguishing in *Tristan.* Whereas the move from unconscious to conscious enacts the direction of idealist philosophy, especially Hegel, who, as we have seen, could describe the ascent of pure thought to the Absolute in terms resembling Isolde's *Liebestod,* the sinking back to unconsciousness mirrors the romantic belief that reason, concept, and "word" were inadequate to the task. At the end of "Das eigentümliche innere Wesen der Tonkunst" Wackenroder puts it thus:

> But why do I, foolish one, strive to melt words into tones? It is never as I feel it. Come, thou musical strains ["Komme, ihr Töne"], draw near and rescue me from this painful earthly striving for words, envelop me in Thy shining clouds with Thy thousandfold beams, and raise me up into the old embrace of all-loving heaven.[48]

In this light, Isolde's succumbing to the metaphysical "Wellen," then to unconsciousness and silence in the *Liebestod* represents her attaining the absolute.[49] The resemblance between Tieck's characterization of instrumental music as "insatiate desire" unable to find rescue and Wagner's description of Tristan and Isolde's inability to transcend desire, in his program notes for the *Tristan* prelude of more than a decade later, attests to the fact that the primary impulse behind *Tristan,* and one of the most characteristic traits of its text—the poeticizing of Schopenhauer—constituted a renewal of Wagner's old urge to comprehend the absolute through the union of philosophy and music. *Tristan,* therefore represents Wagner's extending the idea of absolute music to opera.[50]

Fulfillment of that urge was not forthcoming in the 1840s, however. Instead, whatever influences of Schelling and Hegel might have lingered in Wagner's consciousness were supplanted in the late 1840s by that of Hegel pupil and apostate, Ludwig Feuerbach, whose works Wagner praised for the very quasi-poetic qualities that for him were most opposed to systematic philosophy.[51] Presumably, Wagner's frustration with Schelling and Hegel had gotten the better of him. So far from promoting the search for a metaphysical absolute, Feuerbach's anthropocentric philosophy denigrates all such endeavors, inverting the thrust of Hegel's phenomenology of spirit by viewing religion and the deity as externalizations of human species qualities, above all love and feeling in general.[52] In his *Principles of the Philosophy of the Future,* the work whose title Wagner copied in *The Artwork of the Future* (dedicated to the philosopher), Feuerbach makes a plea for sensuousness in the "new philosophy," which he defines as the "essence of feeling elevated to consciousness," for "in love and feeling generally, every man confesses the truth of the new philosophy."[53] Feeling was for Feuerbach the "key to reality," whereas the abstract, speculative character of the "old," "absolute philosophy" had privileged reason and intellect. Feuerbach's pejorative use of the term "absolute" ("absolute being," "absolute thought," "absolute idealism," "absolute philosophy," and the like) conveyed his disdain for what he viewed as disembodied intellect, all that was opposed to the "heart" as the "whole and real being of man"; feeling was, therefore the "true absolute."[54] Nevertheless, despite Feuerbach's rejection of metaphysical and philosophical absolutes, his giving priority to feeling over intellect and intuition over conception parallels Schopenhauer's work, and even many of his formulations resemble those that later attracted Wagner to Schopenhauer—his association of religious feeling and dreams and his advocating dream interpretation to "reveal the mysteries of religion," for example.[55] And Schopenhauer, too, had no use for the exponents of the "absolute."[56] Around 1850, it was Feuerbach's emphasis on feeling as the true "absolute" that most influenced Wagner. And, for Feuerbach, music had a special role in relation to feeling. In music, which he calls "the monologue of feeling, . . . feeling speaks only to feeling"; as a result, "the complementing of the visual or figural representation with the musical gives the total image [of feeling] its fullest scope." Wagner's early "theory" of the leitmotif is considerably indebted to such formulations.[57]

Understandably, given his frustrated struggles with systematic philosophy, Wagner took over many of Feuerbach's ideas wholesale in the quasi-theoretical writings of the late 1840s and early 1850s: principally "Art and Revolution" (1849), "The Artwork of the Future" (1849), *Opera and Drama* (1851), and "A Communication to my Friends" (1851). Those writings—all produced in the compositional hiatus between *Lohengrin* (1847–48) and the beginning of the Ring (poem completed in 1853, composition begun in early 1854)—represent his closest approach to a systematically conceived aesthetic system. In them, some of the most voluminous prose works of his entire career, Wagner ranges indefatigably over an extensive ground of cultural and political history, both ancient and modern, weaving themes from the arts, myth, religion, and history together in one vast tapestry of quasi-philosophical aesthetic character. Running through them like a golden thread is a story of the opposition and higher union of feeling and intellect, of intuitive and conceptual knowledge, music and poetry, woman and man, a story ultimately of yearning for the perfect oneness of expression and form in the music drama. In many of Wagner's formulations— such as the opposition of conscious and unconscious, freedom and necessity—we perceive the ghosts of Schelling's "terminological pairs," now with a distinct Feuerbachian overlay. In part genuinely theoretical and in part a stream of mythically metaphorical language, those writings constituted what Wagner would descibe soon after the completion of *Tristan* as his "system," an "abstract expression of the artistic process then at work within [him]."[58] There is no question that in the most substantial of these writings, *Opera and Drama*, Wagner forged the conceptual basis of virtually all the most distinctive elements of his mature style. The leitmotif, *Stabreim* (alliteration), the orchestra as equivalent of the chorus of the Greek drama, the figurative and structural roles of modulation and periodic design—these and many other features of Wagner's later style all appear prominently in one form or another, although often in the "abstract" form that has led to difficulties with our describing their exact applicability to the works. In this process, Feuerbach provided Wagner with what might best be termed "aesthetic orientation," manifested in the continual extolling of feeling over intellect and the derision of anything that smacked of metaphysical or philosophical absoluteness.[59] Superficially adopting this element of Feuerbach's work, Wagner created his own long list of mostly pejorative absolutes—"absolute melody," "absolute form," "absolute harmony," and the like—associating many of them with the kind of music he viewed as overly concerned with music's routine constructive devices, such as excessive periodicity, and therefore detached from "poetic intent."[60] In seeking to inject the characters of the Ring with all that was "purely human," Wagner found Feuerbach's anthropocentrism enormously supportive; his sudden rejection of the absolute he had wanted most to comprehend, however, is based on nothing more sophisticated than his own misappropriation of the term to music.[61] In the process of equating his own attitudes toward the routine in music to Feuerbach's critique of idealist philosophy, the link between "poetic intent" and the musico-metaphysical absolute of the romantic writers was temporarily obscured in Wagner's mind. The discovery of Schopenhauer in 1854 would restore it once and for all.[62] Whether or not anything of Schopenhauer's ideas might have leaked into his consciousness before 1854, at the time of his beginning composition of the Ring early that year Wagner remained under the spell of Feuerbach, although by that time its influence had weakened to a degree that justifies us in the view that he was primed for change.[63]

Tristan and Schopenhauer

A S W E K N O W, by late 1854 Wagner's conversion to Schopenhauer was a fait accompli. References to Schopenhauer begin to appear in letters to Wagner's friends and continue over the following years. In one of these, written to August Röckel in August 1856, just a year before he produced the prose draft of *Tristan,* Wagner claimed that his own pre-Schopenhauer understanding of the Ring had been in error, what he called his "Hellenistically optimistic" conceptions in conflict with his pessimistic intuitions:

> Well, I scarcely noticed how, in working out this plan, nay, basically even in its very design, I was unconsciously following a quite different, and much more profound, intuition, and that, instead of a single phase in the world's evolution, what I had glimpsed was the essence of the world itself in all its conceivable phases, and that I had thereby recognized its nothingness, with the result, of course [that]—since I remained faithful to my intuitions rather than to my conceptions—what emerged was something totally different from what I had originally intended.[1]

Wagner went on to explain that his reading of Schopenhauer had enabled him to become conscious of the difference between his conceptions and his artistic intuitions in the Ring. He now viewed even the three operas of the 1840s in Schopenhauerian terms. Feuerbach's anthropocentrism had led Wagner away from romantic aesthetics and the search for the absolute in which his intuitions were deeply grounded, whereas the discovery of Schopenhauer represented a return to those aesthetics, but now within a more explicitly philosophical framework, and one that emphasized both the tragic character of existence and the possibility of redemption from that existence. Schopenhauer provided the exact blend of the poetic, philosophical, and metaphysical that Wagner had been seeking, along with the most substantial metaphysics of music of any modern philosopher. As the embodiment of his Schopenhauerian aesthetics, it was *Tristan,* more than the Ring, that Wagner viewed as the point of no return in his style development.[2]

In its underlying thematic content, *Tristan und Isolde* can be compared with the structure of the two parallel volumes of *The World as Will and Representation* (1819 and 1844), each of which describes a large-scale motion from philosophical analysis of representation (part 1) and will (part 2) to the metaphysics of art (part 3), then, finally, the quasi-religious goal of Schopenhauer's work: denial of the will-to-life and the "road to salvation" (part 4). For Wagner, as we saw, Schopenhauer's principal idea was the theme of his fourth book, which was of "terrible seriousness," but "uniquely redeeming." The design of *Tristan* was directed toward this goal. Although the progression of ideas in *Tristan* cannot exactly parallel the succession of Schopenhauer's topics, it nevertheless succeeds in intertwining most of the major ones with what for Wagner were the key episodes of Gottfried von Strassburg's story (except, of course, for the ending, which is missing in Gottfried).

In his first book, Schopenhauer treats the physical world as the product of the human mind, in which the a priori categories of time, space, and causality (the *principium individuationis*) limit and define our perception. Schopenhauer takes Kant as his starting point, retaining Kant's distinction of reality (noumenon) and appearance (phenomenon), which the idealist philosophers had rejected, but diverging sharply from Kant in the nature of the philosophical system he grounds in it. Intuition and conception remain, as for Kant, the basis of the distinction; but there is now a very different tone, in that Schopenhauer does not center his concerns on the analysis of reason and its limitations with regard to metaphysical knowledge but, rather, demotes reason and concept, claiming that "perception is the first source of all evidence, that immediate or mediate reference to this alone is absolute truth, . . . as every mediation through concepts exposes us to many deceptions."

Because of its analytical character, this part of Schopenhauer's treatise does not lend itself readily to direct poeticizing within the context of a love story. As we have seen, however, its primary thrust, that the world is the representation of the mind, without verifiable objective reality, is easily translated into the poetic trope of life and existence generally as a dream, without real substance. The opening words of *The World as Will and Representation*—"The world is my representation"—echo in the duet "O sink hernieder" when Tristan and Isolde, under the spell of the dream of love, voice Schopenhauer's thesis directly—"Selbst dann bin ich die Welt."[3]

Wagner's carrying over his setting of Mathilde Wesendonck's poem "Träume" (which he called a "study for *Tristan and Isolde*") in "O sink hernieder" and elsewhere in *Tristan* attests to the influence of Schopenhauer's dream theories on his conception of the work.[4] Whereas Wagner's earlier works often give a very prominent place to dreams, after the reading of Schopenhauer Wagner spoke of two kinds of dreams, the "dream of deepest sleep," which can never be understood in terms of the waking world, and the "allegorical" dream, which represents a distortion of the unconscious dream through its translation into the terms of phenomenality. Schopenhauer made these equivalent to the relationship of the noumenal and phenomenal worlds of Will and representation. This dualism, which is shared by Wagner's later conception of the leitmotif and of the relationship of music and drama in general, corresponds to the opposition between the inner and outer dimensions of myth— its archetypal content versus the clothing provided by the fantasy-like storyline.[5]

In "Music of the Future" (1860), Wagner maintains that *Tristan* carried to its limit a principle that had been developing in his works ever since his turning from historical to mythological subjects in *The Flying Dutchman:* the creation of poetic texts that would mirror the freedom and flexibility of symphonic music rather than the traditional forms of opera.[6] The everyday quality of conventional opera texts and the standard forms that accompanied them, both of which Hoffmann had found to be obstacles to music's exhibiting its true elevated nature, now gave way to a conception of opera as a world apart from the dominance of history, reason, and concept:

> The character of the scene, the legendary tone, transport the mind into a dream-like state which soon becomes a clairvoyant vision: the phenomena of the world are then perceived as possessing a coherence they do not have for the inquiring mind in its ordinary waking state, forever asking 'Why?' in order to overcome its fear of the incomprehensible world—that world it now perceives so clearly and vividly. How music should consummate the magic of this clairvoyant vision you will readily understand.[7]

Drawing its impulses principally from Schopenhauer's essays, "On Man's Need for Metaphysics" and "On Spirit Seeing and Everything Connected Therewith," this passage articulates a view of causality in opera that entirely conditioned the composition of the *Tristan* poem. It concerns the way that myth works on the perceiver, transporting him or her into a level of consciousness in which the suspension of disbelief takes over, as in a dream. The question of why Alberich and the Rhine maidens do not drown at the bottom of the Rhine in the opening scene of *Das Rheingold* is not only irrelevant but injurious to understanding the work; for the Ring constitutes a dream world in which ordinary motives and causality apply only in the most limited sense. In comparison to conventional opera texts, Wagner's now centered completely on "psychic motives," eliminating all the intricacies of description and plot that belonged to historical subject matter. This quality reached its apex in *Tristan*:

> I was free of all doubts when at last I threw myself into *Tristan*. Completely confident, I immersed myself in the depths of the psyche and from this inmost centre of the world boldly constructed an external form. You have only to glance at the voluminous text and you will see at once that, whereas the writer of a historical text is obliged to give a detailed exposition of the external events of his plot, obscuring any revelation of its inner motives, in my case the detailed exposition is of just those motives and only those. Life and death, the import and existence of the external world here depend entirely upon inner psychic events. The whole affecting story is the outcome of a soul's inmost need, and it comes to light as reflected from within.[8]

Wagner extends this conception to the view that not only the *dramatic* but also the *musical* motives possess inner and outer dimensions, the processes by which they are varied and developed analogous to the a priori character of perceptual knowledge in Kant and Schopenhauer, and the devices by which they are brought into association with the drama (i.e., as leitmotifs) basically external in nature.[9] Music's ineffability (or absoluteness), is the key to its dominance of the drama, now reduced to a "deed of music become visible."

In a sense, therefore, the direction of *Tristan* is opposite to that of *Die Meister-singer*, in which dreams and dream interpretation furthered the understanding of ordinary reality. In that work, Walther's "morning dream" provides the material that, when correctly interpreted in the terms of the waking world, the rules of external form, becomes the prize song (eventually entitled the "Morgentraumdeutweise"). The mythological content of the Ring, too, has a decidedly dreamlike character; and it has been interpreted allegorically in terms of both its external—that is, political or historical—content (Shaw) and its internal or psychological content (Donington).[10] In *Tristan*, however, the dream of love and the idea of dreams in general serve another purpose altogether: that is, they lead inward instead of outward, from the illusion, the allegorical dream of existence, through the "dream of deepest sleep" to the end of dreaming as the celebration of unconsciousness and the denial of the will-to-life itself. Whereas in *Die Meistersinger*, the internal world of intuitions, dreams, and the unconscious is united with the external one of conscious conceptions (compositional craft), as Schelling had said, in *Tristan* the process of metaphysical understanding is one of increasingly transcending the external, the victory of night over day.[11]

The dramatic subject matter of *Tristan* addresses the very questions Wagner takes up in "Music of the Future," as if it could be considered an *aesthetic* allegory of his new Schopenhauerian beliefs. Thus, the dreamlike character of myth becomes the dream of love that enfolds the lovers in act 2. Its leitmotif, the so-called dream chords of the song "Träume," symbolizes the lovers' longing for the never-awakening state of the metaphysical night. After they are awakened from their dream by the daylight and King Mark's return Wagner even introduces a passage, toward the end of the act, in which the unanswerable question "why" is put by King Mark and answered negatively by Tristan in terms of the Schopenhauerian message of the work as a whole. Tristan's denial that the ground of existence sought by King Mark can be either explained or experienced introduces the music of desire as the "what" of existence, then turns to music associated with the realm of night. Whereas formerly Wagner had veiled his characters' motivations on the grounds that such an explicit presentation of dramatic causality risked destruction of the instinctive side of the drama, now he went further, proclaiming that the search for ultimate causality—centering on the question "why"—was fundamentally unanswerable.[12] In *Tristan*, therefore, love, "this most beautiful of dreams," clothed the unfathomably tragic truth of existence as the Ode to Joy did in the Beethoven Ninth Symphony or Hans Sachs's ethically positive stance did in *Die Meistersinger*. Isolde's succumbing to unconsciousness in the *Liebestod* culminates these themes, rendering the debate over whether or not she dies into exactly the kind of question that Wagner argued should never be asked or answered.

In his second book, Schopenhauer treats of the world according to its second aspect: the universal principle of will, an extension of the direct knowledge of the self to the physical world. Recognition of the all-pervading character of will—the "what" of existence—is the closest anyone can come to knowledge of the world as it is in itself. Human life, and indeed all existence, animate and inanimate, are dominated by will in its various forms, the most extensive of which for living beings are the will-to-life, or the continuance of the species, and the principle of unfulfilled desire in general. As the agency through which the will creates and perpetuates in human minds all that we know as the world of differentiated phenomena—the "world as representation," founded on the *principium individuationis*—desire permeates human relationships in their entirety, especially love and sexuality. It is thus the source of the heights of human pleasure. But because desire can never be fulfilled or satisfied, it is also—and more fundamentally—the deepest source of human suffering, incomprehensible and therefore inescapable. For "while acts of the will always have ground or reason outside themselves in motives," the will itself is "groundless" and in no way subject to motives or causes of any kind. The will objectifies itself in the world of representation as endless striving and suffering whose ultimate cause can never be fathomed, as Tristan proclaims to King Mark (to the music associated with desire) in the passage mentioned earlier.[13] The physical world, permeated and perpetuated by desire in its countless forms, is therefore tragic at its root, despite the fact that the momentary fulfillment of desire might bring the illusion of happiness.

Because desire, under its endless striving, allows neither peace nor real progress toward attainment and satisfaction, existence in Schopenhauer's view is both restless and essentially static, an illusion of motion that in reality is no more than a perpetual circling back to the starting point. In this conception history, central to Hegel, is virtually meaningless. Schopenhauer cites it only to demonstrate that things have always been the same.[14] This is what Wagner recognized in the passage cited at the start of this chapter. This quality underlies the conception of the *Prelude* to *Tristan*, which, as has long been recognized, creates the impression of striving for a tonal form based on modulation that is never achieved. The dynamic of the *Prelude* is an extension of the idea embodied in its first seventeen measures—the music of desire itself—whose harmony, centered on the so-called Tristan chord and the unresolved dominant-seventh chord to which it progresses, never succeeds in attaining the tonal goal toward which it appears to move.[15]

Desire, then, is bound up with the illusion of existence, and the bliss it produces is momentary and deceptive, as Tristan recognizes at the end of act 1 (his cry, "O Wonne voller Tücke! O truggeweihtes Glücke!"—O bliss full of deceit! O happiness consecrated to lies!). Desire is the primary motive behind *Tristan*, its music almost continually present and its signal harmony, the Tristan chord, pervading the sonic world of the entire work. Its apex, in which "desire as fearful torment" reaches its greatest point of intensity, occurs in the third act as Tristan comes, under the influence of music, to awareness of its fundamentally tragic character, cursing the love potion and his own existence and sinking back into unconsciousness. His death, later in the act, is accompanied by the final sounding in the opera of the desire music in something close to its original form, but now reversed in its dynamic character.

Whereas, for Schopenhauer, consciousness of the force and universality of desire and the suffering it brings can lead to the knowledge that the world of representation is no more than an illusion created by the metaphysical will, attaining such knowledge is not possible through the usual intellectual channels. In book 3, Schopenhauer takes up the arts as the means by which human beings can come to some understanding of the universal qualities of existence, via the Platonic Ideas. Artistic contemplation enables us to pass beyond enslavement to the network of causal relationships that is bound up with willing, to enter temporarily a will-less, objective, or disinterested state in which the question "why" is suspended in favor of immersion in the "what" of existence. This idea, the core of Schopenhauer's aesthetics, involves his invoking the Platonic Ideas as the content of all art. In this light, Schopenhauer outlines a hierarchy among the nonmusical arts, ranging from architecture at the bottom to tragedy at the top, according to their nearness to or distance from the physical qualities of existence (the bottom of the scale) and their ability to project knowledge of the essentially tragic nature of existence as the product of the metaphysical will. Tragedy was the "summit of poetic art," whose purpose, "the description of the terrible side of life," represents "the nature of the world and of existence" as the "antagonism of the will with itself."[16] In certain individuals, however, the "light of knowledge" can soften this violence,

> until at last . . . this knowledge is purified and enhanced by suffering itself. It then reaches the point where the phenomenon, the veil of Maya, no longer deceives it. It sees through the form of the phenomenon, the *principium individuationis;* the egoism resting on this expires with it. The *motives* that were previously so powerful now lose their force, and instead of them, the complete knowledge of the real nature of the world, acting as a *quieter* of the will, proclaims resignation, the giving up not merely of life, but of the whole will-to-live itself.[17]

This is, of course, not the classical definition of tragedy. But it is the conception that Wagner followed in *Tristan*. Twice in later years Cosima Wagner recorded his words on that subject, in which he called *Tristan* the "greatest of tragedies, . . . for here Nature is thwarted in its finest work."[18] When, soon after completing *Tristan*, Wagner proclaims the pattern of nature as "broadly speaking a development from unconsciousness to consciousness and Man as the most striking example of that process," it is clear that he does indeed conceive of *Tristan* as a reversal or thwarting of that pattern.[19] The stages of that reversal are explicit in the motion from Tristan and Isolde's coming to consciousness of their love at the end of act 1 to Isolde's ecstatic submission to unconsciousness at the end of the opera ("unbewusst, höchste Lust").

Likewise, Schopenhauer's view that the "true sense of the tragedy is the deeper insight that what the hero atones for is . . . the guilt of existence itself" resonates with Tristan's cursing his own existence in act 3. This process Schopenhauer calls the "conversion" or the "turning" (*Umwendung*) of the will. It might be conveyed primarily by musical means:

> the genuinely tragic effect of the catastrophe, the hero's resignation and spiritual exaltation produced by it, seldom appear so purely motivated and distinctly expressed as in the opera *Norma*, where it comes in the duet *Qual cor tradisti, qual cor perdesti.* Here the conversion of the will is clearly indicated by the quietness suddenly introduced into the music. Quite apart from its excellent music, and from the diction that can only be that of a libretto, and considered only according to its motives and to its interior economy, this piece is in general a tragedy of extreme perfection, a true model of the tragic disposition of the motives, of the tragic progress of the action, and of

tragic development, together with the effect of these on the frame of mind of the heroes, which surmounts the world.[20]

That Schopenhauer cites a musical drama as exemplary of his conception of tragedy must have been of great influence on Wagner. For, in Schopenhauer's view, whereas the other arts provide the possibility of apprehending through contemplation the universal qualities that underlie the individual phenomena of existence, music, because of its inherently nonrepresentational nature offers far more. After his discussion of tragedy, Schopenhauer accords music a unique position among the arts, the only art that provides a copy of the Will and therefore an Idea of the world in its totality rather than in terms of its individual phenomena:

> the (Platonic) Ideas are the adequate objectification of the will. To stimulate the knowledge of these by depicting individual things . . . is the aim of all the other arts. . . . Hence all of them objectify the will only indirectly, in other words, by means of the Ideas. As our world is nothing but the phenomenon or appearance of the Ideas in plurality through entrance into the *principium individuationis* . . . music, since it passes over the Ideas, is also quite independent of the phenomenal world, positively ignores it, and, to a certain extent, could still exist even if there were no world at all, which cannot be said of the other arts. Thus music is as *immediate* an objectification and copy of the whole *will* as the world itself is, indeed as the Ideas are, the multiplied phenomenon of which constitutes the world of individual things. Therefore music is by no means like the other arts, namely a copy of the Ideas, but a *copy of the will itself,* the objectivity of which are the Ideas. For this reason the effect of music is so very much more powerful and penetrating than is that of the other arts, for these others speak only of the shadow, but music of the essence. However, as it is the same will that objectifies itself both in the Ideas and in music, though in quite a different way in each, there must be, not indeed an absolutely direct likeness, but yet a parallel, an analogy, between music and the Ideas, the phenomenon of which in plurality and in incompleteness is the visible world.[21]

Elaborating on this last idea in the second volume of his treatise, Schopenhauer maintains that "there is indeed of necessity no resemblance between [music's] productions and the world as representation, i.e., nature, but there must be a distinct *parallelism*." That parallelism enabled him to introduce analogies between music and certain of the generalized or universal qualities of existence, several of which—such as delayed resolution of dissonance as the counterpart of unfulfilled desire, modulation to a remote key as analogous to death, and the like—are suggestive in light of their prominence in the *Tristan* tonal language. It was this aspect of Schopenhauer's work, above all, that enabled Wagner to come to terms with the dichotomy between metaphysically absolute music and program music, the outcome of which was his two most interesting Schopenhauer-inspired essays, the one—"On Franz Liszt's Symphonic Poems" (1857)—written as Wagner was preparing to interrupt the Ring for the composition of *Tristan,* and the other—*Beethoven* (1870)—written as his contact with the young Friedrich Nietzsche stimulated him to reflect on his Schopenhauerian aesthetics in general.

In both essays, Wagner sets forth the opposition between appearance and essence, the world of phenomena and metaphysical intuition, external and internal, the former associated with conventional views of musical form, rooted in visual-conceptual processes, and the latter with the transcendence of such views. In the Liszt essay, he describes the oppositions that surround Liszt himself—the virtuoso and the poet—in terms recalling the oppositions Wagner had introduced in his 1846 notes on the Beethoven Ninth: between the understanding of music that can be conveyed in verbal description and the "absolute" understanding of music that comes from a personal inner experience. These qualities are analogous to the hilt and the blade of a sword, Wagner's metaphor for the static (conceptual) and dynamic (intuitive) aspects of musical form.

These and other of Wagner's later writings articulate a vision of the relationship of music and drama as one in which music, because of its inherently nonrepresentational nature—its providing a copy of the will, not of individual phenomena—takes priority over the drama at a deep level, even though it may derive from the drama in an immediate sense. Carl Dahlhaus described this aspect of Wagner's aesthetics as its "twofold truth," namely, that music was metaphysically determining of the drama at the same time that it was empirically determined *by* the drama.[22] The shift away from the viewpoint of *Opera and Drama*—in which Wagner proclaimed that music should be a means to the higher entity of drama—was reflected in Wagner's dropping the pejorative view of absolute music he had derived from Feuerbach in the writings of the late 1840s and early 1850s.[23] After Schopenhauer, however, music's metaphysical significance rendered it "absolute" in another sense, even though Wagner did not explicitly set forth the difference. In this view, music, especially in its motivic-developmental nature, paralleled the processes by which the empirical world came into existence as a representation of the mind. As Wagner expressed it in the 1870 Beethoven essay,

> music, in its motives, gives us the character of all phenomena of the world, according to their most inner abstract-self. The motion, shaping, and transformation of those motives, are not only related to the drama analogically and alone, but the idea-exhibiting drama is in truth to be understood, with perfect clearness, only through those musical motives, which thus move, and are shaped and transformed. We might not err, then, if we were to recognize in music man's *a priori* qualification, in general, for constructing the drama. As we construct for ourselves the phenomenal world, by the employment of the laws of time and space which are prefigured *a priori* in our brain, so, again, this conscious exhibition of the idea of the world in the drama would be prefigured in those inner musical laws which unconsciously make themselves valid in the dramatist's mind, just as the laws of causality are unconsciously employed for the apperception of the phenomenal world.[24]

Music thus exhibits inner and outer aspects, or absolute and empirical sides, in a more specific sense than had been set forth by Wackenroder and Tieck, or even Schelling and Hegel. In Wagner's aesthetics, this dualism is bound up with one of the most important ways in which the influence of Schopenhauer came to permeate Wagner's work: the conception of the sublime and its relationship to the beautiful. This distinction has, of course, a long history in aesthetic writings. But for our purposes the starting point is Edmund Burke's famous treatise of 1757, *A Philosophical Enquiry into the Origin of Our Ideas of the Sublime and Beautiful*, which was of great influence on Kant's 1764 treatise on the same subject and, both directly and indirectly, (through Kant) on Schopenhauer and Wagner.[25] We can gain an immediate sense of the relevance of this subject for *Tristan* from the fact that among his many oppositions between the sublime and the beautiful Burke associates the former with darkness and the latter with light, an opposition that Kant presents specifically as "Night is sublime, day is beautiful."[26] And, although both Kant's later formulation of the distinction in the *Critique of Judgment* (1796) and Schopenhauer's in *The World as Will and Representation* are more complex, this viewpoint on the sublime and the beautiful is embodied in the night/day metaphors of *Tristan*, along with several other associations shared by Burke, Kant, and Schopenhauer that Wagner invokes in his post-Schopenhauer aesthetic writings.

Schopenhauer's version of the association between the sublime and pain, fear, darkness, and tragedy, derived from Kant, was bound up with the conflict between the will and its striving, on the one hand, and the condition of will-free aesthetic contemplation, on the other. The more hostile the object of aesthetic contemplation was to the interests (or satisfaction) of the will, and hence the greater the obstacle to such contemplation, the greater the feeling of sublimity in anyone capable of maintaining the state of contemplation. Schopenhauer, therefore, subsumes the opposition of darkness and light beneath that of will and aesthetic contemplation.[27]

Using the afore-mentioned analogy, Schopenhauer describes grades in the progression from the will-dominated to the will-free states of aesthetic contemplation, stages in the transition from the beautiful to the sublime as the contemplative state overcomes increasingly fearful objects of contemplation. In this view, the beautiful is the condition of aesthetic contemplation, its purpose that of liberating the subject from the striving of will. What had been for Burke and Kant its lowest grade, the charming or attractive, is for Schopenhauer the "real opposite of the sublime . . . that which excites the will by directly presenting to it satisfaction, fulfillment." After the liberating effect of beauty, however, the feeling of the sublime arises when "something positively unfavourable to the will becomes object of pure contemplation. This contemplation is then maintained only by a constant turning away from the will and exaltation above its interests; and this constitutes the sublimity of the disposition."[28] The state of greatest sublimity, therefore, is contemplation of what is most unfavorable to the Will, death: "the full impression of the sublime . . . is caused by the sight of a power beyond all comparison superior to the individual, and threatening him with annihilation."[29] "Astonishment," one of the qualities most associated with the sublime by Burke and Kant, is for Schopenhauer what we experience in coming face to face with death, the greatest impulse to metaphysics.[30] For Kant, the sublime was particularly linked to transcendental idealism itself, in that it excited in the subject the feeling of a supersensible faculty. Kant linked the sublime with the infinite, the "absolutely" great, claiming that it led to a sense of a priori principles as the basis of judgment and postulated a susceptibility of the mind for Ideas.[31] Whereas the beautiful prepares us for disinterested contemplation, "the sublime pleases immediately through its opposition to the interest of sense." Understandably, therefore, Schopenhauer praised Kant's treatment of the sublime, calling it the "most excellent thing in the *Critique of Aesthetic Judgment.*"[32]

The complex of ideas that surrounds the sublime in Kant and Schopenhauer was of profound influence on Wagner. Wagner's most extensive discussion of the sublime comes in the 1870 Beethoven essay, in which he associates the beautiful with periodicity, conventional, and visual conceptions of form, phenomality, appearance, and the like, and the sublime with the inner essence of music, "the highest ecstasy of the consciousness of illimitability." Wagner makes an etymological connection between *Schein* and *Schönheit* to underscore his point, which is also a backhanded slap at Hanslick. Wagner extols the sublime over the beautiful because of its embodying the pathology of the Will, the mirror of its inner conflict rather than its appearance or representational aspect.[33] In his notes for the essay, Wagner sets forth the nature of the beautiful and the sublime with particular clarity:

> Terror of inner world basis of sublime. Sublimity. Effect of music always that of sublime: form, however, that of beauty, i.e., in first instance, liberation of individual from conception of any causality,—Musical beauty form in which musician plays with sublime. . . . The objectively beautiful?—Effect of what is beautiful only condition for onset of true effect of work of art, that is to say, the sublime one. In music first effect immediately and universally achieved through its form precisely because it is pure form.—If it does not lead to sublime effect, then that which is beautiful is mere play.[34]

In the poetic text of *Tristan*, Wagner introduces the word "sublime" (*erhaben*) twice and "beautiful" once. In the so-called Tagesgespräch of the second-act love scene, Tristan describes the dawning in his breast of the mild, sublime power of night, ending his commitment to day ("da erdämmerte mild erhabner Macht im Busen mir die Nacht; mein Tag war da vollbracht"). The passage in question is central to the establishing of A♭ major as the key of night in *Tristan*. And in its opening words, the culminating hymn to night and the oneness of love in the act 2 love scene, makes a similar association: "O ew'ge Nacht, süsse Nacht! Hehr erhab'ne Liebesnacht!" Much later, in act 3, at the end of his clairvoyant vision of Isolde, Tristan is overcome by her beauty ("Ach, Isolde! Isolde! Wie schön bist du!"), associating it in the music that follows with all that he has to overcome, namely the qualities associated with appearance, or day.

At the point of Isolde's arrival Tristan converts the visual into the auditory: "Wie, hör ich das Licht? Die Leuchte, ha! Die Leuchte verlischt! Zu ihr! Zu ihr!" (What, do I hear the light? The torch, ha! The torch goes out! To her! To her!). The music that now enters, combining the death motive of act 1, the motive associated with Isolde's extinguishing the torch in act 2, scene one, and the motive associated with the subjectivity of light in "O sink hernieder," all above a G pedal, is the most dissonant in the entire opera, embodying all the qualities associated with the sublime, and giving way to the music that accompanies Tristan's death, the desire music. The desire music is now reversed in its dynamic character, beginning at a point of maximum loudness and progressing to virtual inaudibility as it passes over into the music that symbolizes the origin of Tristan's and Isolde's love, the glance music, to which Tristan dies. The entire passage is the fulfillment of the ending of act 2, scene one, where Isolde had first introduced the theme of the subjectivity of light, associating it with the opera's first climactic anticipation of the transfiguration music of the *Liebestod*.

In the earlier scene, as Isolde gears herself up to extinguish the torch, she invokes the power of Frau Minne:

Die im Busen mir	She who fans the embers
die Glut entfacht,	in my breast,
die mir das Herze	she who causes
brennen macht,	my heart to burn,
die mir als Tag	who smiles on me
der Seele lacht,	as the day of the soul,
Frau Minne will:	Frau Minne wills
es werde Nacht,	that it be night,
daß hell sie dorten leuchte,	that brightly she may illuminate
wo sie dein Licht verscheuchte.	there where your light has banished her.

Here Wagner alludes to Schopenhauer's analogy between the sun's heat, associated with will, and its light, associated with will-free knowledge, giving it a new twist, in that it is Frau Minne (Gottfried von Strassburg's goddess of love), who leads Isolde from the glowing embers of physical passion in the breast, through the burning flames within the heart, to the laughing of "day" in the soul. The climax of the passage is Frau Minne's demand for night so that the subjective inner light of metaphysical intuition can replace that of the day and its symbol, the burning torch. And, as Isolde extinguishes the torch, proclaiming her action a metaphor for death, we hear the basis of the dissonant music that accompanies the lovers' final meeting in act 3, the victory of the sublime (love, night) over the beautiful (appearance, day).

Although the idea that sexual love can lead to transcendence of the will-to-life is in opposition to Schopenhauer, Wagner might have found a measure of support in the final paragraphs of Schopenhauer's metaphysics of music in both the first and second volumes of *The World as Will and Representation*. In the latter, Schopenhauer raises the question of music's seeming to "exalt our minds and speak of worlds different from and better than ours," whereas it "nevertheless flatters only the will-to-live, since it depicts the true nature of the will, gives it a glowing account of its success, and at the end expresses its satisfaction and contentment." Schopenhauer's solution to this apparent contradiction was to cite a passage from the Upanishads, in which human desire and ecstasy are seen to participate in the rapture of the "highest Atman," the sense of oneness with the universal "self" or world-spirit. In the Upanishads *Ātman*, ultimately equivalent to Brahma as the "world-ground," the objective soul that united all existence, was both a unity and a dualistic principle, separating into phenomenon and noumenon, but nevertheless permeating and bonding the two. As one of the Upanishads says, "He who has found and has awakened to the Soul (Self = *Ātman*) . . . the world is his; *indeed, he is the world itself*."[35] In light of Wagner's citing the italicized words at the climax of "O sink hernieder," it is conceivable that he also made the etymological connection beween the Sanscrit *Ātman* and the German "Atem" (breath), as the Grimm brothers did in their dictionary. At the climax of the *Liebestod* the phrase "In des Welt-Atems wehendem All" suggests as much, whereas Isolde's hearing a metaphysical melody that is inaudible to the others seems to mirror the idea that the division into appearance and inner reality of the Brahma involves a Brahma that is sound and one that is nonsound. Nonsound is revealed only by sound; in the highest state of meditation one passes beyond sound into nonsound, from the sensual, the appearance, to the reality.[36] Isolde, likewise, passes from Will to non-Will, Schopenhauer's "transcendental change."

In his third book Schopenhauer introduces the image of humanity bound to the endlessly rotating "wheel of Ixion" (Schopenhauer speaks also of the "wheel of time") to convey its enslavement to will, and that of the cessation of the wheel to suggest how the will-less contemplation of the Platonic ideas in art liberates us temporarily from the tyranny of the *principium individuationis*.[37] These ideas are not wholly original. Behind them, and behind Griepenkerl's invoking similar imagery to characterize the representation of the "sonnenlachende Idee" in the Beethoven symphonies, lies, in all probability, the influence of Wackenroder. In the story that begins the second (musical) half of the *Phantasien über die Kunst*—"A miraculous oriental fairy tale of a naked saint"—Wackenroder described a naked saint obsessed and possessed by the wheel of time, which made him perpetually restless and agitated, appearing to others like a madman in his desperate fear that time might stand still, whereas at the same time oppressed by the continual roaring of the wheel.[38] Finally, one night two lovers who "wanted to give themselves over to the solitude of night" appeared on the river near the cave where the saint lived. "The penetrating moonlight had illuminated and dissolved the darkest, innermost depths of the lovers' souls; their softest feelings melted together and flowed, united in boundless streams." Accompanying them was the "ethereal sound of music, floating in the expanse of heaven itself, sweet horns and I know not what other magical instruments drew out a swimming world of tones," among whose upward surging and subsiding tones a song to love and music was heard. And with this the wheel of time disappeared and the saint's restless, indefinable desire was finally pacified. His "genius" freed from its earthly confines, he ascended to heaven, following the tones of the music among the stars. Wackenroder's description of the saint's transfiguration is remarkably evocative of Isolde's *Liebestod,* which envisions Tristan's ascent surrounded by stars, introduces the imagery of "Wellen" and the sound of a metaphysical tune, and culminates with a symbolic depiction of the stilling of desire.

Whether or not Schopenhauer had Wackenroder's story in mind when he spoke of the wheel of time, it is impossible to believe that Wagner did not. For Mathilde, Wesendonck introduced a poeticized version of the wheel of time in her Schopenhauerian poem "Stehe still," which Wagner set as one of the *Wesendonck Lieder.* It has clear poetic and musical affinities with the character of the *Tristan* love scene, in which the lovers abandon their individual identities in a process mirroring Schopenhauer's pacification of the will. The resonance between Wackenroder and Tieck and Schopenhauer can be felt in both the depiction of the character of unfulfilled striving and the never-ceasing cyclic return of desire in the prelude and that of the pacification of the will and transfiguration through the oneness of love in the love scene (and the *Liebestod*); through the pacification of the will love takes on the character of Schopenhauer's aesthetic contemplation.

Thus, Wagner's amendment of Schopenhauer is rooted in Schopenhauer's metaphysics of music. Although overcoming desire remains essential to Wagner's conception of redemption, Wagner treats love as significantly more than it is for Schopenhauer, retaining links with Feuerbach's vision of love and feeling generally as the true absolute. In this view desire, which is present in *Tristan* right to the final cadence, is not the same as love (as in the Ring, where Alberich renounces love but not sexual desire); love contains the seeds of transcendence and is capable of transformation into metaphysical insight.

At the end of his third book, Schopenhauer, in anticipation of the subject matter of his fourth book, describes the progression of the artist himself toward transfiguration, a quality that for him was mirrored in certain art works. When the artist, whose life is one of deep suffering, "finally becomes tired of the spectacle, and seizes the serious side of things," he progresses to the condition of the saint experiencing a state of transfiguration, as in Raphael's painting of St. Cecilia.[39] In the 1870 essay on Beethoven, Wagner describes Beethoven in exactly those terms, comparing his forms to "transparencies" *through* which the inner light of night shines (as opposed to a painting *on* which the light shines).[40] Beethoven's forms are vehicles of revelatory character rather than objects.

Finally, in his fourth book Schopenhauer directly addresses the qualities associated with what he had proclaimed the "serious side of things" at the end of book 3: denial of the will-to-life as the source of the ecstatic transfiguring experience, the quality that, as Wagner tells us, demanded rapturous expression in *Tristan*. Such denial depends on recognition of the true character of the will in the identity of all phenomena, the overcoming of the *principium individuationis*. In book 3 Schopenhauer had maintained that through artistic contemplation temporary pacification of the will was possible, and through music, the "in-itself" of the world could be expressed. In book 4, subtitled "With the Attainment of Self-Knowledge, Affirmation and Denial of the Will-to-Live," Schopenhauer names knowledge of the inner nature of the world through the Platonic ideas as the means by which "we can also reach that disposition of mind which alone leads to true holiness and to salvation from the world." Such knowledge, however, is not the knowledge of "the whence, whither and why of the world . . . but always and everywhere the *what* alone."[41] Schopenhauer, therefore, emphasizes the nature of human motives, their connection with knowledge and their restriction to the world of phenomena. Ultimately, penetrating the unity behind all motives and of existence in general comes about through self-understanding, after which the Will, previously determined in all its phenomena by motives, can "express itself anew,"

> and that indeed where, in its most perfect phenomenon [humanity], the completely adequate knowledge of its own inner nature has dawned on it. Thus either it wills here, at the summit of mental endowment and self-consciousness, the same thing that it willed blindly and without knowledge of itself; and then knowledge always remains *motive* for it, in the whole as well as in the particular. Or, conversely, this knowledge becomes for it a *quieter*, silencing and suppressing all willing. This is the affirmation and denial of the will-to-live already stated previously in general terms.[42]

Schopenhauer's description of the difference between affirmation and denial of the will-to-life in terms of whether knowledge is a "motive" or a "quieter" is one that Wagner built into the very structure of the third act of *Tristan*, which, as is well known, moves in cycles containing substantial parallels in their sequences. In the first cycle, Tristan seeks release from the pain of desire, but the more he anticipates Isolde's coming to provide that release the more powerfully his vision is infected by the return of desire. The principal motives of the love scene reappear in newly intensified forms dominating Tristan's state of mind. There is an implicit connection between Schopenhauer's motives—that is, human motivations—and musical motives; but, as yet, there is no understanding of their reduction to desire. Tristan's vision of Isolde's arrival, dominated by desire, is not fulfilled. In the second cycle, however, Wagner combines Schopenhauer's metaphysics of music with the process of self-understanding that Schopenhauer describes in his fourth book, leading Tristan to denial rather than affirmation of the will-to-life. Under the influence of music (the so-called *alte Weise*), Tristan comes to understand the role of desire in a life fated for tragedy. Wagner's musical analog is Tristan's recognition that desire underlies the other motives, his cursing the love potion—the symbol of desire—and his own existence. Then following a near-death relapse, he reawakens with the metaphysical insight that enables his clairvoyant vision of Isolde.

Tristan's reawakening at the center of the act is accompanied by a transformation of the desire music that represents the substance of Wagner's purported amendment of Schopenhauer—namely, that through sexual love, or desire, one may attain metaphysical understanding leading to pacification of the will and denial of the will-to-life. Although Schopenhauer would have disagreed, he nevertheless left the door ajar in that in his fourth book he described, as the "last item in [his] discussion, how love, whose origin and nature we know to be seeing through the *principium individuationis*, leads to salvation, that is, to the entire surrender of the will-to-live, i.e., of all willing." Schopenhauer then described the love in question, however, not as sexual desire, but as "compassion or sympathy." And he proclaimed suicide affirmation, not denial, of the will-to-life, the main point of disagreement in the letter Wagner drafted but did not send.[43] Wagner must have thought carefully, and perhaps with ambivalence, about these distinctions. For Tristan's curse of the love potion and his own existence in act 3 replaces what had originally been conceived as a curse of love itself, whereas what had originally followed his awakening was centered on *Treu* (loyalty) and *Mitleid* (compassion).[44] In the final form of the act Wagner shifted his focus on the latter qualities to an earlier point in the act, placing another Schopenhauerian idea, that of the clairvoyant vision, or *actio in distans*, at the center and making it the outcome of a transformed view of desire. Instead of compassion, Wagner affirms (sexual) love as the key to the transcendental change.

If, as Wagner said, act 3 of *Tristan* was the point of departure for the mood of the work as whole, then it is likely that the opposition of "love as fearful torment" and love as "this most beautiful of dreams" dictated the musical character of the opera. Because Gottfried von Strassburg's Tristan poem is incomplete—missing most of what would correspond to Wagner's third act—Wagner would have had to resolve the ending before proceeding with his early prose draft. Although we cannot say exactly how much of the general musical character of act 3 might have been in his mind at an early stage, the fact that Wagner at various times made statements of one kind or another regarding the priority of music over drama, particularly in relation to *Tristan*, is suggestive. Whether or not such statements are taken as indications of the influence of Schopenhauer's metaphysics of music, they represent, I believe, the other side of what was in Wagner's mind when he said that the Schopenhauerian frame of mind was *in part* what inspired him to the creation of *Tristan*. Another vital part of that inspiration came from Wagner's music itself, which, owing to the new motivic-developmental processes in the Ring and the unprecedented scope of the harmonic-tonal qualities that accompanied them, must have encouraged Wagner to think in terms of analogies to Schopenhauer's principal ideas.[45]

By early 1857, while composing the second act of *Siegfried*, Wagner must have sensed the potential of certain aspects of his musical language for the kind of concentrated development demanded by tragedy, and particularly a tragedy in which Schopenhauerian themes would occupy center stage in a way that, owing to the pre-Schopenhauerian text, they could not in the Ring. The first two scenes of the second act of *Siegfried* feature musical qualities whose potential to convey the meaning of the Schopenhauerian oppositions was exactly what Wagner needed for his new work. The opening scene, in particular, centers on the tritone relationship between the "keys" of f minor and b minor, symbolic in that context of the dark forces behind the optimistic heroic surface associated with Siegfried and his bond with nature. In the second scene, the two are confronted, Fafner's tritones offset by the triads and perfect fifths of Siegfried's horn call and the song of the woodbird. Significantly, it is the taste of Fafner's blood that enables Siegfried to comprehend the meaning of the woodbird's song. In these scenes, Wagner confronts musical tendencies towards atonality with triadic symbols of tonality and nature. And the dualism of tonality and atonality carries over into *Tristan*, where, as we will see, it underlies the desire music. Ultimately it determines not only the character of the work's greatest turning point, Tristan's third-act relapse and reawakening—confronting the same tritone-related keys of f minor and b minor—but also the tonal structure of the act as a whole, which begins in f minor and ends in B. The harmonic-tonal qualities we find in the scenes from *Siegfried*, although put to different dramatic purposes from those of *Tristan*, are remarkably prophetic of the language of *Tristan*, where Wagner reveals that they possess aspects suggestive of surface and depth, nature and tragedy, representation and will.

Wagner's Schopenhauerian vision of the world as essentially tragic, and therefore—as Wagner viewed it—more profound, meant that from now on his entire outlook on art was dominated by powerful dualisms expressing the basic opposition of an optimistic surface that clothed the essentially tragic nature of existence. Thus, the finale of Beethoven's ninth symphony, formerly viewed by Wagner as the overcoming of inchoate tragic striving by the emergence of the conscious apperception of joy, now became an expression of the fundamental illusion of existence. The symphony remained tragic, in relation to which the Ode to Joy merely provided what Nietzsche would call the illusory Apollonian surface of the Dionysian tragic depths.[46] This is the character Wagner intended for the ending of the first act of *Tristan*, in which the bliss of the lovers' newly emergent consciousness of love, rendering Tristan's honor and Isolde's shame into a dream, masks the tragic reality that lies beyond. Tristan's closing words—"O Wonne voller Tücke! O truggeweihtes Glücke!" (O bliss full of deceit! O happiness consecrated to lies)—point the way to that reality, musically anticipating the deceptiveness of day in act 2. Ultimately, Wagner's feeling that in the Ring his conceptions were optimistic while his intuitions were the opposite becomes a consciously adopted attempt to mirror the dualism of appearance and essence, the day and night of *Tristan*, as two aspects of a reality that is accessible only through ecstatically intuitive states. *Tristan* is the work in which Wagner first represents both aspects simultaneously.

After *Tristan*, therefore, Wagner could return openly to historical and religious subject matter without contradictions in his new system. The case of his next opera, *Die Meistersinger von Nürnberg*, is very revealing in this regard. In the preface to his 1851 essay, *A Communication to my Friends*, Wagner had explained his inability, after *Tannhäuser* (1844), to find the appropriate tone for what was to have been his next project, *Die Meistersinger*. Although he had produced a prose draft for the latter work that is remarkably close in basic outline to its final version of nearly two decades later, Wagner found that he could only treat the subject ironically, an unacceptable situation. Wagner describes irony as a problem of modern social intercourse, a failure to speak directly that leads to the masking of true meaning, which can never break through the "form" of irony. Wagner links irony to the "purely formal side of my artistic views" rather than to "that core of Art whereof the roots lie hid in life itself."[47] As a form, irony is immediately understandable; hence its widespread acceptance. But it leaves the core of truth unexplored. Irony is resistance to an "element of life" that "primal mirth" cannot seize; its true content is tragedy. After his conversion to Schopenhauer and the composition of *Tristan*, Wagner was at last able to realize his intentions for *Die Meistersinger*. What made such a change possible was his acceptance of the tragic character of existence as the bedrock of truth beneath all optimism. Sachs's *Wahn* monologue gives the idea full expression.[48]

Similarly, in *Tristan*, Wagner often extends the implications of Gottfried's language according to ideas that in the main are far more indebted to his interpretation of Schopenhauer. Thus ideas such as forgetfulness and the "world apart" of love become wholly metaphysical in tone.[49] Likewise, Wagner amplifies Gottfried's expression "lieben tot" to what is ultimately yearning for death as metaphysical release.[50] Wagner's idea of *Liebestod* unfolds from act to act, associated first with Gottfried's vision of the union of love and death in the potion (as is well known, Wagner originally used the word "Liebestod" as a title for the prelude), then with the union of love, night and death—"sehnend verlangter Liebestod" in the duet "O ew'ge Nacht."[51] The third stage, completing the association of night and *Liebestod* with transfiguration, is wholly that of Wagner's amended Schopenhauerian perspective.

Tristan, therefore, describes a Schopenhauerian three-stage progression that I will refer to as desire, night-death, and transfiguration. It appears at many levels within the work, ranging from leitmotif combinations of a few measures duration to the three love scenes as a whole; and it underlies the pairing of the *Prelude and Liebestod*. Its most direct presentation is the passage where King Mark, in anguish over the lovers' betrayal, questions the meaning of human suffering and the deep mysterious ground of existence. His question, and Tristan's answer—"O König, das kann ich dir nicht sagen; und was du frägst, das kannst du nie erfahren" (O king, that I can never tell you; and what you ask you can never experience)—encapsulate many of the key issues of Schopenhauer's philosophy (the essentially tragic nature of existence, the futility of the question "Why," compassion as the basis of morality, the "Grund" of existence, the limits of what can be experienced, and the impossibility of knowledge

concerning the metaphysical noumenon) within a sequence that introduces the desire music of act 1, the music associated with night-death from the act 2 love scene
and, finally, an anticipation of the transfiguration music of Isolde's *Liebestod*. Here
Wagner seems to summarize the Schopenhauerian themes of the work and their
goal, the lovers' denial of the will-to-life as a transfiguring event.

In describing *Tristan* to Liszt as a *musical* conception Wagner adumbrated the
idea set forth in the 1857 essay on Liszt, that music "in no possible alliance ceases to
be the highest, the redeeming art," capable of absorbing and transfiguring any outside influences from the drama without losing its metaphysical absoluteness.[52]
Metaphorically, the source of music's redemptive power is its capacity to dissolve intellectual processes, as the metaphysical *Wellen* dissolve Isolde's consciousness at the
end of *Tristan*. The winding down of the long-drawn-out final cadence from the
major subdominant (E) to the blissful, but passive, minor subdominant (e), as Isolde
succumbs to unconsciousness (the E/e shift sounds beneath her "unbewusst, höchste
Lust"), and the substitution, in the final echo of the desire music, of that same E
minor harmony for the dominant-seventh chord on E are the means by which Wagner represents the dying of life's final illusions in Isolde as a transfiguring event: the
cessation of desire as a *motive* or cause—a representation of the end of dreams.

Wagner clearly intuited the existence in his time of powerful musical oppositions
such as tonality and atonality, romanticism and antiromanticism, qualities that were
of enormous potential in expressing the "terrible seriousness" of Schopenhauer's
principal idea versus its "uniquely redeeming" aspect, in juxtaposing the negating
aspect of the metaphysical night with the vision of love as "this most beautiful of
dreams." In this respect, the *Tristan* style represents at times the exaggeration and at
times the very dissolving of romanticism. Ultimately, the final cadence of *Tristan* became a symbol for the end of romanticism itself.[53]

THREE

Tristan and Gottfried von Strassburg I

Minne

Although to this point I have emphasized the priority of Schopenhauer over Gottfried von Strassburg in the inception of Wagner's *Tristan,* that is not the whole story. We do not know exactly when or in what form Wagner first encountered Gottfried's *Tristan und Isolt,* but it can be said without exaggeration that he penetrated the meaning of Gottfried's poem with a degree of understanding that qualifies him as a serious interpreter of the Tristan legend, as many literary scholars have recognized.[1] His reduction of the poem, drastic, and inevitable from the standpoint of a musical setting, in no way delimits the depth of his artistic involvement with it; and it preserves most of what literary scholars have long recognized as Gottfried's core themes. To be sure, Wagner translates those themes into Schopenhauerian terms, as Nietzsche did with Greek drama in *The Birth of Tragedy.* Doing so does not invalidate his understanding of Gottfried's underlying content, however. I would view it, rather, as comparable to Shelley's description of the sculptor of *Ozymandias* (slightly paraphrased): the hand (or in this case the head) mocking while the heart fed. When Wagner speaks of music as "the direct dream image, . . . the innermost power on which our poets unconsciously fed, whose presence they divined and sought to explain," he is alluding, like Shelley, to the division between the inspired (unconscious) and the craft (conscious) dimensions of creativity, the opposition that permeates *Die Meistersinger.* Understanding it enables Hans Sachs to recognize the validity of Walther von Stolzing's interaction with a voice from the past, that of Gottfried's contemporary, Walther von der Vogelweide. Sachs, like Wagner, has read both Walther and Gottfried, and knows how to divine the inner meaning behind the "allegorical" dream. The truth regarding Wagner's attitude toward Gottfried is not to be found in his rejection of what he would have considered the dated aspects of Gottfried's poem, but in his interaction with the universality of its underlying "music," which emerges in the poetic language, thematic content, and even the structure of *Tristan.* In this and the following chapter I will concentrate on the resonances between Gottfried and Schopenhauer in two of those themes, honor and Minne, which Gottfried elevated to the level of the conflict between love and the world and on which Wagner based much of his conception of *Tristan*.

Remarkably, over half of Wagner's Dresden library comprised works on the subject of German medieval literature and among them were three editions of Gottfried von Strassburg's *Tristan*, two in the original middle high German and one in a modern German version.[2] Gottfried's poem had been discovered in the eighteenth century and first published in 1775, and scholarship and literary criticism continued unabated throughout the nineteenth century. As a cornerstone in the rediscovery of the earliest German literary masterpieces, Gottfried's work sparked not only keen interest but also sharp controversy throughout the first hundred years of its modern reception, attracting the interest of figures such as August Wilhelm Schlegel, Jakob Grimm, and Joseph Freiherr von Eichendorff, to name only some of the most prominent.[3] Almost from the beginning Gottfried's work drew critical attention on two fronts: first, the brilliance of its poetic language, which is widely recognized as one of the greatest achievements in all German literature; and second, the moral issues surrounding Gottfried's very personal and unorthodox view of love and religion, adultery and guilt.

Drawing on the *Tristan* of Thomas of Brittanie, Gottfried paints a picture of love (*Minne*) as an all-consuming passion that is unique for its time, almost for any time. Under its spell, induced by (or symbolized in) the famous device of the love potion, Tristan and Isolde disregard all obstacles, moral and physical, in order to consummate their sexual longing. Their sexual relationship begins soon after drinking the love potion, on board the ship to Cornwall, and continues throughout most of the poem. It is offset by King Mark's continual suspicion and numerous attempts to discover the truth, about which he wavers back and forth for most of the poem. Time and again the lovers trick Mark with the most complex series of deceptions, ranging from substituting Brangaene for Isolde on the wedding night to the most notorious of all, the one known as "the ordeal," in which Gottfried describes the complicity of Christ himself in the lovers' deception, enabling Isolde with a "doctored oath" to redeem her honor. Gottfried's remarks at the end of this episode—especially his description of Christ as "pliant as a windblown sleeve"—raise the question of the lovers' honor as the central one in the morality of the poem as a whole.[4]

Needless to say, the lovers' deceit roused the ire of Gottfried's critics in his own time as well as after the rediscovery and publication of the poem. Gottfried's contemporary Wolfram von Eschenbach alludes, in the preface to his *Parzifal*, to female falsity and lack of honor, punning on the name "Isolde."[5] And in the nineteenth century many literary critics found Gottfried's poem immoral in exactly the same ways. As Rosemary Picozzi indicates, criticism was divided on the question of the lovers' guilt, with those who found Gottfried's treatment of this question either blasphemous or immoral, or both, in a clear majority.[6] It is interesting to note, however, that the minority, who found the lovers guiltless, either "belonged to or was sympathetic to the Mythological school," which tended to find ancient, universal, and religious origins (rather than historical origins) for Gottfried's poem.[7] Among the adherents to this school of thought were Friedrich H. von der Hagen and Hermann Kurtz, whose editions of Gottfried's *Tristan* were in Wagner's library. In light of Wagner's own extensive mythological studies, it is no surprise to find that he shared the view of this school that Tristan and Isolde, as the manifestation of what would later be called mythic archetypes, represented the priority of primal desire over the conventional trappings of the medieval courtly love tradition.

In this view, the magic potion neither created their love nor salvaged their honor. Instead, love reached such a point of intensity in them that it overcame all conventional moral obstacles. Whereas in the two endings written in the late thirteenth century to complete Gottfried's unfinished poem King Mark, having heard the story of the love potion, forgives the lovers and sanctifies their union, Hermann Kurtz's ending goes much further in absolving the lovers from lack of honor. Together Kurtz's last two episodes—"Tristan und Isolde" and "Rose und Rebe"—give his own perspective on the meaning of the lovers' deaths, especially the question of the relationship of love and honor. It is very much of the nineteenth century, of course. Thus, whereas Gottfried can be said to create a "religion of Minne" that is highly provocative, even blasphemous in its relationship to the orthodox beliefs of his time, Kurtz's ending reflects the mythological view of religion that was prominent in both Feuerbach and Schopenhauer, among others. In Kurtz's view the deity, so generalized as to become virtually an extension of nature, is easily invoked to overcome any lingering questions of morality arising from the lovers' deceptions and betrayal of King Mark. Kurtz's narrative ends with a prayerlike monologue of Mark, who, now an old man, visits their graves and, so far from merely granting forgiveness to the lovers, proclaims their honor and reproaches himself for having failed to recognize the divine bond between them and for having driven them from the path of honor to guilt and deception. Mark asks for forgiveness for *himself,* pronouncing that what he took for deceit and loose behavior in Isolde was in reality deep unspoken suffering. In this world, satisfied by what appears to the eyes, like the ivy and vine on the lovers' graves, no one follows the roots to their point of origin (*Grunde*), the suffering within the heart. What is visible to the eyes of humanity is only appearance (*Schein*) and illusion (*Wahn*). God, however, sees the truth: the genuine, divine force of love cannot be renounced. In death, therefore, the lovers, no longer separated by their names (*Getrennt durch Namen*) or by the web of worldly deceit are united in truth and stand free from God's judgment.

In Kurtz's ending, Tristan and Isolde are not only exonerated from any taint of dishonor but also elevated in death to a transcendent sphere, qualities that must have made a great impact on Wagner. Many of Kurtz's turns of phrase and much of his thematic content resemble Wagner's, although in Kurtz their frame of reference is far more conventionally religious than is the case with Wagner's quasi-Schopenhauerian outlook. Nevertheless, Kurtz's vision of the world as appearance and illusion beneath which lies a deeper reality of suffering and beyond which lies a transcendent sphere resonates with Wagner's Schopenhauerian agenda.

The most remarkable parallel in this regard is Kurtz's introducing the metaphor of "day" versus "night" in his penultimate episode, which deals with the deaths of Tristan and Isolde. Kurtz first introduces it in his narrative of the struggle of life and death in the wounded Tristan, where, having alluded to Gottfried's idea that Tristan was fated for death from the start, he describes Tristan as unable to die. The reason, he explains, is that residing within the soul is a "life force," a "mystery" that draws it back from the "black flood," holding death at bay and rendering the final struggle with death a bitter one. This force is a guilt (*Schuld*) that seeks redemption through confession, causing death to seek in vain to release the "fallen soul":

Umsonst! Schwer scheidend von dem Tag,	In vain! Struggling to take leave of Day,
Krümmt unter seinem Sensenschlag	The limbs writhe under Day's
Sich das Gebein. Was innen wacht,	Scythe-blow. The inner wakefulness
Will nicht hinunter in die Nacht.	Will not descend into night.

In such a passage "night" does not have the metaphysical overtones of Wagner's conception of night; rather night and day simply poeticize death and life. But Tristan's being unable to die because of an inner life force that is bound up with guilt and atonement echoes in Wagner's third act, where, kept alive by desire for Isolde, Tristan awaits her coming to drink atonement to him.

Kurtz's Tristan, wavering between life and death, heaven and earth, sends Kurvenal to fetch Isolde, who alone can bring him forgiveness, rest, and *Liebestrost*:

Ich will, ich muss sie noch einmal sehn,	I want, I must see her again,
Vergebung von ihrem Munde flehn. . . .	Plead forgiveness from her mouth. . . .
Mein irrer Geist hat keine Ruh,	My errant spirit cannot rest,
Sie komme denn, sie selbst, herzu. . . .	Unless she, herself, comes hither. . . .
Sie nur hat über mich zu schalten:	She alone has power over me:
Sie soll mich lösen oder halten.	She shall release me or retain me.
Ich kann nicht leben, kann nicht sterben,	I cannot live, I cannot die,
Mag ich nicht Liebestrost erwerben.	Unless I win the solace of love.

In Wagner's poem, Tristan also cries out for rest and finally, in his vision, perceives Isolde as bringing him "Trost und süsser Ruh." But Wagner greatly intensifies Tristan's wavering between life and death in terms of what he called "love as fearful torment"—that is, the force of desire, which keeps him alive against his will and demands Isolde for its resolution. Tristan's curses of day and his own existence, his relapse and reawakening, go beyond anything imagined by Kurtz. For Kurtz, Tristan awaits Isolde's coming as the light that will release him from the dream of earthly existence, whereas for Wagner Isolde is the light that Tristan hears ("Wie! Hör ich das Licht?") bringing him salvation near the point of death.

O Harren, bis der Morgen wacht!	Oh waiting, until morning awakens!
O dunkler Traum der Erdennacht.	O shadowy dream of earthly night.
Der Menschenkinder banges Loos!	Fearful fate of humankind!
So muss in deinem stillen Schooss	Thus in your still womb
Tristan, des Glückes Liebling, nun	Must Tristan, beloved of fortune,
Am Abend seiner Tage ruhn. . . .	Rest at the end of his days. . . .
. . . Dem ist das Loos gefallen,	. . . For him fate has come,
Wie seinen Brüdern allen:	As to all his brothers:
Warten und Harren! Kommt sie nicht?	Wait and hope! Will she not come?
Noch immer Nacht? Verzieht das Licht?	Is it night still? Does daylight dither?

Night is not the desideratum for Kurtz that it is for Wagner, although as the narrative continues it begins to take on something of a metaphysical quality. After Isolde of the white hands declares the flag on Isolde's ship to be black, Kurtz supplies an extended questioning of the cause behind such tragic events, reiterating the word "Warum" no less than four times and supplying as his final answer:

Warum? . . .	Why? . . .
Geht, fragt die alte Hüterin,	Go, ask the old guardian,
Die an dem ewigen Thor der Nacht	Who at the eternal portal of night
Stumm über ihren Räthseln wacht,	Silently guards her mysteries,
Wo blutend, eh sein Morgen tagte,	Where, before its new dawn, bleeding
Manch grosses Herz vergebens fragte.	Many a great heart inquired in vain.

Kurtz's "eternal portal of night" might have suggested to Wagner something akin to Schopenhauer's "veil of Maya," the barrier between the phenomenal and the noumenal or, in Wagner's poetic language, between night and day. Wagner speaks of the portal of *death*, both in the love scene and in act 3, where it is certainly equated with night. Kurtz, however, remains within the religious perspective, describing "night" as the necessary foil to God's light of grace:

Nacht muss er haben, wenn gnadenvoll	Night he must have, if, full of grace,
Das Licht seiner Augen leuchten soll.	The light of his eyes should shine.

It is possible here to perceive a parallel to Wagner's "Frau Minne will: es werde Nacht, dass hell sie dorten leuchte," in which, as described earlier, the poetic concept of night is the condition for the onset of the light of transcendence. In this light, Wagner could be said to transfer the religious associations of the night/day metaphor to his and Gottfried's deity, Minne. In the end, Kurtz describes both Tristan's and Isolde's deaths as yielding to night; and in the final lines of the segment he explicitly joins light and darkness with love at a higher level:

Sie schlummern. Mir ist so wohl für sie	They slumber. I rejoice for them.
Gehören sie nun einander nicht	Do they not belong to each another now,
In Gottes freiem Sonnenlicht,	In God's open sunlight,
Und auch im treuen Schooss der Nacht,	As well as in the true womb of night,
Wo Liebe selig bei Liebe wacht?	Where love blissfully watches over love?

Although Kurtz's conception of the day/night opposition suggests at times his own version of the appearance/reality oppositions, it is not allied so unmistakably with a physical/metaphysical vision of the world as Wagner's. Nevertheless, Wagner's reading of Kurtz probably supplied some of the impetus for his interpretation of night. Several of Kurtz's poetic formulations, such as "Schooss der Nacht," "seelige Träumen," and "Tagesschimmer," appear either directly or in parallel expressions in *Tristan*, whereas others, such as his description of the lovers as "Getrennt durch Namen" (compare Wagner's "Ohne Nennen, ohne Trennen") and his "Scheiden und Meiden" episode (compare Wagner's "Ohne Scheiden, ohne Meiden") resemble Wagner's.

And yet, because of its Schopenhauerian component, Wagner's ending and all that leads to it is far less conventional than Kurtz's. Kurtz's "religious" ending is hardly satisfying as a resolution of the conflicts in the poem that precedes it. Because in his ending Kurtz never mentions Christ, or indeed anything else that would pin God down to a set of specific expectations from humanity, the tension in Gottfried between religious dogma and societal norms, on the one hand, and the intensity of the sexual urge, on the other, is dissipated by the "pliancy" of a religion of love and nature that Gottfried never could have imagined. Kurtz's deity is entirely *ex machina*.

Wagner, of course, avoids introducing God into *Tristan* in any manner. The prayer that Kurtz assigns to Mark at the end of his poem is, therefore, impossible within Wagner's frame of reference in *Tristan* (although it may have provided Wagner with elements of King Mark's solos at the ends of acts 2 and 3). In Wagner's ending King Mark, having heard of the love potion from Brangaene (a detail taken from Kurtz), forgives the lovers, absolving them from guilt, as he does in the Türheim and Freiberg endings. But in Wagner's conception this forgiveness remains worldly. Although it dovetails with the perspective of the *Liebestod*, it remains distinct from it. The redemption of the lovers' honor has another source altogether: Gottfried himself by way of Schopenhauer. Extolling the power of nature was, for Wagner, no longer adequate when he turned to *Tristan* in 1857. A major part of his conversion, in fact, was the recognition that the world was, like Gottfried's poem, innately tragic, its deepest truths in *opposition* to nature. The kinds of connections Kurtz and others perceived between the Siegfried and Tristan myths may well have operated on Wagner when he turned from *Siegfried* to *Tristan*; but Tristan was not to be a natural hero like Siegfried. The intervention of Schopenhauer between Wagner's conception of nature in the Ring and his vision of the opposition of tragedy and nature in *Tristan* was decisive.

Nevertheless, Wagner's ending is not pure Schopenhauer. For, in claiming to have amended Schopenhauer on the metaphysics of sexual love, articulating the view that love could lead to denial of the will-to-life, Wagner turned to Gottfried's conception of Minne, intensifying Gottfried's vision of the union of life and death through love (*Liebestod*) to the point of its becoming a force of metaphysical proportions, overcoming worldly values entirely. Because for Gottfried there was no honor without Minne, the composer who extolled free love in the Ring, including adultery and incest of various kinds, could have no qualms when it came to Gottfried's lovers. Wagner links Gottfried's Minne with the metaphysics of desire, which from act 2 on he links with night, downplaying the deceptions and lies that even some of Gottfried's more sympathetic critics found troublesome by rendering them into manifestations of the metaphoric day. At the same time, however, Minne is more than desire. As Wagner presents her, she embodies the force that leads the lovers to the final outcome, which Wagner described in the original poetic draft of *Tristan* as Minne's "way." Ultimately, Minne is a quasi-religious force, encompassing not only life, desire, and death but also what Schopenhauer called the "path to salvation." Her "way," embodied in Wagner's desire/night-death/transfiguration sequence is the story of *Tristan*, the key to the redemption of honor.

Minne

Wagner, of course, makes explicit the fact that the love potion was, at least from the lovers' point of view, a symbol only, not the cause of their love. Isolde proclaims this openly in act 2 where, in opposition to Brangaene's claim that the lovers' passion was the result of her work in switching the potions, Isolde attributes absolute control of love, life, and death to "Frau Minne," whom she calls "the queen of the boldest spirits, the ruler over the world's becoming" (*des kühnsten Mutes Königin, des Welten-werden's Walterin*). The personification derives from Gottfried, who describes Minne in similar terms. The key to Wagner's interpretation of the potion is the fact that the lovers believe they are drinking poison, which is not the case in Gottfried. Nevertheless, although literary criticism has always been divided on the question of whether the love potion was the cause or the symbol of love for Gottfried, no one has ever failed to recognize that Gottfried's primary interest was in exploring the nature of love in more profound fashion than the authors of earlier Tristan poems (for whom the potion was unquestionably the sole cause of love). And, for Gottfried, recognizing a bond between love and death was essential to that process. Even before the lovers drink the wine Gottfried explains that it will bring their deaths (lines 11,672–75):

nein, ezn was niht mit wine,	No, it held no wine,
doch ez ime gelich waere:	much as it resembled it.
ez was diu wernde swaere,	It was their lasting sorrow,
diu endelose herzenot,	their never-ending anguish,
von der si beide lagen tot.[8]	Of which at last they died!

And Brangaene likewise recognizes death as the outcome (11, 705–06):

ouwe Tristan und Isot,	Ah, Tristan and Isolde,
diz tranc ist iuwer beider tot!	This draught will be your death!

Later, in telling Isolde of the love potion, Brangaene reiterates this (12, 487–89):

'owi!' sprach si 'daz selbe glas	'Alas,' replied Brangaene, 'that flask
und der tranc, der dar inne was,	and the draught it contained
der ist iuwer beider tot.'	will be the death of you both.'

And soon after this (12494–502), Tristan, in one of the most famous passages in Gottfried, and one that has been described as an anticipation of Wagner's *Liebestod*, proclaims

'nu waltes got!' sprach Tristan	'It is in God's hands!' said Tristan
'es waere tot oder leben:	'Whether it be life or death,
ez hat mir sanfte vergeben.	it has poisoned me most sweetly!
ine weiz, wie jener werden sol:	I have no idea what the other will be like,
dirre tot der tuot mir wol.	but this death suits me well!
solte diu wunnecliche Isot	If my adorable Isolde

iemer alsus sin min tot,	were to go on being the death of me in this fashion,
so wolte ich gerne werben	I would woo
umb ein eweclichez sterben.'	death everlasting!'

It was not simply desire, in fact, but Gottfried's broader central concept of Minne that proved of greatest use to Wagner in effecting his amendment of Schopenhauer. And what Gottfried's Minne offered Wagner was the close association between love and death, the idea that death was *within* love itself, as it were.[9] In his prologue, Gottfried speaks of a love that is so powerful as to draw joy and sorrow, life and death together into a union. Such desire creates what Gottfried calls a "world apart" from the ordinary world of those who are incapable of enduring sorrow and wish only to "revel in bliss."[10] Gottfried identifies his ideal readers as those "noble hearts" who understand love this way. To mirror the binding power of love Gottfried introduces a string of oppositions, mostly utilizing *Stabreim* (alliteration) to overcome the antitheses; among them is the expression "lieben tot," perhaps the source of Wagner's famous expression *Liebestod*:[11]

Der werlde und diseme lebene	What I have to say does not concern
erkumt min rede niht ebene:	that world and such a way of life;
ir leben und minez zweient sich.	their way and mine diverge sharply.
ein ander werlt die meine ich,	I have another world in mind
diu samet in eime herzen treit	which together in one heart bears
ir süeze sur, ir liebez leit,	its bitter-sweet, its dear sorrow,
ir herzeliep, ir senede not,	its heart's joy, its love's pain,
ir liebez leben, ir leiden tot,	its dear life, its sorrowful death,
ir lieben tot, ir leidez leben:	its dear death, its sorrowful life.
dem lebene si min leben ergeben,	To this life let my life be given,
der werlt wil ich gewerldet wesen,	of this world let me be part,
mit ir verderben oder genesen.	to be damned or saved with it.

As A. T. Hatto remarks of the passage just cited, "the rhythm of Gottfried's verse, the music of his rhymes binds opposites together triumphantly, strange though it all is in logic."[12] And this quality—the dominance of sound over meaning in the poetry—exhibits the very qualities that Wagner addressed in a famous passage from *Opera and Drama* in which he draws an analogy between *Stabreim* (alliteration) and modulation. Wagner's discussion was influenced by his extensive reading into medieval German literature, of which Gottfried's Tristan poem formed a cornerstone. Wagner describes the role of *Stabreim* in just the way that Hatto does the "music" of Gottfried's rhymes: as binding opposites into a unity in which the intellect "loosens" and the feeling "binds," a theme that links up with the emphasis on feeling over intellect in the Feuerbach-influenced aesthetics of *Opera and Drama*.[13] Wagner's discussion of *Stabreim* and modulation extends the sound-meaning opposition to the binding power of music over poetry, a quality that resonates with both the thematic content of Gottfried's poem and its "musical" style.[14]

That resonance is particularly strong in all that concerns the way that love binds life and death into a higher union in *Tristan*. It first emerges with the death motive of the first act—"Todgeweihtes Haupt! Todgeweihtes Herz!"—which binds the opposition of intellect and feeling together under their association with death. Wagner's music for this phrase sets up an antithesis in the harmony (on "Haupt") that the cadence of the motive resolves on "todgeweihtes Herz," an illustration of the way that feeling binds oppositions together. In addition, Wagner carries over the basic harmony of the desire music as the cadence of the death motive ("todgeweihtes Herz"), deriving its melody from the desire music as well. In this way he merges his quasi-philosophical feeling/intellect dualism with Gottfried's use of *Stabreim* to bind antitheses into a higher union, in particular those that Gottfried uses to identify love as his "world apart"—its embodying joy and sorrow, life and death.

Before proceeding further with how Wagner develops the union of love and death in *Tristan,* we may consider the ways in which "music" of various kinds runs throughout Gottfried's poem. Gottfried appears, in fact, to have associated the music of singing and instrumental playing with the intimate bond between Tristan and Isolde, both before and after the drinking of the love potion, and the musical style of lyric poetry as a means of conveying the same bond (even his narrative of Isolde of the white hands presents music as the cause of love). His use of rhetorical devices— alliteration, repetition, antithesis, word plays such as the turning of nouns into verbs ("gewerldet" in the above passage), and the like—is one of the best-known aspects of his style, and one that aids him enormously in articulating his central theme, the binding power of love.

In this respect, one of Gottfried's most interesting devices is the chiasmus, which appears in the form of word repetitions within a single line or line grouping, within the rhyme schemes of many of his quatrains and, on a larger scale, within the acrostics centering on the names Tristan and Isolde that run throughout much of the poem.[15] The most celebrated instance of word repetition of this kind appears at the point in his prologue where the names of his hero and heroine first emerge from his discourse on the nature of love (lines 129–30):

ein man ein wip, ein wip ein man,	A man, a woman; a woman, a man:
Tristan Isolt, Isolt Tristan.	Tristan, Isolde; Isolde, Tristan.

These lines complete a segment whose first two quatrains begin respectively with the initials T and I (the segment that contains the string of antitheses cited earlier); and they are directly followed by a segment whose first quatrains begin with the reverse initials, I and T. That segment and the prologue as a whole ends with another type of chiastic pattern, involving a double ABBA pattern of line endings (instead of just the normal rhyming couplets):

Deist aller edelen herzen brot.	This is bread to all noble hearts.
hie mite so lebet ir beider tot.	With this their death lives on.
wir lesen ir leben, wir lesen ir tot	We read their life, we read their death,
und ist uns daz süeze alse brot.	and to us it is sweet as bread.
Ir leben, ir tot sint unser brot.	Their life, their death, are our bread.
Sus lebet ir leben, sus lebet ir tot.	Thus lives their life, thus lives their death.
sus lebent si noch und sint doch tot	Thus they live still and yet are dead,
und ist ir tot der lebenden brot.	and their death is the bread of the living.

After Gottfried's emphasis on the power of Minne to bind joy and sorrow, life and death, earlier in the prologue, these famous concluding lines, with their obvious eucharistic allusions, provide a good instance of Gottfried's "fusion of sensuality and spirituality." Gottfried's *Leben—Tod—Brot* sequence is very suggestive of Wagner's desire—night/death—transfiguration sequence.[16] In this sense the lovers' deaths have a kind of redeeming function in terms of the meaning of their story for those readers, lovers, and "noble hearts" who come after and who want to understand the true depths of love. Minne can be said not only to encompass life and death, joy and sorrow, but also to point beyond the question of life and death to a kind of immortality for the lovers.

In the pattern involving the lovers' initials in his prologue, Gottfried provides what was most likely intended as a representation of the intertwining of the names Tristan and Isolde throughout his poem. That is, the TI and IT initial pattern marks the beginning of a fourfold intertwined acrostic of the first four letters in the names Tristan and Isolde (or Isolt): RS and SR in lines 1791–95 and 1865–69; IO and OI in 5099–5103 and 5177–81; SL and LS in 12431–35 and 12503–07. The pattern does not continue beyond this point (which coincides, significantly, with the avowal of love after the drinking of the love potion). According to Gottfried's spelling of the names Tristan and Isolt, the next four initials would all be T, a fact that would break down the chiastic pattern, but that would also have the potential to symbolize the lovers' union. For that reason we might expect it to appear in the lovers' cave scene, where such an ideal union occurs. It does not, however; and neither the full intention behind the acrostic pattern nor the fact that it is itself intertwined with other initial patterns has been fully explained.[17] Gottfried perhaps intended to complete it in the part of his poem that was left unfinished. In linking patterns of word repetition, rhyme scheme, and larger sectional divisions in a manner suggesting progression from musical (sound based) to visual qualities, Gottfried provides the reader with analogs of the lovers' union; the intertwined acrostics were perhaps introduced as a graphic representation of how Minne "knits" hearts together (see later). It presumably underlies the detail of the intertwining ivy and vine that grew on the lovers' graves and took root in Tristan's head and Isolde's heart.

The poetry of *Tristan* is substantially indebted to the binding qualities of Gottfried's poetic language: *Stabreim* (alliteration), word repetition, antithetical compounds (oymoron), and the like. In addition to the idea of *Liebestod*, many expressions of the lovers' union in the love scene derive from similar ones in Gottfried, although Wagner lends them Schopenhauerian associations.[18] One of the most interesting in this regard is the passage where the lovers discuss the word "and" in the title of the opera as the obstacle to their deeper union, an analog of Gottfried's "Tristan Isolt, Isolt, Tristan." Wagner makes it the center of a large-scale structural correspondence involving repetition of an entire dialog between the lovers in which their roles are reversed the second time round.[19]

In Gottfried's poem the theme of Minne is focused at three points above all: the prologue, in which Gottfried introduces his conception of love before beginning the narrative; the drinking of the love potion, in which Gottfried provides a discourse on love; and the episode of the lovers' cave, in which Tristan and Isolde attain the ideal of love as world apart. With great insight into Gottfried's central theme Wagner made these three passages over into his own introductory representation of desire (the prelude) and the first and second of his three love scenes. Since Gottfried's poem is incomplete, for his third love scene Wagner devised his own ending, which combines elements of the two medieval completions of Gottfried's poem that he had at his disposal and that of Hermann Kurtz's translation with Schopenhauer's "path to salvation."

Gottfried's shipboard and lover's cave settings represent the only scenes where love is unfettered by societal restraints, separate from the deceptions and intrigues that play such a large role in his poem.[20] As representations of his vision of the world apart of love they articulate a progression toward the ideals of *Liebeseinheit* and *Minnetranscendenz* (see notes 19 and 26): in the lovers' cave scene he no longer dwells on the antitheses within love—joy and sorrow, life and death—even as oppositions that are resolved into a higher union. Instead, he presents the lovers' existence in the cave as one of harmony and idyllic quasi-religious communion.[21] This quality is bound up with the famous set of allegories around which the *Minnegrotte* scene centers, depicting the fusion of sensuality and spirituality to an unprecedented degree.[22]

Wagner's selection of "three love scenes" from Gottfried on which to base his drama extends the sequence of desire, night-death, and transfiguration to the structure of the work as a whole. His three love scenes progressively open up the meaning of the lovers' "world apart" from the shipboard setting of act 1 to the garden of act 2 and the metaphoric interpretation of Tristan's "home" as the "weiten Reich der Welten Nacht" in act 3. In that sequence, Minne is the force that leads the lovers along the path of metaphysical understanding. Minne is not nearly as prominent in Wagner's poetic text for act 1 as she is in the corresponding parts of Gottfried's poem; nevertheless, at the end of the act, the lines "Sehnender Minne schwellendes Blühen, schmachtender Liebe seliges Glühen" and their A major tonality point ahead to the visionary character associated with Minne in act 2. The love scene, whose spiritual impetus derived, as Wagner said, from the song "Träume," is Wagner's primary representation of Gottfried's lovers' cave scene, often described as a "dream life."[23]

The allegorical aspect of Gottfried's lovers' cave scene provided Wagner with the inspiration for the increasingly metaphoric character of the first two scenes of act 2, as a summary of the setting itself makes clear. In the three scenes of his second act, Wagner preserved elements from three different love scenes in Gottfried's poem—centering on the episodes known as the "Assignation by the Brook," the "Cave of Lovers" (including the "Discovery"), and the "Parting" (see chapter 10). In Gottfried's poem the first and third of these scenes take place in Isolde's orchard at King Mark's court, whereas the second is entirely apart from the court, located in a wilderness nearly two days journey from the court. Common to both settings are shady trees and a brook, lending them the idyllic character of the traditional *locus amoenus* that Wagner retains in his setting. The hunting theme appears in the first two of Gottfried's love scenes, where it is associated primarily with King Mark; in the first scene he returns to spy on the lovers at night, whereas in the second the hunting party strays too far, extending into the night, and is forced to camp overnight. Both the lovers' cave scene and the parting scene involve Mark's discovery of the lovers, but the parting scene, in which he finds the lovers *in flagranto dilecte*, settles all doubts of their adultery once and for all. Wagner conflates the two discovery scenes into one, retaining the nighttime hunting party of the lovers' cave scene and the discovery of the lovers at dawn the next morning. The day/night metaphor, which does not emerge explicitly until scene two, determines the meaning of the dramatic events in the first scene as well. Thus, the burning torch, an addition of Wagner's (replacing Gottfried's floating twigs with the initials T and I), becomes a symbol of desire and day and its extinguishing a symbol of the onset of night; likewise, Frau Minne's will that it be night in scene one becomes her pointing the "way" to night-death for the lovers in the love scene (as is made explicit in the original version of the transition to "O ew'ge Nacht" preserved in the compositional draft). And Isolde's anticipation of physical union with Tristan in scene one becomes the lovers' ecstatic intuition of metaphysical oneness in the love scene. Thus, Wagner's scene succession retains the character of anticipation from Gottfried's brook scene, of an idyllic dream life (*Wunschleben*) from Gottfried's lovers' cave scene, and of discovery and parting from Gottfried's scenes of those names.

Among the allegorical descriptions of the *Minnegrotte* that Gottfried introduces to emphasize his view of love as a world apart are its hidden location, which is not accessible to all, and the additional fact that it is further protected from intrusion by a gate and a door whose locks cannot be opened from without except by those who know the secret. The inner world is one where conventional values of love and honor no longer apply; only Minne—"aller herzen künigen"—shows the way to the cave and permits entrance to love's delights. In Wagner's prose draft Isolde's chamber "through whose wide open door one sees into the dimly lit interior" suggests the interior of the cave, its door open in anticipation; and instead of urging Brangaene to extinguish the torch, Isolde urges her to open the *Pforte* (the gate into the garden) for Tristan.[24] At the end of the scene Isolde refers to a *Pforte* again, this time identifying it as the gate or door of death (*Todes Pforte*), which, as mentioned earlier, Wagner introduces (perhaps inspired by Kurtz) in both acts 2 and 3. And in the poetic draft of the original transition into "O ew'ge Nacht," which Wagner set to music in the compositional draft but later deleted, Wagner also introduced a metaphoric gate (*Tor*) and door (*Tür*), the latter revealed to the lovers by Minne. Although the gate/door symbolism is not present in the final version of the transition, a residue of the parallel with Gottfried appears at the beginning of "O ew'ge Nacht," where Wagner's stage directions describe Isolde's rising ("Ewig währ' uns die Nacht") and Tristan's following her, gestures reminiscent of Gottfried's description of the lovers' retiring into the cave for music and love-making. In this light "O ew'ge Nacht" is a metaphoric equivalent of the lovers' entering the *Minnegrotte*, now under the protection of night. Frau Minne's will that it be night at the end of scene one becomes eternal night, invoking the quasi-religious character of Gottfried's cave episode that has led commentators to speak of his religion of Minne. These details articulate the idea that Minne has a plan for the lovers, a "way," the goal of which is the ecstasy of *Liebeseinheit* and transfiguration in "O ew'ge Nacht" and the *Liebestod*.

In Wagner's earlier drafts of both text and music Minne played a considerably more significant role than in the final version. In all versions, however, Frau Minne takes on special prominence in act 2, scene 1, where Isolde introduces her in response to Brangaene's claim that Tristan and Isolde's love was her "work," brought about through the exchanging of the love potion for the poison intended by Isolde:

Dein Werk?	Your work?
O thör'ge Magd!	O foolish maiden!
Frau Minne kenntest du nicht?	Don't you know Frau Minne?
Nicht ihres Zauber's Macht?	Her magic power?
Des kühnsten Mutes	Of the boldest spirits
Königin,	the queen,
des Weltenwerden's	of the world's becoming
Walterin,	the ruler.
Leben und Tod	Life and death
sind untertan ihr,	are under her control,
die sie webt aus Lust und Leid,	which she weaves from joy and sorrow,
in Liebe wandelnd den Neid.	changing envy into love.
Des Todes Werk	The work of death
nahm ich's vermessen zur Hand,	I took rashly in my hands,
Frau Minne hat es	Frau Minne
meiner Macht entwandt.	took it from my power.
Die Todgeweihte	The death-consecrated
nahm sie in Pfand,	she took in pledge,
fasste das Werk	took the work
in ihre Hand.	in her hand.
Wie sie es wendet,	However she turns it,
wie sie es endet,	however she ends it,
was sie mir kühre,	whatever she chooses for me,
wohin mich führe,	wherever she leads me,
nun lass' mich gehorsam zeigen!	let me now show myself obedient!

In this passage Wagner assigns to Frau Minne more even than Gottfried does, merging qualities derived from both Gottfried and Schopenhauer (and also, perhaps, from Hermann Kurz's describing love as "Der Minne ganzes Werk"). That Minne binds life and death, joy and sorrow, is taken straight from Gottfried's prologue, whereas Isolde's declaring herself obedient to Minne echoes Gottfried's several personifications of Minne, all of which emphasize her control over the lovers' destinies. The *Stabreime* connect up both with Gottfried's and with Wagner's discussion of *Stabreim* and modulation in *Opera and Drama*. And Wagner's music for the passage, to be taken up in a later chapter, matches it in ways that are paradigmatic for the language of *Tristan* in general (see ex. 8.1). At this point, we may observe that in his setting of the lines just cited Wagner intertwines the death and desire motives in an even closer relationship than they exhibit in act 1, anticipating the enharmonic bond between death and desire that will be revealed in the new death motive. The reference to "weaving," both here and in "O sink hernieder" ("Wonnehehrstes Weben"), derives from Gottfried, who describes Minne as the entity who "knits" lovers' hearts together. The phrase "des Weltenwerdens Walterin" (ruler over the becoming of the world), however, combines Gottfried's presentation of Minne as "mistress of the world" with the representational attributes of desire or Will that derive from Schopenhauer. Minne, then, is a personification of desire; and the A major that Wagner associates with her in the ending of the passage cited above can be understood as the idealized "other side" of the A minor of the desire music, the vision of bliss or *Liebeswonne*.

But in this last respect Minne represents desire not as Schopenhauer viewed it, but according to Wagner's amended version of Schopenhauer. Isolde's ecstatic continuation, cited in the preceding chapter, makes that clear. Minne fans a glow in the breast, makes the heart burn, laughs as "day" in the soul and demands that it be night, which she illuminates from within. Her *Busen—Herz—Seele* sequence bonds the sensual and the spiritual in a musical sequence built upon the rising chromatic line of the desire music (in the bass); as Isolde describes how Minne's inner light arises within the night, it leads to a climactic, visionary anticipation of the transfiguration music of *Liebestod*. Minne leads the lovers from sensuality to longing for transcendence.

It is Minne, then, who controls the core sequence of desire, longing for night-death and transfiguration, embodying Wagner's amendment of Schopenhauer. Minne represents the illusion or dream of love, "der Welt holdester Wahn," as Kurvenal will call it in act 3. Isolde's vision of transcendence as the result of Frau Minne's will goes beyond anything in Gottfried; but Wagner's view of Minne's role in the process that leads from desire through night-death to transcendence is nevertheless indebted to Gottfried in some respects. Thus, in the love scene of the second act Wagner refers to the union of night and death as "ew'ge Minne," intensifying in the music the enharmonic language associated with Frau Minne's weaving life and death in the preceding scene. And in the compositional draft Wagner developed this idea in the transition to the final duet of the love scene, "O ew'ge Nacht," in relation to what he called Minne's "way" (Wagner deleted the first fourteen lines of this transition from the final version of the opera, although he included them in the printed text and set them to music in the compositional draft):

[Tristan] Soll der Tod	[Tristan] Shall death
mit seinen Streichen	with its blows
ewig uns	forever
den Tag verscheuchen?	Drive out the day for us?
[Isolde] Der uns vereint	[Isolde] That which unites us
den ich dir bot,	that which I offered you,
lass' ihm uns weih'n,	let us consecrate ourselves to it,
dem süssen Tod!	To sweet death!
Musste er uns	If he [death] had to close
das eine Thor,	the one portal,
an dem wir standen, verschliessen:	at which we stood:
zu der rechten Thür	to the right door
die uns Minne erkor,	which Minne chose for us,
hat sie den Weg nun gewiesen.	She has now shown the way.

These lines might well have been composed at the very time Wagner wrote to Mathilde Wesendonck of his proposed amendment of Schopenhauer (December 1, 1858). A week later (December 8) Wagner referred again to his amendment, remarking that he had become occupied with *Tristan* again on the previous day. Then, on December 22, he relates that for three days he had been "plodding at the passage 'Wen du umfangen, wem du gelacht' and 'In deinen Armen, dir geweiht,' etc.—" after having been "long interrupted."[25] Because the passages he identifies appear within "O ew'ge Nacht," just before the point of modulation to B, it is very likely that Wagner could not have been far from the transition into the duet when he wrote of the amendment.

When we look at the text and musical setting of the original transition, we find that it features interesting musical gestures and combinations that appear nowhere else in any version of the opera (see appendix 1 for facsimile and transcription). As Isolde refers to death as the bond between the lovers, and to her having offered Tristan death—that is, in act 1—we hear the death motive of the first act, associated with suicide, and in close to the specific form that Wagner had used in the *Tagesgespräch* of the act 2 love scene to illustrate Isolde's reflecting back on the poison drink as her attempt to attain "ew'ge Minne":

dort dir zu trinken	there to drink to you
ew'ge Minne,	eternal love,
mit mir dich in Verein	in union with me
wollt' ich dem Tode weih'n.	I wanted to consecrate you to death.

And as she sings "lass ihm uns weih'n, dem süssen Tod" (let us dedicate ourselves to it, to sweet death), we hear the first death motive merge into the new death motive (on "sweet death"). This is the only place in any version of the opera where Wagner makes immediately clear that the two views of death are equivalent. He then reiterates the cadence of the first death motive twice more, making clear that it is also a variant of the cadence of the second death motive, before leading it enharmonically into the beginning of the desire music, exactly as he had, earlier in the act, when referring to Frau Minne's control over life and death, joy and sorrow. This gesture, which reappears in act 3 for Tristan's death, accompanies Isolde's reference to a metaphoric gate that death had to close for the lovers, and that the music identifies as the gate of desire.

Wagner now presents the first two phrases of the desire music in a version that is transformed in a manner that, as will become clear later, corresponds to his claim, in the unfinished letter to Schopenhauer, to having discovered "in the beginnings of sexual love itself a path to salvation." On the third phrase the chromatic melody line continues upward as Isolde now refers to the "right door" that Minne has chosen for the lovers and to which she now shows the "way." The "way," of course, is the one Wagner described to Mathilde Wesendonck as the basis of his amendment: the way to salvation (*Heilsweg*) arising from desire.[26] On the word "Weg" Wagner makes an enharmonic shift to A♭, bringing in the motive known as the "love's peace motive," corresponding to the "pacification of the will" described by Wagner in his amendment. And from there the music (now much the same, although transposed, as the version of the transition we know from the published score) moves through a new combination of the motives associated with day and death, which lead directly into the transfiguration music for the beginning of the duet.

Thus, the transition traverses the path from the first-act view of death, which Wagner described as a "lower grade," to what he called the "highest and most perfect instance of the resolution of the Will." Musically, it can be viewed as a kind of microcosm of the lovers' metaphysical progression as a whole. That progression derives from Wagner's interpretation of Gottfried's goddess of love, Minne, as joining joy and sorrow, life and death. In appropriating two of Gottfried's allegories of the "lovers' cave" scene, those of the gate (*Tor*) and door (*Tür*) that bar entrance to the cave from all except those who enter through love, Wagner makes the gate into an allegory of desire and the door into one of transfiguration through pacification of the will, both entranceways descending from what he had called the portal of death (*Todes Pforte*) in the prose draft.

Not only was the transition into the duet "O ew'ge Nacht" reworked by Wagner from its original to its final form but also the duet itself was substantially recomposed in relation to the version Wagner produced in December 1858 at the time he wrote of his amendment. Its original form, which will be discussed in a later chapter, confirms the fact that Wagner's amendment formed a three-stage progression from the theme of suicide as "lower grade" in the resolution of the Will (act 1) to longing for death as transcendence of the individual will (act 2) and, finally, the "highest and most perfect instance of the resolution of the [species] will" (act 3). "O ew'ge Nacht," as Wagner wrote it in December 1858, was not as close to the *Liebestod* as is its final version, bringing back the so-called glance music of the prelude to the opera, which also had reappeared in the duet ending the first act. In this respect, "O ew'ge Nacht" looked backward to the first act as well as forward to the third—that is, it occupied an intermediate role in which the transfiguration music was much less present than in the *Liebestod*. In all this, the change from the "bewusst" of the first act duet, to the "einbewusst" of the second and the "unbewusst" of the *Liebestod* could be said to be more clearly articulated musically in the older version.

One reason that Wagner revised the original versions of the transition and the duet was probably that they made his intentions too explicit. Such an explicit presentation of intentions was something that Wagner had resolved to avoid in the Ring.[27] Beyond that, Wagner had returned to the theme of Minne's "way" once more at a later point in the act and, even there, had removed lines of text. After the breaking off of the love scene, King Mark's extended solo had culminated in his questioning Tristan regarding the "deep, mysterious ground" of suffering, and Tristan's reply had chained together in succession a presentation of the desire music (as he had declared Mark's question unanswerable), and music associated with night that featuring the second death motive prominently (as he had described his intention of journeying to the "wondrous realm of night" and asked if Isolde would follow). Isolde's response had then ended with an anticipation of the transfiguration music of the *Liebestod* as she asked Tristan to show the way; in concept, the sequence is close to that of the deleted transition. After that Tristan had kissed Isolde (as he does in Gottfried's parting scene), provoking Melot's intervention, and events had moved swiftly to Melot's fatal wounding of Tristan, clearly what Wagner meant by Tristan's showing the "way." Soon afterward, Tristan's final solo in the act had concluded with his explanation that Melot was the agent of Minne, his actions serving the sole purpose of showing Tristan Minne's way:[28]

Der Minne Macht	The power of Minne
hat's vollbracht!	Has brought it about!
Die Minne hat ihn erwählt	Minne has chosen him

der Minne Weg mir zu weisen,—	to reveal to me Minne's way,—
den letzten Weg, Isolde,	the last way, Isolde,
das ich dich führen sollte.—	that I shall lead you.—
[Wehr dich, Melot!]	[Guard yourself, Melot!]

Wagner deleted these lines (except the bracketed last one) from the original poetic draft without setting them to music, presumably because, again, they make the message of Minne's control too explicit as well as being somewhat redundant. Wagner had, in fact, adumbrated the meaning of this passage much earlier in the act, in scene one, where Isolde tells Brangaene that "he [Melot] opens up for Tristan what you [Brangaene] close off for me," a prefiguring of Melot's opening up the realm of night-death for Tristan. At that point as well as at the point at which Tristan kisses Isolde before Melot's intervention the transfiguration music enters in G♭, its only appearances in that key.

The one remaining reference to Minne in the text of *Tristan* is the one described in the preface as the fulfillment of Wagner's amendment, the turning point of act 3. Before that event Tristan, mortally wounded, reviews the events of his life in terms of his being fated for death and of the role of desire in his life. The latter part of this solo is dominated, as we will see, by his interpreting a series of the opera's leitmotifs— seven in all—in terms of the music associated with desire. At the climax of the solo, Tristan introduces a new motive in association with his rejection of desire, cursing the love potion as symbol of desire and eventually combining the curse and desire motives and cadencing to F as he curses his own existence as the "brewer" of the potion. This entire process is an extended allegory of Tristan's coming to recognize the force Schopenhauer called the "species will" behind the world of representation. Saturated with diminished-seventh chords, a symbol of negation, Tristan collapses unconscious to an F cadence that is neither major nor minor. This point, symbolically completing the first half of the act, which began in F minor and returned to that key repeatedly, marks the negative aspect of Wagner's amendment.

Simultaneously with Tristan's F/f cadence, Kurvenal enters with the pitch B, at first continuing the harmonic style of the preceding pages, but soon moving to B minor. The point where the modulation begins, at least in terms of Wagner's changing the key signature, is the near-exact center of the act from the standpoint of the measure numbers: Kurvenal's outcry "Schrecklicher Zauber! O Minnetrug! O Liebeszwang! Der Welt holdester Wahn!" (Frightful magic! O deception of love! O the power of love! The world's dearest delusion!). Wagner introduces the new signature on the word "Wahn" (delusion), which is the downbeat of measure 849 in an act of 1,699 measures. I do not believe for a moment that Wagner counted the measure numbers and contrived this detail, which in terms of the timing of the act is about five minutes beyond the center. The numerical exactness is a coincidence. But it is an enormously meaningful coincidence. For Kurvenal's pronouncing love "the world's dearest delusion" is the central pivot of the act, corresponding to what Schopenhauer says in his essay "On the Metaphysics of Sexual Love," the chapter that Wagner was responding to when he spoke of amending Schopenhauer's philosophy.

In his essay, Schopenhauer demystifies and deromanticizes love in every possible way. He does not deny the force of romantic love and its delusions, but he insists that beneath it lies the pure biological urge of a blind willing force, directed entirely toward the continuance of the species. In pronouncing love "the world's dearest delusion," therefore, Kurvenal agrees entirely with Schopenhauer. Tristan's subsequent reawakening, however, indicates the path to salvation and pacification of the will that Wagner described as the goal of his amendment. After singing the phrase "der Welt holdester Wahn," Kurvenal seems to address the audience rather than Tristan, whom he believes to be dead: "Hier liegt er nun, der wonnige Mann, der wie Keiner geliebt und geminnt. Nun seht, was von ihm sie Dankes gewann, was je Minne sich gewinnt!" (Here he lies now, the blissful man, loved and desired as no other. Now see what thanks she got from him, what Minne always gets!). In claiming that Minne receives no thanks from Tristan, Kurvenal is, of course, referring to the fact that before his collapse Tristan had cursed the love potion and his own existence as the agency of desire (the species will). But there is an irony here, in that directly following Kurvenal's words the desire music reenters, now transformed after the manner that depicts, as I will argue, the path to salvation. Tristan reawakens to this music, which leads to B for an anticipation of the transfiguration music. The irony is that this is *also* what we are being asked to "see"; and it bids fair to be considered the author's message. Tristan now experiences the clairvoyant vision described earlier, in which Isolde drinks atonement, to him—"wie sie hold mir Sühne trinkt"—a symbol of the "other side" of the love-death potion of the first act, where Isolde had spoken of it as such while concealing its true nature (poison). The parallel between the drink of desire and the drink of atonement becomes a focal point for the juxtaposition of the pessimistic Schopenharian view of love and the transcendent view of Wagner's amendment.

From Tristan's clairvoyant vision to his death events move swiftly. And, bound up with the interpretation of Tristan's death as the fulfillment of Minne's way is another of Gottfried's personifications of Minne that greatly influenced Wagner, as a "physician." It first emerges after the lovers drink the potion and, as is the case with Wagner's Frau Minne, it represents Minne as an active force before which the lovers are entirely passive:

> That night, as the lovely woman lay brooding and pining for her darling, there came stealing into her cabin her lover and her physician—Tristan and Love [Minne]. Love the physician led Tristan, her sick one, by the hand: and there, too, she found her other patient, Isolde. She quickly took both sufferers and gave him to her, her to him, to be each other's remedy. Who else could have severed them from the ill which they shared but Union, the knot that joined their senses? Love the Ensnarer knit their two hearts together by the toils of her sweetness with such consummate skill and such marvelous strength that in all their days the bond was never loosed.[29]

Gottfried is talking here, of course, of the physical union of the two lovers, personifying Love or *Minne* as healing them of lovesickness by knitting their senses together. But healing has another association in Gottfried; and it is one that Wagner developed ingeniously in *Tristan*. At the beginning and ending of their relationship, Isolde "heals" Tristan, the first time from the wound received from Morold (a wound in the loins, inviting sexual connotations in Gottfried), whereas the second time she comes to Kariol ostensibly to heal him from the wound received from Melot at the end of act 2. And Wagner, borrowing from Gottfried's description of Love as "physician," adds a dimension to this theme, in that he derives the theme associated with "Frau Minne" in Isolde's solos in act 2, scene 1 from that of Isolde's narrative in act 1, scene 2, in particular from the form of that theme that sounds when Isolde refers to her having healed the one who slew Morold. Both are based on the desire music. And in act 3, when Kurvenal reveals to Tristan that he has sent for the one who healed Tristan from Morold's wound to heal him again, Wagner makes the connection explicit by sounding first the theme of Isolde's narrative and then the Minne theme in immediate succession over their common quasi-ostinato bass. When Kurvenal refers to Isolde as "die beste Ärtztin," he is referring, of course, to Isolde's healing Tristan from Melot's wound; but later, when Tristan calls Isolde "die ferne Ärtztin," he means that Isolde alone can heal him of the sickness of life and desire.

In act 3, after making an association between his bloody wound in the fight with Morold and his intention to encounter Isolde with another bloody wound, Tristan rips off his bandages and staggers forward to meet Isolde:

Die mir die Wunde	She who my wounds
ewig schliesse,	closes forever,
sie naht wie ein Held,	she approaches like a hero,
sie naht mir zum Heil!	she comes for my salvation!
Vergeh' die Welt	Let the world pass away
meiner jauchzender Eil'!	to my jubilant haste!

"Heil" means both healing and salvation in German. Just as certain Bach cantatas develop the ancient metaphor of Jesus as the "physician" who heals the believer's soul from the sickness of sin, so the ending of *Tristan* depicts Isolde as the "physician" who heals Tristan of life.

The point of that healing is Tristan's death. As the lovers meet for the last time, Wagner brings back the music associated with Isolde's extinguishing the torch in act 2 (the torch and death motives combined), merging it with the motive of the subjectivity of light from "O sink hernieder." Then, recalling the music associated with Frau Minne's weaving life and death in act 2, scene 1, he leads it into the last appearance of the desire music in its basic form, a symbolic closing of the cycle of desire. In the deleted transition to "O ew'ge Nacht," Wagner had bonded the death and desire music in the same way, associating the desire music with the metaphoric "gate" that had to close before Minne could reveal the way to the right "door," that of pacification of the will and eternal night. There it led on to the transfiguration music in B for the beginning of the duet. Here Wagner reserves the move to B for Isolde's *Liebestod*, the completion of Minne's way, now equivalent to Schopenhauer's "road to salvation."

FOUR

Tristan and Gottfried von Strassburg II

Honor

WHEN HERMANN KURTZ IN HIS ENDING had King Mark exonerate Tristan and Isolde from dishonor, proclaiming them free from God's judgment and united in God's truth, he had no direct source in Gottfried von Strassburg's narrative, but he certainly knew that for Gottfried there could be no honor without Minne. Gottfried's allegories of the lovers' cave make abundantly clear that deceit was an abhorrence for him where love was concerned. The essence of his religion of Minne was that in *that* world, the world apart of the cave, ideals were of the highest. The crystalline bed carved with the name Minne signified the transparency and translucency of love, the roundness of the cave walls its simplicity, without any corners of cunning and treachery, and their whiteness its integrity; the green marble floor represented constancy; and the latch on the door, which was worked from the inside without any lock or key, prevented treachery and deceit: "for when anyone enters at Love's door who has not been admitted from within, it cannot be accounted Love, since it is either Deceit or Force."[1] There are other allegories of like kind. Finally, at the end of his discussion of the allegories, Gottfried assigns a special, indeed a culminating place to honor, explaining that the interior of the cave itself was illuminated by three little windows carved in the rock overhead through which the light of honor shone: "through these three, the sweet light, that blessed radiance, Honour, dearest of all luminaries, smiled in and lit up that cave of earthly bliss."[2]

Given all that leads to this point in the story—especially the last and most problematic of the deception episodes, the "Ordeal"—it is significant that the question of honor emerges more prominently in the episodes that surround the lovers' cave scene than at any other point in the narrative. Gottfried describes a kind of honor that is mere semblance in the episode that precedes the lovers' banishment ("Petitcreiu"). Here Tristan's honor is at its peak, yet it is not real honor. And in the narrative of the banishment Mark recognizes his own lack of honor. When the lovers are discovered within the cave, they are spotted through one of the windows of honor.

And, having heard the sound of the horns throughout the day, they have prepared for the possibility of discovery by lying at a distance from one another on the crystal bed, with Tristan's sword placed between them. They are illuminated by honor in the *Minnegrotte* because they are at last free from Mark's surveillance and their own need for deception. Nevertheless, the idyll comes to an end owing to Mark's discovery of the cave and the return of his doubts. Mark cannot enter the cave, but he can look in from the outside, from the very windows that should admit only the light of honor. And what he sees is the semblance only. Captivated by Isolde's beauty, "Love's gilding, golden innocence," he deceives himself out of attraction for Isolde. In a remarkable description of Mark's rising sexual feeling for Isolde, on whom a tiny sunbeam shone in, Gottfried has him cover up the window of honor with leaves and twigs so as to keep it from marring her beauty. He goes away in tears, after saying a prayer for Isolde's good keeping, but soon afterward he takes the lovers back to the court, "where his court and his household were devoted to their honour."[3] But nothing could be the same again, for the lovers were now under surveillance. Mark possesses Isolde physically, but has none of her love. As Gottfried describes it, he was entirely without honor, for Tristan and Isolde did not deceive him; he could see with his own eyes that Isolde did not love him, yet, deceiving himself out of lust and appetite, he persisted in a sham marriage, his life "bare of honor." His discovery of the lovers soon afterwards *in flagrante dilecto* is not so much another story of deception as it is the manifestation of a truth that has been there all along.

In all this it is important to recognize that Gottfried knows two kinds of honor, external and internal, the former concerned with appearances only, while the latter is completely indifferent to appearances and incapable of being separated from love. And this distinction was virtually unique for its time, in which honor was exclusively of the extrinsic kind.[4] Gottfried's bonding honor with sexual love was the root of the offense to Wolfram von Eschenbach and the majority of the nineteenth-century critics.

Wagner understood all this perfectly. The theme of honor and its relationship to love was, in fact, central to his design for *Tristan*. And it appears virtually certain that he worked it out at an early stage in the genesis of the work, even before beginning the compositional draft of the first act. For on a document in his hand appears the earliest surviving version of the desire music, containing details that Wagner had already altered before beginning the compositional draft, along with the music associated with Tristan's honor in act 1, scene 5.[5] In this manuscript the honor music also appears in a version that precedes that of the compositional draft and is then altered, below on the page, so as to conform to its final version (exx. 4.1 and 4.2).

The desire music and the honor music are versions of one another, each based on a sequence of three phrases ending with dominant-seventh chords built on the tones of the dominant triad (in relation to the key of the sequence as a whole): in the desire music the minor dominant of a, with dominant-seventh chords on E, G and B; in the honor music the major dominant of b/B, with dominant chords on B flat (A sharp), C sharp and F sharp. In the desire music the melodic units of the first and second phrases outline chromatic ascent from g#' to b' and b' to d", respectively, while the third phrase extends the pattern to the major third from d" to f#", to conform to the fact that the dominant seventh chord of the third phrase is a major third above

Example 4.1. Beginning of the *Tristan* Prelude, mm. 1–17: the "desire" music

that of the second phrase. The boundary tones of the three phrases—g♯′, b′, d″, and f♯″—describe a Tristan chord. In the honor music the three phrases outline a diminished-seventh chord in three minor-third units: f′ to a♭′, a♭′ to b′, and b′ to d″. The revision that Wagner made to the honor music on the document we are considering involved his adding to the first and second phrases an extension whose bass line arpeggiated the Tristan chords of the first two phrases of the desire music, those on F and G♯ (the final two measures of those phrases, 6–7 and 12–13, plus their upbeats; see exx. 4.1 and 4.2).

In deriving the honor music from the desire music, Wagner shifted the dominant-seventh chords of the first and second phrase endings at the tritone, that of the third phrase at the perfect fifth (or fourth). Because the desire music arpeggiates the dominant triad, beginning from its root, then progressing to the third and the fifth, its key is announced, albeit indirectly, from the start. In the honor music, however, the initial phrase does not indicate what the key will turn out to be. It begins from a cadence to F and moves toward what we take to be the dominant of E♭; only when the arpeggiation is completed over all three phrases, do we relate it, by hindsight, to b/B. Its overall F/b tritone shift is all the more meaningful, in that the F cadence at the beginning of scene 5 is unprepared and inexplicable except in terms of the shift itself. Antithesis and conflict seem to be bound up with honor, which is not what it

Example 4.2. Beginning of act 1, scene 5: the "honor" music

seems on the surface, a quality that we might also infer from the disparity in the
honor music between its melodic arpeggiation of the F diminished-seventh chord
and harmonic arpeggiation of the F♯ triad. The relationship between the melodic
contour of its three phrases and that of the "deceptive" cadence of the desire music
suggests that honor is a version of desire in which self-deception plays a central role.
Extrinsic honor leads to the denial of desire, whereas intrinsic honor acknowledges
desire. Thus, with all their talk of honor and shame in act 1, Tristan and Isolde deceive
each other and themselves, burying the truth of their desire beneath a facade of honor
until the end.

In act 1, scene 2, Wagner presents the desire music in yet another form, this time
outlining the diminished-seventh chord from d′ to d″ in a four-phrase sequence. In
this version the first unit, from d′ to f′, is not harmonized, but the remaining three

all follow the pattern of the first two phrases of the basic version (transposed): that is, they all outline a rising minor third melodically and they feature Tristan chords on D, F and A♭ with dominant-seventh chords on D♭, E and G. The three Tristan chords are those of the basic version, but now rotated (in 3, 1, 2 instead of 1, 2, 3 phrase order). This version of the desire music fulfills a crucial role in the act, even though it is never heard again in this form: it introduces the first death motive— Isolde's "Todgeweihtes Haupt! Todgeweihtes Herz!"—which follows immediately. And the latter motive features, as its cadential half ("Todgeweihtes Herz!"), the melodic contour of the deceptive cadence of the desire music and the honor music, but with its whole tones replaced by semitones. As mentioned earlier, its harmony is that of the second phrase of the desire music which directly precedes its entrance (ex. 4.3).

In other words, Wagner created three versions of the desire music, all of which appear in the first act, in association with desire, death, and honor, respectively. From the purely harmonic standpoint, one version arpeggiates the minor triad in the roots of the harmonies of its phrase endings, one the diminished triad and one the major triad. The first is associated with the key of a, the second with c and the third with b, three of the keys that have most to do with the structural design of the act (see chapter 9).

Wagner's view of honor in act 1 corresponds to the relationship of desire and honor in Schopenhauer's treatment of the two: desire (or will) is one of the deepest principles of existence, whereas honor is just the opposite. In scene 5, in which Tristan and Isolde debate the question of honor, Wagner uses the same melodic contour for both the honor music and the deceptive cadence of the desire music. Throughout the scene, the orchestra plays the death motive beneath Isolde's superficial talk of reconciliation and atonement. As Tristan comes to realize, however, that the drink that Isolde is offering him is, in fact, poison, he proclaims his honor—"Tristan's Ehre—höchste Treu'! Tristan's Elend—kühnster Trotz!" (Tristan's honor, highest truth! Tristan's anguish, boldest defiance!)—making the connection between the melodic contour of the honor music and that of the cadence of the death motive explicit. At the point in question Tristan understands suicide as the means of clearing his honor; the passage culminates in his singing the death motive, for the only time in the act, immediately before drinking the potion.

With the drinking of the potion Wagner articulates the relationship of desire, death, and honor in a manner that is prophetic for much of the design of *Tristan*. He brings back the music of the prelude not from the beginning, but from a point analogous to its climax, where the tonality shifts toward the key of e♭, a tritone away from the beginning of the prelude. And, to effect that shift, he sounds the first phrase of the desire music with its dominant-seventh chord transposed at the tritone, as occurs in the first phrase of the honor music, a gesture that seems to intensify the merger of death and honor.

In act 1, scene 5, honor is a high ideal for Tristan and Isolde, the code of chivalry to which they belong. Reconciling this with an unacknowledged passion that smolders beneath the surface of their tense encounter would seem to be impossible. Death is apparently the only answer; but death through suicide is, as Schopenhauer claimed, a deception, affirmation not denial of the will-to-life. Desire must be acknowledged.

Example 4.3. Act 1, scene 2: the desire music and death motive

And the return of the prelude music makes this clear. Wagner reinterprets the move toward e♭ enharmonically as at the climax of the prelude, casting the lovers back to where they were: in the midst of desire and its A minor tonality. What had seemed the gateway to redemption of honor and love in death, turns out to have gone nowhere at all. The potential for the union of honor and death to express transcendence of desire is not fulfilled. After the lovers have drunk the potion and the first phrase of the desire music dies away in the orchestra, we hear the cadential half of the death motive, the part that derives harmonically from the desire music and that resembles the honor music, dissolve into the desire music deep in the bass.

And after the lovers have awakened to consciousness of their desire, as Tristan sings "Was träumte mir von Tristan's Ehre?" and Isolde "Was träumte mir von Isolde's Schmach?" Wagner accompanies them with the first two phrases of the desire music in a version that projects a very different character from the one that followed the drinking of the potion. Now both phrases are in major (A and C) rather than minor, beginning from major triads rather than Tristan chords, and extended melodically, as if to clothe the otherwise somewhat abstract qualities associated with the basic form of the desire music. Within their melodic surface the honor theme sounds in passing, now hardly more than secondary figuration, stripped of all the terrifying force it has on its first appearance for the lovers' confrontation and intermingling with the themes of the glance and the drink of atonement. The blissful dream of love—symbolized in the easy adoption of the major mode—overwhelms all contradictory dreams. Ultimately C major, associated with the arrival at Cornwall, overcomes the key of death in the first act, C minor, making clear that a new set of values has taken over. In the midst of the excitement only the reappearance of the deceptive cadence on Tristan's final words, "O Wonne voller Tücke! O truggeweihtes Glücke," hints that something is wrong.

That something is the quality that Wagner calls "day" in act 2.[6] Tristan's honor and Isolde's shame (female honor in Schopenhauer's view) center, of course, on their treatment of King Mark—that is, their adulterous relationship. Honor therefore constitutes a devalued quality associated with day throughout the first half of the love scene of the second act. The beginning of the scene returns to C as the lovers revel in what Wagner described as "life overflowing with all the most violent emotions."[7] And in the subsequent Tagesgespräch (dialogue on day) honor stands in opposition to the deeper realities of night that result from the merging of love and death in the potion. Tristan and Isolde reflect back on the events of act 1, interpreting them now in terms of the day/night antithesis. That opposition is at first absolute. Its climax is Tristan's solo, beginning "Was dich umgliss mit hehrster Pracht, der Ehre Glanz, des Ruhmes Macht,—an sie mein Herz zu hangen hielt mich der Wahn gefangen" (What shone around you with the noblest splendor, the sheen of honor, the power of renown,—on these to hang my heart the delusion held me captive). In this solo, Wagner sets up a powerful antithesis between honor and night, in which, for the climax of Tristan's merging honor and day—"der Welten-Ehren Tages Sonne, mit ihrer Strahlen eitler Wonne" (the daylight sun of worldly honor, with its rays of empty bliss)—the harmony settles on B and its dominant for six measures, before passing to A♭ as Tristan continues, "durch Haupt und Scheitel drang mir ein, bis in des Herzens tiefsten Schrein. Was dort in keuscher Nacht dunkel verschlossen wacht, was ohne Wiss' und Wahn ich dämmernd dort empfah'n, . . ." (penetrated through my head and skull right to the deepest recesses of the heart. That which awakened there in the chaste night, sealed in darkness, that which, without knowledge or delusion I dimly perceived there, . . .).

Tristan's initial phrases ("Was dich umgliss mit hehrster Pracht, der Ehre Glanz, des Ruhmes Macht") are based on a motivic combination that otherwise appears once only in the opera: the merging of the day and second death motives that appears in the transition to "O ew'ge Nacht." There it sounds twice in succession, both times leading into the transfiguration music. The second time it passes over into the beginning of the duet itself. In "Was dich umgliss" the transfiguration music is less in evidence (although it is anticipated), but otherwise the music is the same (transposed in the case of the first phrase). Wagner had not conceived this combination when writing "Was dich umgliss" in the compositional draft; he carried it back from the transition to "O ew'ge Nacht" to the earlier solo when producing the final version. The connection between the two points is of great significance for our understanding of his treatment of honor in the love scene. For the sharp antithesis between "der Welten-Ehren Tages Sonne, mit ihrer Strahlen eitler Wonne" and "bis in des Herzens tiefsten Schrein"—the opposition of worldly, external values associated with honor and the concealed spirituality of love and night—involves the juxtaposition of the two keys that will come to symbolize for Wagner the passage from night to transcendence in the love scene, and eventually the *Liebestod*: A♭ ("O sink hernieder" and "So stürben wir") and B ("O ew'ge Nacht," which reiterates music of both earlier duets and also contains an A♭–B modulation within it). In "Was dich umgliss" the two keys are not fulfilled—that is, they are adumbrated, but not defined as such by cadences—and they appear in reverse order (B followed by A♭). More seriously, B appears with reverse associations: the emptiness of honor and day not the transcendent qualities of night.

Just as Wagner described the love scene as a broad progression from "life overflowing with all the most turbulent emotions" to the "most sincere and heartfelt longing for death," he makes clear in the relationship between Tristan's "Was dich umgliss" and the transition to "O ew'ge Nacht" that the meaning of honor reverses from the beginning to the end of the love scene. From the debased, hollow virtue of the ending of act 1 and the *Tagesgespräch*, honor takes on transcendent qualities: it is redeemed by its association with night rather than day; that is, it changes from extrinsic to intrinsic honor. The change is inseparable from two musical processes that are central to the love scene: the establishment of A♭ as the key of night, and the passage from A♭ to B as an allegory of the transcendent qualities that arise through night.

It would take us too far afield at this point to trace the processes just mentioned. After the key of A♭ is established (in "O sink hernieder"), there is very little direct discussion of the question of honor in the love scene. Having come to terms with day, the lovers center their dialogue on the question of oneness and separation, the physical world as barrier to the union of night, and how it can be transcended. But in articulating that transcendence Wagner takes pains to account for the redemption of the lovers' honor. He does this by bringing back the honor motive in "O ew'ge Nacht" and, indeed, in giving it a culminating, transcendent role analogous to the role of honor, "dearest of all luminaries," in Gottfried's lovers' cave scene. The result is a convergence of Minne and honor, as in Gottfried.

As mentioned earlier, in the compositional draft of the second act of *Tristan* not only the transition to "O ew'ge Nacht" but also the duet itself underwent revision and recomposition from its original to its final form (the original version of the duet is reproduced in facsimile in the appendix, "Excerpts from the Original Version," with transcription of the passages that were later revised). In December 1858, perhaps intent on articulating the second stage of his amendment of Schopenhauer, Wagner created a version of "O ew'ge Nacht" that harked back to the duet ending act 1 as well as anticipating the *Liebestod*. Emphasizing its relationship to the act 1 duet, Wagner brought back the second theme of the prelude, the glance music, at three points. The first occurred at the lines "Wen du umfangen, wem du gelacht, wie wär' ohne Bangen [aus dir er je erwacht]" (the one whom you embrace, on whom you smile, how could he ever awaken from you without fear), and the second at "In deinen Armen, dir geweiht" (In your arms, consecrated to you), the two parallel passages that Wagner mentioned in the Venice Diary entry of December 22, cited earlier.[8] Wagner's three-day struggle with the two passages is clear from the compositional draft. His first thought for both passages, evident in the melody and bass line, was to bring in the first two phrases of the glance music beginning from g♯', instead of the original a. Then he crossed out the bass notes, leaving the melody intact, and wrote in harmonies based on the dream chords of "O sink hernieder" (and the song "Träume"), anticipating the fact that in the second of these passages the glance music merges into a full statement of the dream chords with the aid of the whole-tone appoggiatura shared by both themes. (Although both passages contain the glance music and the dream chords, which cannot, of course, sound together, the Venice Diary entry refers only to the latter, Wagner's final solution at that point.) Then, just before the climax of the duet, as the lovers sing "heiss erglüther Brust," Wagner brought back the glance music in full and *in its original key* (and notated in $\frac{2}{4}$ against the $\frac{2}{2}$ of the voices and the movement in general), interrupting the motion of the harmony toward B. On its completion, he moved back toward B, sounding the transfiguration music once, then leading the orchestral line upward in sequences based on the honor music; the harmony seemed ready to articulate the union of honor and transfiguration (as in the *Liebestod*) but was broken off by King Mark's return.

In the new year of 1859 Wagner revised both the duet and the transition that led into it, removing the glance music completely. At "Wen du umfangen" he retained the dream chords in the orchestra, but substituted sequences based on the honor motive in the vocal lines. And at "In deinen Armen dir geweiht" he brought in the dream chords in full, several measures earlier than before. He also replaced the original A♭/B modulation (see below); in the new one a brief allusion to the honor motive sounds just before the shift to to B. Mostly, however, the dream chords precede and the honor music follows the A♭–B modulation, an analog of the passage from night (A♭) to the subjective light of Minne, honor, and transcendence (B). After the shift to B, he introduced references to the honor music, *in both versions,* at several points. The first, accompanying the lines "fern der Sonne, fern der Tage Trennungs Klage" (distant from the sun and from the daylight's complaint of separation), introduces a melodic succession that begins with the day motive ("fern der Sonne"), but that, as it goes on, brings out a musical relationship that has been latent to this point, that between the honor motive and the transfiguration cadence. As the lovers distance themselves from the day and the pain of separation—an analog of their entering the cave in Gottfried's narrative—the day motive gives way to honor and finally transfiguration. Wagner articulates the relationship of honor to desire and transfiguration more and more as the movement goes on, especially at points where the harmony settles on the dominant of B. At "ohne Meiden, ohne Scheiden" the honor motive ("ohne Meiden") and the chromatic unit of the desire music ("ohne Scheiden") appear in immediate succession, impelling the music to its arrival on F♯, while at "Ohne Nennen, ohne Trennen, neu Erkennen, neu Entbrennen," the honor music ("ohne Nennen," "neu Erkennen," "neu Entbrennen") comes to dominate the desire music ("ohne Trennen"). In the original version of the duet the dominant pedal to which this passage led gave way to the glance music ("heiss erglüther Brust"); in the final version, however, Wagner introduces a threefold sounding of the transfiguration cadence, extending the words "endloß, ewig einbewusst," and making its relationship to the honor motive explicit. Then, returning to the dominant of B, he builds for what on its reappearance in the *Liebestod* is the climax, in which Isolde succumbs to the "world spirit's infinite breath" (Welt Atems wehendem All). At the latter point the transfiguration cadence finally resolves to the root position B major chord and the honor-transfiguration music dominates until the end.

In all that I have just described Wagner completes what is the most significant sequence of interrelated motives in the opera, its very core: desire, deception, death, honor, and transfiguration (ex. 4.4). His revisions to the duet clarify the merging of the last two qualities. Transfiguration, however, is not attained in "O ew'ge Nacht."

Example 4.4. Motivic relationships: deception, death, honor, transfiguration

In the act 1 honor music the disparity between the F diminished-seventh-chord pattern of the melody and the F♯ dominant-triad arpeggiation of the harmony mirrored the conflict between honor and desire in the lovers, a conflict that was overcome in the victory of the deeper principle, desire. Now King Mark's return shatters the musical affirmation of the lovers' union in the most dramatic fashion: with the substitution of the F diminished-seventh chord beneath the final tones of the honor-transfiguration motive. In the scene that follows, Mark inverts the honor motive within his principal theme, afterwards turning to a key—D minor—derived from the F diminished-seventh chord harmony as he proclaims that Tristan has behaved dishonorably[9] (ex. 4.5). His reproach forces the question of honor back into the foreground of the drama.

In the final lines of his solo, however, Mark opens up the wider context to which the question of honor belongs in *Tristan:* "Die kein Himmel erlöst, warum mir diese Hölle? Die kein Elend sühnt, warum mir diese Schmach? Den unerforschlich tief geheimnisvollen Grund, wer macht der Welt ihn kund?" (Why this hell for me which no heaven can redeem? Why this shame, for which no suffering can atone? The unfathomably deep mysterious cause, who can reveal it to the world?) Mark's existential question prompts a Schopenhauerian response from Tristan. Wagner's stage directions specify that Tristan, who has lowered his eyes during Mark's solo, now "raises his eyes to Mark in compassion" ("mitleidig das Auge zu Marke erhebend"), thereby invoking the quality that Schopenhauer named as the basis of morality—compassion (*Mitleid*)—because of its necessitating identification with another person's suffering, a form of transcendence of the *principium individuationis.* Compassion was, for Schopenhauer, one of the deepest principles of existence, in comparison to which honor was bound up with "other people's opinion of our worth" (its objective side) and "our fear of that opinion" (its subjective aspect).[10] In a series of essays that were of great influence on the *Tristan* poem Schopenhauer set up a progression from the most internal qualities to the most external, or representational: from what a man is, through what he has (including friends) to what he represents (chiefly concerned with honor).[11] If we ask how, then, can the lovers' honor be redeemed, the answer is through their coming to understand the fundamental oneness of existence, which Schopenhauer equates with compassion, uniting magic and sexual love within itself.[12]

Wagner's understanding of honor was indebted to both Schopenhauer and Calderón while composing Tristan. Very soon after completing act 1, Wagner wrote to Liszt on the question of the conflicts surrounding honor in a way that suggests that the honor music was devised to represent those conflicts. Wagner was overwhelmed by how in the works of Calderón the "fine and deeply passionate spirit" of Spain had "seized upon the concept of 'honour' to express an idea in which all that is most noble and, at the same time, most terrifying assumes the form of a second religion."[13] Wagner took the conflict surrounding the question of honor to represent that between the world and a "deeply human sense of fellow-suffering (*Mitleid*)" that sought refuge "in an almost unspoken melancholy which, for that very reason, is the more deeply embracing and the more truly sublime: in it we see how terrible and how empty is the world's true essence." The concept of honor led to "denial of the

Example 4.5. Act 2, scene 3: Mark's theme, with inversion of the honor motive

world," which was confirmed in the lives of "almost all the great Spanish poets," which revealed their "complete spiritual victory over life." Honor, therefore, has both worldly and religious qualities, a negating and a transcendent aspect.

Wagner's view of Calderón was, of course, heavily conditioned by his reading of Schopenhauer, who had also praised Calderón highly and who had dealt with the question of honor in this manner in the afore-mentioned essays.[14] Through Calderón, Wagner came to the view that the particular profundity of the "Spanish view of life" in those works lay in their revealing the nature of the world through the antithesis of honor and fellow feeling (i.e., compassion, or *Mitleid*). In this context exaggerated honor, although linked to the values of day, nevertheless revealed truths about the meaning of the world—above all, its fundamental illusoriness. Calderón's masterpiece, *Vida es Sueño* (Life is a Dream) comes to mind immediately. Tristan's answer, therefore, sets a deeper principle of existence up against Mark's worldly one. And the musical sequence accompanying his answer—the "core sequence" of the desire music, followed by the music of night-death from act 2, then a brief anticipation of the transfiguration music—moves to a♭/A♭, a tritone away from the D minor tonal region of Mark's solo and the ending key of the act in general, as Tristan turns to Isolde. A♭ is the key of night in the love scene, an association that Tristan brings back to represent the lovers' distance from the world of day and honor represented by King Mark's question, their inhabiting in effect what Gottfried calls the world apart created by love. The meaning of Tristan's answer, therefore, is that metaphysical intuition (night), manifested in compassion, takes precedence over worldly values such as honor. Its source, the "teif geheimnisvollen Grund" of existence, can never be the object of knowledge or experience, and Mark's question "Why" is futile.[15]

Wagner's drawing the honor motive into the transfiguring perspective of the B major music of "O ew'ge Nacht" (and ultimately the *Liebestod* as well) means that in amending Schopenhauer's views on the relationship of love and metaphysical intuition Wagner was amending or expanding his conception of honor as well. Honor could in this view be redeemed metaphysically. Honor in *Tristan*, therefore, has two aspects, one which is superficial and illusory, whereas the other links it to the deeper qualities associated with Gottfried's world apart, above all the transcendent view of love.

Wagner presumably had this idea in mind from the beginning, for the act 1 honor music prefigures a series of transformations that take place in the latter part of the love scene of act 2, leading to the duet "O ew'ge Nacht," transformations that are, however, not completed until act 3. They are all bound up with establishing the key of B as the one that will symbolize Isolde's transcendence of the physical world in the *Liebestod*. Wagner's conception unfolds in three stages, at each of which the desire music is progressively modified according to the tonal pattern of the honor music. In act 1, only the first phrase is modified, its dominant-seventh chord shifted at the tritone, from E to B flat, at the climax of the prelude and again at the point where the lovers drink the potion. At both points it is followed by an enharmonic relapse back to its original form. In act 2, Wagner introduced this modification for *two* phrases of the desire music in the version of the transition to "O ew'ge Nacht" that he later replaced. In that version (see the appendix, "The Original Transition") the de- sire music initiated a sequence of tonal and motivic transformations in which the desire, night-death, transfiguration sequence featured music in A♭ from the love scene, ending with the sounding of the transfiguration music in B major (the key of the lead-in to "O ew'ge Nacht" in the original version). The keys of A flat and B marked the beginning and ending points of Minne's "way" in the transition.

Perhaps to further link the A♭/B modulation to the desire music, yet at the same time to make the point that sexual desire could lead to the denial of the will-to-life, Wagner's original modulation from A flat to B in "O ew'ge Nacht," alluded to earlier, introduced a symbolic modification of the desire music once again, this time settling on the dominant of B. Now the Tristan chord enters as a deceptive resolution of the dominant of A♭. And Wagner's modulation is an "inverted" form of the desire music, the chromatic melody descending instead of ascending, and the bass rising instead of descending a semitone (ex. 4.6). This was perhaps intended as a symbolic com- pletion of the arpeggiation of the F sharp major triad within the desire music. After sixty measures, however, it could hardly be heard as such. But the appearance of the transfiguration music in B major as the lead-in to the duet (instead of C sharp, as in the final version) certainly announced that key as the goal of both the transition and the duet.

In the final version, Wagner rewrote the modulation to B within the duet, he re- moved the desire music from the transition (along with other passages), and he transposed the combined day-death-transfiguration phrases, which he retained, to B flat and C sharp (keys corresponding to the dominant-seventh chords of the honor music's first two phrases as well as those of the first two phrases of the transformed version of the desire music).[16] This was part of a larger design in which the arpeg- giation of the F sharp major triad would be adumbrated at several points but not completed until Tristan's reawakening in Act Three. At that point Wagner makes a symbolic shift from the f/F with which the act began (the cadence of Tristan's sink- ing into unconsciousness) and the b/B of his reawakening, a gesture that represents an enormous expansion of the F/B juxtaposition of the honor music in act 1 and that mirrors the beginning and ending keys of act 3 as a whole. As Tristan revives we hear the transformed version of the desire music arpeggiate the dominant of B in its three phrases, as in the honor music of the first act, then lead into a prefiguring of the transfiguration music in the latter key. Desire and honor converge at a deeper level than before, leading Tristan to his clairvoyant vision of Isolde, the opera's ultimate instance of the metaphysical character of compassion: *actio in distans*.

Example 4.6. The original A♭/B modulation of "O ew'ge Nacht"

Despite the pivotal role of Tristan's reawakening and clairvoyant vision in the design of act 3, the poetic text of the act makes very little reference to honor. Instead, another quality of Gottfried's poem that Gottfried couples with honor comes increasingly to the fore, *Treu* (loyalty). *Treu*, or in Gottfried's German, *triuwe*, has received attention from Gottfried scholars as the "one and only virtue specifically mentioned in the prologue," where Gottfried presents it as the sign of the inner bond (*inneclichiu triuwe*) between the lovers that runs throughout the poem.[17] Gottfried lends loyalty the inner quality he also assigns to love (Gottfried used the adjective *inneclichiu* to characterize *Minne, Liebe,* and *guot*), making an association between *êre* and *triuwe* and the lovers' immortality in death, which emerges at the end of the prolog. But for most scholars, it is much later in the narrative after the lovers' separation that, "*triuwe* becomes, so to speak, of the essence."[18] Although Gottfried's poem is incomplete, in linking *triuwe* and *êre* with the lovers' immortality, the prologue anticipates those places in the narrative where Gottfried emphasizes the union of love and death. Thus, Max Wehrle interprets the ending of the prolog as Gottfried's assertion that "*triuwe* and *êre* are conveyed to us in the *Liebestod* of Tristan and Isôt."[19] With *Liebestod* he means, of course, the *liepen tot* of Gottfried's prologue, not the ending of Wagner's opera; but, in fact, Wagner's emphasis on *Treu* in act 3, especially after Tristan's death, makes the same connections.

In this light, loyalty, like honor, has two forms in *Tristan*, the first centered entirely on Tristan's loyalty to King Mark, which is what he proclaims with his "Tristan's Ehre, höchster Treu" in act 1, and the latter centering on his bond with Isolde, the equivalent of Gottfried's *inneclichiu triuwe*. The former quality, like honor, loses its meaning for the lovers in act 2. This is clearest in the version of the compositional draft. There, in Tristan's solo "O nun waren wir Nachtgeweihte" (O if only we were now consecrated to night), which proclaims the illusoriness of honor and day for the last time, bridging to the onset of night in "O sink hernieder," Wagner introduced the first eight of the following lines of text, setting them to music but later deleting them. They connect up musically and spiritually with Tristan's "Was träumte mir von Tristan's Ehre" in Act One, which refers to his extrinsic honor, his duty to King Mark.[20]

Selbst um der Treu'	*Even with the delusion*
und Freundschaft Wahn,	*of loyalty and friendship*
dem treu'sten Freunde	*for the most loyal of friends*

ist's getan,	*it is done,*
der in der Liebe	*he who has gazed*
Nacht geschaut,	*into the night of love*
dem sie ihr tief	*to whom she has entrusted*
Geheimnis vertraut.	*her deep secret.*
In des Tages eitlem Wähnen	In the vain delusions of day
bleibt ihm ein einzig Sehnen—	remains for him only one longing—
das Sehnen hin	the longing for
zur heil'gen Nacht,	holy night,
wo ur-ewig,	where eternally primal
einzig wahr	uniquely true
Liebeswonne ihm lacht!	The bliss of love smiles on him!

With the lines that he retained, culminating in the transition to "O sink hernieder," Wagner introduced the second death motive, the beginning of the desire music and an anticipation of the transfiguration music, thereby creating a musical analog of the joining of desire and death under the rubric "night." The sequence makes the point that loyalty means nothing to anyone who has looked into the mystery of the night of love.

Wagner, perhaps, changed his mind, deleting the lines on the illusoriness of loyalty and friendship in "O nun waren wir Nachtgeweihte" after completing the love scene. For when King Mark anguishes over Tristan's lack of loyalty, raising the question of the "deep mysterious *Grund*" behind human suffering, Wagner specifies Tristan's compassion. And when, after his response, Tristan turns to Isolde in the hope that she will follow him "loyally and sweetly" (*treu und hold*) into the realm of night, loyalty takes on a deeper meaning; that is, in coming under the influence of night rather than day *Treu*, like honor, exhibits an intrinsic rather than an extrinsic character.

Wagner thought carefully about the placement of his Schopenhauerian themes; and *Treu* and *Mitleid* were not only prominent among them but also related to one another. *Treu* comes into the foreground in act 3 owing to the lovers' separation. In the prose draft of the third act Wagner had not yet planned to make a central pivot around Tristan's reawakening with a clairvoyant vision of Isolde. Instead, after Tristan's awakening, he had placed Tristan's praise of Kurvenal's loyalty, adding a marginal note in praise of his *Mitleid* as well.[21] At what must have been a later time he added another marginal note—"Treue. (hier)"—earlier on, at the point at which the themes in question appear in the final version of the act. In the final version *Treu* is at first associated with Kurvenal and with *Mitleid*, just as in the prose draft, but is no longer placed after Tristan's awakening. In joining desire and honor at the latter point, Wagner suggests a deeper (but purely musical) reflection on *Treu* and *Mitleid*, qualities connected now to the idea of *actio in distans*. The point at which *Treu* emerges most clearly is now in the solo sung by Isolde in response to Tristan's death. Isolde's solo begins with a new leitmotif, "Isolde kam, mit Tristan treu zu sterben" (Isolde came to die loyally with Tristan), whose melodic contour, sinking by thirds through the upper tones of a minor dominant ninth chord, then rising again by thirds through the upper tones of the Tristan chord on the same bass tone (on "treu zu sterben"), moves at the peak of its ascent into the melodic shape that is shared by the honor and death motives—the tones c″, d♭″, f♭″, e♭″. The orchestra intones the motive very

Example 4.7. Act 3: The ending of Isolde's first solo in the version of the compositional draft

softly and slowly, making the point of the union of honor (now called *Treu*) and death in Isolde's mind. The very shape of the line as a whole suggests the process of death and rebirth with honor in death as its goal (see ex. 15.2).

Isolde's solo (discussed in chapter 15) anticipates the music of the *Liebestod* at several points. Its ending marks the beginning of Wagner's final realization of the idea behind Gottfried's world apart. As Isolde, who has finally accepted the fact of Tristan's death, hears him awaken to the metaphysical night, her "treu zu sterben" motive, which has been heard several times throughout her solo, instead of turning downward to end with the semitone appoggiatura, continues upward to introduce the music that anticipates the beginning of the *Liebestod*. In the compositional draft Isolde sings the additional word "Nacht"—the last in her solo—as she sinks unconscious to a vision of Tristan's reawakening: "Ha! Horch'—Er wacht! Geliebter! *Nacht!*" (Ha! Listen—He wakes! Beloved! *Night!*). This occurs in the final measure as the minor-third rotational pattern of the music of "So stürben wir," beginning on B, reaches F (see ex. 4.7). But before it can proceed to the next stage, A♭, Wagner interrupts it abruptly, making the shift to scene 3, as Kurvenal enters to announce the arrival of King Mark's ship, bearing Isolde, Mark, and Melot. In the original version this music continually ascends, but in its final form it *descends*, through the same sequence of keys: B, D, and F. Were it to continue, its next phrase would be identical to the beginning of the *Liebestod*; in fact, the ending of Isolde's solo was used around the turn of the century as an introduction to the *Liebestod*.[22] The interruption has the effect that from this point on the stage divides into what we must view as two separate groups. One centers on the altercation between King Mark's and Kurvenal's men; it represents the external action—day. The other centers on Isolde and Brangaene (who arrives with Mark's ship and ministers to Isolde). This division represents the fact that Isolde now exists in a world apart—identified explicitly as night—oblivious to the events on stage. The music of her two solos forms a continuity on the metaphysical plane, whereas that continuity is interrupted on the physical level by the altercation and the various explanations of Brangaene and King Mark, including their own perspectives on *Treu* (see chapter 15). Ultimately, they all converge on the *Liebestod*.

Thus, Wagner articulates the belief of the mythological tradition of Gottfried scholarship that Tristan and Isolde are guiltless of adultery and deception by asserting the metaphysical underpinning of their love, his version of Gottfried's world apart. The primary sequence of leitmotif interrelationships in *Tristan*—that which bonds the themes of desire, deception, death, honor and transfiguration—proclaims that the lovers' honor is redeemed by their deaths, their loyalty and their love (Minne), which bonds the opposites of joy and sorrow, life and death. Wagner intensifies the interrelatedness of desire, death and honor in relation to Gottfried's story by merging desire and death in the love potion, by elevating desire to the status of a metaphysical force, and by uniting desire and intrinsic honor as the path to salvation.

FIVE

The Desire Music

W RITING TO MATHILDE WESENDONCK soon after the completion of *Tristan,* Wagner cited the initial rising chromatic unit of the beginning of the prelude— the tones g♯′, a′, a♯′ and b′—as symbol of the "Buddhist theory of the origin of the world," the breath that "clouds the clear expanse of heaven." What he meant, as Thomas Mann perceived, was that the beginning of *Tristan,* like that of the Ring, was essentially a "myth of the world's creation," one in which "love's desire," the "focus of the will," was the principle behind existence itself.[1] The prelude unfolds the music from which the four tones are extracted—the desire music—and a few other themes derived from it in a manner that Wagner described in his program notes as analogous to the emergence of love, its search for transcendence through death, and its inevitable return to its starting point. Then, as the curtain goes up on the first act, we hear, as the first texted music of the opera, an unaccompanied sailor's song, commenting, so it seems, on Isolde's lovesick condition. The breath is now the sighing of tormented love, propelling the drama forward with all its contradictions:

Westwärts	Westward
schweift der Blick:	wanders the glance:
ostwärts	eastward
streicht das Schiff.	speeds the ship.
Frish weht der Wind	Freshly blows the wind
der Heimat zu:	towards home:
mein irisch Kind,	my Irish child,
wo weilest du?	where do you linger?
Sind's deiner Seufzer Wehen,	Is it the breath of your sighs
die mir die Segel blähen?	that swells my sails?
Wehe, wehe du Wind!	Blow, blow you wind!
Weh, ach wehe, mein Kind!	Sigh, ah sigh, my child!

Irische Maid,   Irish maiden,
Du wilde, minnige Maid.   You wild, passionate maiden.

Behind the sailor's puns and antitheses lies the first and most universal of Wagner's "psychic motives," desire, or will, the ground of human life and all existence. Passage from the first to the last of the four tones—g♯ (a♭) to b—expands throughout the opera to the level of harmonic successions, bass lines supporting transposing phrases, and, finally, modulation from A♭ to B. Focused in Isolde's transfiguration, but adumbrated at many earlier points, the A♭/B modulation symbolizes completion of the lovers' metaphysical journey. At the climax of the *Liebestod* Isolde returns to the cosmic breath, now the "Welt Atems wehendem All" into which her consciousness dissolves. Through the series of transformations indicated in the preceding chapter, the breath of desire has become one with the "highest *Ātman*," or world soul. As if fulfilling Wagner's claim to have found in the beginnings of sexual love a path to salvation and denial of the will, the four tones sound one last time before being absorbed into the final cadence.

Tristan is about the meaning of desire, its origins, universality, and, as human love, its urge to transcendence. At several points Wagner makes connections between the desire music and the lovers' intuitions regarding the nature of the world. As they sing "Selbst dann bin ich die Welt" in "O sink hernieder," he brings in the beginning of the desire music in combination with the day motive on the word "Welt," underscoring the subjectivity of the world as representation. Similarly, at the peak of his disgust with life and his own existence in act 3, Tristan introduces a new leitmotif, the so-called curse motive, for his realization that he "brewed" the love potion himself, that is, that the external events of his life had an inner cause: "ich selbst hab' ihn gebraut!" (I myself brewed it). Derived from the desire music, it combines with all three phrases of that music in preparation for Tristan's cursing his existence. And at two other points Wagner associates the desire music with a mysterious cause or "secret": Tristan's response to King Mark's search for the hidden ground of existence, and—its last appearance as a three-phrase unit—Brangaene's relating that she explained the secret of the love potion to King Mark. The former, as mentioned earlier, is motivated by compassion, whereas Brangaene's explanation reflects the way she has understood the potion from the beginning: as magic. These are two of the three phenomena through which, Schopenhauer maintained, the metaphysical identity of the will as thing-in-itself was manifested, the third being sexual love itself.[2] Thus, the desire music appears in different versions according to the dramatic circumstances, but is to be understood, nevertheless, as expressing an underlying unity. In this respect, it fulfills the inner/outer dualism of the motives just as Wagner described that quality.

The desire music of *Tristan* is probably the most frequently analyzed passage in the entire corpus of western music, even today. One reason is that it embodies patterns that suggest a high degree of symmetry—phrase parallelism, mutually inverting ascending and descending chromatic scalar units, transposing Tristan chords and dominant-seventh chords (also inversions of one another), and retrograde elements—in dialogue with qualities that suggest the breaking of that symmetry for "expressive" purposes. In this respect, the desire music embodies an important tendency of its time; for, as is well known, in the latter half of the nineteenth century and the early years of the twentieth symmetry emerged as a major topic in German music theory, particularly in association with the idea of dualism.[3] As David Bernstein indicates, this tendency appears to have first emerged in Moritz Hauptmann's *Die Natur der Harmonik und Metrik*, written in 1853, where its association with the Hegelian dialectic lent it something of the status of a "metaphysical" quality; this speculative dimension characterizes much of the continuing tradition of dualism, especially as it is associated with Hugo Riemann and Arthur von Oettingen.[4] At the same time, the more pragmatic idea of symmetrical inversion appeared in Simon Sechter's *Die Grundsätze der musikalischen Komposition* (1853–54), which recognized symmetrical inversion around the D axis as a compositional device of diatonic as well as chromatic music.[5] Later theorists, such as Bernhard Ziehn and Hermann Schröder, articulated theories of symmetry that united the more abstract forms of dualism with the more practical compositional inversion techniques, one turn-of-the-century theorist, Georg Capellen, analyzing the first two phrases of the *Tristan* Prelude in that light.[6]

In this context, Wagner's desire music is an ingenious invention, a more complex statement on the origins of existence than its counterpart in the Ring, embodying ideas of symmetry and asymmetry, pessimism and yearning for transcendence within it. In the opera, any of these qualities may be emphasized. We have seen that Wagner devised three forms, all of which appear in the first act. The first of these, beginning the opera, constitutes the most general statement on desire, whereas the other two, associated with death and honor, respectively, tend toward the pessimistic and transcendental aspects of love. It is a premise of this study, however, that these different, even opposite tendencies, which are bound up with the arpeggiation patterns of the diminished-seventh chord, the minor triad and the major triad, are embodied within the basic version itself. That is, within the pessimistic or death-centered version the diminished-seventh chord dictates both the melodic and harmonic patterns of the phrases, whereas within the version that appears at Tristan's reawakening in act 3 (derived from the honor music) the major triad provides the harmonic underpinning and the melodic units are altered so as to outline the major third on all three phrases (in the honor music the melodic units remain bound to the minor third). In the basic version, however, we find a mixture of the two; there is a strong component of the diminished-seventh chord, especially in the first and second phrases, whereas the third phrase marks a departure from that framework. This, I believe, is best interpreted in terms of a diminished-seventh-chord "background" that is manifested in the phrase patterning—an external quality—against which there is an inner tendency to break with the diminished seventh chord. In this view, the diminished-seventh chord symbolizes perfect symmetry and closed cyclicity, ultimately an analogue of what Wagner and Schopenhauer called "the nothingness of the world," whereas the elements that break with it—analogous, perhaps, to the "breath that clouds the clear expanse of heaven"—tend toward, first, the physical fulfillment of love, giving life its meaning (the basic version), then the urge toward transcendence, in Wagner's view love's metaphysical fulfillment (the third-act version).

We must therefore distinguish between what remains the same and what changes in the different versions of the desire music. Limiting ourselves to the three versions of act 1 (exx. 4.1, 4.2, and 4.3), we note that while the arpeggiation patterns of the dominant-seventh (or -ninth) chords are different among the three, the Tristan chords and diminished-seventh-chord patterns of the melodic line are very closely related. The basic version and the death-related version are closest in this respect, because the pattern of the first two phrases of the basic version is that of all three phrases in the death-related version; also, these two versions feature the same three Tristan chords—on F, A♭/G♯, and D (in different order)—whereas the honor music features only those on F and A♭/G♯ horizontally in the bass of the first two phrase endings. The death-related version and the honor music outline the same diminished-seventh chord in the melody, whereas the basic version alters it in the final phrase. Thus, it appears that, despite the difference in their arpeggiation patterns, the Tristan chord/diminished-seventh-chord element changes the least among the three versions.

One of the most telling features of the basic version is the common-tone element among the first five chords, which relates entirely to the diminished-seventh chord on F. The pitch class F appears in chords 1, 4, and 5, G♯ or A♭ in 1, 2, 3, and 5, B in 1, 2, 3, and 4, and D in 2, 3, 4, and 5. Three of the four pitches of each of these five chords come from the F diminished-seventh chord, whereas none of those that do not is heard more than once. And many other features of the desire music invoke the idea of the diminished-seventh chord as their harmonic background or "referential sonority."[7] The most obvious of these are the long-held melody tones, f', g♯', b', and d", the minor-third transposition between the first two phrases, the division of the ascending and descending chromatic motives into minor-third units whose boundary tones are those of the diminished-seventh chord on F, the common tones shared with the three Tristan chords and the dominant-sevenths of the first two phrases (including a minor third voice exchange between each of the pairs of chords in those phrases), and the semitone descent of the bass in all three phrases to the root of the dominant-seventh chord. Even the fact that the d♯'. resolves downward to d. in phrase one and the f♯' to f' in phrase two belongs within this perspective. It may be mentioned that the basic form of the desire music throughout the opera features the major sixth (a♭–f') or diminished seventh (g♯–f') for the first phrase as well; only the *Prelude* and one other point in the opera begin with the minor sixth (a–f'). And in the first draft of the movement Wagner had used tritones from the F diminished-seventh chord instead of sixths as the rising intervals that lead into the first two phrases.[8]

From this standpoint, the three Tristan chords of the desire music belong to a harmonic sphere that, in fact, comprises *four* Tristan chords, the one on B having been omitted (or "replaced" by that on D in phrase three) so as to facilitate the three-phrase triadic arpeggiation pattern of the dominant-seventh chords. At several points in the opera, however, Wagner introduces patterns involving all four Tristan chords, thereby bringing out their relationship to the diminished-seventh chord from which each of them differs only by a single semitone. The music that precedes Tristan's curse in act 3 offers a particularly clear instance (see ex. 14.4, discussed in chapter 14). And Brangaene's understanding of the magic of the love potion, both in her act one "consolation" and in her explanation of the "secret" of the potion in act 3 (see ex. 15.3, discussed in chapter 15), depends on its containing the B Tristan chord.

In this context, the most significant aspect of the Tristan chord is the single semi-tone that breaks with the perfect symmetry of the diminished-seventh chord. It is this difference, viewed vertically, that renders the Tristan chord and the dominant-seventh chord inversions of one another (that is, reading the intervals of both chords in close position from bottom to top, the former consists of two minor thirds and a major third, the latter the reverse; in this sense the two are symmetrical "around" the diminished-seventh chord). From the horizontal standpoint the principal departure from the diminished-seventh chord in the basic version is the change in transposition interval for the third phrase. In this version the arpeggiation of the minor triad with the dominant-seventh chords that end the phrases means that the dominant-seventh chord of the third phrase transposes at the major instead of the minor third, a feature that underlies the fact that the three melodic units outline the Tristan chord on G♯ with their beginning and ending tones: g♯′–b′, b′–d″, d″–f♯″. The pattern of the Tristan chord is closely bound up with the phrase succession, creating the impression that the minor-/major-third difference generates the tonal character of the three phrases. Also, the difference between the tritone (two minor thirds) and the perfect fifth (a minor and a major third) not only underlies the character of the desire music, but is also played out extensively in the key relationships of the opera. For this reason, it may be useful to consider very briefly and broadly the historical role of the tritone and its relationship to the perfect fifth in Western music.

From a theoretical standpoint, the most telling quality of the tritone in tonal music is a negative one: the fact that it is not a perfect fifth. That fact, which underlies its great instability, can be used as the basis for an "evolutionary" description of the various subsets of the Western tonal system from its origins to the twentieth century. Such subsystems—symbolized in models such as the medieval-Renaissance gamut and the enlightenment circle of keys—had repeatedly sought to provide closure and comprehensiveness for tonal practices that had always been deeply rooted in the perfect fifth as the basis of tonal relationships. The perfect fifth is the first interval in the harmonic series that we perceive as two pitch classes rather than one. It thus became the generative basis of the diatonic scale. But for both mathematical and acoustic reasons, the perfect fifth could not be the basis of a closed circular system of diatonic pitch relationships, which was inevitably rendered imperfect by the acoustically impure tritone. At one or another level (melodic, harmonic, tonal), the tritone was an obstacle to perfect symmetry and closure within such theoretical systems. Hence, its coming under the strictest control in music before 1600: the transposition scales (hexachords) were six-tone patterns that contained no tritones, the tritone and diminished fifth were "corrected" in certain modes such as the Dorian and Lydian and virtually prohibited from counterpoint, where they were characterized pejoratively as nonharmonic relations. From the beginning of the modern tonal era, however, a change took place with respect to the tritone and diminished fifth, as the urge to expand the tonal system admitted imperfection at local levels. Now more evident in melodic lines, these intervals also were accepted in harmonic configurations (such as the dominant- and diminished-seventh chords). Above all, the seven-tone major and minor scales (derived at least as much from the transposing scales or hexachords as from the modes) completely legitimized the tritone and diminished fifth within a system of keys that eventually formed a fully closed system of transpositional perfect-fifth levels: the eighteenth-century circle of keys.[9]

The widespread acceptance of the enharmonically closed circle of keys as the basis of the Western tonal system might seem to have settled the problem of the tritone once and for all. Yet, the very closure of the circle introduced a new set of problems. Until the nineteenth century, the implications of the disparity between notation (rooted in sharp/flat differentiation) and the inevitable ability of a symmetrical circle of keys to "rotate" (i.e., so that C is no longer the neutral center of the system and other keys sharp or flat) were not much explored. The priority of fifth relationships—always perceived as the most "natural" ones—meant that the pitch differences involved in most key changes were introduced gradually, most often by means of adjacent key signature levels. Because the perfect fifth (and its inversion the perfect fourth) are the only intervals that do not divide the octave equally, modulation to distant tonal regions pointed up the underlying imperfection of the system as a whole—that is, the necessity of enharmonic notation—the old tritone problem in new guise.

The outcome of this was that beginning with the romantic era the wide range of modulation opened up by the circle of keys created situations in which the priority of fifth relations was again seriously challenged, now at the *tonal* level. It had now become possible for the first time for compositions to abandon the priority of the fifth at both local (harmonic) and tonal (structural) levels. Some of the music that was most influential on Wagner—Weber's *Der Freischütz* with the tritone-related keys of its "wolf's glen" scene, and a significant part of Liszt's work in general—falls into this category. Expansion of the predominant tonal system (the circle of keys) so as to accommodate such distant relationships (as the major and minor scales had accommodated formerly inadmissable melodic and harmonic elements such as the tritone) could only take place through increased acceptance of the enharmonic region of the circle (that is, keys with more than four sharps or flats, J. S. Bach's normal limits, for example) and the consequent weakening of the distinction between flat and sharp notations, an analog of the break with rationalism. Although limited use of the devices of enharmonicism might be seen to fit the patterns by which the scope of tonal relationships had been extended in earlier eras, their widespread use introduced a strong tendency toward ambiguity—in some cases even destruction of the tonal sense. Such ambiguity was appealing in an age when the ineffable was so highly prized over the concrete and definite. In *Opera and Drama*, Wagner's comparing key relationships to the entire family of human relationships and his claiming that the principal key comprised all the others in itself asserts that the scheme of diatonic key relationships described in the enlightenment circle can no longer be taken for granted as the norm.[10] Rotation of the circle is, in fact, a means by which we may come to understand Wagner's propensity for modulation and immediate transposition by intervals that divide the octave equally: the semitone, major second, minor third, and tritone (the major third, prominent in *Die Meistersinger,* is less used in *Tristan*).[11] Certain of the most characteristic key relationships in *Tristan,* such as those between A♭ and A, A♭ and B, F and B, derive from enharmonic equivalencies and reinterpretations rather than the measuring of tonal distance by fifths (implied or actual) that underlay the rationalistic modulatory procedures of the early circle of keys. Pitch class equivalency is the last in a series of enharmonic equivalencies and the one that marks the final annihilation of flat/sharp directional dualism.

The tonal dynamic of the *Tristan* prelude and the harmonic language of the work as a whole raise this issue in the most overt manner. At the climax of the prelude the tendency of the tonality towards e♭, a tritone away from the tonic, a, involves pitch relationships whose extensive enharmonic overlap with a has been noted by a number of authors.[12] More than twenty years earlier, Chopin's G minor ballade had created a similar effect with the same "Tristan" chord in the same spacing as the beginning of the *Tristan* prelude, using it to shift from A to E♭. Wagner introduces this particular tritone relationship (in reverse) at three points in the first act, all of which are based on the music of the prelude: the prelude itself, the central dialogue between Isolde and Brangaene over the magic potions, and the final love duet. At another point of great structural and symbolic import in the act—Brangaene's preparation of the "drink of atonement"—Wagner shifts from the B minor tonal sphere that has held to this point in association with the dialog on honor, to the key of death, C minor. Amplifying the opposition embodied in the shift, Wagner makes a powerful melodic cadence to f♯ before the transition to C/c ("Nun lass' uns Sühne trinken"). He had set up a cadence to F at the close of scene four, specifically to effect a tritone shift within the honor music to the B minor with which scene five began. Act Three pivots around the same F/B tritone.

Wagner's music exhibits instances of tritone relationships that are sometimes immediate (the F/B shifting in the second act of *Die Meistersinger*, the abovementioned f/b shifting in *Siegfried*) and at other times more extended (the circle-of-fifths transposition pattern from D to A♭ at the end of *Parsifal*; the extended move from G♭ to C in the third act of *Die Meistersinger*), but that are always imbued with the poetic character of antithesis and transcendence, often paradoxical in nature, and that always retain at some level a sense of departure from the perfect fifth. After Wagner, a series of major milestones in the emergence of modern music, such as Debussy's *Prelude to the Afternoon of a Faun* and the first movement of Bartók's *Music for Strings, Percussion, and Celesta*, exhibit many of the same tonal relationships and devices, at first in an unmistakably dialectical relationship to tonality centered on fifth relationships (Debussy), but gradually more and more independent of them altogether. Alban Berg's *Lulu* is an outstanding example of a dramatic work in which the tritone plays a paramount role at many levels of composition, including the confrontation of tonal and atonal music.[13] The many symmetrical structures in Berg's work relate conceptually and musically to such qualities in the basic musical material itself. The fundamental difference between the unequal division of the octave in tonal music (i.e., perfect fifth and fourth) and the equal division that encourages a higher degree of intervallic permutation is as relevant to Wagner as it is to Scriabin, Bartók, and Webern. In act 3 of *Tristan*, the shepherd's *alte Weise* highlights the tritone division of the octave and its substitution for the perfect fifth, featuring inner symmetrical relationships, whereas the *frohe Weise* that appears later in the act reverts to the purely diatonic perfect fifth exclusively. Symmetry (the diminished-seventh chord in much tonal music, the chromatic scale in *Tristan*, the augmented triad in *Die Meistersinger*, the whole-tone scale in Debussy, and so on) is conceptually and aurally related to atonality and asymmetry to tonality.

Interestingly, among the analytical "literature" on these aspects of the *Tristan* harmonic sphere there is one item that might, directly or indirectly, have descended from Wagner himself. On the single sheet that preserves the compositional sketch for the concert ending of the prelude on one side and the orchestral sketch on the other there appears a series of harmonic and scalar patterns that the *Wagner Werk-Verzeichnis* describes as "harmony lessons."[14] These patterns are not in Wagner's hand but appear to have been placed on the sheet during the nineteenth century. Wagner produced the concert ending in Paris in 1859, the time of the *Tannhäuser* revisions that are, as is well known, closely related to the *Tristan* harmonic language. In 1860 he gave the sheet in question to the German Kapellmeister, Louis Schlösser, who published it in facsimile, two years after Wagner's death, along with an account of the occasion of his meeting with Wagner.[15] Unfortunately, Schlösser did not publish the lower half of the page on which the patterns appear, either because the patterns were not in Wagner's hand or because that part of the page was still blank, the patterns having been added only after 1885. But it is conceivable that they came about as the result of an explanation or rationalization of elements of the *Tristan* harmonic style by Wagner himself (ex. 5.1).

In example 5.1, each of the three lower chordal sequences, scale patterns and cadences is the exact inversion of the pattern immediately above it. Not only do the individual voices invert, but the intervals of the chords do as well. Thus, the f'/g' major second between the alto and soprano voices of the initial chord becomes the minor seventh, b'/a'', of the chord below; this procedure is carried out exactly throughout all the chords. Likewise, the ascending C scale is inverted by the descending E "Phrygian" scale (written in letters rather than notes), and the two quasi-cadential patterns in C and a invert one another.[16] The first chord in the upper group is in the closest possible spacing, maximizing the contrast when it is inverted. Next, the harmonies of the initial sequence comprise dominant sevenths on G, B♭ (spelled as an augmented-sixth chord, with g♯' instead of a♭'), and C (chords 1, 2, and 4), plus two F major chords (3 and 5), whereas those directly below comprise Tristan chords on B, G♯ (A♭), and F♯ (chords 1, 2, and 4) and two e triads (3 and 5). The two sequences point out the inversional relationship of major to minor triads and of Tristan chords to dominant sevenths. The basis of the inversion of the sequence as a whole is the note d', long recognized as the axis of symmetry of the tonal system. In this particular series of harmonies, the pitch d' remains constant in the original and inverted patterns, whereas the members of the diminished-seventh chord that are symmetrical above and below it, f and b, a♭ and g♯, exchange with one another. The d/g♯ and f/b tritones and the diminished-seventh chord on F emerge as a framework for the overall pattern. Embedded in the chordal patterns, therefore, are a number of the basic features of the desire music and, more generally, of the *Tristan* harmonic language, all deriving from the diminished-seventh chord background.

Intuitively, Wagner seized on and intensified the inner dialectic of tonality and atonality in nineteenth-century music as the analog of the Schopenhauerian aspect of the story of Tristan and Isolde. In this interpretation, the diminished-seventh chord lies "behind" the Tristan chord and the dominant-seventh chord as an analog of how the Schopenhauerian principle of negation lies behind the principle of desire. On the score of why Wagner altered the diminished-seventh chord to the Tristan

Example 5.1. Symmetrical patterns from the original manuscript of the concert ending of the prelude

c d e f g a h c
e d c h a g f e

chord by raising one of its pitches (if we can speak this way), we may remember that Hanslick, in his first published review of Wagner's music, a very favorable and lengthy coverage of *Tannhäuser* that he sent to the composer, had noted Wagner's tendency toward "diminished-seventh chord music," one of the stereotypes of nineteenth-century music.[17] Wagner responded to Hanslick, acknowledging the criticism in a back-handed way by associating the device ("that object of general censure, 'diminished-seventh music'") with earlier composers (Spontini and Weber) and maintaining that his own works, present and forthcoming, were attempts to demonstrate the continuing feasibility of opera.[18] Wagner implies that his goal was to escape such routine means of expression. Interestingly, Hanslick's criticism of the *Tristan* prelude makes a very similar complaint, "incessant diminished-seventh chords." There are, of course, a considerable number of diminished-seventh chords in the *Tristan* prelude; but in describing them as "incessant," Hanslick might well have intended to include the Tristan chord under the same rubric.[19]

The qualities I have described are clearly seen in the passages mentioned at the outset of this chapter. Thus, at the climax of "O sink hernieder," the diminished-seventh chord changes to the Tristan chord (and the beginning of the desire music) on the word "Welt" in the line "Selbst dann bin ich die Welt." At that point, Wagner has the desire music emerge from the F, A♭, C♭, D diminished-seventh chord, arranging that the E♭ (D♯), entering as the uppermost tone, introduce the day motive simultaneously with it. The symbolism is unmistakable: existence (day) and desire are bonded inseparably, as in Wagner's view of the Buddhist theory of creation. The change from d to e♭ suggests what Wagner called "the breath that clouds the clear expanse of heaven"—that is, the break with the symmetry and neutrality of the diminished-seventh chord background as the analog of emergent desire. The reverse procedure comes in act 3 in the motive Tristan introduces for his curse of desire and his own existence. There, Wagner turns the Tristan chord into its chord of "origin," the diminished-seventh, a device that he had introduced in several earlier passages in the same span. When Tristan combines the curse motive with the desire music, we hear the diminished-seventh chord mediate between the Tristan chord and the dominant-seventh. Saturated with diminished-seventh chords, the solo finally cadences on F as Tristan lapses into unconsciousness once more; at the threshold of night, his denial of existence and desire renders the F "atonal."

In the desire music and throughout much of *Tristan* the diminished-seventh chord and tritone serve as harmonic symbols of atonality and negation, whereas the Tristan chord and the dominant-seventh chord reflect the urge toward key centers that remain largely unfulfilled until the end. At the climax of the prelude, Wagner's transposing the dominant-seventh chord of the first phrase at the tritone casts the Tristan chord in what is its most pronounced functional role: that of the half-diminished supertonic seventh chord (in e♭). But what is tonal at the local level is not at the higher level; the tritone relationship collapses back to the original key. However, when Wagner also transposes the dominant harmony of the second phrase ending at the tritone—to C♯, as in the deleted transition to "O ew'ge Nacht," and as adumbrated in the first and second phrase endings of "So stürben wir"—the potential for shift to B is increased, although Wagner does not fulfill it until act 3. But in the honor music and the version of the desire music that accompanies Tristan's reawakening in act 3 replacement of the tritone by the perfect fifth in phrase three effects an overall tritone shift from beginning to end (f/F to b/B) in which the tonal sense increases from the first to the third phrase. The sequence from Tristan's curse and relapse to his reawakening and clairvoyant vision is a focal point for the idea of a progression from negation to ecstatic vision, amplifying qualities that we recognize in the desire music itself, above all the increasing sense of a tonal center that emerges from a diminished-seventh chord background. We might even speculate that Wagner drew the large-scale tonal design of act 3 from the first Tristan chord itself, because the pitches that form its lower third—f–g♯/a♭—suggest F minor and those that form its upper third—b–d♯'—B major. Certainly, the vertical pattern of the Tristan chord—minor thirds and diminished triad below, minor triad with major third above, in addition to the f/B tritone antithesis—suggests dualistic qualities that Wagner makes horizontal in the opera, above all in conjunction with progressions from negation to transcendence and their musical counterparts: atonality to tonality, diminished and minor to major harmonies.

In my opinion, the sense that the Tristan chord mediates between the neutral diminished-seventh chord and the tonal dominant-seventh chord underlies the multiplicity of functional-tonal interpretations that have been assigned it. Among such interpretations (among which, apart from the diminished-seventh chord, the augmented-sixth chord, the incomplete dominant-ninth chord, and the altered dominant-seventh chord on B are the most prominent) is one of the oldest ones: that the chord is a complex of tendencies toward more than one key (the tone f relating to a and the d♯' to e, for example).[20] Shared by these interpretations is an essential feature of the opening measures: the major third within the F Tristan chord (b–d♯') prefigures the arrival on the dominant at the end of the third phrase (i.e., B^7 as V^7 of E). At that point the pitches b and d♯' sound within the B^7 chord in the same register as they had in the first Tristan chord. And that arrival is an overcoming of the atonal implications of the minor-third transposition between the first and second phrases. That is, the d♯' of the first Tristan chord and its equivalent, f♯', in the second, both components of the B^7 chord of the third phrase, are the only elements in those chords to suggest that the third phrase will be tonal, ending on B^7 rather than atonal, ending on B♭^{7} (which would result had Wagner continued the minor-third transposition pattern). The third phrase can be said to legitimize the d♯′ and f♯′ of the preceding two Tristan chords by completing their implications. The B major ending of the opera fulfills this tonal tendency toward B.[21]

Thus, the change of pitch spectrum on the B^7 chord intensifies the sense that this phrase pushes to overcome the prior tendency of the harmony toward the diminished-seventh chord. The upper voices of the first two phrases fill out the chromatic octave d′–d″ in alternating descending and ascending minor-third units, whereas the e♯″/f♯″ of the third phrase makes a point out of the extending of the next such unit (d″–f″) by a semitone (d″–f♯″). After the B^7 chord, Wagner's reiterating the ending of the third phrase, then his echoing its final two pitches, e♯″/f♯″, in different registers consolidate the shift from the diminished-seventh common-tone region of the first five chords to one that is a semitone away (i.e., a perfect fifth rather than a tritone), enabling the V^7 of V harmony to sink in, as it were. That the e♯″/f♯″ appoggiatura then becomes the starting point of the fourth unit of the desire music (a fourth phrase that is in some ways a cadential appendage to the third phrase), shifting the rhythmic weight to the second tone of the melody, means that the next stage in the chromatic ascent also extends a semitone beyond the f″–g♯″ that would complete the chromatic octave in the top voice. And Wagner's beginning this unit with the E^7 chord on which the first phrase had cadenced confirms the tone a″ as its goal. Wagner gives added weight to the "extra" tone a″ by means of the appoggiatura b″/a″.

With the famous deceptive cadence to F that completes the desire music, the e–f bass motion, as is often remarked, reverses that of the first phrase, a gesture that, because of the suggestion of return via a circle-of-fifths progression, invites interpretation as the continual return of desire. The semitone ascent of the bass contracts the fifth descent from the B^7 to E^7 harmony to a tritone relationship between the F and B^7 chords. As the melody reaches its highest tone, b″, Wagner gives the greatest possible legitimacy to the tone F that the B^7 chord had struggled to overcome in phrase three by making it the root of the harmony. More than avoiding an A (or a) cadence (which it is highly doubtful that we expect in any case), this "Lydian" effect disperses the tonal thrust of the third phrase, affirming a world in which such normal forms of tonal fulfillment as dominant-tonic cadences are no more to be taken for granted than is conventional worldly happiness to be expected for Tristan and Isolde. This quality of the cadence is not so much owing to the F harmony per se as to the sounding of the tone b″ above it; that is, it articulates the relationship of that tone to the tone (F) it has seemingly passed beyond, but with which it is inextricably bound up (as components of the same diminished-seventh chord). The b″ increases the openness of the cadence, the need for something further, which the entrance of the glance music supplies.

We will examine the relationships among the various themes of the prelude in the following chapter. At this point, however, we may note that the glance music serves as a kind of counterbalance to the ending of the desire music, giving us a perspective on the desire music itself. The glance music, that is, leads toward a cadence in the subdominant, d; and the way in which its melodic curve pivots around the tone b♭', turning downward to f' for the cadence to d, offsets the dominant character of the ending of the desire music (on its first appearance the glance music continues to a half close in d, introducing the Neapolitan E♭⁶ chord before the cadence, a gesture that intensifies the subdominant character of the motive). The glance music picks up on the subdominant implications of F, confirming in its shift to d the pitches that the ending of the desire music had moved away from (ex. 5.2).

Poetically, the glance music is associated with the beginning of Tristan's and Isolde's love; hence its directly following the desire music in the prelude. It is, therefore, less abstract in nature than the desire music, its rhythm pervading the prelude and its melodic character suggest the raising, then lowering of the lovers' eyes. Behind its gestural component, however, lies a quality of motivic derivation from the desire music that Wagner probably developed *directly* from Schopenhauer, who emphasized the metaphysical meaning of the glance as a manifestation of the principle of compassion (which is exactly its association when Isolde introduces it in act 1).[22] On its first appearance, therefore, Wagner immediately (but freely) transposes its subdominant cadence up a tone to a half close on the dominant of e/E, then moves on to A, to prepare the momentary bliss of the third theme of the prelude, the E major drink of atonement (*Sühnetrank*) motive (ex. 5.3). Behind this gesture we hear a delayed echo of the tendency of the desire music's third phrase toward the dominant. The E, however, although momentarily blissful, is illusory, giving way to the glance music on its two appearances, then dropping out, whereas the glance music remains to merge with the desire music at the climax. There, instead of the dominant of E (V of V), Wagner emphasizes tonal motion toward the dominant of e♭, seemingly fulfilling the implications of the avoided minor third transposition in phrase three of the desire music. The enharmonic relapse back to A minor reveals that the minor third, tritone cycle of the diminished-seventh chord has no potential for transcendence.

Thus, the desire music suggests a symmetrical, "atonal" procedure at the outset that the asymmetrical, tonal character of the third phrase seems to overcome, only to be undermined as the melodic ascent reaches its peak. Already these seventeen measures suggest Wagner's description of the dynamic of the prelude as a series of yearning/relapse patterns.[23] The third phrase is the crucial one, because of its breaking out of the circular minor-third transposition pattern. Psychologically, the complementary relationship of the first two phrases echoes in the alternating e♯"/f♯" in the upper and lower registers of phrase three. This gesture seems almost to describe the two lovers hesitating or holding back, then, with the entrance of the E⁷ chord, pressing forward as if to consummate the tonal implications of the foregoing measures. The dissipating quality of the cadence, however, suggests more than the qualities of surprise or denial routinely attributed to the deceptive cadence. The loss of energy that comes with the F major chord can be considered, metaphorically, a point of release from conventional expectations. In other words, the idea of deception is given a degree of reality that goes beyond the idea that it simply denies the true cadence. Although the conventional view of the deceptive cadence as substitute for an expected tonic cadence cannot satisfy as an explanation in light of Wagner's continual use of the device, the idea of deception was very probably an important musicopoetic factor in Wagner's ending the desire music in this way. This is analogous to

Example 5.2. The glance music: mm. 17–22 of the prelude

the fact that the idea of deception in Wagner's poem goes beyond its association with the lovers' intrigues in Gottfried's *Tristan,* coming ultimately to characterize the world of representation (day) in general. Not only are ideas such as deception, illusion, and the like, central to all that Wagner will include under the pejorative conception of day in act 2, but this cadence sounds innumerable times as their particular symbol, emerging at the end of the first act in association with Tristan's reference to the "truggeweihtes Glücke," then again, at the end of the so-called *Tagesgespräch* of act 2, in conjunction with the day motive.[24]

The transfiguration cadence that Wagner introduces in the prelude to act 2 to replace the deceptive cadence of the desire music represents a new stage in the lovers' understanding. As the act unfolds, they long, increasingly, for closure without the return of further desire, for the end of their enslavement to repeated tension and release as a cyclic pattern. In the concert ending of the prelude, therefore, Wagner brings in the transfiguration music to close off the final appearance of the desire music, illustrating the point that he made in his program notes for that version of the prelude: exhausted after an endless series of yearning-relapse patterns, of strivings without attainment, the lovers are granted a vision of the transcendent beyond,

Example 5.3. The *Sühnetrank,* or drink of atonement, music: mm. 25–30 of the prelude

Example 5.4. Act 2, scene 3: Tristan's answer to King Mark

the realm of night-death. At that point, the transfiguration cadence substitutes directly for the deceptive cadence and the chromatic ascent leads to closure in A. In the opera, however, the prelude turns at that point to C minor instead, a shift that is unmistakably bound up with the implications of the second phrase of the desire music and its minor-third transposition. The version of the desire music that precedes Isolde's introduction of the death motive is its culmination, whereas the honor music, much later in the act, picks up on the ideal character of the tendency toward the dominant. As in the prelude, the music that accompanies the drinking of the love potion brings out the minor-third/tritone framework once again. Although the lovers' consciousness of desire and the overcoming of the key of death, C minor, by C major, at the end of the act, seem optimistic, Tristan's final words reveal that the lovers remain locked with the cyclic framework of the first two phrases of the desire music; only their mode, now major, has changed, not their potential to suggest transcendence, which Wagner associates with the tendency of the third phrase toward b/B.

Many of the qualities I have described can be seen clearly in the version of the desire music that Wagner introduced to accompany Tristan's answer to King Mark's existential question near the end of act 2 (ex. 5.4). There Wagner adds one further harmony to the endings of phrases one and two, second inversion chords on g♯ (phrase one) and b (phrase two), respectively. This change causes the bass of each phrase as a whole to mirror the chromatic descent of the alto—f, e, d♯ in phrase one, and a♭, g, f♯ in phrase two—causing the alto to return to d♯' in phrase one after its f', e', d♯', d' descent and, similarly, to f♯' in phrase two. The changes from d♯' to d' and f♯' to f' that I have described above are thus reversed at the phrase endings. But the vocal lines with which Tristan answers King Mark overlap the three orchestral phrases, returning to the diminished-seventh chord pitch framework once more and making an obvious analogy between that and Tristan's expressions of negation: "O König, das kann ich dir *nicht sagen*" and "und was du frägst, das kannst du *nie erfahren.*" At the end of each line Wagner places the tritone that contradicts the raised pitch—g♯'−d' the first time and b'−f' the second—reminding us that in its original version the first two phrases of the desire music began with b−f' and d'−g♯' tritones.

SIX

The Prelude

A Musico-poetic View

THE *TRISTAN* PRELUDE IS CELEBRATED for its gradually unfolding, variation-like form, beginning almost without a beginning, and creating the impression of a seamless dynamic of tension and resolution rather than a sequence of clearly de-marcated sectional divisions. Wagner describes it as a dynamic of yearning, increasing intensification and relapse:

> From the timidest lament in inappeasable longing, the tenderest shudder, to the most terrible outpouring of an avowal of hopeless love, the sentiment traverses all phases of the vain struggle against inner ardor, until this, sinking back powerless upon itself, seems to be extinguished in death.[1]

Wagner wrote this 1863 description of the prelude (heading it *Liebestod*), for its pairing with the *Liebestod* (headed *Verklärung:* transfiguration). A few years earlier (1859), he wrote Mathilde Wesendonck that he had found a concert ending for the *Tris-tan* prelude, enclosing a copy of that ending along with a program that was used when that version was performed in Paris early the following year.[2] The earlier description is fuller, characterizing the prelude as "one long-articulated impulse" involving a string of antitheses—hopes/fears, laments/wishes, raptures/torments—within its basic dynamic pattern of a series of "attainments," each followed by languishing back to re-newed desire. The goal of these tension/relapse cycles—the climax of the prelude—represents the lovers'"most powerful effort" to find the breach [*Durchbruch*] that will reveal the path to endless love. This time, their relapse—"final exhaustion"—is re-warded by a glimpse into the "attainment of highest rapture," that of night-death, a "wondrous realm from which we stray the furthest when we strive to enter it by force."[3]

If Wagner meant his remarks as a close analog of the climax of the prelude, then the shift of tonal focus toward e♭ perhaps corresponds to the lovers'"straying" to the fur-thest point on the circle of fifths, the tritone, whereas the several reiterations of the beginning of the desire music mirror both their striving "by force" and their failure to progress to a higher level, bringing about the enharmonic relapse to the original tonal context, A minor. In this view the prelude is basically cyclic in form, always returning to the desire music, whereas the two endings, which diverge from the same point—the deceptive cadence of the version of the desire music that follows the climax—move in opposite directions. The ending in the opera moves to the key associated with the second phrase of the desire music, c, an extension of the diminished-seventh chord background and the minor-third transposition pattern. Wagner effects the shift by harmonizing the "glance" motif with the D Tristan chord of the third phrase of the desire music instead of the original dominant D harmony—that is, by restoring the harmonic framework the B^7 chord had broken with. The change from a to a♭ and f♯ to f in that chord are telling signals of the change (ex. 6.1). In a copy of the

Example 6.1.   The ending of the prelude in the opera

prelude dated November 5, 1857, Wagner wrote in the words "Vorhang auf" (curtain up) at the entrance of the glance music.[4] Then, in the final measures before the curtain to the first act, Wagner reiterates the first and second phrases of the desire music, setting both phrases entirely in a C minor context: he replaces the initial a by ab, and reinterprets the g♯' of phrase two, still notated as such, as ab. The c tonality holds for the first scene and the first half of the second; its meaning is revealed at the beginning of scene 2, in which Wagner leads the diminished-seventh chord version of the desire music into the death motive (its first appearance). When the music of the prelude reappears for the drinking of the love potion, it is preceded by the final full appearance of the death motive in the act (the only time it is sung by Tristan); after its c, Wagner shifts toward eb, so that the prelude music returns from a point analogous to the climax and enharmonic relapse.

The poetic idea behind the prelude and its reappearance at the drinking of the love potion is, as Wagner said, the lovers' "vain struggle against inner ardor," associated in act 1 with their seeking death as an escape from desire. They fail because, as Schopenhauer maintained, suicide is the affirmation not the negation of the will. In act 1, c is an extension of the a associated with desire in the first phrase of the prelude; its intensification toward eb at the climax of the prelude and the drinking of the love potion, and the subsequent relapse back to a depict their failure to break with desire, to find the "breach" into night. In this light, the design of act 1 can be considered an extension of the prelude, its tritone relationships and overall a–C tonal design deriving from the first two phrases of the desire music, whereas its keys of e (Isolde's narrative) and b (the first half of scene five) are extensions of the perfect-fifth motion between the first and third phrases (and in a meaningful sense prefigurations of the E of Tristan's clairvoyant vision and the B of the Liebestod).

In contrast, the A of the concert ending draws on the transfiguration music from the final pages of the opera (modified considerably and transposed down a tone to A) to depict the glimpse into night. Wagner's 1859 program note therefore carries the summary description of the story beyond the first act. A prefatory paragraph attributes the lovers' plight to "the goddess of love," referring not only to the love potion but also to Isolde's affirming Frau Minne's control of the lovers' destinies in act 2, scene 1, and ending with lines reminiscent of Tristan's solo "O nun waren wir Nachtgeweihte." These are all points that culminate in ecstatic visions of night involving adumbration of the transfiguration music, which Wagner introduced in the prelude to act 2 as substitute for the deceptive cadence of the desire music. Because the melodic contour of the transfiguration cadence outlines the same pitches as the deceptive cadence—in A major the tones f♯", g♯", b", a"—it was a simple matter for Wagner to lead the desire music into an A major version of the ending of the Liebestod (with substantial changes, as described below), replacing the turn to C minor that continues from that point in the opera.

The Glance Music

The most conspicuous common element in both Wagner's programs is that the prelude represents the dynamic of desire arising almost from nothing and expanding toward a climactic point at which there is a relapse. The 1859 notes suggest more than one tension/relapse pattern, a series of "attainments," in fact, each of which "brings in its wake only renewed desire." Wagner's descriptions are broad and general in outline; yet they are not vague or ambiguous. What they do not specify is how the tension/relapse patterns operate within and among the principal themes, to create the dynamic of the prelude as a whole. I have described the desire music (mm. 1–17) from that standpoint, emphasizing its dualism of tonality (yearning) and atonality (negation). On a larger scale, the same idea underlies the interaction of the main themes and the form of the whole.

Basically, the thematic material of the prelude falls into three main groups that, for convenience, may be designated as A, B, and C. The first is the desire music (mm. 1–17; see ex. 4.1), the second the so-called glance motive (mm. 17–22, extended on its first appearance to m. 24; see ex. 5.2) and the third the E major *Sühnetrank* or "drink of atonement" motive (mm. 25–28; see ex. 5.3). The last of these themes is associated with the dualistic nature of the potion. That is, it mirrors the fact that the potion is understood in part as a love potion and in part as a death potion (mm. 25–28 constitute the theme proper, whereas an appendage of transitional character introduces what is sometimes known as the "poison" motive in the bass: mm. 28–32). As is well known, all three theme groups are closely interrelated in ways that suggest variation of the desire music.

As a beginning the desire music depicts the link between desire and the emergence of the world itself, affirming a tonal world, but one in which we must be alert to the possibility of enharmonic double meanings and negations. In this light, the glance music, although building on elements of the desire music, offers a new, more human, perspective on desire. The motive of its first five tones, the most detachable element, introduces the ♪♪.♪ | ♪♩ rhythm that pervades the prelude after this point. Although that rhythm arises from the ♪♩ rhythm of the desire music, in the desire music it comes at the ends of the phrases, whereas in the glance music it initiates the basic forward motion of the rhythm, an impulse that is missing in the more abstract patterns of the desire music. Continuing, the glance music replaces the chromatic lines of the desire music by diatonic ascent, the rising appoggiaturas by descending ones, the initial rising sixth by the falling seventh, and the long silences between phrases by an uninterrupted rising-third motion. In addition, it contains its own form of rhythmic acceleration that leads to the rising seventh from c' to b♭' in the middle of the phrase. This gesture, whose rising interval recalls the beginning of the desire music, turns the line back down to a cadence on the subdominant (d).

Poetically, the glance of love is an important theme in both Gottfried von Strassburg and Schopenhauer, and Wagner's conception is indebted to both: to Gottfried for its place in the story of Tristan and Isolde, and to Schopenhauer for its metaphysical meaning. Two chapters of the second volume of *The World as Will and Representation* are of particular interest in this regard, "On the Primacy of the Will in Self-consciousness" and "On the Metaphysics of Sexual Love." The latter chapter, as we know, is the one Wagner was responding to when he wrote of his amendment, probably around the time he composed the duet "O ew'ge Nacht," which in its original version had introduced the glance music prominently. In the former chapter,

Example 6.2. Act 1, scene 3: excerpt from Isolde's narrative

Schopenhauer poses the question "On what does the identity of the person depend," concluding that the "expression of the glance" mirrors the "unalterable character" of the will.[5] The primacy of the will, commonly identified with the heart as opposed to the head, or the intellect, is manifested in the glance. In this chapter, we encounter the kind of thinking that underlies not only the conception of the glance in *Tristan* but also its relationship to the juxtaposition of head and heart in the death motive ("Todgeweihtes Haupt! Todgeweihtes Herz!"). In his chapter on the metaphysics of sexual love, Schopenhauer goes further, linking the "longing glances" of lovers to their enslavement to the species will, that is, their looking one another over as potential parents of the next generation.[6] Thus, the true meaning of lovers' glances is their looking through the individual to the will that lies beyond.

The glance, then, is closely bound up with passing beyond the *principium individuationis*, seeing into the depths of another, whether or not this is recognized consciously. It is the beginning of love, which, as Wagner describes it in act 1, is the outcome of Isolde's compassion for the wounded and suffering Tristan. In her narrative, accompanied by the glance music in the orchestra, Isolde recalls the origins of their love, singing "er sah mir in die Augen. Seines Elends jammerte mich; das Schwert— ich liess es fallen!" (He looked into my eyes. His suffering tormented me; the sword— I let it fall!) to a rising sixth followed by a chromatic descent, thereby making clear the bond between compassion and love (ex. 6.2). That event took place in Isolde's chamber; and it came to symbolize the inner world, all that Isolde kept hidden in the first act, as opposed to the public events of the reconciliation between Ireland and Cornwall and, above all, Tristan's seeking her out as bride for King Mark. Thus, as Dieter Borchmeyer remarks, "the love between Tristan and Isolde bears the marks of fellow-feeling [*Mitleid*] from the very outset."[7] In a letter to Mathilde Wesendonck, written soon after he sent the completed first act of *Tristan* to his publisher, Wagner linked compassion and the glance in a characteristically intricate manner; that is, he wove together a critique of Goethe's *Faust*, which he considered had failed to deal adequately with the "great compassion" of the individual's redemption through absorption by the world, with the glance of love. The glance, representing the primacy of the internal over the external, was thereby universalized to the level of "active participation [*Mitleid*] in the world's suffering," which was what Wagner felt Goethe had failed to depict in *Faust*.[8]

Wagner's interpretation of Gottfried von Strassburg's story in Schopenhauerian terms means that many of the leitmotifs have, *even in their purely referential aspects*, what we might call an inner (philosophical) and an outer (dramatic) meaning, the inner aspect deriving in some cases directly from passages in Schopenhauer. The dream chords of "O sink hernieder" are an obvious symbol of the passage between inner and outer worlds (i.e., night and day) that Wagner based on Schopenhauer's dream theories. Likewise, the motive associated with the torch in act 2, scene 1 perhaps derives from Schopenhauer's describing the torch as a metaphor for the limited light of human understanding surrounded by the great expanse of night.[9] In this light, the glance is bound up with the question of identity from inner and outer standpoints. After their return to consciousness following the powerful effect of the drinking of the love potion it is to the glance music that Tristan and Isolde sing each other's names (and again in the duet that follows); likewise, Tristan dies to the beginning of the glance music as he sings Isolde's name. In act 1, when Isolde relates the story of the original glance of love (her so-called narrative), it is in the context of the wounded Tristan's having hidden his identity behind the name "Tantris." In his vulnerable condition Tristan "wounded" Isolde herself with his glance; Isolde healed him out of compassion, so that his glance would no longer torment her: The wounds that Morold struck, I healed them, so that he would return home,—with his glance no more torment me ("Die Morold schlug, die Wunde, sie heilt' ich, dass er gesunde, und heim nach Hause kehre,—mit dem Blick mich nicht mehr beschwere!"). But when he returned to claim Isolde for King Mark, it was in his identity of Tristan, the hero, avoiding all glances. In the dialogue with Tristan in scene 5, Isolde describes the other meaning of the glance, the one Schopenhauer had linked to the delusion of the species will, the self-deception surrounding love; what makes it all the more tormenting for Isolde is that the "measuring glance" (*messender Blick*), Schopenhauer's symbol of how lovers size one another up as potential parents of the next generation, was applied by Tristan on behalf of King Mark ("als dein messender Blick mein Bild sich stahl, ob ich Herrn Marke taug' als Gemahl").[10]

The basis of Wagner's narrative of the glance is the episode in Gottfried known as "The Splinter," in which Isolde first discovers Tristan's identity from the missing piece of his sword that was embedded in Morold's head. It begins with a remarkably erotic passage in which the glance is associated with Isolde:[11]

> Isolde kept on looking at him; she scanned his body and his whole appearance with uncommon interest. She stole glance after glance at his hands and face, she studied his arms and legs, which so openly proclaimed what he tried to keep so secret. She looked him up and down; and whatever a maid may survey in a man all pleased her very well, and she praised it in her thoughts.[12]

In addition, Isolde has a servant polish Tristan's armor, which she covertly examines, taking up Tristan's sword in a passage that leaves no doubt of the underlying eroticism.[13] After discovering the meaning of the splinter Isolde recognizes the identity of the once vulnerable Tantris with Tristan, the slayer of Morold. And that leads her to confront Tristan in another state of vulnerability: naked in his bath. Here, with the latent eroticism of the situation as a background, Gottfried makes no mention of glances. Instead, he provides a very wordy series of dialogues as Isolde confronts Tristan and he responds, not only to her but also to her mother (who enters soon afterward), attempting to deflect Isolde from her purpose by bringing up the question of honor both to Isolde and to her mother. Gottfried describes Isolde as racked by conflict between her anger, which leads her to attempt to kill Tristan three times, and her "tender womanliness," which prevents her. Ultimately it is the victory of Isolde's "sweet womanhood" over her anger that saves Tristan's life: she flings the sword away and bursts into tears, "Alas, that I ever lived to see this day." The outcome is Tristan's promise to secure marriage to the king of Cornwall for Isolde.[14]

In the Gottfried literature this episode is a mainstay of the view that Tristan and Isolde love one another, although unconsciously, before they drink the love potion. Wagner clearly viewed it that way, for he links the glance to the sword in Isolde's narrative and her confrontation with Tristan. In contrast to the heroic upward-shooting triadic character of the sword motive of the Ring, the falling seventh in the glance motive of *Tristan*—literally suggestive of Isolde's looking down at Tristan on the sick bed—became associated with the fall of the sword from Isolde's hands and the fall of Isolde's honor with respect to Morold, all symbols of the priority of the inner life over the external, and of Tristan's abandoning his heroic stance. From Wagner's perspective, Gottfried's scene needed severe editing and compression; and, even more, it needed to be recounted as a memory, not presented directly on stage. As Dieter Borchmeyer points out, in later years Richard and Cosima Wagner recognized the parallel between the scene of the glance as it appears in Wagner's *Tristan* and a similar scene in Schiller's *Die Jungfrau von Orleans*.[15] Common to both was the heroine's dropping the sword because of the glance that passed between her and her lover at the very point of readiness to kill. As Cosima relates, both she and Wagner considered Schiller's presentation of Joan's glance and dropping the sword ineffective, feeling that only as narrative could the scene remain faithful to the living truth of myth (that is, as an internalized event).[16]

In Isolde's narrative, Wagner conflated Gottfried's episode of the splinter with that of Tristan's healing, making Isolde's memory of the association between the sword of vengeance and the glance of compassion and love into the source of her inner conflict throughout the first act. Additionally, Wagner carries over something of the meaning of the sword as a symbol of manhood and heroic identity as well as vulnerability that it exhibits in the Ring. Instead of a clever poetic tension between the naked man in the bath surrounded by three beautiful women (Gottfried eventually brought Brangaene into the scene as well) and debating questions of honor with them, he created an opposition between the intimacy of the chamber, where the healing of Tantris and the sword/glance episode took place, and the public character of Tristan's identity as knight and hero. When Isolde recollects all this in her confrontation with Tristan, it leads to Tristan's abandoning that identity, offering his sword to Isolde to the accompaniment of the glance motive. Wagner invests this point with great symbolic significance in that the glance motive enters in E flat minor, the key toward which it leads at the climax of the prelude and in which it initiates the reprise of the prelude music at the drinking of the potion. Later the glance motive reappears at the same pitch as Isolde offers the drink of atonement in place of the sword.

In Gottfried the glance has multiple meanings. In addition to eroticism as the beginning of love between Tristan and Isolde, Gottfried describes the glances between them at King Mark's court as evidence of the passion about which King Mark deceives himself. And in the lovers' cave scene he describes the lovers' glances as their sustenance, lending it something of a metaphysical character that is bound up with the theme of *Liebeseinheit*.[17] This last association, viewed in Schopenhauerian terms, underlay Wagner's bringing the glance music back in the original version of "O ew'ge Nacht" (see appendix). As mentioned earlier, Wagner introduced the be-

ginning of the glance music at several points in the duet—in g♯ at "Wem du umfangen, wem du gelacht, wie wär ohne Bangen [aus dir es je erwacht?]" (The one
whom you embrace, on whom you smile, how could he awaken from you without
dismay?), and again at "in deinen Armen, dir geweiht" (in your arms, consecrated to
you)—before bringing it in full, and at its original pitch, at "ewig einbewusst, heiß
erglüther Brust" (forever of one consciousness, hotly glowing breast). The last of
these points parallels the climactic final phrase of the act 1 duet, where the glance
music accompanies the lovers' ecstatic "einzig bewusst, höchste Liebeslust." In the
original version of "O ew'ge Nacht" the glance was invested by Wagner with metaphysical signficance, furthering the idea of a progression in the lovers' metaphysical
understanding from the first act to the second. But, at the climax of the duet its return at its original pitch interrupted the motion of the harmony toward B major utterly. Wagner perhaps intended the return to B after the glance music to overcome
the flashback to the first act duet and the individuality that underlay the motive's association with the lovers' names (as the second act duet denies the relevance of
names and individual identities). But the restoration of B involved some very routine sequences that rendered the climax ineffective as such. In his revision, Wagner
removed all references to the glance from "O ew'ge Nacht," increasing the references
to honor, as described in chapter 4.

The role of the glance motive in the prelude, where it is most prominent of all,
illuminates the poetic and formal character of the movement. There the glance
music comes into ever closer relationship with the desire music. The glance motive
initiates the climax, introducing for the first time the countermelody derived from
the desire music that will be associated with Isolde's expression of compassion in her
narrative; as the tonality moves toward e♭, the glance motive combines with the first
phrase of the desire music in a manner that suggests a "deep" relationship—that is,
a motivic and harmonic oneness. After the enharmonic relapse back to a for the final
return of the desire music Wagner makes the relationship between the desire and
glance music clear by interposing the glance motive between the phrases of the desire music. Suddenly we know that the glance motive was created as a variant of the
desire music, and that behind both motives lies the diminished-seventh chord. The
harmony of the Prelude is saturated with the sound of Tristan chords, which relate,
of course, to the desire music, whereas the rhythm is pervaded by that of the glance
music, a reflection of the fact that in Wagner's and Schopenhauer's metaphysics of
music harmony is internal and rhythm external. We may conclude, therefore, that
Wagner understood the glance as the cause of Tristan's and Isolde's love in the phenomenal world, whereas behind it lay the principle of desire and, ultimately, their
recognition of metaphysical oneness. The glance was a gateway to the inner life, as
Schopenhauer described it.

This is why for the drinking of the potion the reprise of the music of the prelude
begins from the point where it moved toward e♭. At that point, the glance music had
seemed to open the door to death, or what Wagner would call night in act 2. In Schopenhauerian terms, recognition of the identity of the will underlies the glance, but the
will, manifested in desire, retains control of the lovers' destinies. Their emerging
consciousness brings "only desire in its wake," to paraphrase Wagner's program notes

for the Prelude. With the return of the desire music the cadential element of the death motive, now transposed from c to a, dissolves symbolically in the bass; and as the music of the Prelude unfolds, it is more and more influenced by the C of the arrival at Cornwall. The final appearance of the glance music is forced to take on the character of that music. The lovers sing each other's names to the glance music, after which Wagner immediately shifts the meter and tempo to the rapid ²⁄₂ (*Lebhaft mit Steigerung*) that will turn out to be closely associated with day in act 2.[18] As the music of the prelude begins over again from the desire music—at "seliges Glühen"—Wagner adjusts the order of the motives of the prelude, keeping the tonality in C. Now the *Sühnetrank* music precedes the glance music so that the duet ends with the latter: "einzig bewusst, höchste Liebeslust" (the point that Wagner intended to parallel when he brought back the glance music to "endloß ewig einbewusst" in the original version of "O ew'ge Nacht"). Thus, the recall of the music of the Prelude at the end of the act begins and ends with the glance music, the beginning associated with death and forgetfulness (c/eb) and the ending with desire, life, and consciousness (a/C).

For this reason, Wagner brings back the glance music for the last time as Tristan dies. As the C/c of the lovers' meeting passes directly back to a, the desire music sounds for the last time in something close to its original form but with its dynamic character reversed, as mentioned earlier. As it reaches the deceptive cadence, Wagner prolongs the cadence itself for three measures then holds the tone a, the starting pitch of the opera, for two measures, marking a tempo change (*Sehr langsam*) for the beginning of the glance music. As Tristan looks into Isolde's eyes and speaks her name, the glance music reaches upward to the pitch bb′, then breaks off as Tristan dies.[19] Wagner had chosen exactly this point in the glance music to initiate the motion toward eb that occurs at the climax of the Prelude. There he took the pitch bb′ and, instead of turning it downward, as he always had before, he extended it upward in ever-rising sequences based on the desire music. Parallel to the drinking of the potion at the end of the act, this passage represented the lovers' striving to enter night by force—that is, suicide—as Wagner put it in his notes for the Prelude. The enharmonic shift back to a then made the point that desire could not be escaped in this way. At the point of Tristan's death Wagner returns to harmonize the bb′ of the glance music with the same C Tristan chord that he had introduced at the beginning of the climax of the Prelude, this time following it by silence.

Wagner chose exactly this point for Tristan's death so as to complete the cycle of desire by referring back to Isolde's healing Tristan; Tristan and Isolde's love in the physical world ends just as it began, with his looking up from a near-death state into her eyes. Only the direction is different. The point at which Isolde had dropped the sword, healing Tristan physically but wounding him (and herself) with desire, becomes the point of Tristan's dying of another sword wound. That wound, as we know, was given by Melot as the agent of Minne. But in his long solo anticipating Isolde's coming Tristan made clear that his *Heil* would come from his final battle with Isolde; that he would encounter Isolde once again with a bloody wound, this time to be truly healed. With Tristan's death, finally, the metaphysical meaning behind the glance and Isolde's healing is complete.

The Drink of Atonement Music

On its first appearance in the prelude, Wagner extends the cadence of the glance music downward through eb' (the Neapolitan sixth chord, which suddenly darkens the harmony) to c♯' for a half close in d. Continuing, he leads the cadence sequentially up a tone, and from the melodic d♯' of this half close he leads the melody chromatically upward in sixteenths to c♯", a suddenly optimistic gesture that reaches a weakly accented A cadence, then turns immediately to E, for the "drink of atonement" (*Sühnetrank*) theme. On the downbeat, the prior melodic arrival on the third of the A major chord gives way to a downward leap from c♯" to d♯' within a D♯ Tristan chord, from which the line once again rises, this time beginning diatonically but incorporating the chromatic ascent from g♯' to b' as it settles on the E harmony, then continues in sequence without the chromaticism. Its rhythm is that of the glance motive, and its melodic ingredients are derived entirely from the desire and glance music, but its character is new, that of a blissful point of attainment, a secure though momentary arrival on E. After the minor subdominant of the glance music, the return of the pitch sphere associated with the arrival on B⁷ in the desire music is entirely without struggle.

The E is short-lived, however, because of the "poison" motive, which enters in the bass at the end of the second phrase. Consisting of a rising semitone followed by a falling sixth (usually major) or seventh (usually diminished), it is a more truncated retrograde of the initial tones of the desire music than that of the glance motive. The rising B–c semitone turns the dominant of E into a diminished seventh, and against the drop from c to D♯ in the bass the melody begins to describe a more intense kind of sequence, now rising chromatically, undermining the simplicity of the diatonic melody and turning the brief "attainment" of E back into renewed desire.

In act 1, the *Sühnetrank* music appears only at those points where the music of the Prelude returns more or less in its entirety: the scene that deals with the magic potions at the center of the act and the scene that follows the drinking of the potion at the end. In the first of these scenes Wagner sounds it in C as Brangaene draws forth what in her view is the noblest of the magic potions, the drink of love: "Den hehrsten Trank, ich halt' ihn hier!" Isolde however, disagrees. As the blissful melodic surface of the *Sühnetrank* motive disappears and the bass moves into the poison motive, she proclaims "Du irrst, ich kenn' ihn besser" (You're wrong, I know it better), drawing forth the drink of death. The poison motive introduces a series of enharmonically dissolving harmonies that culminate in the key of death, c, a contradiction of Brangaene's C (ex. 6.3).

After this point, the *Sühnetrank* music does not return until near the end of the act. But the poison motive does, at several points, always lending an ominous tone to the dramatic situation. At the beginning of scene 5, it undermines the honor motive, forecasting the outcome of the scene. Perhaps its most significant appearance, however, is to accompany Brangaene's preparation of the death potion on Isolde's orders. Here its role is structurally significant, as this is where the tonality of act 1, scene 5 shifts from b/B to c/C. Isolde's prior words, "Nun lass' uns Sühne trinken,"

Example 6.3. Act 1, scene 3: the drink of atonement and poison motives

close in f♯, the last tie to the B minor tonal framework. After the poison motive has done its work of dissolution, however, Tristan's disoriented outcry "Wo sind wir?" prompts Isolde's response, "Hart am Ziel" to the death motive. Although Isolde speaks of atonement (*Sühne*) to Tristan and presents the drink in that light, the shift to c reveals the underlying truth.

The *Sühnetrank* motive reappears, along with the rest of the music of the Prelude, at the end of the act; and Wagner associates it (now without the poison motive) with another blissful expression of the lovers' union: "Welten entronnen du mir gewonnen, Tristan!" (Escape from the world, I have won you!). Now it appears toward the end of the music recalled from the Prelude, leading into a rapid version of the glance music as the lovers proclaim consciousness of their love—"einzig bewusst, höchste Liebeslust"—and the ending of their duet merges into C.

The *Sühnetrank* motive does not appear in the second act or the first half of the third (although the poison motive does, briefly, at a few points). Its reappearance in act 3, however, is very telling in relation to the Prelude. For it now enters in the segment directly following Tristan's curse of the love potion, his relapse and rebirth, accompanying his vision of Isolde's arrival. After the turn to B following Tristan's reawakening, anticipating the transfiguration music and transforming the nature of

Tristan's curse, we hear the *Sühnetrank* music for the first time since the end of the first act, now in B, in a three-phrase sequence and without the poison motive and its disrupting sequences. Instead, its new third phrase sounds to the only appearance of solo violin in the opera. Tristan sings "wie sie hold mir Sühne trinkt" (how dearly she drinks atonement to me) to this music. The threatening character of death and desire is over. Before his relapse Tristan had cursed the love potion and his own existence; now the drink of atonement provides the other side of the love potion, the quality that Alfred Lorenz described as the idea of love in the Platonic-Schopenhauerian sense. The E is the fulfillment of all that lies behind the E of the prelude: the lovers' vision of transcendent union.[20]

Wagner's conception of the desire, glance and *Sühnetrank* motives and their interrelationships forms a logical succession that underlies the poetic character and musical dynamic of the first half of the Prelude. From the universal principle of desire through the specific origins of Tristan's and Isolde's love (the glance music), to an expression of their longing for transcendent union, the sequence moves more into the sphere of human love, its hopes and illusions. All three motives contain something of the tension/relapse idea within themselves, the desire music leading to the hopeful arrival of the B^7 chord then sinking back into the deceptive cadence to F, the glance music beginning as if in C and rising to the pitch b♭', then returning to a close in the subdominant, d, and the *Sühnetrank* motive attaining a momentary point of bliss in E, which the poison motive undermines as it introduces tensions based on the desire music. Although it picks up on the tonal implications of the third phrase of the desire music, its E seems like a glimpse into the potential future, an ideal, not a reality. Hence, Wagner's bringing it back in association with Tristan's clairvoyant vision in act 3.

Only two other themes from the Prelude need be mentioned, both variants of the desire music. Measures 36 to 43 introduce a variant of the desire music that begins from an augmented-sixth chord instead of the Tristan chord; it moves by semitone bass descent to the root of a dominant-seventh chord in a manner that suggests at times parallel dominant-seventh motion (ex. 6.4). Its transposition pattern is that of the rising major second and its rhythm is entirely that of the glance motive; also, the shape of its first three melody tones derives from the glance motive, whereas that of the remaining two return to the appoggiaturas of the desire motive. In conjunction with the semitone appoggiaturas that end the first two phrases (f♯'–g' and g♯'–a'), the rising-second transposition pattern causes the successive phrase endings to outline a rising chromatic scale. Wagner moves directly to the glance motive for its third phrase, so that the glance now enters *before* the deceptive cadence. Thus, this music merges the desire and glance themes, a musico-poetic idea that suggests Schopenhauer's explanation of the glance as key to the identity and continuance of the Will within the individual.[21]

The only other theme of distinct character in the prelude accompanies a reprise of the desire music that begins in the tonic major (mm. 63–74). Its active melodic surface is again based on the rhythm of the glance motive, and its successive units end with rising chromatic appoggiaturas that accumulate to form an ascending chromatic line, as we saw in the theme just described (ex. 6.5).

Example 6.4. Measures 37–44 of the prelude

If we designate the last two themes A′ and A″, acknowledging their derivation from the desire music, we are in a position to diagram the sequence of themes and variants of the prelude in a manner that reveals a permutational side to its form (fig. 6.1). The desire and glance motives are not only the two that appear most often but also those that articulate most clearly the dynamic of the movement; the harmonic and interval content of the one and the rhythm of the other pervade the Prelude. Although the *Sühnetrank* motive derives from both the desire and glance motives, it appears only in the first half of the Prelude and is not involved in the climax.

Along with its tendency toward the flat (subdominant) direction, the glance music contradicts the tendency toward the dominant in the desire music. Both themes have a character of yearning and relapse, but only the glance music expresses this quality by means of the melodic curve. As the movement unfolds, the variant forms of the desire music adopt features of the glance music until, finally, they merge at the climax of the movement, and again after the enharmonic relapse. Wagner harmonizes the uppermost tone of the glance motive, b♭″, first with a minor seventh chord (m. 77), then with a Tristan chord (m. 78), forcing the line to continue upwards. This change not only brings about a closer merging of the two themes, it sets up the tonal motion toward e♭ whose enharmonic transformation to a constitutes the final relapse back to the starting point.

In this view the desire music begins each of the major subdivisions of the prelude, the first two of which end with the glance motive, whereas the third leads to a merging of the desire and glance themes at the climax and again after the relapse back to desire. In the first and second sections, the downward tendency of the glance music constitutes the relapse from which point the next section begins. Thus, the dynamic

Example 6.5. Measures 63–73 of the prelude

Figure 6.1. Scheme of the prelude to *Tristan und Isolde*

A: mm. 1–17 (desire music)
B: mm. 17–24 (glance music, extended)
C: mm. 25–32 (*Sühnetrank* music)
B: mm. 32–36 (glance music, basic form)

A':   mm. 36–44 (variant of desire music, leading to A)
C: mm. 45–54 (*Sühnetrank* music, in E)
B':   mm. 55–58 (glance music, up a major third)
B: mm. 58–63 (glance music, normal pitch, with extension)

A":   mm. 63–74 (desire music beneath new theme in A)
B":   mm. 74–83 (glance music, extended upward and incorporating elements of the desire music—climax of prelude, suggesting e-flat, with enharmonic shift back to a)

A"':   mm. 83–94 (desire music, incorporating glance motive and A' variant)
B: mm. 94–100 (glance music, leading to c)

A"":   mm. 100–106 (desire music, first two phrases only, above a G pedal; leading to a linear form of the first Tristan chord in the bass, arranged so as to settle on the dominant of c)7

of those sections can be described as a curve from the desire music through the glance music to the *Sühnetrank* theme, then back through the glance music to a new variant of the desire music. Because Wagner has carefully closed the seams between sections, there is always a certain artificiality to such partitioning.[22] But measures 36 and 63 (the points at which the desire music reappears in variant forms following statements of the glance music) are useful in drawing our attention to a number of details. The twenty-seven measures between these two points consist entirely of the three principal themes of the opening section in varied form and slightly shuffled order. The glance music (B) appears twice in each of the two sections and the desire (A, A') and *Sühnetrank* (C) music once each. If we reorder the units of measures 37 to 63 after the pattern of the first thirty-seven measures (with the omission of most of the transition from d to E in mm. 21–24, which is no longer necessary), it is clear that Wagner's changes to the three principal themes in these measures effect an intensification of the "sharp" or dominant character that the E major theme introduced briefly in the first section.

Altering the transpositional interval of the successive phrases of the A' variant of the desire music to the major second enabled Wagner to shift up a major third for the deceptive cadence in measure 45 (i.e., to A instead of to F: V⁷–VI in c♯). He now changes the key signature to three sharps, retaining it for twenty-eight measures. If we follow the traditional view that the earlier cadence to F constitutes avoidance of a cadence to a or A that is set up by the third phrase of the desire music, then it is possible to view this cadence to A as a completion of the tonal motion that the earlier cadence had interrupted, a higher level of attainment. After measure seventeen, the glance motive had turned the music in the subdominant direction, from which it moved again toward A and E for the *Sühnetrank* music (mm. 22–29); after that the glance motive had turned back toward d once again (mm. 32–36). Now, beginning from a variant of the desire music, measures 36 to 44 use the deceptive cadence to A to establish the sharp framework more securely. As a result, the E major *Sühnetrank* music follows both the glance motive and a cadence to A, as it did in the opening section. Now, however, the sense that this A cadence is the sixth degree in c♯ (or, to put it differently, the fact that the tone D♯ is established for four measures before the cadence) means that the E major *Sühnetrank* theme is far more stable tonally the second time round. And its ending continues the sequential pattern that begins with the entrance of the poison motive for the two and one half extra measures that are necessary to permit the glance motive also to sound a major third higher than before, now in f♯ (mm. 53–56). Wagner's ending this version of the glance motive with a deceptive cadence to D (m. 56), however, enables it to repeat immediately at its original pitch level (mm. 57–60). Wagner then repeats its cadential descent pattern up a tone, ending with a half close to E and bringing in the next variant of the desire music (A″) over the dominant pedal (E⁷). This variant, beginning on the dominant of the major mode (A) will lead, via the glance music, to the climax of the movement.

The events just described (36–63) can be viewed as realizing the tonal implications of the motion toward the dominant (E) within the desire music as well as that from the subdominant minor cadence of the glance motive (d: measure 22) to the dominant major (E) of the *Sühnetrank* motive (mm. 25–28). In this light, the *Sühnetrank* motive affirms the dominant while the glance motive turns away from it. This is in keeping with the fact that behind the glance lies compassion (*Mitleid,* bound up with suffering), whereas the *Sühnetrank* music depicts the vision of transcendent union. In linking the *Sühnetrank* motive with the establishing of the sharp tonal area of the second section of the prelude, Wagner hints at the blissful fulfillment of love that a satisfying extension of the major dominant key and a resolution to the tonic major could provide (and that Wagner's concert ending further hints at).

The return of the glance motive to its original pitch level (mm. 60–64) between its transposition up a third and the A major reentry of the desire music (A″) seems to merge its d into a continuum of sharp music, where it functions as the minor subdominant of A. It appears now that the downward-turning character of the glance music has been overcome by the E/A relationship. The return of the desire music within an A context and beneath the most animated theme of the prelude invites the hope that this music will move toward the goal of the sharp transpositions of the preceding section, perhaps a visionary B comparable to that of Tristan's reawakening in act 3; and that, in turn, would render the E secure. Wagner brings in the return of the desire theme after three and one half measures of dominant harmony, sounding the opening phrase twice in conjunction with the prolonging of the dominant of A (the F/E bass alternation now intensifies the dominant of A for several further measures).

This is the most hopeful passage in the prelude, anticipating the key of Wagner's concert version, with its overtones of transcendence. Yet, in Wagner's language, the climax of the prelude represents failure to find the breach into the realm of night, a realm "from which we stray the furthest when we attempt to enter it by force." Despite its optimistic character, the new animated string theme introduces increased emphasis on the descending chromaticism of the desire music. And the desire music, although beginning in A, does not transcend the diminished-seventh chord harmonic sphere. The second phrase transposes at the minor third, to C/c, as before, causing a shift away from the A major tonality (and a canceling of the three-sharp key signature). Even more momentous is the fact that Wagner telescopes the third phrase, simultaneously sounding the chromatic descent and ascent elements, limiting the B^7 harmony to half a measure, and overlapping the deceptive cadence to F with the beginning of the glance motive (mm. 74–75), so that the entire phrase occupies only two measures (instead of eight). It initiates the motion toward e♭ at the climax, denying completion of the E/A music that had begun as far back as the third phrase of the desire music, and that had steadily increased through the first appearance of the *Sühnetrank* motive (mm. 25–32) and the sharp transposition of the second segment. In other words, the sharp music functions as the backdrop to a climax that denies its optimistic tendencies altogether.

To initiate the motion toward e♭, a tonality that is diametrically opposed to A, yet at the same time intimately bound up with it, Wagner introduces a chromatically descending line that continues from the b″–a″ appoggiatura of the deceptive cadence, creating a syncopated contrary motion against the melodic ascent of the glance music. This is the melody that (prefaced by a rising sixth) Isolde sings in her narrative as she recalls the original glance of love. Its text—"Seines Elends jammerte mich"—links the sorrowful aspect of the desire music with compassion and the glance. As the glance music continues in the Prelude Wagner also substitutes c♮ for the bass tone c♯ that usually sounds beneath the tone b♭′, erasing its tendency toward d and flattening the harmony still more by introducing a c minor-seventh chord at that point (m. 77). His original intention (which survives in the earliest version of the Prelude) was to bring in the half-diminished-seventh chord (or Tristan chord) on C at that point. His delaying the change from g to g♭ until the second half of the measure enables the voice leading to proceed more gradually and clearly. The harmony settles on vii^7 of B♭ first and the Tristan chord on C on the first beat of the next measure, before landing on the dominant of B♭. Meanwhile, the glance motive has shifted at the tritone, beginning now on e♭′ (m. 78) and lending weight to the pitch g♭′.

In the music that follows, leading to the climax, the pitch overlap between key areas a tritone apart prompted Alfred Lorenz to characterize the e♭ as illusory. The desire and glance motives answer one another at the tritone, completing the pitches of a single diminished chord before transposing down the fifth. When the desire music finally enters at pitch, beginning in measure 80, it seems to push beyond the minor third of the glance motive, c♭″, introducing the major third and major dominant-ninth chord as in the music that accompanies Tristan's reawakening in act 3, whereas the insistence of the glance motive on the minor third forces the enharmonic relapse.

The move toward the climax of the Prelude can be considered to begin with the arrival on the dominant of A major (m. 63) for the entrance of the desire music and to extend from there until the enharmonic relapse in measure 84. The rhythmic and melodic activity of the musical surface (like the major mode) clothe the inescapable fact that the underlying harmonic framework has not changed. From the point of overlap between the desire and glance music (m. 77), this span comprises an unbroken melodic ascent from a' to ab''', as the normal turning point to melodic descent, the bb'' of measures 78–79, now initiates instead a development of the ascending elements of the desire and glance motives. The harmonization of the bb'' was, as I mentioned, originally a Tristan chord, the first of a series of seven on the first beat of every measure through the climax. As it stands, the Tristan chord sounds on the first beat of each of the following six measures, on C in measures 78–79 and on F in measures 80–83, a tremendous allegory of the "attempt to find the breach" by insistent reiteration. The climax can be viewed as a tonal motion from a/A to eb (both "keys" articulated by their dominants), followed by the enharmonic revelation that it has not really gone anywhere. Melodically, the tones a' and ab'' circumscribe an ascent that, like the chromatic ascent from g#' to a" in the opening seventeen measures, represents a striving that is undermined at its peak by reinterpretation of the harmony at the tritone.

After the climax, the return to the desire music in a reveals relationships and options that Wagner has not presented explicitly until this point. The glance motive sounds within the same diminished-seventh common-tone framework as the desire music, appearing as a form of inversion of the rising sixths and descending chromatic thirds. For the third phrase, Wagner begins by continuing the minor-third transposition of the preceding phrases, utilizing the "missing" Tristan chord in the diminished-seventh-chord sequence, b, d", f', a', to introduce the A' variant of the desire music as a replacement for the remainder of the phrase. Instead of ushering in a sharp-key transposition of the glance and *Sühnetrank* themes, it leads to the original deceptive cadence to F. In the process, the impact of the potentially transcendent B harmony is once again greatly lessened.

The deceptive cadence now marks the point of divergence for the two endings of the prelude, that of the opera (and the *Prelude and Liebestod*) turning toward C minor, and that of the concert ending to A. In the concert ending the turn to A and the transfiguration music, in substituting for the F cadence, seemingly makes the point that the blissful vision of transcendence has finally been realized. Wagner's notes suggest as much. They also make clear that the vision itself is not the result of the lovers' "striving to enter it by force"—that is, by any direct effort—but, rather, by the opposite: abandonment of will. The opera itself has the scope to make this point clear. In the Prelude, however, Wagner was faced with a special problem— namely, that the Prelude itself was designed *not* to fulfill the lovers' search for transcendence. From this standpoint, the pairing of the *Prelude and Liebestod* is a far more satisfactory representation of the opera in microcosm, as it duplicates one of the core tonal sequences of the opera—a (desire), c/Ab (the two views of death and night) and B (transfiguration). In the Prelude, the series of progressively stronger articulations of the E/A relationship—the third phrase of the desire music, the transition between the glance and *Sühnetrank* motives on their first appearances, the sharp transpositions of the second "section," the return of the desire music in A at the beginning of the third section—gives way to the enharmonic relapse of the climax followed by a version of the desire music that lacks its former articulation of the dominant of E. As a result, the concert ending is not sufficiently "motivated" by the music that precedes it. Wagner therefore emphasized its standing apart from the main body of the Prelude. Within its twenty-five measures, he changes the time signature four times, a striking event considering that the remainder of the prelude has sounded entirely in $\frac{6}{8}$ meter.[23] The concert ending follows eight measures of $\frac{4}{4}$ by two of $\frac{5}{4}$ (further subdivided by dotted barlines into alternating $\frac{3}{4}$ and $\frac{2}{4}$ measures), an additional three measures of $\frac{3}{4}$ and, finally, twelve measures of $\frac{2}{4}$. The denial of rhythmic regularity goes hand in hand with changes in the orchestration (increased emphasis on the upper winds and the introduction of harp for the first time in the prelude) to create a visionary aura to the A major ending, but not one that can mirror the Schopenhauerian character of redemption as "denial of the will-to-life."

In order to end the concert version in A, Wagner had to transpose the final sounding of the first phrase of the desire music down a tone at the end of the prelude, a highly questionable gesture in light of its basic untransposability in the remainder of the Prelude and throughout the opera in general. As a result, the A major ending does not provide the stages by which we come to experience the transformations of desire within the opera itself. This is undoubtedly the reason that it has never competed with the *Prelude and Liebestod* as a concert piece. Underlying the latter is Wagner's conception of what the attainment of transfiguration involves, which is bound up with the transformation of the desire music so as to establish the B of its third phrase as the tonal goal of the opera, preceded by its own dominant F♯ (and even *its* dominant: the C♯ dominant ending of the second phrase of the transcendent version of the desire music). All this is anticipated in Tristan's reawakening in the middle of act 3; but the point where it is achieved is the *Liebestod,* in which the A♭ beginning, carried over from the duet "So stürben wir" of the love scene, retains the diminished-seventh chord framework of the desire music, yet nevertheless serves as a tonal preparation for the main body of the duet, in B (see chapter 15).

The concert ending of the Prelude is, therefore, gratuitous in a way that the ending of the *Liebestod* is not. And although the idea that the desire-exhausted lovers are *granted* a vision of the transfiguring night rather than earning it by conscious effort fits with the message of the opera as a whole, its lack of preparation eliminates the character of ecstasy that, in Schopenhauer's and Wagner's views, is the state of mind that leads to metaphysical intuition and transcendence of the world. Only the *Liebestod* provides that quality in the perfect balance between causality and mystery with which the A♭ music passes over into B major; after that the increasing emphasis on the dominant, F♯, in preparation for the B major transfiguration cadence bears the association of Isolde's being drawn into something greater than herself, even if it must remain fundamentally a vision only.

In the Prelude, then, Wagner adumbrates the lovers' vision of transcendence, mostly associated with the E major *Sühnetrank* music, as a momentary emotional state only. The cyclic character of desire remains dominant, owing to the tendency of the glance music away from the dominant region toward which the third phrase of the desire music moves, and which represents the lovers' vision of overcoming the negating diminished-seventh framework of the pessimistic, tragic nature of desire in the world. Significantly, it is the glance music that turns the prelude toward C minor, whereas the association of the *Sühnetrank* music with B and E as the outcome of the transformation of desire is realized at the point of Tristan's clairvoyant vision.

~

SEVEN

Tragedy and Dramatic Structure

WHEN WAGNER CLAIMED that *Tristan* was "the greatest of tragedies because in it nature was thwarted in its highest work," he was following what Schopenhauer called the "fundamental truth" behind the world's great religions: "the need for salvation from an existence given up to suffering and death, and its attainability through the denial of the will, hence by a decided opposition to nature."[1] For Schopenhauer, nature was the Will objectified. Wagner, as we saw, viewed nature as "broadly speaking a development from unconsciousness to consciousness," a conception mirrored in the Ring, whose Prelude and opening scene symbolized the emergence of the evolutionary processes of nature from their point of origin to the ever more differentiated and dissonant qualities of human existence. On the largest scale, the dramatic structure of *Tristan* enacts a reversal of this process, in Tristan's death and Isolde's final "unbewusst, höchste Lust."

In Schopenhauer's view, of all the poetic forms only tragedy could turn the will away from nature, first by presenting events that oppose the will, then by arousing the awareness that

> there is still left in us something different that we cannot possibly know positively, but only negatively, as that which does *not* will life. Just as the chord of the seventh demands the fundamental chord . . . so every tragedy demands an existence of an entirely different kind, the knowledge of which can always be given to us only indirectly, . . . At the moment of the tragic catastrophe, we become convinced more clearly than ever that life is a bad dream from which we have to awake.[2]

And elsewhere, again pursuing the analogy to music, Schopenhauer maintains that

> in the whole of music there are only two fundamental chords, the dissonant chord of the seventh and the harmonious triad, and all chords that are met with can be referred

to these two. This is precisely in keeping with the fact that there are for the will at bottom only dissatisfaction and satisfaction, however many and varied the forms in which these are presented may be.[3]

In developing the musical language of *Tristan*, Wagner would not have needed the various analogies that Schopenhauer offers in support of the idea that music provides a copy of the will. Nevertheless, *Tristan* exhibits many of the general qualities of Schopenhauer's analogies, none more pronounced than the sense of dissatisfaction that pervades the work in association with prolonged and unresolved dominant harmonies. This quality emerges with the desire music, its ambiguities, avoidances of closure, deceptions, dissonances, all very closely allied to the extraordinary emphasis on the dominant—Schopenhauer's "dissonant chord of the seventh." It is the source of some of the largest-scale dramatic and musical correspondences in the work.

One of the greatest of these sets of correspondences involves the events leading to the tragic catastrophe, Tristan's death, which Tristan views as Isolde's healing him from life, and which Isolde describes, in her subsequent solo, as his awakening from life (her "Horch! Er wacht! Geliebter! Nacht!"). That it also represents the thwarting of nature is clear from the fact that much of the music that follows Tristan's clairvoyant vision and leads to Isolde's arrival is based on the most conspicuous example of "natural" music in the opera, the shepherd's so-called joyful tune (*frohe, fröhliche* or *lustige Weise*), which Wagner said was inspired by an alphorn tune and described as an expression of the naive view of existence.[4] Wagner limited the melody to six diatonic tones, wanting it to be played on a specially constructed instrument made of wood, modeled after a Swiss alpine horn, with a coarse sound and capable of playing only the C major "Naturskala"[5] (Ex. 7.1). In lieu of such an instrument Wagner assigned the *frohe Weise* to the English horn; but his remarks in the published score admitted other possibilities, so important was the quality of the sound at that point. C major already had associations with day in *Tristan* (the end of act 1 and the beginning of the second act love scene). In act 3, Wagner presents it entirely above a prolonged dominant (G) pedal—an enormous extension of Schopenhauer's chord of the seventh—creating an analog of Tristan's awaiting Isolde's arrival to heal him from life. For more than 150 measures following his clairvoyant vision the *frohe Weise*—sounding sometimes from the English horn on stage, sometimes from the orchestra—dominates the harmony, which returns continually to the dominant of C. And after the *frohe Weise* comes to an end, the dominant pedal continues to define

Example 7.1. Act 3, scene 1: the *frohe Weise*

most of the tonal center for another 150 measures, culminating in Isolde's arrival directly before Tristan's death.

These events are the fulfillment of a much earlier sequence of events: Isolde's extinguishing the lighted torch at the end of act 2, scene 1, and the subsequent transition into the act 2 love scene, which begins with the lovers' meeting. Just before extinguishing the torch, Isolde proclaims that gesture a metaphor for death—"Die Leuchte, und wär's meines Lebens Licht, lachend sie zu löschen zag' ich nicht!" (The light, even if it were the light of my life, I would not hesitate laughingly to extinguish it)—on which the music associated with her longing to extinguish the torch throughout the preceding scene (the "torch" motive) combines with the death motive in a huge decrescendo above the dominant (F) pedal (ex. 7.2). In act 3, Wagner makes this music and the measures that precede it—now transposed up a tone—the basis of the lovers' meeting. As described earlier, he increases the already disso-

Example 7.2. Act 2, scene 1: the torch and death motives combined

nant character of the combined death and torch motives by layering above them another theme, associated with the inner light of night in the love scene (the melody that enters to the words "Barg im Busen uns sich die Sonne" in the duet "O sink hernieder," which Wagner called the motif of the "Tristanesque night"), and by causing the entire passage to lead into the desire music by means of an enharmonic change derived from the music associated with Frau Minne's weaving of life and death in act 2, scene 1. In this way, the dissonance above the dominant pedal (G) intensifies the tragic catastrophe enormously in relation to its earlier counterpart; the enharmonic change turns the dominant of c into the a of the desire music, whereas the decrescendo completes the turning of the will in Tristan, ending in the silence that follows his death. Tristan's death is the fulfillment of Isolde's extinguishing the torch, an analog of the thwarting of nature (ex. 7.3).

The parallel between these widely separated points involves their reliance on extended dominant pedals, on F in the music of act 2, scene 1, G in the music that pre-

Example 7.3. Act 3, scene 2: the lovers' meeting, leading to Tristan's death

cedes the lovers' meeting in act 3. To intensify the metaphoric foreshadowing of death and transfiguration that underlies the extinguishing of the torch, Wagner constructed the entire "torch" scene as a rondolike form built around regular recurrence of the dominant, often as an extended pedal point. Underscoring the association with nature and the dissatisfaction of existence, one of the most prominent means by which Wagner prolongs the dominant in that scene is with another obvious symbol of nature, the hunt music, which always sounds on the dominant (ex. 7.4). As in the case of the natural instrument intended for the *frohe Weise,* Wagner wrote a prefatory remark in the published score of *Tristan* in which he made known his preference for natural horns.[6]

Recurrence of the dominant of B♭ in this scene is associated with three kinds of music: the principal theme of the prelude, the theme associated with Isolde's longing to extinguish the torch, and the hunt music. The first of these themes is associated with anticipation of the lovers' meeting, whereas both of the others symbolize the artificial extension of day into night. As the hunt continues on into the evening, its music prolongs the dominant; likewise, as Tristan later complains, the lighted torch extends the day beyond its normal time. Recurrence of the dominant pedal throughout the scene accompanies Isolde's longing for night and tonal closure, associated poetically with the extinguishing of the torch, and musically with the emergence of the transfiguration music of the *Liebestod* in this scene. The cadential potential of the transfiguration music, however, is never fulfilled in the torch scene, largely because of the rapid tempo to which it accommodates. The music that follows the extinguishing of the torch returns to the principal theme of the Prelude to the act, as if to articulate formal closure, but soon becomes increasingly anticipatory. At the point of the lovers' meeting we hear a move toward the transfiguration cadence, in B♭. Its potentially transcendent character is, however, swallowed up by the rhythmic momentum, which pushes the tonality away from B♭ and on to the C

Example 7.4. Act 2: the hunt music

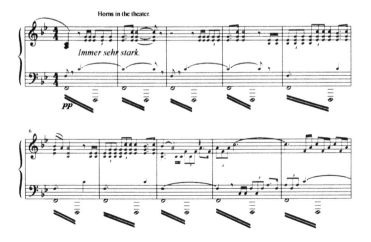

major beginning of the love scene, itself articulated by another extended dominant (G) pedal. As a result, the idea of incomplete formal closure in the scene as a whole mirrors the dominance of nature, desire, and day (as symbolized in Wagner's placing the day motive at the head of the act).[7] Throughout the scene, we may speak of Wagner's using the chord of the seventh (or the ninth) to intensify both Isolde's dissatisfaction and her vision of an "existence of an entirely different kind" (night) from the reality in which she finds herself (day).

Wagner's building the three hundred measures that precede the lovers' meeting in act 3 around the *frohe Weise* and the dominant of C, deflecting the tonality at the last moment to a, suggests the tragic catastrophe of Tristan's death as the turning of the will away from nature. Breaking with the framework of nature and day is, of course, what *Tristan* is all about. So Wagner introduces conspicuous symbols of nature in all three acts, making them coincide with the raising of the curtain: the sailor's song in act 1, the hunt music in act 2, and the shepherd's *alte Weise* in act 3. Throughout act 1, the natural music (the sailors' chorus and the music associated with the ocean voyage) returns at several points, always in opposition to Isolde's thoughts of death, finally dominating the ending of the act as it turns to C. In acts 1 and 2 the natural music is associated with King Mark and the qualities Wagner associated with day. In act 3, however, Wagner introduces *two* forms of natural music: the *alte Weise*, symbolizing the tragic character of existence, and the *frohe Weise*, which sounds after Tristan's reawakening, mirroring what Schopenhauer called the one "inborn error": belief in happiness as the goal of existence.[8] Whereas the *alte Weise* is in minor and features a considerable amount of chromaticism, the *frohe Weise* is entirely diatonic and in major (exx. 7.1 and 7.5). And that opposition, embodied to some extent in the *alte Weise* itself, was latent in the sailor's song of act 1 as well. In act 1, the diatonic music of the sailor's song eventually triumphed as the C major music of the ocean voyage and the arrival at Cornwall, symbols of day. In act 3, however, the C major *frohe Weise* does not determine the ending. Instead, Isolde's reference in the *Liebestod* to a *Weise* that only she can hear affirms the inner quality of music that is the core of Schopenhauer's metaphysics of music. It is the counterpart to Isolde's *not* hearing the music of nature—the hunting horns—in act 2, scene 1.

In addition to the presence of natural music in all three acts, Wagner introduces prolonged dominant pedals in all three acts, always in association with the lovers' meetings. In the first half of act 1, scene 5, the honor music and the B minor tonality associated with it are projected by constant return to the dominant (F♯), whose tendency not to cadence in the tonic mirrors the unfulfilled character of honor, ultimately revealed as a hollow ideal that is overcome by nature (the sailors' chorus). After the dominant of B♭ in act 2, scene 1, and the dominant of C in the beginning of the love scene, the duet that ends the latter scene—depicting what Wagner called "the most sincere and heartfelt longing for death"—emphasizes the dominant of B at key structural points in preparation for its apparent resolution into the transfiguration cadence. Once again, however, that event is deflected by the return of day, symbolized in King Mark's return. Only after the reappearance of the dominant of C, leading to Tristan's death as the thwarting of nature, will the *Liebestod* fully resolve the chord of the seventh (F♯) into its fundamental chord (B).

Example 7.5. Act 3: the *alte Weise*

All the points I have described in connection with this idea are interrelated, affirming the opposition of nature and metaphysical intuition within the dramatic structure of *Tristan*. The basic direction of nature is outward, that of increasing consciousness, desire, life, and day. Its most prominent symbol in Wagner's work is the prelude to *Das Rheingold,* source of the nature motives of the Ring, in which the idea of *creatio ex nihilo* recalls Schopenhauer's analogies between the harmonic series and the physical world—that is, nature. In his Schopenhauerian aesthetics, Wagner viewed various forms of natural music, such as the alphorn he heard on one occasion and the Venetian gondolier's song that awakened him on another, as equivalent to the "cry of tone" that accompanied an awakening in terror from the "dream of deepest sleep."[9] The cry of tone was a metaphor for the origins of music in the fundamental conflict of the will with itself; it affirmed the fact that music, in contrast to what Hanslick believed, had pathological origins, rooted in expression rather than beauty.[10] The differentiation it underwent in the phenomenal world represented a softening or dissipation of the terror, an attempt to clothe the tragedy of existence with what Nietzsche called "metaphysical comfort." This, ultimately, became Wagner's view of the entrance of the voice in the finale of the Beethoven Ninth Symphony, a "deed of music" in which resistance to the tragic truth of existence, the "cry of horror" that began the movement—"O Freunde, nicht diese Töne"—gave way to Beethoven's vision of the emergence of music from the metaphysical night in the diatonic melody of the Ode to Joy, another creation metaphor.[11]

In one of the *Wesendonck Lieder*, "Stehe still," alluded to in chapter 2, Wagner gave his own interpretation of the overcoming of nature through understanding its meaning. "Stehe still" begins in c and ends in C, associating the change of mode with the poet's reference in the last line to "solving the riddle of nature."[12] As described earlier, the song deals with an image taken directly from Schopenhauer, very probably by way of Wackenroder, the "wheel of time," whose endless revolving symbolizes the cyclic nature of existence and desire. Schopenhauer, for whom the circle was the universal symbol of nature, referred to the " wheel of Ixion" as a symbol of the endless process of willing, the subject of "Stehe still."[13] The title of "Stehe still" is a cry for the wheel to cease, bringing an end to existence itself. The relationship of this theme to *Tristan* can be gathered from the endings of Wagner's first two strophes, both set to a circular perpetual-motion-style accompaniment of running sixteenth notes: "genug des Werdens, laß mich sein!" (enough of becoming, let me be: strophe 1); "ende, des Wollens ew'ger Tag!" (end, eternal day of willing: strophe 2). In Wagner's song, there are two stages in the slowing and eventual cessation of the wheel's motion. The first comes in the third strophe, in which Wesendonck introduces the "sweet forgetfulness" of love and the oneness of two "souls" who "sink into one another" as a key to transcendence of the endless motion. Here Wagner changes from sixteenth-note to eighth-note motion. For the line "Seele in Seele versinken" the music modulates in the flat direction to eb, at which point Wagner shifts enharmonically from cb (B) to E ("Wesen in Wesen sich *wiederfindet*": being finds itself in being again), changing the key signature. The enharmonic equivalence makes the point of the identity of inner being. Soon afterward, we hear the final stage in the cessation of the wheel: "keinen Wunsch mehr will das Inn're zeugen: erkennt der Mensch des Ew'gen Spur, und lös't dein Rätsel, heil'ge Natur!" (the inner being desires to form no more wishes; one recognizes the trace of eternity and solves your puzzle, holy nature).[14] Here the accompaniment virtually comes to a halt; and Wagner introduces his symbol of nature: a series of very slowly moving seventh chords beginning from A^7 and moving through the circle of fifths through D^7, G^7, C^7 to F^{+7}, before cadencing in C major (on "Natur"). Thwarting nature meant progressing backward from chromatic through diatonic music to silence, the association underlying the three *Weise* of act 3.

The parallels I have described point up one of the largest-scale correspondences in *Tristan:* Wagner's defining the boundaries of his three love scenes in terms of the keys of b/B and C, and his reversing their order in acts 2 and 3 in relation to that of act 1. In act 1, the love scene (scene 5) begins with the first meeting of the lovers in the opera and ends with the arrival at Cornwall immediately after their drinking the love potion. The beginning of the scene and much of its first half are in B minor, associated with the honor music, whereas its ending is in C. The blatant C triads of the trumpets can be considered to depict the victory of nature and day over honor and death. Although the scene as a whole cannot be described simply as a progression from B to C, the choice of those keys and the shift from the one to the other are very meaningful in terms of the question of tonal symbolism in *Tristan*.

In act 2, the love scene returns to C major at the beginning for the first of its four duets, the point that Wagner meant when he referred to the beginning of the scene as "life overflowing with all the most violent emotions." The scene ends with the B major duet, "O ew'ge Nacht," which he referred to as "the most intense and heartfelt longing for death." Behind the scene lies, of course, the lovers' increasing metaphysical intuition, embodied in the transition from day to night and life to death. Thus, the scene divides into two principal parts, the *Tagesgespräch*, or dialogue on day, and the night scene, which begins with the second duet, "O sink hernieder," and extends to "O ew'ge Nacht." The change in the lovers' feelings from the ideal of honor to the victory of day in act 1 becomes that from day and life to night/death and intuition of transcendence in act 2.

Finally, in act 3 the idea of a love scene is far less literal than in act 2. But again the boundary keys of C and B are vital to its definition. And C is again associated with nature and day (the stretch that involves the *frohe Weise*), B with transcendence (the *Liebestod*). None of the three love scenes can simply be described as a progression from C to B, or vice versa, of course. In particular, the sequences of tonalities in acts 2 and 3 are highly complex. And it is very important to note that the relationship of each love scene to the design of the act in which it appears as well as to the other two love scenes introduces important parallels involving other keys and key relationships than those between the boundary keys of C and B.

In each of the three love scenes the relationship of love and death determines the meaning of the shift from B to C or vice versa. In act 1, Wagner sets up an opposition between C major and C minor, the former associated with the sailors' chorus and the arrival at Cornwall and the latter with Isolde's plan for the lovers' deaths. Wagner highlights the symbolic nature of the shift from the B minor segment of scene five to c/C by cadencing in the dominant, f♯, as Isolde completes her ironic fantasy on the drink of atonement she is offering Tristan. And from there the music shifts to c/C as Brangaene prepares the drink to the sound of the poison motive. This is one of many tritone shifts in the opera that Wagner introduces to represent the idea of opposition—but generally opposition that turns out to be only a "surface" phenomenon, subsumed under a larger sense of union. C minor is the principal recurrent key throughout the act, associated with death and offset several times by entrances of C major from the sailors or from Kurvenal, always with the opposite association. Its return after the most extensive digression of the act is enormously symbolic. Tristan's words "Wo sind wir?" (Where are we?) echo Isolde's from the beginning of the act (also in c), and Isolde's response—"Hart am Ziel!" (Near the goal)—brings in the death motive, which reappears soon afterward with the same associations to frame a segment in that key. Her subsequent C major solo likewise returns to the minor mode as she fails to hold to her ironic, mocking mode and cadences in c. Most of all, however, the C minor music of this part of the scene reveals Tristan's increasingly coming to understand both Isolde's hidden intentions and their underlying motive. Accompanying his disoriented and distracted orders to the sailors, therefore, the semitone ascent of the beginning chords of the death motive continues upward in the orchestra, following the pattern of the desire music. The culmination of C minor occurs soon afterward with Wagner's revealing the close relationship between the honor motive and the death motive ("Tristan's Ehre") and Tristan's singing the death motive itself for the only time ("Vergessens güt'ger Trank, dich trink' ich sonder Wank"). After this, the return of the music of the Prelude and the final affirmation of C symbolize the victory of desire, nature, and day over death and honor.

In act 2, the return of C major at the beginning of the love scene restores the framework of day even as the extinguishing of the torch opens up the possibility of night. Throughout the *Tagesgespräch*, the lovers' interpretation of the past involves the increasing encroachment of physical and metaphoric night as Tristan and Isolde reject honor and day. Gradually the key of Ab emerges as the principal recurrent tonality, associated with night. And, at several points, Wagner introduces it to replace the key of c in highly symbolic fashion. Thus, Ab takes over from c as the key of the lovers' new perspective on death: longing for night as the result of their perception of the bond between love and death, instead of simply death (suicide) as escape from a love that can never be fulfilled. The introduction of the new death motive encapsulates the change directly before "O sink hernieder," and the climax of the duet gives it symbolic status. Already in the transition to the duet Wagner had intended, in a rejected version from the compositional draft, to foreshadow the next stage in the lovers' metaphysical understanding—the motion from night-death to transcendence—by having the transfiguration music sound first in Ab, then in Cb (B) in immediate succession. He subsequently changed his mind, reserving that modulation for "O ew'ge Nacht"; but the Ab/B relationship remained as his symbol of the lovers' overcoming the dream of love. Immediately after they cry out "Sehnend verlangter Liebestod" to the new death motive in "O ew'ge Nacht," Wagner shifts back to Ab for the dream chords of "O sink hernieder" and at their close ("von Erwachen's Not befreit") shifts to B for the main body of the duet.

Thus, the reversal of the B–C tonal boundaries of the act one love scene in the C–B of act 2 is bound up with the change in the lovers' viewpoint on death and of its key from c to Ab. In act 1, the minor third from a to c—extending the keys of the first and second phrases of the desire music—depicts the idea of death in apparent opposition to desire, whereas the change to the major mode, C, reveals the bond between desire and life, or day. In act 2, the emergence of Ab as the key of night-death, replaces the C major with which the love scene begins and the C/c life-death antithesis of the first act by the bond between desire and night, after which Wagner reintroduces the rising minor third relationship, now from Ab to B, to represent the bond between night-death and transfiguration. In the *Tagesgespräch* and in the transition to "O sink hernieder" and the duet itself, Wagner brings out a considerable degree of shifting between pitches and tonal emphases on A and Ab, finally revealing at the climax of the duet that Ab, the beginning tone of the desire music, is the "ground tone" of night to which a/A has to return before progression to the next stage—shift from A♭ to B as the motion from night to transcendence—can take place. Behind these relationships lies the desire, night-death, transfiguration sequence that controls the three act succession and the pairing of the *Prelude and Liebestod*. The a–C relationship of act 1, expressive of desire as a manifestation of nature and day, gives way to the A♭–B succession of act 2—prefigured in "So stürben wir" and accomplished in "O ew'ge Nacht"—as the deeper one, expressive of the progression from love to the union of night-death and transfiguration. The process is completed In the *Liebestod* with the joining of "So stürben wir" to the B major music of "O ew'ge Nacht."

To relate all this to his amendment of Schopenhauer—that love as sexual desire could itself lead to denial of the will-to-life and transfiguration—Wagner needed to reveal that the key of transcendence in *Tristan*, B major, was linked via its primary pitch to the same diminished-seventh chord that lay behind the desire music, yet at the same time was the symbol of transcendence of that chord. He therefore widened the antitheses of c/b in act 1 and A♭/B in act 2, to that of f/B in act 3. C minor represented the key of death in apparent opposition to desire but in actuality only an extension of desire that was not recognized as such; A♭ represented the key that bonded desire and death within the poetic night; now f represented the key of tragic suffering leading to denial of desire and the will-to-life as the gateway to the metaphysical beyond. Even the tonic pitches of the three keys of death—C, A♭, and F—spell out the F minor triad. The b–c/C shift in act 1 affirms the original framework of desire (the return of the prelude at the end of the act), the A♭–B shift in "O ew'ge Nacht" represents the visionary passage from night to transfiguration, whereas the f/B shift in act 3 places that visionary ecstasy in the context of denial of the will-to-life. In all three acts, C is closely allied with the diatonic framework of nature and day; it is finally overcome by the increasingly complex and transformational tonal relationships surrounding desire, death, and transfiguration—the realm of night.

Among the three acts parallel sequences of events amplify the opposition of nature and tragedy. Directly following the natural music in each act Wagner introduces a scene in which one of the lovers opposes the conventional views of a secondary character (Isolde and Brangaene in acts 1 and 2, Tristan and Kurvenal in act 3). Wagner contrasts the musical styles associated with the primary and secondary characters; in act 1, Brangaene, and later Kurvenal, create overtly periodic designs, always in major keys, from the music of the ocean voyage, whereas Isolde parodies and distorts both the ocean music and the principle of periodic forms. In act 2, Isolde and Brangaene disagree over the question of whether or not the hunting horns are audible, over Melot's faithfulness or treachery and over Brangaene's substitution of the love potion as the cause of the lovers' dilemma. In act 3, Tristan and Kurvenal likewise differ in their perceptions of reality: Kurvenal sings in F and even brings back the superficially periodic music associated with Tristan's honor and heroism as he rejoices in Tristan's return to life and his home, Kariol, whereas the *alte Weise*, in f symbolizes Tristan's longing for death and his true home, night.

In addition, each act devotes a substantial segment (or segments) to reinterpretation of the past as an essential part of the process through which understanding moves forward. The reinterpretations become progressively more internal and dreamlike from act to act. In act 1, Isolde (in the segment known as Isolde's narrative) recounts to Brangaene the history of her relationship with Tristan prior to the events of act 1 itself. At its close, she makes the association between C minor and death explicit. After their meeting, Tristan and Isolde go back over some of that history in light of their present relationship. In the final stages of their dialogue Tristan finally accepts Isolde's plan of death, singing the death motive in c. In the second act, Wagner devotes the entire first segment of the love scene, the so-called *Tagesgespräch*, to the lovers' reinterpretation of past events, especially those of act 1, in light of their new metaphysical insight, symbolized in the opposition of night and day. Throughout this process A♭, emerges as the new key of the dream world of night-death, replacing the c of act 1.

Finally, in act 3, Wagner provides us with the most extensive reinterpretation scene in the opera and one of the most impressive such scenes in his work as a whole (see chapter 14). Over two cycles Tristan, tormented by desire, curses first the day, then the love potion and his own existence. His memory stimulated by the sounding of the shepherd's tragic *alte Weise* (the English horn on stage), then by his own internalized form of the song, Tristan comes to recognize the force of desire in the continuance of his life and his own part in the creation of the world (symbolized in his proclaiming that he brewed the love potion). In the terms of Wagner's amendment, Tristan comes to consciousness of his life as agency of the species will, symbol of nature, which he rejects, relapsing into unconsciousness to the highly symbolic f/F cadence that forms the act's central pivot. The rejection of nature enables his reawakening and acceptance of day, culminating in Schopenhauer's tragic catastrophe, his death. Together with the ending of the *Liebestod*, these events make the point that the highest form of knowledge not only derives from the unconscious but also leads to renunciation of consciousness: the thwarting of nature.

The greatest correspondence among the three acts is, of course, that of the three love scenes, each of which begins with the lovers' meeting after a period of anticipation, and ends with an action related to death. In each case, the focus on death is offset by King Mark's presence, symbolizing the perspective of day. In the first act, the drinking of the love potion brings about an intermingling of love and death, the key to Wagner's disagreement with Schopenhauer regarding the possibility that desire might lead to denial of the will-to-life. The second act features three points of culmination in which, increasingly, death moves from metaphoric to literal reality: the extinguishing of the torch, a prefiguring of death; the duet that ends the love scene, in which Tristan and Isolde proclaim their longing for death; and Tristan's wounding by Melot at the end of the act. The last of these actions prepares for the metaphysical insight of the first half of act 3, after which Tristan's death and Isolde's transfiguration complete the process, bringing about the fact that for the only time Mark's presence does not determine the character of the ending. Behind these events, we might well perceive parallels to the kinds of Christian symbolisms that some commentators have felt underlie Gottfried von Strassburg's poem, the gesture of Tristan's acceptance of the drink of death corresponding to Jesus' acceptance of the "cup" at Gethsemane, that of his wounding corresponding to that of Jesus in the Passion; and, finally, that of his and Isolde's deaths (and rebirths, literary rather than physical in Gottfried) as the goal of the Passion itself. Schopenhauer opened the door to such religious allegories in his describing the death of the tragic hero as atoning for the guilt of existence. Thus, the common view of *Tristan* as a religious drama, according to which the love-death potion is a kind of forerunner of the grail of *Parsifal*, is appropriate so long as we recognize its Schopenhauerian tragic character.

EIGHT

The Two Death Motives

Inner and Outer Worlds

In Wagner's Schopenhauerian aesthetics, for which *Tristan* was the focal point, the leitmotifs mirror the dualisms associated with the world as representation and will. Following Wagner's lead (see chapter 2), we recognize that for him the leitmotifs exhibited two distinct sides, the one referential and the other based on "inner musical laws." Because the latter had metaphysical priority, the drama was equivalent to "deeds of music become visible" and the musical motives took over the role of "motivating" the dramatic events (in the Schopenhauerian sense of providing their "inside").

Wagner's claim that the motives "give us the character of all the phenomena of the world according to their most inner abstract-self," means that the motives possess qualities analogous to the interpretation of phenomena as Platonic Ideas. This seems to contradict Schopenhauer, who said explicitly that "music does not, like all the other arts, exhibit the *Ideas* or grades of the will's objectification, but directly the *will itself.*"[1] But Schopenhauer nevertheless recognized the existence of "an analogy, between music and the Ideas, the phenomenon of which in plurality and in incompleteness is the visual world."[2] He therefore drew parallels between music's individual elements and the phenomena of the world, some of which influenced Wagner's conception of the language of *Tristan*. Although for Schopenhauer music was independent of dramatic motivations, when combined with a dramatic text, as in opera, it became "the expression of the inner significance of all those incidents, and of their ultimate and secret necessity that rests on this significance." For "with the language of the feelings, our faculty of reason does not willingly sit in complete idleness. From its own resources, music is certainly able to express every movement of the will, every feeling; but through the addition of the words, we receive also their objects, the motives that give rise to that feeling."[3] For Wagner, symbolizing those "objects" and "motives" was the role of the leitmotif, which had the capacity to suggest both inner and outer aspects of reality, the former tending toward union with the other motives and the latter toward their differentiation and individual associations.

Thus, Wagner's vision of the musical motives distinguishes between what we would call their motivic and *leit*motivic aspects. The former are rooted in everything that binds them to the other motives—their intervallic, gestural, harmonic, or rhythmic content. Analogous to the fact that in heightened states of awareness individuals could perceive the coherence of all phenomena that was normally closed off, Tristan, in the agitated state that precedes his curse in act 3, perceives the role of desire behind reality and the principle of negation behind desire itself. The *alte Weise* and the desire music combine with a series of other motives in which Tristan chords continually dissolve into diminished-seventh chords. The curse motive is the outcome of this new insight. At the same time, its striking individuality depicts its phenomenal presence, its subordination to the *principium individuationis;* in some motives, this quality may extend to pictorial qualities but more often it mirrors the generalized affective sphere associated with the phenomenon in question.

In conceiving the motives of *Tristan*, Wagner often had direct recourse to Schopenhauer, molding the events of Gottfried von Strassburg's poem into vehicles of quasi-philosophical content. Gottfried's treatment of love is, of course, the most obvious instance of this process, becoming the symbolic agency of Schopenhauer's universal principle of desire or will, the ultimate motivation behind events in the phenomenal sphere. Consequently, Wagner's desire music has a far wider set of associations in the drama than that of the love potion, its variant versions representing the manifold forms that desire takes in the world. As such they often coincide with the greatest dramatic climaxes of the work, at which points the desire music makes an impact as a quasi-periodic design, whereas at other times its more generalized aspects— above all, the rising chromaticism and the Tristan-chord/dominant-seventh chord relationship—permeate the fabric of the music in more "internal" fashion. Tristan's answer to King Mark's question regarding the "deep mysterious cause" behind existence and his curse of the love potion proclaim desire as the symbol of causality in the phenomenal world underlying other causes and even existence itself. Analogous to the fact that even desire is not a final cause, but only the appearance or phenomenon of the will, behind which lies the veil of ultimate negation, in the passages just cited Wagner reveals that behind the Tristan chords and dominant sevenths lies a single diminished-seventh chord as the harmonic symbol of negation. Its enharmonically paradoxical character is analogous to the "veil of Maya."

Wagner's emphasizing the motion, shaping and transformation of the motives suggests that the motives should not be defined, either musically or poetically, as fixed entities with finite associations. Yet, there is often a physical object, event, or quality that lends its name to the motive; we speak of the honor motive, the torch motive, the glance motive, and the like. In the Ring, many of the motives are more closely identified with physical objects or props than in *Tristan:* the Ring, Valhalla, the sword, Wotan's spear, and so on. Even there, however, the specific names and associations of the motives clothe ideas that extend beyond their phenomenal presence. The naming of objects, even people, coincides in many cases with the greatest dramatic climaxes; and the names themselves very often have symbolic or allegorical meanings. We need think only of the naming of Valhalla, of Siegmund and Sieglinde, and the sword (*Nothung*) in the Ring and the *denial* of names in *Tristan* ("ohne Nennen, ohne Trennen," "nicht mehr Tristan, nicht mehr Isolde") to get a sense of how important this question was for Wagner, for whom the essence of objects, events, people—in a word phenomena—was not to be identified with static conceptions or names, but with motion and process.[4] Tristan and Isolde move backward through the names to the reality beyond.

Wagner's most interesting statement on this question, bridging the gap between the leitmotifs and form, came on the eve of his beginning the composition of *Tristan*, in February 1857, in the essay "On Franz Liszt's Symphonic Poems." In it, Wagner develops the idea of the sword as metaphor for musical form, its hilt, or *Griff*, representing the static conception (etymologically related to *Begriff*), and its blade the dynamic quality that constituted the essence of true form. As Wagner saw it, the most common misconceptions of form—"Swords without blades!"—were analogous to judging the hilt to be the most valuable part of the sword, the part that attracted attention when the sword was not in use. When the sword was in use, however, the intimate fit between the hand and the hilt rendered the latter invisible, with the result that form—analogous to the motion of the blade—could not be perceived as such. This was particularly true in the case of a composer such as Liszt, whose conceptions were unusually dependent on his individual poetic sensibility. The only way to grasp such forms was through identification with the composer's poetic intent, which Wagner described as analogous to love. Thus, in its primary subject matter, *Tristan and Isolde* became a metaphoric enactment of Wagner's Schopenhauerian aesthetics.

Wagner hints in this essay that his friends have heard him speak out on this subject, meaning, perhaps, that the sword in the Ring somehow embodies the qualities he is addressing (Wagner was composing *Siegfried* at the time of writing the Liszt essay).[5] In the Ring the sword and its motive, which are to be found in all four operas, coincide with some of the most momentous events and dramatic climaxes in the entire tetralogy, ranging from Wotan's announcing his "great plan" at the end of *Das Rheingold*, to Siegfried's death in *Götterdämmerung*. The sword motive is a key element in the climactic endings of *Das Rheingold*, the first act of *Die Walküre* and the first act of *Siegfried*. And in the first two of these it is associated with naming: *Valhalla* at the end of *Das Rheingold*, Siegmund, Sieglinde, and the sword itself (*Nothung*) at the end of the first act of *Die Walküre*. After that, it becomes a symbol of Siegfried's heroic identity with his reforging the sword in the first act of *Siegfried*. Then it represents his quasi-Oedipal confrontation with Wotan in the second act of that work and, finally, his awareness of sexual identity as he encounters Brünnhilde's womanhood in the third act. It would take us too far afield to consider this question here. But Wagner's viewing the sword as what I would call an aesthetic metaphor is a quality that is shared by many of the motifs of the Ring. Metaphorically, the sword represents a dynamic conception of form that is analogous to emerging consciousness, an artistic deed, as Wagner described the entrance of the voice in the Beethoven ninth symphony. This conception underlies the ending of the first act of *Tristan*, in which emerging consciousness and names are again very prominent.

The analogy between the musical motives and the "idea-exhibiting drama" is rooted in the mythological qualities of the latter, which are sufficiently general to permit interpretation in terms of underlying psychological, political, or aesthetic ideas. In other motives from the Ring, Wagner does not draw analogies with his aesthetic ideas so openly, perhaps, as in the case of the sword. But they are not difficult to perceive. The ocean/land metaphor that runs throughout Wagner's aesthetic writings and that underlies the setting of the first act of *Tristan* is particularly evident in *Das Rheingold*, especially in all that concerns the Rhine river, on the one hand, and Valhalla, on the other. From the first to the second scene of *Das Rheingold* the motion from the depths of the Rhine to the mountaintop on which the castle stands is symbolic of the distance between unconscious drives and conscious designs (in Robert Donington's terms), but also of the fluidity of musical transition in comparison to the rigidity and symmetry of musical periodicity and architecture. The Valhalla music is the first such architecturally periodic form in the Ring, arising from the ring motive (a symbol of the lust for power), which it forms into an image of permanence and grandeur. It represents the faultiness of imposed form as the castle itself symbolizes all that is wrong with Wotan's desire for power. Wagner's allegory recalls Schopenhauer's placing architecture on the lowest scale of the arts and music on the highest for essentially the same reasons that underlie Wagner's poem and its setting. Wagner, in later years, made reference, pejoratively, to excessive musical periodicity as "quadratic construction," arising from the faulty analogy of music with architecture. In Valhalla the fluid motives of the prelude and opening scene of the Ring freeze into a monumental symbol of the intellectual construct or conception. As the Rhine maidens cry at the end of *Das Rheingold*, "Traulich und treu ist's nur in der Tiefe: falsch und feig ist was dort Oben sich freut!" (Only the depths are trustworthy and true; false and fearful is what rejoices up above).

Wagner's choosing the ocean voyage from Ireland to Cornwall as the setting of the first act of *Tristan* invokes some of the same oppositions, symbolizing the shallowness of the world of conventional honor inhabited by the lovers in relation to the depths of their unspoken desire. Revealing the force of desire and its connection with the process of increasing consciousness is the poetic goal of the first act. At this stage desire, in union with nature, controls events from beneath the surface, emerging in full only at select points where there is a "motive" or "object" to call it forth: the appearance of the potions of love and death at the center of the act, and the drinking of the potion at the end. There are two distinct groups of leitmotifs in the first act; and the oppositions they represent emerge with the dualisms within the sailor's song at the rising of the curtain. The motives of the ocean voyage and Tristan's heroism ("Hei unser Held, Tristan"), even of the name "Tristan" (as opposed to "Tantris"), do not derive overtly from the desire music (although they will combine with it in act 2). But all others do, and four of them—the motives of death, the glance of love, Isolde's narrative, and Tristan's honor—can be traced directly to Schopenhauer. Underlying all of them is the opposition that arises from the inner/outer qualities that Wagner casts in the terms of a division between intellect and feeling, or head (*Haupt*) and heart (*Herz*). That division is manifested primarily in the glance and death motives, both of which emerge from the desire music.

The First Death Motive

What I have outlined for the glance music in chapter 6 is true of the core motives of *Tristan*. Above all, the two death motives relate to two different perspectives on death as Wagner interpreted and "amended" Schopenhauer. The first, in act 1, is an extension of desire. Emerging from desire, it returns to desire just before Tristan's death, its last appearance in the opera. The second, which arises at the onset of night in act 2, incorporates on its first appearance the set of Tristan chords that appear in the desire music's three phrases. It then leads through the first phrase of the desire music and the transfiguration music in A and from there to A♭, the key of night in *Tristan*, replacing the C minor of the death motive in act 1. The pivot between the two views of death is the turning point in the lovers' metaphysical understanding. It reflects Wagner's amendment in its bonding desire and longing for death as the source of metaphysical insight.

In the first act of *Tristan* death appears at first to be opposed to desire. In scene 2 the close relationship between the two motives identifies c, the key of death in act 1, as an extension of desire (see ex. 4.3). Throughout the act, c is the principal recurrent key. At several points its juxtaposition to an optimistic C (the sailors and Kurvenal) reinforces the opposition of life and death that Isolde perceives as absolute. With the drinking of the love-death potion the music moves toward e♭, recalling the climax of the prelude. The sinking back of this gesture to the A minor desire music once again, however, and the replacing of c by C, mean that, metaphorically, the move from a to c/C represents both life and death (as it is conceived in act 1) as extensions of desire, the framework in which the first act is contained.

Despite the fact that Tristan and Isolde remain dominated by nature and the progression toward increasing consciousness, the first act represents an initial stage in the lovers' odyssey of metaphysical understanding, to be completed by Isolde's succumbing to *unconsciousness* at the end of the opera. Although in act 1 that understanding is equivalent to Schopenhauer's view of suicide as affirmation rather than negation of the will-to-life, the fact that the lovers face death is decisive. As Schopenhauer explained, human consciousness, because of its separating will (heart) and intellect (head), enables reflection on existence. In animals,

> will and intellect are not separated widely enough for them to be capable of being astonished at each other when they [i.e., will and intellect] meet again . . . and in them the whole phenomenon is still firmly attached to the stem of nature from which it has sprung, and partakes of the unconscious omniscience of the great mother. Only after the inner being of nature (the will-to-life in its objectification) has ascended vigorously and cheerfully through the two spheres of unconscious beings, and then through the long and broad series of animals, does it finally attain to reflection for the first time with the appearance of reason (*Vernunft*), that is, in man. It then marvels at its own works, and asks itself what it itself is. And its wonder is the more serious, as here for the first time it stands consciously face to face with *death*. . . . Therefore with this reflection and astonishment arises the *need for metaphysics* that is peculiar to man alone; accordingly, he is an *animal metaphysicum*.[6]

Because facing death gives "the strongest impulse to philosophical reflection and metaphysical explanations of the world," the greatest claim that *Tristan und Isolde* has to being what Nietzsche called "the actual *opus metaphysicum* of all art" is that it reveal this basic insight. Its initial symbol is the first death motive, "Todgeweihtes Haupt, todgeweihtes Herz," which proclaims the division between intellect (*Haupt*) and will (*Herz*) and the power of death to overcome it.

Wagner's addiction to the opposition of intellect and feeling preceded his discovery of Schopenhauer. *Opera and Drama* gives enormous attention to the dualism, often linking music to the one (feeling) and poetry to the other (intellect) and characterizing the former as feminine and the latter as masculine. But Schopenhauer, too, was enormously suspicious of conceptual knowledge; and feeling, viewed as Will, was close to the "true absolute" for him as well.[7] In fact, one passage in Schopenhauer's essay "On the Primacy of the Will in Self-Consciousness" (alluded to in chapter 6 in relation to the glance motive) seems to have influenced the character of the first act of *Tristan*. Schopenhauer asserts that the "universally used and generally very well understood expressions *heart* [*Herz*] and *head* [*Haupt*] have sprung from a correct feeling of the fundamental distinction in question" (between Will and intellect). Having represented the heart as the "symbol, indeed the synonym of the *will*," Schopenhauer further asserts that it is through the "expression of the glance" that "the *identity of the person*" depends; "the identity . . . rests on the identical *will* and on its unalterable character; it is also just this that makes the expression of the glance [*Blick*] unalterable. In the *heart* is the man to be found, not in the head."[8] Heart, will, and feeling are equivalent.

Wagner might well have derived the idea behind his glance motive from the passage just cited. When the death motive first appears, in act 1, scene 2, he links it with the desire music, and the glance music, all three of which appear in close succession. At this point none of the motives projects the metaphysical tone of act 2. But because death is bound up with the lovers' struggles between their hidden feelings and their outward actions in the first act, its motive centers on the antithesis of head and heart that underlies Schopenhauer's view of death as the impetus to metaphysical understanding. Isolde's "Todgeweihtes Haupt, todgeweihtes Herz" is a point of insight into the dominance of suffering and death in the world and their relationship to desire.

On its first entrance, the death motive introduces the antithesis of intellect and feeling as a symbol of the lovers' separation, both physical and psychological (see ex. 4.3). Because of what in act 2 will be described as Tristan's domination by day—that is, conventional views of honor—Tristan and Isolde are estranged from their former feelings of love, now pushed below the surface, for Tristan more than Isolde. Two external events precipitate Isolde's bringing her deeper thoughts to the surface on the first appearance of the death motive. The first is the opening of the dividing curtain that had formerly cut off her view of the stern and Tristan (the action that marks the division between scenes 1 and 2). The second is Wagner's beginning scene 2 with a truncated version of the sailor's song that had sounded to the rising of the stage curtain in scene one. Wagner sets up Isolde's state of mind in each of the first two scenes with the sailor's song. In the first scene its last line, "Du wilde minnige Maid" (You wild, passionate maiden), resonates with Isolde's anger, which culminates in her invoking the forces of nature to destroy the ship. In contrast to Brangaene's attempt to console her with conventional formal devices, Isolde bends the normally periodic character of the ocean motive (phrases two and three of the sailor's song) to her will, as she also does with the desire music throughout the first scene. In the second scene, Wagner drops the final two lines of the sailor's song so that it ends with "Weh', ach, wehe, mein Kind" (Sigh, ah, sigh, my child), commenting on Isolde's torment and setting up a change in tone for the scene as a whole.

At the beginning of scene 2, Wagner adds a G pedal below the sailor's song, then intensifies the sorrowful character of the ending phrases by moving the bass down by semitones, [G], F♯, F, pausing on F for "Wehe, wehe, du Wind," moving down through F, E, E♭, and pausing on E♭ for "Weh', ach, wehe, mein Kind," and finally ending on D as the chromatic descent in the melody moves from a♭' to f♯'. Seeming to emerge from this descending chromaticism, Isolde's line begins from the upper octave (d') of the final bass tone and reverses the chromatic motion of the bass descent. Meditating gloomily on the loss of Tristan's love, Isolde sings the chromatic ascent of the desire music, adjusted so as to outline a series of minor-third transpositions spanning an octave (d'–f', f'–a♭, a♭'–b', b'–d"). Although Wagner begins the melodic ascent from d', he does not harmonize the motive until the unit that begins from f'. This allows him to utilize the three Tristan chords of the three phrases of the prelude in an ascending minor-third transposition pattern, but, as described earlier, in the "rotated" order of phrase three, followed by phrase one, then phrase two. The final phrase of the sequence leads towards a half close on the dominant of c (the Tristan chord on A♭ followed by the dominant seventh on G), as normally occurs on its second phrase.

In the orchestral accompaniment Wagner overlaps the descending and ascending chromatic motives of the desire music, thereby linking the chromatic descent in the sailor's song to the intermingling of suffering and desire in Isolde. Isolde begins her slow chromatic ascent with references to her condition, "Mir erkoren, mir verloren" (chosen for me, now lost to me), changing as the sequence ascends to the contrast with Tristan, "hehr und heil, kühn und feig" (noble and acclaimed, bold and fearful). At the peak of the ascent, the death motive summarizes the antitheses in terms of the opposition of head and heart. Entering a semitone above the high d, it creates the effect of a barrier to further ascent. Isolde excludes the original third phrase of the desire music, whose tendency toward B would break with the circular rotation pattern, pointing to a potentially transcendent outcome (ex. 4.3).

The A♭⁶ chord with which the death motive begins ("todgeweihtes") relates to the c of the preceding phrase, after which the root-position A major chord that follows (on "Haupt") has no real tonal point of reference.[9] It therefore suggests both the idea of disembodied intellect that Feuerbach and Schopenhauer rejected and also, perhaps, the astonishment that accompanies the consciousness coming face to face with death. The initial harmonies of the death motive—A♭⁶ and A—suggest the first two tones of the desire music (later in the act Wagner first alternates, then extends, the pattern of the first two harmonies of the death motive up the chromatic scale—G♯⁶, A, B♭⁶, B, C⁶, D♭, D⁶, E♭—thereby intensifying the bond between death and desire as Tristan comes to understand Isolde's hidden intentions). In the context of c, however, their immediate relationship is one of opposition. Because the heart, Schopenhauer's "synonym" of the will, is more fundamental than the head, it is the word *Haupt* that introduces the antithetical quality, its A harmony juxtaposing sharply with the A♭⁶ chord of "todgeweihtes." Wagner emphasizes the highly provocative character of the A major harmony by leaping up a major sixth in the voice—emphasizing the tritone e♭'–a'—and changing the orchestration from woodwinds to brass with a drum roll in the bass. The f⁶ chord to which it gives way, however, introduces the A–A♭–G bass motion that draws the harmony back to the dominant of c for "todgeweihtes Herz."

The shift from the A harmony to the f⁶ chord is not nearly so disrupting as the introduction of A after A♭⁶, since it effects a return to the key of c (half close). The A–A♭–G bass motion reverses the semitone antithesis of the initial A♭/A harmonies, returning to the harmony of the desire music from which the motive had emerged. The pitch e♭' above the dominant harmony and the return of the woodwind orchestration for the cadential "todgeweihtes Herz" create a sense of closure that confirms the key of c and overcomes the foreignness of the A harmony. Not only does the cadence of the motive duplicate the harmony of the preceding phrase of the desire music, but also its melodic contour—the pitches b, c', e♭', d'—is also a variant of that phrase (a fact that is instantly apparent when the melodic e♭' on *Herz* is replaced by a c♯').[10] The descending e♭'–d' appoggiatura of the cadence returns the pitch of Isolde's line down the octave to its starting point. The analogy is that Isolde's thoughts of death are an extension of desire.

The sense of closure at "todgeweihtes Herz" mirrors the instinct of the heart for death as opposed to that of the astonishment and resistance of the intellect. In *Opera and Drama*, Wagner had described the role of *Stabreim* in overcoming the opposition of feeling and intellect in commonly used expressions such as "Wohl und Weh," "Lust und Leid" (and, of course, "Haupt und Herz," the one that underlies them all):

> At bottom of this thrust of his [the poet's] there lay an instinctive knowledge of feeling's nature, which takes in alone the homogeneous [i.e., the verbal connections made through *Stabreim*], alone the thing that in its oneness includes alike the conditioned and the conditioner; which seizes the imparted feeling according to its generic essence, so that it refuses to heed the opposites contained therein, qua opposites, but is guided by the nature of the *genus* in which those opposites are reconciled. The understanding loosens, the feeling binds; that is, the understanding loosens the genus into the antitheses which lie within it, whereas the feeling binds them up again into one harmonious whole.[11]

In the terms of *Opera and Drama*, the *Stabreim* between *Haupt* and *Herz* in the death motive reveals the generic essence behind the antithesis of head and heart. In the terms of Gottfried von Strassburg's Tristan poem, it depicts the fact that life and death both come under the control of Minne, here depicted as desire. But music, as Wagner maintains, has the potential of revealing the idea of opposition in unity more effectively than poetry. This it does by means of periodic designs in which departure from and return to the original key coincide with antithesis and resolution in the poetic text. Thus, in the case of a line such as "Liebe bringt Lust zum Leben" (Love brings joy to life) a single affect holds throughout the musical phrase, and the composer is not prompted to change key. In the line "Die Liebe bringt Lust und Leid" (Love brings joy and sorrow), however, the musician is impelled to modulate between *Lust* and *Leid* in such a way that the music of *Lust* utilizes the leading tone of the new key demanded by *Leid*. In this way the music illustrates the connection between the antithetical terms. And if the poetry should continue with "doch in ihr Weh auch webt sie Wonnen" (yet in its sorrow it also weaves bliss), the word *webt* (weaves) brings about a return to the original key in the same way. Here, the music surpasses the poetry in representing the generic nature of the feelings, since the latter has no return of the original *Stabreim* to express the unity of the whole. The poetry expresses only the *sense* of the return, whereas the realization of the *feeling* is left to the musician. The split between sound and meaning in the poetry is resolved into a unity by the music.

In this light the death motive resembles a small-scale period in its division into two parallel halves with an antecedent/consequent relationship, each half beginning with an octave leap downward in the voice (e$\flat$″–e$\flat$′ the first time; c″–c′ the second).[12] Although it is certainly a gesture of opening rather than closure, the A major harmony is not, of course, a modulation, but an instance of the bolder harmonic style of *Tristan* that Wagner had not envisioned in 1851 when he wrote on modulation. In this sense the motive is a good illustration of Wagner's claim to have transcended his "system" in *Tristan*. The particular antithesis of *Haupt* and *Herz*, however, resonates with Wagner's remark concerning the understanding and the feeling. With the A major chord, Wagner produces a musical analog to the "loosening" quality of the understanding, whereas the "binding" quality of the feeling follows in the C minor half close. Isolde's solution to her misery, the plan of suicide that will be closely associated with this motive throughout the first act, is mirrored in the way that the pitch A$\flat$ draws the A back to c, as if absorbing the errant intellect back into its point of origin in feeling. Will and intellect come to a provisional level of union in Isolde's intuition of death. Intellect emerges as less real than feeling.

Wagner's first death motive represents the opposition of intellect and feeling as much as it does death. Throughout the act Isolde, because of the depth of her suffering, stands apart from the other characters, even Tristan, a degree of opposition that Wagner mirrors musically by various means, among which her association with the key of c and the death motive are central to the structure of the act. Because at first Isolde keeps her plan of death hidden from Brangaene and then Tristan, Wagner lends many of her solos an ironic cast. And because irony for Wagner was symbolic of how the "form" of language covers up the tragic content of existence, Isolde's fixation on death represents an intuition of that tragic content that is not shared by the others. At several points, therefore, the death motive accompanies Isolde's ironic pronouncements, such as her response "Hart am Ziel" to Tristan's disoriented "Wo sind wir?" in scene five, and her "[Wir sind am Ziel: in kurzer] Frist stehn wir vor König Marke," soon afterward, both of which depend on our recognition of the hidden tragic meaning that is given by the motive alone.

In addition, Wagner mirrors Isolde's irony by means of the juxtaposition of conventional periodic forms, associated with Kurvenal and Brangaene, and Isolde's parodies of such forms. In this way he lends much of act 1 an aspect of surface versus depth that extends the *Haupt/Herz* antithesis in his death motive. In the second act love scene, however, there is no more irony, no more opposition of feeling and intellect, at least between the lovers. Instead, the antithesis of day and night represents a new form of surface/depth opposition in which desire, night, and death intermingle and finally merge. This quality underlies the new death motive, which projects a more internal nature than the first, in keeping with its association with night. Before its entrance Wagner prepares for it by presenting the original death motive in contexts that increasingly emphasize what we might call its inner, transitional, rather than its external, periodic nature.

We have already seen that Wagner's discussion of *Stabreim* and modulation in *Opera and Drama* resembles the way Gottfried von Strassburg describes the power of love (*Minne*) to bind antitheses—particularly life and death, joy and sorrow—into a unity. As described in chapter 3, Wagner develops the relationship of the death and desire motives in the solo from act 2, scene 1, in which Isolde extolls Frau Minne's power to Brangaene. The passage draws on the very *Stabreime* Wagner used in *Opera and Drama:*

Leben und Tod	Life and death
sind untertan ihr,	are subordinate to her,
die sie webt aus Lust und Leid,	which she weaves from joy and sorrow,
in Liebe wandelnd den Neid.	turning envy into love.

In this solo, Isolde recalls the thwarting of her plan of death by desire at the end of act 1 and attributes it to Frau Minne, not Brangaene or the love potion. In the lines just cited Wagner not only weaves the motives of death (c) and desire (A) together, but he also introduces the leading tone, $g\sharp$, of the new key, A, by reinterpreting the pitch ab'' enharmonically; and he extends that process to reinterpretation of the eb of the death motive as the $d\sharp$ of the Tristan chord (ex. 8.1). Significantly, however, he sets the antithetical terms "Leben und Tod" entirely within the death motive, and without any harmonic juxtaposition or modulation between the two; likewise, after the modulation to A, the entire line "die sie webt aus Lust und Leid" sounds in the new key. Obviously, Wagner could easily have adhered to the modulatory principles of *Opera and Drama*, by mirroring the immediate verbal antitheses in music. That he does not is because, although there are certainly strong elements of periodic design in Isolde's solo, its function is to reveal the gradual emergence of the A with which the solo ends: a representation of the heightened emotion of her avowal of obedience to Frau Minne's will. The primary level of antithesis is not that between life and death (or *Lust* and *Leid*), for, as Isolde proclaims, they are united under Minne's control; rather, it is between Isolde's attempt to take over that power in her suicide plan of act 1 and Frau Minne's revealing desire as Isolde's real motive: that is, the opposition of *Haupt* and *Herz.*

In the solo that continues from this one (following opposition from Brangaene) Isolde brings back Minne's A major music in B, an unmistakable gesture of escalation, especially when it leads to the transfiguration music for Isolde's ecstatic vision of Minne's union of night and the inner subjective light of *Liebeswonne.* When soon afterward those ideas yield to another climactic presentation of the death motive in bb for the extinguishing of the torch, we recognize the separation of Isolde's intu-

Example 8.1. Act 2, scene 1: death and desire music joined enharmonically

ition of Frau Minne's power of transcendence from the astonishing, fearful aspect of death. Isolde overcomes the latter with sheer bravado as she pronounces her readiness to face death as willingly as to extinguish the torch (see ex. 7.2).

Behind the bravado, however, is a deeper intuition of the meaning of death than that of act 1. And Wagner's transitional style binds the ecstatic quality of Isolde's "Minne" music and its sharp-major keys with the b♭ death motive by means of voice leading that renders the opposition itself secondary to Isolde's twofold intuition into night.[13] The force of Isolde's will, more than any sense of obedience to an outside agency, binds this particular sequence of ideas into a whole. At the same time, Isolde's music draws on the imagery of light and burning passion (desire) in a manner that affirms both the life force and the desire for transcendence within her.

In preparation for the emergence of the new view of death and its association with A♭, Wagner's introduction of the death motive in the *Tagesgespräch* links it with the principal poetic theme of the segment, the onset of night. Now the death motive is entirely transitional in nature, more deeply enharmonic than any earlier appearances; and, as such, it binds musically equivalent regions of sharp- and flat-notated key areas into a continuity in which they can no longer be distinguished from one another. Significantly, this music deals with death as "*ew'ge* Minne" (see ex. 11.3). Wagner presents the death motive in the context of the continual "nontransformational" enharmonicism that results from frequent shifts between flat and sharp key areas; out of this increasingly undifferentiated world of enharmonic relationships the A♭ of night eventually emerges.

The Second Death Motive

The solidifying of A♭ as the key of night, in "O sink hernieder," follows a solo in which Wagner effects a symbolic shift from the first death motive to the second. In this solo, "O nun waren wir Nachtgeweihte," Tristan, after proclaiming the deceptive qualities of day for the last time, describes the state of mind that overcomes anyone on whom night has consecrated her glance.

Wer des Todes Nacht	He who lovingly
liebende erschaut,	looks upon the night of death,
wem sie ihr tief	on whom she entrusts
Geheimnis vertraut,	her deep secret,
des Tages Lügen,	the lies of day,
Ruhm und Ehr',	fame and honor,
Macht und Gewinn,	power and attainments,
so schimmernd hehr,	which shimmer so nobly,
wie eitler Staub der Sonnen	like the pure dust of the sun
sind sie vor dem zersponnen!	for him they disappear!
In des Tages eitlem Wähnen	In the pure delusion of the day
bleibt ihm ein einzig Sehnen,—	there remains for him one single longing,
das Sehnen hin	the longing
zur heil'gen Nacht,	for holy night,
wo ur-ewig, einzig wahr,	where eternal and primal, the only truth,
Liebeswonne ihm lacht!	love's bliss smiles upon him!

In this solo Wagner's harmonic symbol of the idea of consecration to night is the Tristan chord, which sounds in dramatic, emblematic form—sustained for three measures—on Tristan's initial outcry, "O nun waren wir *Nachtgeweihte*" (Oh, if only we were *consecrated to night*) and permeates the harmony after that point. The initial phase of the solo characterizes the emptiness of day, leading into two successive presentations of the first phrase of the desire music to bridge with the lines cited earlier. The first is harmonically identical to the beginning of the prelude (ending on the dominant of a), whereas the second ("Wer des Todes Nacht") leads the Tristan chord on F into the dominant of c. On the word "Nacht" Wagner introduces the first act death motive, setting it entirely above an F pedal, and altering the harmonies of its cadence to the two Tristan chords on D and F (ex. 8.2). In other words, Wagner links the first death motive to Isolde's conception of the relationship of desire and

Example 8.2. Act 2, scene 2: the first death motive in Tristan's "O nun waren wir Nachtgeweihte"

death in the first act. In embodying the sounds associated with desire, it now reflects the broader change Wagner is preparing in the lovers' understanding of death. The new death motive is his symbol of that change. At the end of the solo, therefore (on "das Sehnen hin zur heil'gen Nacht, wo urewig, einzig wahr [Liebeswonne ihm lacht!"]), Wagner introduces the new death motive, twice in succession, the first appearance featuring *all three* Tristan chords of the desire music in the rotated order G♯, D, F (we remember that the entrance of the first death motive had been preceded by those harmonies—within the desire music—in the rotated order D, F, A♭), and the second nearly identical, except that this time the F Tristan chord moves directly into the first phrase of the desire music (on "wahr"). This then progresses to the transfiguration music in A ("Liebeswonne ihm lacht"), which then, in one of the most beautiful transitions in the opera, gives way to the A♭ of night and dreams (ex. 8.3).

The convergence of poetic and musical events at this point in the drama led Wagner's friend Heinrich Porges to view it as a turning point.[14] The change between the two death motives symbolizes the lovers' passing from a view of death that arose within the framework of desire as day to one that expresses the bond between desire and night. Instead of consecration to death arising from the division of head and heart, they long for consecration to night, in which such distinctions dissolve. In the middle section of the duet, a series of phrase transpositions upward by semitones from A♭ extends the visionary aspect of love—an inner subjective light ("Barg im Busen uns sich die Sonne")—to an expression of the subjectivity of the world itself:

Example 8.3. Act 2, scene 2: the emergence of the second death motive and the transition to "O sink hernieder"

"Selbst dann bin ich die Welt." The day motive now merges with the beginning of the desire music, introducing another recollection of the *Stabreim* of *Opera and Drama*: "Wonne hehrstes Weben, Liebe heiligstes Leben" (noblest weaving of bliss, love's holiest life). Above the bass E Wagner introduces an A major sonority combining both the music associated with Tristan's earlier "Liebeswonne ihm lacht" melody and the "Barg im Busen" theme, leading the passage through the new death motive ("Liebe heiligstes Leben") to the A♭ cadence and the return of the "dream chords," Wagner's symbol of the inner world. In that world life and death intermingle.

Thus, the second death motive articulates a relationship between A and A♭, in which A, corresponding to the blissful vision of *Liebeswonne* granted by Minne, belongs within the greater unity defined by the A♭ of night, a softening of the antithetical relationship behind the initial harmonies of the first death motive and a per-

Example 8.3. (Continued)

fect analog of how night dissolves all sense of antithesis. In accompanying "Liebe heiligstes Leben" by the death motive Wagner makes the point that life and death become equivalent through the bond between love and night, after which the lovers' motion inward to the world of dreams virtually dissolves the meaning of language into alliterative sound: "Niewiedererwachen's wahnlos hold bewusster Wunsch" (united in the blissful delusion-free wish of never reawakening). That world is one of enharmonicism, endless multidirectional tonal relationships, and the seemingly infinite intermingling of musical motives.

"O sink hernieder" describes a curve that subordinates all sense of contrast keys and motivic surface events to its Ab core. Like the *Tristan* prelude, it contains no real modulations. It merely expands and contracts, largely by chromatic voice leading and scalar motion of the outermost voices, away from and back to Ab. Throughout the movement the Tristan chord provides a referential sonority associated with the bond between desire and night. With its tritone relationships and latent G#/Ab enharmonicism, the second death motive eliminates the idea of antithesis and resolution that surrounds those pitches in the first death motive. In this context, the blissful A major vision of desire and transcendence is purely illusory in terms of anything related to musical structure. Both it and the the day motive are absorbed into A♭, the ground-tone of night and dreams.

The continuing history of the second death motive in act 2 reveals that Wagner used it in conjunction with passages in which the relationship of periodicity to transition is paramount, the former a symbol of day and the latter of night. Wagner depicts a world in which the idea of surface and depth is a consciously exhibited poetic idea, not, as it usually is in musical analysis, a measure of the capacity of the analytical system to penetrate hidden or unconsciously operating unifying principles. In this sense musical analysis after Wagner is incalculably indebted to his depiction of the idea of the world as consisting of two natures: a horizontal (temporal, rhythmic) individuated surface and a vertical (atemporal, harmonic) oneness. The arpeggiation pattern of the desire music (like the beginning of *Das Rheingold*) and the tonic-dominant pillars of the bass line of "O sink hernieder" represent the latter, the endless transposition patterns of the musical surface the former.

In the most overtly periodic part of the love scene, Wagner uses the death motive, in combination with the love's peace motive, to articulate the dissolving of individual identities. In each of two nearly identical but separated segments following the two A♭ duets and Brangaene's two warnings, Wagner combines the love's peace and death motives into a single phrase that he then transposes upward by whole tones in a threefold succession (ex. 8.4). The love's peace motive, the most melodically "beau-

Example 8.4. Act 2, scene 2: the love's peace and second death motives

tiful" line of the opera, holds out the promise of a periodic design that was, in fact, its original form in Wagner's sketches.[15] As it proceeds, however, its character becomes associated with the dissolving of melodic purpose (an analog of the pacification of the will), until finally it leads directly into the death motive, which closes it off. In the two parallel segments first Tristan and later Isolde sing the lines "Lass' mich sterben," "Nie erwachen," and "Lass den Tag dem Tode weichen" to the threefold appearances of the death motive at the ends of these phrases. Like "O sink hernieder," the second A♭ duet, "So stürben wir," circles away from and back to A♭ without any real modulation. And, in response to the warnings from Brangaene that follow the two duets—"Habet Acht! Bald entweicht die Nacht!" and "Habet Acht! Schon weicht dem Tag die Nacht!" respectively—the two parallel dialogues of the lovers transpose the death motive to six different pitch levels, thereby providing all twelve Tristan chords, as if to symbolize the permeation of the world by the union of death (night) and desire.

On one level, these details represent the character of the world as a superficial quasi-architectural symmetry, the false image of unity—day—which gives way to the lovers' intuitions of a deeper oneness in the final duet, "O ew'ge Nacht." Directly following Tristan's "Lass den Tag dem Tode weichen" (Let the day give way to death) Wagner opens up the love scene to some eighty-five measures of freer, more improvisational dialogue between the lovers, in which, for the first time in the love scene the time signature shifts away from the basic slow $\frac{3}{4}$ that has held since the introduction to "O sink hernieder" (see chapter 10, "The Tempo of Day" p. 181). Along with it Wagner sets up a wavering between the pitches e″ and e♭″ (or d♯″) that is resolved several times by the death motive at its basic pitch, which involves a chromatic f♯″–f♮″–e″–e♭″ descent in the melody. Wagner even gives some prominence to the key of e for the purpose of reinterpreting half closes involving the melodic pitches e″ and d♯″ as f♭″ and e♭″. The most prominent instances of this occur on the phrases [Tristan] "Doch, stürbe nie seine Liebe, wie stürbe dann Tristan seiner Liebe?" (Yet, if his love never died, how then would Tristan die to his love?) and [Isolde] "Doch, dieses Wörtlein: und—wär' es zerstört, wie anders als mit Isolde's eig'nem Leben wär Tristan der Tod gegeben?" (Yet, this little word 'and'—if it were destroyed, how other than with Isolde's own life could Tristan be given to death?). That is, they aid in articulating the question of oneness and separation as symbolized in the word "and" in the title of the opera. Wagner allows the A♭ tonality and the slow $\frac{3}{4}$ meter to disintegrate, only to bring them back with the lovers' increasing "consecration" to death, which is bound up very closely with the sound of the second death motive.

At the close of the second set of parallel dialogs involving the love's peace and second death motives, therefore, Isolde's "Lass' den Tag dem Tode" weichen," is followed by the transition into "O ew'ge Nacht," which Wagner shortened considerably from the compositional draft to the final version. In both versions, however, the music and text that lead directly into the duet are substantially the same (except for transposition changes, to be described below). Tristan questions Isolde as to whether the threats of day can be defied and Isolde answers with the solution, eternal night:

Tristan: Des Tages Dräuen nun trotzten wir so?	Could we so oppose the threats of day?
Isolde: Seinem Trug ewig zu flieh'n!	Its deception flee forever!
Tristan: Sein dämmernder Schein verscheuchte uns nie?	Its dawning light never separate us?
Isolde: Ewig währ' uns die Nacht!	May the night protect us forever!

For the first of these lines Wagner created a musical allegory of the transformation of day into night. Beginning with a hint of the love's peace motive, then leading it into the day motive, which he retains as the basis of the melody, Wagner now accompanies it by two dominant-seventh chords (C$\flat^4_3$ and F^7) whose roots are distanced by a tritone. This change enables him to make the day motive into a variation of the death motive (founded in two tritone-related Tristan chords), a literal analog of the line "lass den Tag dem Tode weichen."[16] Placing the first of the dominant-seventh chords in its second inversion—C$\flat^4_3$: that is, with G$\flat$ in the bass—facilitates his using the F^7 harmony to bring in the transfiguration music in B$\flat$, the key associated with Isolde's longing to extinguish the torch in the first scene of the act (ex. 8.5). The sequence as a whole carries that of the preceding segment—the love's peace and death motives—a step further, into the anticipation of transfiguration, fulfilling Isolde's longing for night in the opening scene of act 2, in which the transfiguration music had first emerged in close association with B$\flat$. Now Wagner transposes the composite phrase just described up a minor third, moving into the transfiguration

Example 8.5. Act 3, scene 2: excerpt from the transition to "O ew'ge Nacht," final version

music in C♯ for the start of the duet. The next stages are the modulation from A♭ to B, bringing back the thematic material of "So stürben wir," which comes some fifty-seven measures into the duet, and the sounding of the transfiguration music in B some sixty-seven measures after that again.

To clarify the meaning of those stages "O ew'ge Nacht" begins with the second death motive ("O ew'ge Nacht, süsse Nacht") at the same pitch as the closely related day-death motive (Isolde's "Ewig währ uns die Nacht"), eight measures earlier. Wagner then transposes it up a semitone for the next phrase, "Hehr erhab'ne Liebes-nacht," then, after sixteen measures, up yet another semitone for "sehnend verlangter Liebestod." The latter phrase, the final appearance of the second death motive in the love scene, passes directly into the dream chords of "O sink hernieder"—notated in G♯ instead of A♭—and they lead in turn into the final modulation, from A♭ (G♯) to B.

The chain of events that leads to this point is one of the most remarkable in the entire work by virtue of the way in which, towards its close, Wagner leads the music toward its goal: the dominant of B. After "So stürben wir," the threefold transposi-tion upward by whole tones of the phrase comprising the love's peace and death mo-tives initiates a rising motion of the uppermost line of the orchestra that continues through the upward transposition of the combined day-death and transfiguration phrases in the transition to "O ew'ge Nacht." Its completion is the three-fold trans-position of the death motive in the first section of the duet culminating with "sehn-end verlangter Liebestod." At that point, the return of the "dream chords" amplifies the G♯ on which the death motive has arrived to a recall of the A♭ pedal of "O sink hernieder," which then passes through G to the dominant, F♯. In all that leads to this point the articulation of individual keys is decidedly secondary until the arrival on the dominant of B in the duet. This Wagner identifies symbolically as the goal of the lovers' desire never to awaken ("vom Erwachen's Not befreit"), a prolonged passage inward culminating in the dream chords and the A♭–B modulation.

In this latter part of the love scene, Wagner introduces so much immediate trans-position of phrase units that both Nietzsche's characterization of him as a minia-turist and Schönberg's dissatisfaction with periodic, transpositional elements in his leitmotifs seem entirely justified. Yet, when Wagner claimed that the form of the love scene exhibited a "clarity over an expanse that encompasses every detail" (see chap-ter 11), we sense that the very repetitive devices that I have just described belong to that clarity. That is, they enable us to hear the progression of poetic ideas through-out the large expanse that Wagner viewed in terms of form as transition. The large-scale motion to the dominant of B in "O ew'ge Nacht" completes what Wagner de-scribed as the goal of the love scene: the "most sincere and heartfelt longing for death." The transposing sequences, therefore, all involve the night-death motive, which sounds some thirteen times between the climax of "O sink hernieder" and its culmination in the phrase "sehnend verlangter Liebestod" in "O ew'ge Nacht." It is the principal element in articulating both the static idea of symmetrical corre-spondence rooted in the idea of periodicity and the dynamic one of directed for-ward motion—form as "becoming" or transition—that eventually overcomes it.

The revisions Wagner made to the latter part of the love scene from the compo-sitional draft to the final version of the opera involve transitions (to "O sink hernieder" and "O ew'ge Nacht") as well as points of structural articulation (the A♭–B modulation in "O ew'ge Nacht" and the arrival at the transfiguration cadence in that duet). They highlight what Carl Dahlhaus called the "twofold truth" of Wagner's aesthetics—between composition with leitmotifs as the empirical derivation of music from the drama and the idea of a metaphysically prior "absolute" music—in that Wagner lessened what were initially leitmotif-oriented conceptions in favor of reworkings that brought the quality of directed forward motion to the fore. Referential detail was discarded in the interest of rendering the form more pronouncedly transitional in nature. The original versions of those passages, however, provide us with a wealth of information regarding Wagner's musico-poetic intentions that is not invalidated by the subsequent changes. Rather, the changes document Wagner's search for a clarity of form that would convey the primary conception with a minimum dependence on intellectual processes.

As described earlier, the original transition to "O ew'ge Nacht" began, immediately following Isolde's "Lass' den Tag dem Tode weichen," with a musical relationship that appears nowhere else in the opera in either version: that between the two death motives. Thus, Wagner makes the point that the two views of death—suicide and longing for night—are united. As outlined in chapter 3, the joining of the two death motives (see the appendix) leads into the desire music (partially transformed, as indicated earlier), which leads in turn into the love's peace motive followed by the music of the transition as we know it from the final version (transposed). Both the transition from the death motives to the desire music and that from the desire music to the love's peace motive involve enharmonic shifts, the former duplicating Frau Minne's enharmonic weaving from scene 1, and the latter explicitly linked to Frau Minne's "way." In scene 1, only the first death motive was present, and the enharmonicism was audible as such. Now, as a result of the new perspective on death within the love scene, embodied in the second death motive, the enharmonicism is less "transformational"—that is, it involves transition rather than the juxtaposition of distantly related (or unrelated) keys. The A♭ of the love's peace motive is the outcome of continued sharpward motion from the B^7 chord of the third phrase of the desire music, after which the change from sharp to flat notation is no longer a visual symbol of great distance but an expedience. The meaning of the change from the first to the second death motive is presented in microcosm. Subsequent deletion of the passage, therefore, does not represent any alteration of the poetic content of the work. Rather, it reflects Wagner's concern not to make his intentions too explicit. And even more important, it reveals his awareness that at such a point what was needed was not a sudden increase in the intellectual associative qualities of the leitmotifs but, rather, a sense of large-scale motion leading to the B major part of the duet. The new transition lessens the leitmotif content substantially, carrying the ascent of the uppermost voices of the orchestra from the music that followed "So stürben wir" on into the A♭/B modulation in "O ew'ge Nacht."

In his revisions Wagner focuses on large-scale motion in preference to leitmotif processes, bringing out qualities of transition more than of dramatic juxtaposition. In first conceiving a series of intricate leitmotif combinations Wagner can from one standpoint be viewed as (or accused of) simply translating the phenomena of the dramatic world into musical units that, however ingenious their combinations, created the impression of being chained in sequence, a distinctly unpoetic conception of composition. In other words he overemphasized the empirical derivation of the music from the drama. In the final version, what Wagner viewed as the inner form-generating potential of the motives is more successfully realized.

NINE

Musico-poetic Design in Act 1

T HE FIRST ACT OF *TRISTAN* differs from the others in one very important respect: it contains, on the surface at least, nothing of the metaphysical themes of
the second and third acts. The drinking of the love-death potion at the end of the
act is the catalyst to the emergence of those themes in act 2, especially the night/day
opposition and the idea of transcendence through the merging of love and night-
death (*Liebestod*). Nevertheless, there is a strong sense that the events of act 1 mask
an underlying deeper reality, that qualities of surface and depth are built into Wagner's interpretation of the setting and constitute its true meaning. In this light the
ocean voyage from Ireland to Cornwall is the beginning of a metaphoric journey, the
confined space of the ship symbolizing the fragility and restrictedness of consciously
held conventional ideas or conceptions (*Haupt*). These are set in opposition to the
underlying source and ultimate goal of the journey: the ocean as symbol of the unconscious, to which Isolde returns at the end of the opera.[1]

The mythic, or metaphoric dimension of the first-act journey is conveyed in important ways by means of the tonal design, which is a very logical one, built largely
around relationships and oppositions derived from the desire music, and therefore
suggesting the conflicts of desire or Will itself. It involves three "spheres" that can be
traced separately throughout the act and that converge or are juxtaposed at key points.
The first is the role of C minor as the principal recurrent key of the act, associated
entirely with Isolde until just before the drinking of the potion. It is focused and intensified at many points by recurrences of the death motive. The second involves the
set of fifth-related major keys, E♭, B♭, F, and C, which are associated primarily with
the secondary characters, Brangaene, Kurvenal, and the sailors, with the motive of
the voyage to Cornwall, and conventional ideals of chivalry, heroism, and the like.
Through the relationship of its boundary keys to Isolde's c, as relative major and
tonic major, respectively, it describes a motion, culminating in C, that from the literal (diatonic) perspective is increasingly antithetical to Isolde's state of mind, but

from another (the chromatic bond between c and C) is prophetic of the deeper union of life and death through desire (the derivation of both c and C from the second phrase of the desire music). And the third set is that of the fifth-related minor keys, a, e, b, and f♯, related by tritone to the preceding major-key set and associated primarily with Tristan and Isolde themselves, their past and present relationship (the Prelude, the narrative, and the first half of scene 5); it functions to a considerable degree as an extension of the motion to the dominant in the desire music. Although within these sets of keys the principle of extension is the perfect fifth, the boundary keys—E♭, C/c, a, f♯—describe the intervals of the diminished-seventh chord, not that of the set of Tristan chords but of the keys in which they function: the F Tristan chord within the keys of a and e♭, for example. The latent opposition between the perfect fifth and the tritone, described in terms of nature and the metaphysical in chapter 7, is built into the tonal design of act 1, in which Wagner outlines tritone shifts at momentous dramatic points.

A Narrative of the Tonal Design of Act 1

In each of the three acts a figure representing the conventional world occupies, at least for a time, a position higher than the events on stage, and therefore commanding a kind of "objective" viewpoint: in act 1 the sailor on the mast, in act 2 Brangaene in the turret, and in act 3 Kurvenal in the watch tower. In each case the figure above sees further than those below, forecasting events to come. And what is seen is always a form of day. In act 2, Brangaene perceives the coming day literally and metaphorically, turning the day motive into a slowly moving cantus firmus that floats above the scene below; and in act 3 Kurvenal's ascent to the tower coincides with the beginning of the *frohe Weise*, another version of the perspective of day. In act 1, the symbolism of day has not yet been made explicit; but in introducing the various layers of symbolic conflict behind Isolde's glance toward the west and the direction of the ship towards the east, the sailor's song adumbrates several of its characteristics. Picking up from the C minor ending of the prelude, the phrases associated with Isolde's torment are either in or allude to c, forecasting the principal recurrent tonality of the act and its association with death. The major-key phrases, by contrast, center on the motive of the journey to Cornwall and the motive, as yet undefined, that will be associated with Tristan's heroism in act 1 and with day from act 2 on (ex. 9.1). At first in E♭, then in B♭, in which the song ends, they initiate the sequence of fifth-related major keys that are associated with the goal of the ship.

Directly following her reaction to the sailor's song in scene one Isolde poses an existential question, "Wo sind wir?" (Where are we?), settling on the dominant of c. Brangaene's literal response, however—that the ship is approaching "Kornwalls grünen Strand" (Cornwall's green shore)—completes a solo in which the motive associated with the journey to Cornwall in the sailor's song ("Frisch weht der Wind der Heimat zu") expands to the dimensions of a small-scale musical period in E♭, a symbol of the world of conventional values that Isolde finds constricting in the opening scene (and that Wagner found constricting in the periodic set pieces of opera). Whereas Isolde had picked up on the c in which the prelude ended and from

Example 9.1. Musical relationships among the sailor's song, Kurvenal's mocking song, and the day motive

which the sailor's song began ("Westwärts schweift der Blick"), Brangaene echoes the key with which it was immediately juxtaposed ("Ostwärts streicht das Schiff"). The opposition remains throughout the first scene, Isolde singing in c and Brangaene in Eb. Much later, in scene 5, Tristan echoes Isolde's question as the artificial security of his self-enclosed world finally crumbles, symbolized in the downward plummeting of the motive of the ocean voyage in the orchestra directly preceding his words. The collapse is mirrored in the tonal structure as well. The first half of the latter scene, primarily in b, is occupied with hollow ideals of honor. Centered largely around the dominant, and tending increasingly toward that key, it reaches a full melodic cadence in f#—the limit of the fifth-related set of minor keys—as Isolde offers Tristan the drink of atonement. Deceived by the ominous entrance of the poison motive in the orchestra, this begins an enormously symbolic shift towards c for Isolde's answer—"Wir sind am Ziel: in kurzer Frist steh'n wir vor König Marke!"—sung to the death motive.

What I have just described illustrates several of the principles around which Wagner formed the design of act 1. The journey is bound up with the c/C dualism, symbolic of death and life. At the end of the prelude C minor emerges from the desire music; in the opening scene it comes into relation with E♭ and in the second scene with the death motive. Throughout the act its recurrence, often in the context of other tonalities, mirrors Isolde's fixation on death, whereas C major, associated with the sailors, Kurvenal, Brangaene's false view of the love potion and the festive character of the arrival at Cornwall, is associated with a set of ideas that are directly contrary to Isolde's state of mind. In scene 5, after the final return to c, Isolde attempts to sing an ironic C major solo, anticipating the arrival at Cornwall, but the encroachment and eventual return of the minor mode mirror her failure to sustain the deception. C minor dominates until the drinking of the love potion, at which point the symbolic intensification toward e♭ collapses enharmonically for the return of the desire music in a. From this C *major* emerges victorious for the arrival at Cornwall.

Wagner initiates the processes that will eventually culminate in C in the disparity between Isolde and Brangaene in the opening scenes. At the beginning of scene 2 the truncated version of the sailor's song drops the B♭ cadence on which it had originally ended, and Isolde moves through the diminished-seventh chord version of the desire music to introduce the principal tonal association of the act, that between the death motive and the key of c. After this, Wagner widens the opposition between Isolde and Brangaene by assigning Brangaene another brief periodic design, this time centering on praise of Tristan's heroism, in F. Isolde's scornful parody of this solo ultimately restores c, attaining a point of culmination in her "Befehlen ließ dem Eigenholde Furcht der Herrin ich, Isolde" (Command this self-sufficient one that he fear his mistress, me, Isolde); but the damage is done: a hint of C, picked up from Brangaene, has crept in. As Isolde orders Brangaene to go to Tristan her c cadence becomes the dominant of F, in which key the initial ten measures of Brangaene's first E♭ solo return in the orchestra to accompany her proceeding to the stern.

Brangaene's dialogue with Tristan is largely in F, with secondary key areas, and a distinct tendency toward its dominant, C, that Brangaene affirms by repeating Isolde's command, as cited in the preceding paragraph. But its climax, Kurvenal's insulting solo, also in praise of Tristan the hero, ends in B♭ with the motive that will be associated with Tristan's heroism (and its initial four tones with "day" as well) for the remainder of the opera ("Hei! unser Held Tristan": "Hei! our hero Tristan"). It derives from the sailor's song, whose concluding key it echoes.

To this point the keys have centered on C minor and the fifth-related major keys, E♭, B♭, and F. In scene three, following Brangaene's return from Tristan, Isolde relates the background of her relationship with Tristan, introducing references to Tristan's combat with Morold, his wounding, her healing "Tantris," the episode of the sword and the glance and, finally, Tristan's return under his true name to claim her as King Mark's bride. This solo—her narrative—is set in e, a tonality that has not been heard to this point in the drama (apart from its role as the dominant of a in the prelude). The music of the glance now appears transposed at the fifth, to e. For this and other reasons, such as the derivation of the narrative theme from the desire music and Isolde's recounting the story of Tristan's and her love beyond the more abstract narrative of the prelude, the e tonality can be considered an extension of the a in which the opera began. At the close of the narrative, Wagner has Isolde turn back suddenly to C minor for her curse of Tristan as her betrayer: "Fluch dir Verruchter! Fluch deinem Haupt! Rache! Tod! Tod uns Beiden!" (A curse on you, traitor! A curse on your head! Vengeance! Death! Death for us both!). The sheer force of the c tonality restores the fixation on death.

And once again Brangaene's response is to turn to E♭, for the three-strophe solo known as her consolation. This piece has been called a *Reprisenbar* (barform with tonal reprise) because its first and second strophes (the two *Stollen*) are in E♭ and F, respectively, after which the third (the *Abgesang*) returns to E♭, creating an ABA tonal design (within an AAB strophic pattern). In its poetic character, tonality and periodic design it represents an extension of Brangaene's E♭ and F in the first and second scenes. Its first and second strophes echo her earlier attempts to console Isolde (scene 1) and her vision of Tristan as a hero (scene 2), merging them with her view that Tristan has Isolde's best interests at heart in seeking her out as bride for Mark. Significantly, Wagner does not simply transpose the first strophe from E♭ to F but shifts to B♭ as a bridge to the F of the second. The latter strophe is then followed immediately, although fleetingly, by C (the beginning of Isolde's solo between Brangaene's second and third strophes, which takes the second phrase of the glance music as its starting point). Isolde's tormented view of her condition, however, turns the tonality back, toward e♭, enabling Brangaene's third strophe to complete the ABA tonal design.

But within that third strophe Brangaene makes a striking shift in the tonal character of the solo. The circle-of-fifths motion over the first two strophes from E♭ to B♭, F and (briefly) C can be considered to depict the positive and utterly conventional views of Tristan and Mark with which Brangaene attempts to console Isolde. In the third strophe, however, Brangaene, who has now caught a glimpse of the depth of Isolde's torment, begins to unveil her solution. Beginning from a Tristan chord that is sustained for three measures before resolving, she disputes not Isolde's claim that she is unloved (by Tristan), but that Isolde need *remain* unloved (by Mark). Reintroducing music associated with Mark in her second strophe, she alters the tonal landscape in a highly symbolic manner by bringing out the tritone relationships that belong to the desire music and particularly those that had emerged at the climax of the prelude: between e♭ and a.

The theme that prompts this change is magic, Brangaene's vision of a happy marriage for Isolde by means of a love potion that will overcome any coldness or straying on Mark's part. Her initial words in this part of the solo, "Doch, der dir erkoren" (Yet the one who chose you . . .), however, are clearly reminiscent of Isolde's earlier "mir erkoren, mir verloren," and its melody is a variant of the principal theme of the consolation and particularly of the form in which it referred to Mark in the second strophe. What Brangaene now reveals is that it is also a variant of the glance motive, a further connection to the climax of the prelude. Having heard Isolde's narrative of the glance and been recently reminded of it in Isolde's solo, Brangaene suggests that it will be redirected, as it were, to Mark. In this passage we observe that the three phenomena that Schopenhauer described as manifestations of the identity of the will—sexual love, compassion (the glance), and magic—are intertwined with one another. For Brangaene, magic is the dominant one. In her third strophe, she normalizes the tritone relationship of the prelude and the implied enharmonicism of the desire music, proclaiming triumphantly with her powerful E♭ close that through magic Mark will be brought to love Isolde, even against his will. In effect, she is affirming that such modulations are no modulations at all, their enharmonicism not opening up new tonal regions but confirming the closed cycle of relationships based on the diminished-seventh chord. The analog is that in a world ruled by magic it does not matter who is Isolde's husband; by means of the love potion he will be held within the circle of desire.

Brangaene has understood that Isolde's torment is caused by desire. Musically speaking, she has grasped the enharmonic relationship between Isolde's deep flat harmonies and their sharp counterparts in the desire music; she has made an emblematic association of the first Tristan chord and Isolde's desire; and she has echoed the enharmonic shift of the climax of the prelude, explaining its transformational quality in terms of the power of Minne to create love in the unwilling, by force, as it were. And Brangaene believes that she controls that force, the solution to Isolde's torment, in the box of magic potions given to her by Isolde's mother. As she closes her consolation in E♭, a deceptive cadence to C♭ (B) effects another enharmonic shift, to the beginning of the desire music at its usual pitch, a. This gesture is the continuation of Brangaene's understanding of magic, now more specifically presented in terms of the magic potions, which Brangaene brings forth. As the E♭ of the consolation gives way to a of the desire music, Wagner's stage directions—"mit geheimnissvoller Zutraulichkeit ganz nah zu Isolden" (with mysterious confidentiality approaching close to Isolde)—make clear that Brangaene thinks of desire as susceptible to secret magic, as, in fact, she will reveal in act 3. There, having explained the secret of the potion to Mark—"Des Trankes Geheimnis entdeckt ich dem König" (I revealed the secret of the drink to the king)—she narrates how it effected his forgiveness and willingness that Tristan and Isolde be married. At that point, Brangaene brings in the last three-phrase version of the desire music in the opera, and the only one in which all four Tristan chords of the diminished-seventh chord cycle appear—that is, the only one to feature the B Tristan chord in addition to those on F, G♯, and D. It is followed by Mark's bringing back the music of the third strophe of her act 1 consolation, its only other appearance in the opera. Mark brings back the measures from Brangaene's strophe that took up the question of magic, effecting a tritone shift from a to E♭ by means of the B Tristan chord as he confirms Brangaene's explanation: "Dem holden Mann dich zu vermählen, mit vollen Segeln flog ich dir nach" (In order to marry you to the noble man I raced after you with full sails). Clearly Brangaene and Mark both recognize that the tritone enharmonic shift from a to E♭ or vice versa represents a magical transformation that the lovers could not resist and that therefore absolves them from guilt. Hence, Mark's willingness that they marry.

Underlying what I have just described is one of the principal tonal-allegorical features of the Tristan style: the interaction of perfect-fifth and tritone relationships (and diatonicism with chromaticism). The E♭–B♭–F fifth motion of Brangaene's consolation is the framework within which her tritone-based harmonic shifting is contained. The latter represents manipulation of the circle of nature. After her enharmonic shift, in association with her bringing forth the magic potions, Brangane leads the third phrase of the desire music seamlessly toward the dominant of C major, as if leading Isolde away from her private obsession with death toward the goal of the journey to Cornwall. In the scene that follows the various themes of the prelude all reappear, along with two additional three-phrase versions of the desire music itself, their transpositional intervals and other details manipulated in quasi-systematic ways, but all now directed unequivocally toward c/C. In the midst the death motive appears for the second time, also in c, to expand on the emotions of its earlier appearance: "Rache für den Verrat! Ruh' in der Not dem Herzen!" (Vengeance for the betrayal! Rest for the need of the heart!).

In this segment diatonic and chromatic music intermingle freely, chromaticism appearing often as the inner motion of the voices beneath the diatonic melodic surface. This is particularly clear when the *Sühnetrank* music enters toward the end to symbolize the disparity between Brangaene's and Isolde's views over which is the most potent of the potions—for Brangaene the love potion and for Isolde that of death, as described in chapter 6. Throughout this segment and the one that follows there is a sense that the keys of C major and minor, associated with life and death, the former carefully assigned to Brangaene and Kurvenal and the latter to Isolde, can be said to define a single tonic pitch of two differentiated modes, the allegorical details suggesting that although it arises from the A minor of the desire music the latter key is now subordinated to it. The relationship of a to both C and c renders the C/c juxtaposition an aspect of surface only.

But Wagner needs that surface differentiation to make his dramatic points. The final turn to c and the juxtaposition of the poison motive to the *Sühnetrank* motive as Isolde identifies the death potion, reveal the true nature of the disagreement between Isolde and her maid. Brangaene makes yet another enharmonic shift as she describes the love potion as the antidote to the poison of desire such as Isolde is suffering. Leading from the dominant of D♭ to the beginning of the desire music (ab′ changing to g♯′ in the melody), then to a straightforward articulation of C, her enharmonicism is transformational, the result of a conjunction of distinct but unrelated diatonic keys, whereas Isolde's, which follows her picking up on the poison motive, is increasingly nontransformational, the result of the breaking down of key distinctions in highly chromatic music. Brangaene's enharmonic change describes the power of magic in terms of antithesis: "für böse Gifte Gegengift." The diatonic surface of the *Sühnetrank* motive to which it leads is Brangaene's vision of the outcome of such a transformation. In order to represent differentiation and oneness in act 1, Wagner, paradoxically, had to separate the major and minor modes even as he affirmed the wider tonal world in which that difference would not exist. His symbol of that paradox was the combined *Sühnetrank* and poison motive, its melodic surface periodic and diatonic, and its bass line motivic and potentially enharmonic, even atonal. The entrance of the poison motive at the end of the *Sühnetrank* phrase (its first appearance after the prelude) puts an end to the dialogue between Isolde and her maid, dissolving all traces of the diatonicism Brangaene has struggled to uphold, placing Isolde's C minor ending in the context of its tendency toward atonality (see ex. 6.3). The potentially comforting periodic aspect of the entire dialogue is undermined by fearful irrational undercurrents, none of which is more terrifying to Brangaene than the association between desire and death.

The segment that follows rivets the meaning of the c/C juxtaposition in place. Directly following Isolde's C minor close, the sailors enter on the dominant of C major and Kurvenal pushes through the curtains to announce the immanent arrival at Cornwall, singing a distressingly brusque C major strophe based on the music of the sailors' chorus and the journey to Cornwall. This unmistakable anticipation of the ending of the act fulfills the meaning of Brangaene's fifth motion.

In response, Isolde restores the original tonal framework with two strophes ending respectively in a and c—both demanding that Tristan come to her—the second of which ends with the death motive ("für ungebüsste Schuld:—die böt' ihm meine Huld": for unatoned guilt, now offer him my grace). After Kurvenal's departure to deliver her message Isolde prepares for death, intensifying the tragic tone by moving from c/C toward e♭ (as she had in the solo that intervened between the second and third strophes of Brangaene's consolation and as she will again in dialogue with Tristan in scene 5 and again, finally, at the point where she drinks the potion). Brangaene's misunderstanding deflects the tonality with another C♭ chord, and the poison music returns, once again dissolving the tonal sense. The dialogue that follows reiterates the c/e♭ music up a tone (d–f), further weakening all sense of c. What ultimately gives focus to the segment as a whole is Isolde's returning to the beginning of the desire music as she scathingly reiterates Brangaene's earlier words— "Kennst du der Mutter Künste nicht?"—initiating a truncated version of the dialogue with Brangaene on the magic potions, now vastly more chromatic than before and culminating in Isolde's explicitly revealing her plan of death to Brangaene: "für tiefstes Weh, für höchstes Leid gab sie den *Todestrank. Der Tod nun sag' ihr Dank!*" (For the deepest sorrow, for the greatest suffering she gave the *drink of death. May death now thank her*). Singing the death motive to the italicized words, Isolde cadences decisively in c, putting the seal of finality on the entire episode. The seventeen measures that follow echo elements from the dialog, eventually turning to f for the beginning of scene 5.

The music of the dialogue on the magic potions, although severely truncated on its second appearance, frames the exchange between Isolde and Kurvenal. For both Alfred Lorenz and Robert Bailey it identified the center of a symmetrical design encompassing ultimately the entire first act, with the prelude music at the beginning, middle, and end. In this view, Wagner worked extensively with periodic designs that he grouped in hierarchical fashion to lend the act its structural stability. Lorenz, however, recognized that the proportions of the parallel passages are seriously skewed, the part of the act that follows the centerpiece much shorter than its earlier counterpart, as is the case with the parallel passages within the central segment itself.[2] Although the parallels cannot be denied, there are tremendous psychological differences between the corresponding points. When Isolde mockingly repeats Brangaene's words ("Kennst du die Mutter Künste nicht . . . ": Don't you know your mother's arts . . .), she brings back the desire music without the enharmonic change or any sense of transformation. Isolde intends no magical event. And as she begins to reiterate the first set of permutations of the desire music, Wagner makes changes of the most telling kind. In the earlier dialogue, the ruling principle behind those permutations had been that of patterned transposition. Now it is chromatic voice-leading. Isolde links the phrases together with quasi-functional harmonic glue, replacing the third phrase by the poison motive, dropping all the C major music and clipping the text. Isolde's conception of the antidote (*Gegengift*), unlike Brangaene's, is not transformational but dissolving in nature. The melodic surface of the *Sühnetrank* motive is gone, replaced by its tragic undertone, the poison music, which leads directly into the death motive.

Isolde's modification of the desire music at this point, instead of relying on an external device (transposition), reveals inner harmonic relationships, quasi-functional connectors, in which chromatic voice-leading takes precedence over tonic centricity, now reduced to a residue only. The poison music sounds for only six measures before moving to the death motive, as its counterpart (the third phrase of Isolde's variant of the desire music) had in the earlier scene. But these six measures are enormously informative. Isolde's "für tiefstes Weh', für höchstes Leid" (for the deepest sorrow, for the greatest suffering) illustrates how the progressive motion of a single part by semitones forms the basic harmonic relationships of the desire music including the diminished seventh that mediates between the Tristan chord and the dominant seventh to which it progresses. The chromatic logic of this entire segment reveals that Isolde understands as a transitional process what Brangaene apprehends only from the standpoint of diatonic tonal relationships, as magic. In fact, Isolde's introduction of the poison motive *does* present the enharmonic change between g♯' and a♭', as Brangaene's *Gegengift* had; but, because of its absorption into the poison music, we do not hear it as a transformational event that magically links two discrete keys. Its essence is disintegration. Isolde's antidote is not to change King Mark's or her own feelings by magical, transformational means but, rather, to allow the tonally dissolving nature of the poison music to take its course.

In compressing the music related to Brangaene's and Isolde's very different understandings of the potion, in merging the desire and poison motives, dropping out much of the transpositional element and the diatonic themes from the prelude that were transposed to C, Wagner makes the point that this scene is an intensification of Isolde's state of mind as opposed to Brangaene's, adding dimensions of meaning that do not emerge in its earlier counterpart. In adhering to the diatonic framework, even for magical tritone relationships, in resisting all thoughts of death, Brangaene remains securely within the physical interpretation of reality (nature). In contrast, Isolde's strained chromatic and enharmonic relationships, like her thoughts of death, represent what Schopenhauer called the "impulse to metaphysics." Bracketing the obvious parallels between the two dialogues on the potions does not convey the vital fact that Wagner employs two different tonal and harmonic styles for Brangaene and Isolde. Isolde's leans far more in the direction of atonality; its attempt to connect disparate events by means of traditional modes of understanding mirrors her inner struggle. Her enharmonicism is nontransformational, revealing aspects of the *Tristan* style that are only fully developed at large from the act 2 love scene on. These harmonic features become more prominent from this point on in act 1 as well, with the disappearance of Brangaene from the foreground of the drama and Tristan's gradually coming to understand Isolde's purpose.

Following Isolde's cadential presentation of the death motive, Brangaene echoes Isolde's words, then Isolde leads the tonality abruptly toward F for Tristan's entrance and the beginning of scene five. Her F cadence—"Herr Tristan trete nah'" (Sir Tristan, approach me)—mirrors the c cadence of the death motive in its melodic falling fifth. The two cadences are both of great symbolic significance in that regard, but very different in character. The c cadence is the culmination of the middle segment of the act, in which c is established irrevocably as the key of death. The F cadence, by contrast, is sudden and unexpected. In the eighteen measures between the two Brangaene's response to Isolde's fourth introduction of the death motive and Isolde's "Bist du mir treu?" (Are you loyal to me?) suggest a motion toward e♭ that Kurvenal's entrance to announce Tristan's arrival turns into major, breaking Isolde's intensifying thoughts of death. Isolde's turning to F, after what Wagner's stage directions describe as "a terrible effort to compose herself," represents her force of will in retreating from her anguish into the demands of a superficially polite encounter. This is exactly how the cadence sounds, detached from all that precedes it tonally, and contradicted immediately by the move toward b in the honor music.

The F was not casually chosen. It echoes not only the F of Brangaene's consolation, but her original F, associated with Tristan's heroism and, most of all, the F that accompanied her earlier attempt to fetch Tristan for Isolde. (The fulfillment of its associations, to leap ahead in the drama, is Kurvenal's F in the opening scene of act 3.) Isolde steels herself with this F for Tristan's appearance in his heroic guise. That event, beginning the first "love" scene, is even more terrifying and forbiddingly distant than she, or we, could expect. The honor music with its three powerful crescendi, its emphatic diminished-seventh chord melodic units, the stiff formality of its dotted rhythms and, above all, its tritone shift to B minor, presents nothing of the character of Isolde's former lover, but a figure completely controlled by all Isolde understands by the word *Haupt*.

The honor music is the counterpart for Tristan of what the version of the desire music that introduced the death motive in scene two was for Isolde. There Isolde was obsessed by thoughts of death, as Tristan now is with honor. Both are intensely fearful points, expressing fixations that blot out all else. Both involve the shallow denial of desire, whose controlling presence is all too apparent in the music. As Isolde contemplates Tristan "with fearful agitation," the poison motive undermines his facade by initiating a circle-of-fifths motion in the flat direction for the beginning of the lovers' dialogue. Throughout the first half of the scene that follows the harmony, as described earlier, continually settles on the dominant of b, symbolizing the fact that honor is an unfulfilled ideal, until, after Tristan's offering his sword to an f♯ cadence, Isolde leads her response to closure in that key as she offers him the *Sühnetrank* instead. Both cadences are introduced by the glance motive at the same pitch, beginning from e♭, with its association of the dropping of the sword.

In scene 5 Wagner does not present the desire music itself—that is, in its primary version—until its reappearance along with the remainder of the prelude music from the point where the lovers drink the potion. But he reveals progressively that the initial A♭/A harmonies of the death motive, those associated with "Todgeweihtes Haupt," are a thinly veiled manifestation of desire. Throughout the first half of the scene he drops the cadential half of the death motive (associated with the heart) on all its appearances, an allegory of the fact that Tristan and Isolde bandy words and concepts (honor, shame, custom, and the like) rather than speaking from the heart. Beyond this, he transposes the motive immediately at the minor third on its first appearance, bridging the two by means of a B♭ dominant-seventh chord, so that for six measures the harmonic sequence becomes the following: A♭⁶–A–[f⁶]–B♭⁷–B⁶–C. In other words, he uses the death motive to articulate a series of rising triads on the pitches of the rising chromaticism of the desire music.

On its next appearance the death motive again features only its antithetical first half, this time transposed down a semitone so as to fit with the B minor tonal center; Wagner leads it directly to a presentation of the honor music that is set entirely above an F♯ dominant pedal. These gestures set up the theme of Isolde's retelling her desire to avenge Morold's death, which moves increasingly toward f♯ for Tristan's offering his sword and Isolde's countering with the offer of the drink of atonement. Isolde's f♯ cadence marks the end of the B minor initial segment of scene five, after which Branaene's preparing the drink leads the tonality along the first stage of the return to c for Tristan's "Wo sind wir?" The chorus of sailors bridges to c with their usual circle-of-fifths based harmonies (nature). And Tristan's "Wo sind wir?" marks his reaching the state of mind that has dominated Isolde from the beginning. C minor is reaffirmed as the principal tonal center of the act.

The f♯–c tritone shift depicts the collapse of the lovers' ideals of honor and shame; they both accept death at this point. The f♯ tonality represents, as suggested earlier, an extension by progressive fifths of the a of the desire music, the e of the narrative, and the b of the beginning of scene five. In the honor music, the move from F to the dominant of b was accomplished by transposition of the dominant harmonies that ended the first two phrases of the desire music at the tritone—E⁷ to B♭⁷ and G⁷ to C♯⁷—after which the transposition of the dominant harmony of phrase three at the perfect fifth (B⁷ to F♯⁷) provided the tonal perspective of the F♯ triad. Viewed as an anticipation of the music that accompanies Tristan's reawakening in act 3, this music embodies transfigurational potential. That potential is realized in Wagner's "amendment"—that is, in the revelation that honor is deeply related to love's urge to transcendence. Tristan and Isolde do not perceive this in act 1. The collapse of their ideals and of the tonality from b/f♯ to c will certainly bring Tristan to an intuition of the relationship between desire and death, but he will continue to believe that honor and desire are opposed to one another, ultimately proclaiming that his honor is fulfilled in his voluntary death (the C minor segment that precedes the drinking of the potion).

With the return to c the death motive reappears in full at the beginning and ending of a segment in which Tristan sings a solo whose harmonic underpinning is another rising chromatic pattern: (C⁶–D♭⁶–D–E♭). In this solo, Tristan reveals his understanding of Isolde's meaning, responding directly to her singing the death motive to "Hart am Ziel! Tristan, gewinn' ich Sühne? Was hast du mir zu sagen?" (Near the goal! Tristan, do you grant me atonement? What have you to say to me?). And at the close of the segment Isolde again refers to the goal—"Wir sind am Ziel: in kurzer *Frist stehn wir vor König Marke*" (We are at the goal: in a short *while we will stand before King Mark*)—the death motive again underscoring her meaning. Finally, as Isolde closes again in C minor at the end of a solo of blatantly ironic character in C major, the orchestra introduces several measures of alternating G♯⁶ and A harmonies that finally continue upwards chromatically: [G♯⁶–A]–B♭⁶–B–C⁶–D♭–D⁶–E♭–e, extending the pattern of Isolde's "Todgeweihtes Haupt" and merging it with the desire music. Wagner retains the alternating woodwind and brass orchestration of the death motive to emphasize that Tristan is now divided between head and heart, his head occupied with calling out orders to the sailors and his heart coming to fully understand the connection between death and desire. All that remains in this process is for Tristan to merge the honor and death motives before grasping the goblet with the potion and singing the death motive himself. From that point the glance motive initiates the return of the music of the prelude from a point corresponding to its climax.

The intensification of c toward e♭ as the music from the prelude returns to accompany the drinking of the potion is the event that ultimately opens the door for the C major ending of the act. The final tritone relapse in the act, from an unfulfilled e♭ to a, overcomes the extension of desire to the c of its second phrase—the meaning behind the a–c shift at the end of the prelude and the c tonality of the opening scenes of the act—by restoring the original tonality, a. The new perspective on desire then turns to C instead, confirming the conventional, worldly perspective of the sailors, Kurvenal and Brangaene, and directing it toward King Mark and the arrival at Cornwall. The initial a–c motion of the desire music, manifested in the shift to c at the end of the prelude, was extended to an e–c shift in Isolde's narrative and curse, and finally, to the b/f♯–c shift in scene 5. The tendency toward the dominant in the third phrase of the desire music, extended by fifths toward e, b, and f♯, is the story of desire between Tristan and Isolde; it belongs to the scene in which Isolde narrates that story and the scene in which they come face to face. It is countered each time by relapse to the key of the second phrase, the c of death, until, finally, the relapse to the key of the first phrase brings in the major rather than the minor mode of the second phrase.

The various keys of the first act, therefore, comprise a network whose starting point is the a/c relationship of the first two phrases of the desire music and whose end point is the a/C of those same two phrases, interpreted differently—that is, diatonically instead of chromatically. The diatonic fork in the path of desire leads to the conventional view of nature, manifested in Brangaene, Kurvenal, and the sailors, the chromatic-enharmonic one to Isolde's thoughts of death as the impulse to metaphysics. At the beginning (the prelude and first scene), the motion from a to c and e♭/E♭ initiates motion by progressive fifths from the tritone-related keys a and E♭ that echoes in the F/b of the honor music and widens to the opposition of b/f♯ and c/C in scene 5, then collapses via another tritone relationship (e♭/a) to the starting point. The dynamic of the desire music and of the design of the prelude expands to that of the act as a whole. Only act 3 will realize the tritone motion over the course of an entire act.

On Period Divisions in Act 1

In this light many other musicopoetic aspects of the first act come into sharper focus. In particular, symmetry and periodicity, the latter of which has been viewed as the "secret" of Wagner's form, but which Wagner spoke out unequivocally against, turn out to be less problematic than they might otherwise be. It is not their absolute

status as constructive devices (which Wagner viewed pejoratively) but their interaction with the principle of transition that gives them their true meaning. Periodicity unquestionably has a vital role in the design. At the same time, however, it yields
ground to other musical and poetic processes that Wagner's aesthetic writings invite
us to interpret as the deeper ones and that are often, therefore, out of phase with it.
The leitmotifs and key design are the most general manifestations of the latter.

It might be useful at this point to recall, briefly, certain of Wagner's remarks on
the surface/depth aspects of musical periodicity and transition, because the ocean/
land metaphor that he uses to describe them is such a prominent poetic theme in
the first act of *Tristan*. The metaphor goes back much earlier in his aesthetic writings than the Ring and *Tristan*, it probably underlies the conception of *The Flying
Dutchman*, and it is explicit in the 1846 program notes for the Beethoven ninth symphony. In the Feuerbach-influenced writings of the late 1840s and early 1850s, especially *Art-Work of the Future* (1849) and *Opera and Drama* (1850), then, after *Tristan*,
in *Music of the Future* (1860) it is treated at considerable length. Basically, Wagner describes music as analogous to the ocean that binds and separates the land masses of
dance and poetry, and harmony as the ocean that flows between the continents of
rhythm and melody.[3] The ocean is immeasurable, bottomless, fluid and infinite,
comparable to the "depth and infinity of Nature herself, . . . nature is, however, none
other than the nature of the human heart itself, which holds within its shrine the
feelings of desire and love in their most infinite capacity." The *Haupt/Herz* opposition of *Tristan* is linked through the ocean/land metaphor to the opposition of periodic set pieces and the fluid processes of transition. In contrast to the infinity of nature and the human heart, reliance on "eye" and intellect rather than the heart leads
one to grasp only the already manifested, the "fulfilled"—that is, the predetermined
form, or set piece. By nature humankind seeks closure and satisfaction, attempts to
render the infinite measurable and finite, to lead endless yearning towards a definite
object. Yet, contact with the infinite, "peering down into the depths," widens "won-
drously" the human heart with the "sense of marvel and the presage of infinity." In
this view, the ocean represents the true, infinite musical expression of desire that the
romantics saw as directed toward the absolute; and harmony expresses the struggle
of music (*Ton*) to "shape itself from the exhaustless depths of its own liquid nature."[4]
Harmony is internal, without beginning or end, whereas rhythm enables its extension through time. Although Wagner sometimes condemns excessive rhythmic
periodicity, setting the concept of intelligibility and its correlates such as understanding and logic up against feeling and inner fantasy, he nevertheless describes
periodicity as unavoidable for the comprehension of melody.[5] At the same time,
music's ability to convey the ineffable, longing quality postulated by the romantics
depends on the extent to which it escapes the routines of musical periodicity, linked
with a false idea of musical autonomy.[6] The well-known concept of endless melody
arose within this context.[7]

Wagner's concept of periodicity as described in *Opera and Drama* undergoes a
reorientation after the discovery of Schopenhauer and the rift with Hanslick's conception of musical autonomy. Basically, periodic forms become even more subordinate to transitional processes than before; and wherever overt periodicity predomi-
nates, the pejorative, Feuerbachian notion of absolute music is in force, especially at

points where the dominance of intellect over feeling is a poetic theme. That such designs exist is undeniable. But once we move into the level of close detail questions surrounding their divisions (and hence over their number and roles in the overall design of the act) become acute. One reason is that Wagner seldom provides clear-cut boundaries between scenes or periods. Another is that the periodic designs are, like the ship floating on the ocean of the first act, to be viewed as self-contained only at the smallest scale, embedded in the vastly more fluid world that Wagner himself called the secret of his musical form, transition. In this light, the search for definite boundaries between periods is often doomed to failure because Wagner continually overlaps the parameters we need to define such periods. Carl Dahlhaus has pointed out this overlap—or out-of-phase character—in the case of the relationship between the motives and the phrase designs. It is even more pronounced in the case of the tonal designs.

I will confine discussion of these points to two passages where Robert Bailey and Alfred Lorenz disagree: the opening two scenes and Isolde's narrative. In the first instance, arguments can be made for both interpretations, but they cannot provide unequivocal evidence of period definition. Basically, Lorenz considered that the initial C minor span came to an end with Isolde's "Todgeweihtes Haupt! Todgeweihtes Herz!"—the death motive—whereas Bailey, noting that this motive ended with a half close, puts the period ending some fifty-five measures further along, to coincide with Isolde's restoration of c with a full close as she orders Brangaene to fetch Tristan. The shift to F at that point would seem decisive in marking off a division between periods.

In light of Wagner's claim to have transcended his "system" in *Tristan* (that is the theoretical writings of the late 1840s and early 1850s, especially *Opera and Drama*, in which the concept of the musico-poetic period on which Lorenz and Bailey rely is described), and even more, his extolling transition as the secret of his musical form, we may well wish to consider exactly what periodicity means in his music. At issue is not whether periodicity and symmetry are present, but whether they are deeply rooted principles that pervade the music or devices introduced for particular allegorical purposes. Thus, whereas Lorenz describes both of the first two periods as symmetrical designs, the first with the sailor's song at the beginning and near the end and the second drawing Brangaene's repetition of Isolde's "Befehlen liess dem Eigenholde Furcht der Herrin ich, Isolde" into correspondence with its first appearance, Bailey sees the first period as ending at the first of these places ("Befehlen liess . . .") with the sailor's song appearing at the beginning and midpoint. For both scholars, articulation of beginning, middle, and end symbolizes the idea of structure.

Yet, if we were to search for another set of parallels involving the sailor's song it would not be hard to find. Simply following Wagner's scene division yields another set of correspondences. The sailor's song begins each scene, and is followed by a reaction from Isolde that moves to c before a solo from Brangaene of the type Lorenz called a "metric-rhythmic-period" (E♭ in the first scene and F in the second; there is, therefore, a transition from Isolde's c to F in the second scene that is not necessary in the first). The next event in each scene is a solo of Isolde that reacts to Brangaene's superficial solo (in both cases introducing the desire motive and distorting the thematic material of Brangaene's solo); both these solos make strong culminations in c.

In the first scene, Brangaene sings another solo in E♭, whereas in the second the F major of her solo reenters along with the motive of the voyage to Cornwall in the orchestral passage that accompanies her motion to the helm to deliver Isolde's message (as mentioned earlier, the first ten measures of the orchestral transition are equivalent to the first ten of Brangaene's first E♭ solo transposed up a tone). Beyond this point the parallels cease. They do not confirm a large tonally closed design, but they could easily be diagramed in a manner that would bring out, say, the increasing disparity between Isolde's and Brangaene's states of mind (F being more distant than E♭ from Isolde's c).

I draw these parallels to emphasize that in a style involving much varied repetition of music many different forms of bracketing are usually available. The point is that all three possibilities suppress some very important relationships and favor others. All of them involve decisions regarding suspension of the dominant tonal center for passages of varying lengths. In scene two the emergence of the death motive is a very important psychological *Gefühlsmoment,* after which Isolde's change of tone can be considered a delayed reaction to the opening of the curtain that had cut off the view from bow to stern until scene 2. The entrance of the E⁷–F deceptive cadence marks the change; and Wagner's adding an e″–a′ fifth as Isolde sings the word "Helden" above the F major chord, anticipates the interval with which the motive associated with Tristan's heroism will begin as well as the major seventh chord of the day motive of act 2. We do not know these facts at this point, but the pitch e″ introduces a very striking shift away from the e♭′ of the death motive. Nevertheless, Wagner's bringing in the glance motive in the form in which it enters at the *end* of the prelude initiates an apparent tonal motion towards c again. The glance motive now appears in rising minor-third sequences (from d′, f′, and a♭′) that recall the rising minor thirds of the desire music earlier in the scene. Instead of moving to c, however, Wagner picks up on the dominant implications of the D♭⁷ chord, bringing in a G♭ harmony that Brangaene, misunderstanding Isolde altogether, and undoubtedly thinking of the F of the deceptive cadence, interprets as the Neapolitan harmony of F major, leading it back to the D♭⁷ chord, which now functions as an augmented sixth chord in F. She then trivializes both the desire and the glance motives by forcing them into an F major solo, making them serve as the diatonic melodic material of a four-phrase period of the most conventionally balanced kind as she praises Tristan's heroic qualities. The device parallels the manner in which her E♭ solo in scene one had given a literal, and hence false, answer to Isolde's "Wo sind wir?" (ex. 9.2).

Brangaene's conventional responses have the effect that Isolde turns immediately to recitative style, then to a parody of Brangaene's periodic aria style for ironic purposes. In so doing she herself trivializes the desire music, first by leading her parody of Brangaene's solo into the first phrase of the prelude with a diminished seventh instead of the Tristan chord (d′ instead of d♯′), then by forcing the chromatic ascent of the desire music into recitative. Thick with *Stabreim,* her words, "Dünkt es dich dunkel, mein Gedicht," express a bitterly mocking attitude towards periodicity of the conventional kind (the word "Gedicht" is used contemptuously here, unlike its use in *Die Meistersinger,* to indicate a constructed rather than an inspired or poetic idea). In his setting of this line and, indeed, throughout the scene Wagner plays with the idea of conventional operatic diminished-seventh music as he does with recita-

Example 9.2. Act 1, scene 1: Brangaene's periodic solo

tive and aria styles. Despite her mocking, however, Isolde reveals a characteristic inability to sustain the external tone (this failure characterizes all such attempts of hers
in the first act). Having added Tristan chords, diminished sevenths and deceptive cadences to her rhyming parody of Brangaene's solo, Isolde attempts to sing yet another such strophe. As in her mocking of Tristan later in the act, however, Isolde's
tone becomes deadly serious; and as it does, her ability to sustain the periodic design
breaks down: she clips a phrase from her strophe, breaks the rhyme and intensifies
the chromaticism, introducing a series of Tristan chords over a C pedal and ending
with another clump of *Stabreim* for her bitter assertion that Tristan willfully avoids
her glance, "O er weiss wohl warum" (ex. 9.3).

The half close to c with which she utters these words marks a return to that key.
Isolde now sings in conventional recitative again, for the obvious purpose of making clear her intentions to Brangaene. The orchestral punctuation is disconcertingly

trite, and, as we might predict, Brangaene's question "Soll ich ihn bitten, dich zu grüssen?" sounds the major rather than the minor third. Isolde's answer ("Befehlen liess' . . . ") is imperious and unequivocal, beginning from Brangaene's e" and shifting back to c.

On the whole Bailey's period division is, perhaps, superior to Lorenz's, as the F major that now enters to accompany Brangaene's trip to the helm has the character of an orchestral transition, that, as I mentioned, parallels most of Brangaene's E♭ solo in scene 1 a tone higher. A parallel that neither period division brings out, however, exists between the sounding of the deceptive cadence of the desire music at Isolde's change of tone (to the words "Dort den Helden") and again at Tristan's words on his being informed of the message from Isolde (a fifth higher the second time). This phrase, which suggests the deception involved in their relationship, ushers in both times a dialogue passage of external character that centers on F major periodic phrase groupings. The transposition of the motive up a fifth on its second appearance (B^7–C) sets up the fact that the dominant of F figures more prominently in the exchange between Brangaene and Tristan than it did in that with Isolde; as a result the key of F is more clearly presented at the beginning of the latter exchange (because Isolde is not present to turn the tonality back to c). Later, Tristan repeatedly uses the dominant to evade Brangaene's questions, until, finally, Brangaene, in frustration, reiterates Isolde's "Befehlen liess' dem Eigenholde" phrase, in C/c as before.

Isolde's first "Befehlen liess' . . . ," as Bailey's period division asserts, is a point of culmination, returning to the principal key of the first scene and of Isolde's death motive, whereas, on Brangaene's repeating it to Tristan in the scene that follows, the recall of c/C is subordinate to the surrounding F tonality. This difference between Isolde's and Brangaene's pronouncing the same words is decisive. What makes it so is that the figure-to-ground relationship between F and c reverses between the two places. Isolde's presence causes the F to appear as an intrusion on her inner thoughts, represented by c; in the Tristan/Brangaene dialog F (and later C, a, B♭, and d) becomes, by virtue of the orchestral transition that introduces it, the new ground against which the return of c is mere figure, an appropriate relationship, because Brangaene has no understanding of Isolde's meaning and Tristan is even more politely conventional than Brangaene. Between them they shift the tonal center away from c. The entrance of F, first as a deceptive cadence, then as a secondary key (Brangaene's solo), and finally as principal key (the orchestral passage and the earlier part of the scene with Tristan), is a process of transition that no single period division reflects accurately. Isolde's c is interrupted three times until, finally, it loses its power altogether. Isolde is forced out her private obsession with death by Brangaene, Tristan, and Kurvenal.

In the structure of act 1 as a whole the process just described is essential to Wagner's returning to c after tonal regions of increasingly contrasted character, the last and most intense being, of course, the b and f♯ of the earlier parts of scene 5. Brangaene's E♭ and F, the d/D and B♭ of scene two, the e of the narrative, and the b of scene 5 all function as local tonic keys that can serve as the basis of periodic structures. But the many recurrences of c establish another scale of tonal recurrence that is central to the act as a whole. Periodic recurrences exist at several levels, a feature that both

Example 9.3.   Act 1, scene 3: Isolde's parody of Brangaene's periodic solo

Bailey and Lorenz recognize. What does not emerge from the necessary decision-making process of defining periodic boundaries and diagraming hierarchical structural overviews is the enormous extent to which Wagner's prefiguring and recollecting processes bring about a continual process of overlapping between the perspectives of local and large-scale events, or what I have called figure and ground. Without a strong sense of that process, the substance of Wagner's "art of transition," emphasis on period divisions has limited usefulness.

Isolde's narrative and curse provides another case in point. There Lorenz describes two successive periods, the first in e and the second in C, the latter featuring contrast tonalities that include a very prominent reappearance of e before the c of the curse closes the second period. Bailey recognizes the same keys and divisions, but sees the connection between Lorenz's e period and the return of e after the shift to

Example 9.3. *Continued*

C as decisive; the c curse that follows the final e/E, he argues, is not part of the narrative itself.[8]

Lorenz's division nevertheless makes clear that the curse follows logically from music heard within the second main section of the narrative, a fact that makes its role in the narrative essential. Wagner, in fact, permits both the e and c tonalities to cadence decisively, so that Isolde's force of will in returning to c receives the greatest possible emphasis. In other words, there is a definite sense of struggle and conflict between tonalities here that is the outcome of conflict within Isolde herself rather than simply between her fixation on death and the superficial attitudes of the external world represented by Brangaene, Kurvenal, and Tristan. Isolde has to overcome her own contradictory feelings toward Tristan in order to carry out her death plan. And an essential part of her feelings is expressed in the music that characterizes Tristan's heroism and is symbolized above all in Kurvenal's "Hei! unser Held, Tristan" phrase, ending scene 2. The overlapping transitional element that culminates in the narrative and curse traces from a series of recurrences of this music, the first of which is Isolde's response to Brangaene's return to tell how Tristan had avoided Isolde's message with polite words. Isolde's bitter repetition of Tristan's words "Wie lenkt' er sicher den Kiel zu König Marke's Land," leads into an angry outburst set to the "Hei! unser Held, Tristan" music in a sudden introduction of the dominant of e. The tune reappears at the end of the two major phases of Isolde's narrative, the first time in C, just before the e cadence and the second time in E just before the c of the curse. Whereas, C is easily absorbed into e, the same is not true of E and c. In fact, the last of these points sounds the "Hei! unser Held" phrase in E, C, and B major before making the massive juxtaposition of E and c for the shift from Isolde's ironic mocking to her deeply serious curse. Isolde's irony appears as the surface that masks the tragic truth of her curse.

The question of whether e or c should be taken as the closing tonality of the narrative and curse misses the main musico-dramatic point of the passage. Locally e is the predominant key, but the thematic and tonal relationship of the curse to passages of the narrative that are *not* narrative in nature, reveals that the intrusion of Isolde's contradictory feelings in the second half of the narrative are its most important subject matter, eventually overcoming the e with the return to c.[9] The tonality of the first, quasi-narrative part of the segment is securely in e, perhaps, as I have suggested, an extension at the fifth of the a of the desire music, from which its thematic material derives. The C major "Helden" motive that appears just before the e cadence marking Lorenz's first period division anticipates the encroachment of tonal regions that relate more directly to c/C than to e, as Isolde's feelings of torment and anger surface more directly. At the end of the narrative, the tonal juxtaposition of e/E and c reveals that the conflict within Isolde herself is far greater and more momentous at this point in the drama than that between her inner feelings and the external world.

After the prominent appearances of c at the end of the prelude and throughout much of the first two scenes, its recurrence at the end of Isolde's narrative recalls the conflicts that prompted the entrance of the death motive. Isolde curses Tristan as her betrayer, crying vengeance and invoking death on Tristan and herself. Significantly, she curses Tristan's head—"Fluch deinem Haupt"—for the preceding measures, primarily in e/E, had made a substantial recall of the "Hei! unser Held, Tristan" motive as Isolde mockingly imagined Tristan's assurances to King Mark that he would bring Isolde back as Mark's bride. Isolde's line rises to the high a″ ("Rache"), followed by ab″ ("Tod") and g″ ("Tod uns beide"), doubling the a, ab, g bass line of the C minor cadence (which recalls that of the death motive) and anticipating the next appearance of the death motive (sung to "Rache für den Verrath, Ruh' in der Not dem Herzen"). The curse and one other passage later in the act in which Isolde mocks Tristan both set Isolde's fixation with death (in c) in opposition to the mocking itself (in keys that juxtapose to c); in the latter passage Isolde introduces the death motive to articulate a point of culmination in c.[10] The interpretation of Isolde's narrative as a musico-poetic unit in e that ends before the curse can be sustained by traditional analytical means only if we take the narrative out of its dramatic context; the curse intensifies a psychological truth that runs throughout the narrative and takes precedence over its sense of periodic closure. Isolde's curse is an essential and climactic outcome of the principal tonally contrasted segment of the narrative, from which its music derives. That segment, beginning in C, expresses Isolde's deep bitterness and anger at Tristan's deception and her regret at her own weakness in dropping the sword of vengeance. After Isolde's mocking, the curse restores the serious tone required for Isolde's first full expression of her intent: death for herself and Tristan. In these and a string of other instances, Wagner establishes the key of c as the primary recurrent key of the act, whereas the e of Isolde's narrative, although more extended locally than the c of the curse, is, by virtue of the fact that it does not recur (other than as a facet of b in scene five), a secondary key in terms of the act as a whole. The concept of the closed musical period is subordinate to the psychological climax associated with the recurrence of the dominant emotion (and key) of the act.

In a Schenkerian analysis of the narrative Matthew Brown makes a number of important points relating to these questions.[11] Following the basic division of the narrative into two parts, Brown argues that part 1 is continuously in E minor, whereas, because of the much increased chromaticism of part 2, the latter segment is in E "only in some more remote, discontiouous sense." Nevertheless, part 2 makes a strong closure in e/E, after which Isolde's curse, although dramatically articulating the key of c, functions as "a transition to E♭, the key of Brangäne's Consolation." Along with Schenker, Brown doubts that tonal coherence of the kind that is usually associated with period closure is sufficient to account for Wagner's formal procedures. Unlike Schenker, however, he does not view Wagner's subverting the tonal middleground structure as an aesthetic defect. Rather, "by weakening the tonal framework of part 2, Wagner is able to preserve the overall continuity of scene 3. What we see, in effect, is that while an extensive use of tonal models may provide coherence on one level, on another it may prevent unity." Brown's concept of a "tonal model" is therefore very different from both the token bracketing of key recurrences that constitutes the greatest pitfall of Lorenz's analyses and the tightly constructed tonal designs that identify self-contained periodic units. It acknowledges, in effect, that Wagner may set up something approaching a self-contained period only to undermine its tonal coherence as it unfolds, yet at the same time to demand that the structurally weaker continuation be understood in relation to what precedes and follows it. I would add that in many of his period designs Wagner consciously subverts the idea of closed tonal structures for dramatic purposes. In *Tristan,* it is more the rule than the exception.

TEN

Act 2, Scene 1

Night and Minne

As DESCRIBED IN CHAPTER 3, Wagner developed the succession of three scenes that constitute the second act of *Tristan* from the three love episodes that appear in Gottfried's *Tristan* between the drinking of the love potion and the lovers' separation, binding them into an overarching day-night-day sequence. Of Gottfried's three scenes Minne is prominent only in the lovers' cave scene, where she is the focus of Gottfried's quasi-religious allegories. Wagner moves her forward to the torch scene; toward the end, she leads Isolde to its goal: the extinguishing of the torch.

In this scene, Isolde recognizes the day as an artificial framework she longs to escape. Her extinguishing the torch is Wagner's means of setting up the meaning of the day/night opposition that permeates the *Tristan* poem from the love scene on. In the dramatic and musical structure of the torch scene it is the culmination of a series of three groups of dialogues—all disagreements between Isolde and Brangaene—around which the scene is built. Underlying them all is the question of whether or not the torch should remain lit (Brangaene) or be extinguished (Isolde). The first exchange, on whether or not the hunting horns can be heard (mm. 102–199), directly follows the Prelude and offstage hunt music; the second, on whether Melot is Tristan's friend or his betrayer (mm. 200–342), culminates in Isolde's extended solo on night at approximately the center of the scene; and the third, on whether or not the love potion caused Tristan and Isolde's love (343–496), climaxes in Isolde's proclaiming Minne's will that it be night. The direction of the scene is toward ever more subjective interpretation of reality, as Isolde's perceptions overcome Brangaene's and night replaces day. All three dialogues culminate in powerful articulation of the principal key, B♭, chosen perhaps because of its association with day in act 1, and now associated with Isolde's longing to extinguish the torch. The last one finally accomplishes that goal, associating it with death (see ex. 7.2). The way to night now open, the ensuing orchestral transition begins as if it were a reprise of the prelude to the act, and leads toward what appears as if it will be a climactic cadence in

Bb at the point of the lovers' meeting. Instead, it is deflected toward C for the beginning of the love scene. The design of the torch scene thus centers on digression from and return to Bb—articulated primarily by its dominant, which is often prolonged as a pedal in the bass. Along with the orchestral prelude and reprise/transition, it creates the effect of a quasi-symmetrical rondolike form, the image of symmetry and periodicity—day—that is, never permitted the fulfillment of closure in the tonic.

The extensive reliance on the dominant throughout this scene is introduced in the prelude, where, after an initial emblematic sounding of the day motive, Wagner chains three themes together in sequence, binding them all by their gravitation toward F. The first, a three-phrase variant of the idea behind the desire music, projects a sense of anticipation, rising from the depths, and halting at the end of the first and second phrases, before continuing upward on the third, then returning to the dominant to begin again (ex. 10.1). Above its continuation, Wagner brings in a second

Example 10.1. Act 2: main theme of the prelude

theme (the torch theme), whose initial rapid descent from the chromatically descending tones of the desire music (f″–e″–e♭″–d″) above the dominant pedal, is mirrored by its settling on a series of chromatically ascending diminished-seventh chord harmonies (D–E♭–E–F) that lead back to the dominant (ex. 10.2). Its association with Isolde's longing to extinguish the torch lends it overtones of the metaphoric night to come (and ultimately death).

In this context the desire music itself enters, also above the dominant pedal, but now harmonized with the diminished-seventh chord on F (ex. 10.3). Rhythmically compressed, marked crescendo, with each of its units echoed immediately in the upper octave before transposing upward at the major second, and accommodated to the rapid duple meter of the scene, this version of desire is restless in character. Its most momentous change is Wagner's replacing the deceptive cadence by the first appearance of the transfiguration music, leading it into the key of the starting pitch A♭. As mentioned earlier, nothing at this point suggests the character this music will have in the *Liebestod*. The rapid rhythmic motion swallows up the cadential potential, turning it into a series of sequences, all *fortissimo*, that work their way back to the starting point, this time in the tonic, B♭. The A♭ tonality is also submerged by the rapid motion, exhibiting nothing of the character of night that Wagner assigns it in the love scene. Thus, the prelude as a whole circles around the dominant of B♭ without reaching a point of closure. And the first sounds we hear after the rising of the curtain are those of the offstage hunt music, presented entirely on the dominant of B♭. Isolde's first words, claiming that the sound of the horns has died out, are accompanied by the new desire-transfiguration combination in B♭, making once again a point out of its impatient return to F. In Schopenhauerian terms the emphasis on the dominant mirrors Isolde's dissatisfaction—unfulfilled desire.

Wagner's symbol of attainment and closure is the transfiguration cadence, as his substituting it for the deceptive cadence of the desire music in the concert ending of

Example 10.2. Act 2, scene 1: the "torch" motive

Example 10.3. Act 2, mm. 39–46 of the prelude: the desire music with the transfiguration music replacing the deceptive cadence

the *Prelude* makes clear. If deception characterizes the values of the physical world, then the transfiguration cadence increasingly represents the opposite—the stages in the lovers' attainment of night—reaching a point of culmination in act 2 with the B major music of "O ew'ge Nacht." Its unfolding throughout the opera accompanies the lovers' following a path that ultimately diverges from the deceptiveness and circularity of a world dominated by unfulfilled desire. In the torch scene, however, its *immediate* impression is of *increased* deceptiveness and circularity—of rapid motion that never seems to go anywhere. The transfiguration music appears some eight times, always as the continuation of the desire music in some form, and always without fulfilling its cadential potential. In the earlier part of the scene, it appears at the ends of Isolde's solos, in association with her longing for night. Only toward the end, as she gears herself to extinguish the torch, does Isolde intuit the deeper meaning of her action, namely, that the onset of darkness is a metaphor for the metaphysical night-death the lovers increasingly long for through the course of the love scene. Naming Minne as the force behind life, death, and love, Isolde announces that her goal is night, which she illuminates with a light of her own: "Frau Minne will, es werde Nacht, dass hell sie dorten leuchten." These words, which impel Isolde to extinguish the torch, sound to the first appearance of the transfiguration music that is not given forth at breakneck speed, the first one to anticipate something of how it will sound at the climax of the *Liebestod*. Even so, the sense of fulfillment that comes at the ending of the opera is absent here, undermined by the lack of any corresponding tonal preparation and by the fact that Isolde's ecstasy is part of a transitional motion that leads ultimately to the return of day. The ending of the scene, therefore, sets the idea of closure (return to Bb) and transition in sharp opposition. Closure becomes a prefiguring of the passage from night-death (the extinguishing of the torch) to transfiguration (the lovers' meeting). At the latter point the transfiguration music sounds for the last time, overwhelmed by physical excitement as the torch scene passes over into the love scene. Thus, the torch scene remains very much within the framework of the "truggeweihtes Glücke" of day foreseen by Tristan at the end of act 1 and symbolized by the day motive in the opening measures of act 2.

The Tempo of Day

In this light we must consider two aspects of the Tristan style that have never been given their due: meter and tempo. Corresponding to the large-scale day/night/day motion of the second act, the music moves in three basic tempi following a fast, slow, moderate (duple, triple, quadruple) pattern that, modified slightly from time to time for local purposes, serves as the basic metric framework. The first real point of change from the starting tempo and meter comes in the transition to "O sink hernieder," where it coincides with the emergence of Ab in association with night.

The original tempo of the act, *sehr lebhaft*, is a rapid $\frac{2}{2}$ that carries over from act 1, where it was used extensively for music representing what would be called day in act 2. Particularly interesting in this regard is Wagner's instantiating this tempo for the final 149 measures of the act coincident with the lovers' consciousness of desire after drinking the love potion. It is closely associated with the sailors' chorus of greeting to King Mark and the turn to C. In carrying this basic rapid $\frac{2}{2}$ motion into act 2 Wagner does not change or even significantly modify it until the point where Brangaene reintroduces the beginning of the desire music in scene 1 for the first time in the act. There Wagner indicates a slight slowing of the tempo: *ein weniger mässiger im Zeitmass*. Then, in the next solo, as Isolde herself introduces the desire music to accompany her vision of Frau Minne's magic power, Wagner slows the tempo somewhat by stages. After that, from the point of Brangaene's return to the dominant of Bb to the beginning of the love scene Wagner again indicates tempo increase by stages while continuing to hold to the $\frac{2}{2}$ meter, until reaching *sehr lebhaft* for the duet that begins the love scene. At that point he changes to $\frac{2}{4}$, remarking that the quarter-note is now faster than the previous half-note (the half-note of the original *sehr lebhaft*) and adding that "the tempo should always be modified according to the fiery or tender expression." If we think of the tempo change in terms of bar lengths, then it represents an *accelerando*, but, of course, the quarter note is now *slower* than the preceding *quarter* note. The change was made to mirror the lovers' short breathless outcries, which move in rapid alternation. Twenty measures past the meter change, as the duet reaches the dominant of C, ending the transitional quickening of the tempo that began in the preceding scene, Wagner marks a *molto accelerando* in order to effect a return to $\frac{2}{2}$. Here he remarks that the half-note is the same as it was in the earlier $\frac{2}{2}$ (that is, the original tempo and meter).

At the point of return, completing the arrival on C, the lovers cry out "O Wonne," their lines moving into unison (octaves) for the first time. Here Isolde reaches up to c‴ for the first time in the opera, completing an ascent of her highest tones that reaches back into the preceding scene, its beginning coinciding with the beginning of the abovementioned "Frau Minne" solo. And from the point at which the original tempo and meter return through the entire span of more than four hundred measures that follow until the end of the *Tagesgespräch* and the transition to "O sink hernieder" Wagner retains the basic $\frac{2}{2}$ meter and the fast tempo, which he underscores with many verbal reminders, but modifies only twice for passages of particular intensity relating to anticipation of the emergence of A♭ as the key of night.

Thus, the original *sehr lebhaft* $\frac{2}{2}$ constitutes a basic meter and tempo that should be modified according to the immediate expression but that must remain in place as the overall framework. It is tempting to view it as an analog of day. At the end of the *Tagesgespräch*, with the completion of the lovers' reinterpretation of their past relationship in terms of the night/day antithesis, Wagner makes a sudden though brief shift to a "much slower" tempo, as Isolde casts back to the ending of act 1, her words— "um einsam in öder Pracht schimmernd dort zu leben" (in order to live there isolated in empty, shimmering splendor)—describing Tristan's situation as the outcome of his former domination by day. As her cadence leads into the day motive, in a form that recalls its appearance as a motto for the beginning of the second act, Wagner restores the basic tempo (*wieder lebhaftes Zeitmass*); and in response to two mottolike presentations of the day motive in the orchestra, Isolde juxtaposes past and present: "Wie ertrug ichs nur? Wie ertrag' ich's noch?" (How did I bear it? How do I bear it now?) This moment is highly symbolic, representing a powerful reminder of the framework of day that has been the subject of the preceding one thousand–plus measures of the act. Tristan's response—"O nun waren wir Nachtgeweihte"—strikingly replaces the sound of the major-seventh chord with that of the Tristan chord, initiating the solo that will finally bring about the next stage in the lovers' metaphysical progression: longing for night.

I have described how the latter part of Tristan's solo effects a symbolic change from the first death motive to the new one. At the point at which it turns into the transition into "O sink hernieder," Wagner introduces the second death motive for the first time, preparing it with a sudden *accelerando* surge to *fortissimo*, then modifying it immediately with the heading *etwas gedehnt*. As the desire music emerges from the death motive and passes over into the A major transfiguration music, the dynamic level rapidly and progressively softening, Wagner slows the tempo further with the heading *langsamer, und allmählig immer langsamer*. And as the A major tonality of the transfiguration music begins to give way to the move toward A♭, Wagner anticipates the syncopated rhythmic pattern of "O sink hernieder" in the bass, which reiterates the tones f, e, e♭—that is, the descending chromatic motion of the beginning of the desire music—as a slowly moving pedal, above which the day and desire motives seem to merge. The orchestral line weaves its way downward while the dynamic level moves toward its *ppp* goal. Finally, with the arrival on the dominant of A♭ Wagner completes the process of tempo and meter change, shifting to $\frac{3}{4}$ with the indication *mässig langsam*, which from this point on becomes the basic framework of the part of the love scene that surrounds the two A♭ duets. Owing to the anticipation of the rhythm of "O sink hernieder" throughout the preceding measures, the $\frac{2}{2}$ meter passes almost imperceptibly over into the $\frac{3}{4}$ meter of the duet. With the shift from A to A♭, we might speak of something akin to a transitional "metrical modulation."

The first modifications of this new tempo-meter framework correspond to the next stage in the lovers' metaphysical odyssey: longing for death, following "O sink hernieder" and Brangaene's first warning. Significantly, the modifications now appear *within* the basic slow $\frac{3}{4}$ framework. Wagner indicates *immer sehr ruhig* at the point where the love's peace motive enters; but, like the motive itself and its G♭ tonality, the tempo change is anticipated within the preceding solo, Brangaene's first warning. The dialogue that follows remains at first in $\frac{3}{4}$, but, as it takes on a rather more intellectual character, Wagner indicates several time-signature changes within the basic tempo—($\frac{3}{4}$), $\frac{4}{4}$, $\frac{3}{4}$, $\frac{4}{4}$, $\frac{6}{8}$, ($\frac{3}{4}$)—specifying the equivalence of either the quarter note or the eighth note at the principal points of change. The return to the basic tempo and meter coincides with the reappearance of an earlier, more patterned dialogue (transposed up a semitone), now associated with the lovers' intuitions of oneness (Tristan singing what Isolde had before, and vice versa). Wagner anticipates the return to $\frac{3}{4}$, by notating the viola part of the second strophe of "So stürben wir" in $\frac{3}{4}$ against the $\frac{6}{8}$ of the remaining parts. The music of this segment leads by stages—"immer mehr belebend," then "immer belebter," and finally "lebhaft, mit Steigerung"—to a larger scale of return: to the original rapid $\frac{2}{2}$ for the duet "O ew'ge Nacht" (reprising the tempo and meter Wagner had indicated for the ending of act 1). Ultimately, the slow $\frac{3}{4}$ of night is enclosed within the framework of day. And within the duet itself appear two further stages of tempo increase—"immer etwas drängend," which coincides with the first appearances of the transfiguration cadence, and "noch drängender," which arises with the final arrival on the dominant in preparation for the climax of the movement.

The return to the fast $\frac{2}{2}$ for "O ew'ge Nacht" underscores the parallel between the endings of the torch scene and the love scene, both of which lead toward a climactic presentation of the transfiguration music. Whereas in the ending of the first scene the transfiguration cadence is totally submerged by the rapid motion, in "O ew'ge Nacht" it is much close to the ending of the opera, suggesting that it might finally attain closure. The tempo, however, brings out a crucial difference between the B major music of "O ew'ge Nacht" and its recurrence in the *Liebestod*. In "O ew'ge Nacht" the approach to the climax is not only very rapid but increasingly loud, reaching *fortissimo* at the first set of transfiguration cadences and marked *più forte* after that, then dropping to *piano* and increasing again to *fortissimo*. The *crescendi* coincide with the points of tempo increase. In the *Liebestod*, however, night, as Isolde makes clear, is attained beforehand, with Tristan's death and with Isolde's own collapse and revival and her isolation from the physical events on stage. Neither the dynamic nor the tempo markings increase through the course of the movement; the meter is $\frac{4}{4}$, not $\frac{2}{2}$, and the maximum dynamic level is *forte*. In contrast, the return of day immediately following "O ew'ge Nacht" suggests that the lovers' longing for death remains bound up with the will-to-life.

The Formal Design of the Torch Scene

In this scene Isolde's solos, seven in number, basically increase in length and scope from her initial disputations with Brangaene over whether the hunting horns can be heard or not (ten, sixteen and forty-one measures, respectively) to her disagreement with Brangaene over Melot's friendship with Tristan (fourteen and sixty measures) and finally, her proclaiming Frau Minne as the true cause of her and Tristan's love (two paired solos of sixty and thirty-eight measures respectively, linked by a solo of Brangaene). Each of these dialogues involves a digression from and return to B♭, the first relatively brief and the second and third progressively more extended and ecstatic in nature. Only the latter two digressions are of structural significance in the scene, and both are initiated by Brangaene, who in the first instance warns Isolde of Melot's treachery, and in the second reflects back on her own role in exchanging the death and love potions in act 1. In all three cases, what Brangaene maintains is objectively true: the horns *can* be heard, Melot *does* betray Tristan, and the substitution of the love potion *was* her work. Yet, Brangaene's truths represent the day, whereas Isolde's disagreements bring about increasingly powerful returns to B♭, all three associated with night.

Over the five solos of their dialogue on the horns Isolde and Brangaene accuse each other of being deceived. Isolde's first solo leads directly into the transfiguration music as she announces that the sound has disappeared in the distance ("Mir schwand fern der Klang"). Her second leads into a slightly altered version of the transfiguration music (now in F), as she claims that the sound is merely the rustling of the wind, and Brangaene maintains that she is deceived by desire. And with Isolde's third solo, considerably longer than the preceding two, the offstage horn music ends, dissolving back into the orchestra. Muted violins transmute the dominant-ninth chord of the hunting music into a Tristan chord that leads to the dominant of D♭. To this point, "objective" truth regarding the horns is clearly associated with Brangaene. With this solo, however, Isolde introduces the theme of silence in association with night—"In Schweigen der Nacht nur lacht mir der Quell: Der meiner harrt in schweigender Nacht" (In the silence of night only the brook smiles on me. My beloved waits in the silent night)—conspicuously broadening the rhythm of her line as the torch music returns to B♭. With her concluding phrase—"als ob Hörner noch nah' dir schallten, willst du ihn fern mir halten?" (as though horns were still sounding near you, will you keep him away from me?)—the transfiguration music sounds again, contradicted only by the final words, "fern mir halten," which halt abruptly on the dominant.

From this point the dispute over the horns ends, and we conclude that the silence is now objectively real. The only digression from B♭ in these first two hundred measures of the scene was the brief D♭ that Isolde led back to B♭ after some twenty measures, initiating the return with her reference to the silence of night. The first sustained digression comes when Brangaene, after a period of tonal ambiguity that matches her dark hinting, shifts suddenly to B minor, warning Isolde of Melot's treachery. Their dialogue on this subject leads, once again via the key of D♭, into Isolde's fifth solo, the most extended to this point (sixty measures). Beginning at almost exactly the midpoint of the scene, Isolde now personifies night (feminine) just as Tristan will personify day (masculine) in the *Tagesgespräch* of scene two. Her solo is a focal point for the idea of closure in scene one and its association with the key of B♭. The last traces of the hunt music now recede in favor of night (as the horn music is taken over in D♭ by the clarinets of the orchestra and finally disappears); Isolde, greatly broadening the rhythmic character of her line, prepares the metaphoric interpretation of night to come.

Isolde's solo draws the key of D♭ back into the framework of B♭ by introducing the transfiguration music in G♭ as she retorts to Brangaene that Melot opens up for Tristan what Brangaene closes to her: "Besser als du sorgt er [Melot] für mich; ihm [Tristan] öffnet er, was mir du sperrst" (He [Melot] cares for me more than you; he opens up for [Tristan] what you close off for me). Isolde means, of course, that Melot aids Tristan in his nighttime visitations to Isolde; what he opens up, therefore, is night as the time of the lovers' secret meetings. But toward the end of the act the transfiguration music appears again in G♭ (its only other appearance in that key), as Isolde indicates to Tristan her willingness to follow him into the realm of night. And the action that accompanies the passage in question, Tristan's bending to kiss her, immediately prompts Melot's angry intervention, the action that leads to the wound from Melot that will eventually prove fatal for Tristan. What Melot opens up for Tristan is the Schopenhauerian night-death, which Isolde intuits in scene 1. She therefore draws the G♭ tonality into the framework of B♭ by way of harmonic motion through the diminished-seventh chord on e (sustained for eight measures), followed by a thirty-one measure dominant (F) pedal culminating in a powerful melodic cadence to B♭. In scene 1, Brangaene's view of Melot is worldly wise, her truth more objectively real than Isolde's, who does not perceive Melot's treachery. Isolde's self deception regarding Melot is, however, true at a deeper subjective level that only the appearance of the transfiguration music confirms as such.

In all this, it is clear that Isolde attempts to bring about closure in B♭, associating it with the transfiguration music, whereas Brangaene leads the tonality in new, often contradictory seeming directions. Brangaene's response to Isolde's solo now initiates the third and most momentous of the scene's digressions from B♭ and what is certainly one of the most impressive achievements of the entire work in terms of its confronting transition and closed form for poetic purposes. Brangaene deflects Isolde from extinguishing the torch by opening up a subject that engages her in more than mere disagreement: the substitution of the love potion in act 1, which Brangaene describes as her work. The outcome is Isolde's angry retort that Brangaene has misunderstood matters entirely, failing to account for Frau Minne's intervention. Here she brings out Gottfried von Strassburg's view that love (Minne) bonds life and death, as described in Chapter Three (see also ex. 8.1). Reintroducing the death motive, and a series of third-related harmonies—G, E♭, C, A♭, A, f♯—deriving from the death motive at "Leben und Tod sind untertan ihr," Isolde makes the enharmonic change from the death to the desire music described earlier. Her goal is A, the outcome of Minne's weaving power—"die sie webt aus Lust und Leid, in Liebe wandelnd den Neid"—which attains a strong point of cadential articulation (though "deceived" by f♯ in the bass) for "Frau Minne hat es meiner Macht entwandt." After a brief digression, Isolde completes the move to A, in which key we hear the theme that will be associated with the tumultuous character of love in the beginning duet of the love scene. With this theme, which should probably be designated the "Minne" theme, A major emerges in all its glory for Isolde's proclaiming her obedience to whatever Minne decrees (see the text on p. 61).

In act 3, Wagner reveals the derivation of this theme from the theme of Isolde's first act narrative, in particular the point at which Isolde tells of the events that immediately preceded the glance of love between her and Tristan—that is, the events that caused their love. He also affirms the derivation of both the narrative theme and the Minne theme from the desire music, associating them with Isolde the physician. In this light, the A tonality of the Minne theme is connected conceptually with the a of the desire music. The Minne theme describes a visionary quality, an expression of the way that love weaves an illusory spell around the more elemental quality of sexual desire. This quality is manifested musically in the fact that the new theme sounds to a quasi-ostinato circling bass pattern made up of three ascending semitones (a, a♯, b: derived, of course, from the desire music) and a dominant-tonic cadence (e, a). There is, therefore, a sense of the momentary articulation of a single key by means of the repetition of a short cadential unit. Isolde's first presentation of this theme forms a miniature period of twelve measures, entirely in A, an externalizing of the transcendent aspect of Isolde's desire. And from this point Isolde's desire is dominant in our minds, owing to the mounting excitement that is embodied in her lines, supported now by the equally directed character of the orchestral melodic line. The voice leading is at its most purposeful here, as Isolde and her accompaniment together ascend step by step towards the high a″ that sounds just before her cadence ("nun *lass'* mich gehorsam zeigen!") (ex. 10.4).

In this wonderful solo Isolde overcomes Brangaene's objections with the sheer power of her strongly directed line. It may be mentioned that at two points in the solo Wagner introduces harmonies contradictory to the prevailing A major, both times associated with death and both times referring to the key of the scene, B♭: "Des Todes Werk [nahm ich's vermessen zur Hand] and "Die Todgeweihte nahm sie in Pfand." In temporarily subsuming the tonic harmony of the scene as a whole beneath Isolde's A, they suggest Isolde's subordinating life and death to her sense of oneness with Minne's will.

The last twelve measures of Isolde's solo mark the beginning of what will become the transition into scene 2, its momentum increasing from here on until the C major duet. Isolde's melodic cadence to A is deceived by the F⁷ dominant harmony with which Brangaene's response and the return to faster tempi (*sehr bewegt*) begins. Beneath Brangaene's line the orchestra develops a motif from the Minne theme in a purposefully rising line that moves toward the pitch a″ as if it might become the leading tone to the tonic in the upper register. Gradually, however, the dominant character of Brangaene's F is overcome by diminished-seventh chords, and she moves, instead, toward C minor, turning the a″ back to a♭″ in her descent to a melodic cadence in c that is deceived by the A♭ beginning of Isolde's final solo (as Isolde's A cadence was by F).

From the first appearance of the "Minne" theme, Wagner, for the only time in the scene, uses a single theme to bind together a succession of solos. It holds until Isolde's arrival on the word "night" ("Frau Minne will, es werde *Nacht*"), at which point the transfiguration music replaces it. The escalation of ideas throughout this

Example 10.4. Act 2, scene 1: the "Minne" music

sequence is matched by the fact that the key sequence is based on the tones of the desire music: A (the new Minne theme), B♭ (Brangaene's response), A♭ (the beginning of Isolde's final solo) and B (the second key of Isolde's solo). Thus Isolde begins her final solo with the minor-third relationship that will become the basis of the motion from night to transcendence in the love scene and the *Liebestod:* A♭ to B. As yet it is not articulated as a full-fledged key succession, but merely as a phrase transposition built on the tones of the desire music in the bass: A♭, A, B♭ (A♯), B. But the arrival on B returns to the Minne theme in full, associating it with Isolde's heightened ecstasy and leading to the climax of the scene, her proclaiming Frau Minne's will that it be night to the first truly visionary appearance in the opera of the transfiguration music (ex. 10.5). This climax precipitates the extinguishing of the torch and the final return of the F pedal, now seemingly preparing for an arrival on B♭ to coincide with the lovers' meeting.

Example 10.5. Act 2, scene 1: from Isolde's final solo

On the largest scale this third digression spans Isolde's B♭ personification of night and her return to B♭ to extinguish the torch. Wagner draws a parallel between the two points by recalling the harmony of the earlier solo for the extinguishing of the torch. There he had presented the transfiguration music, associated with Melot's opening up "night" for Tristan, in G♭, drawing it into the return to the dominant of B♭ by means of eight measures of diminished-seventh chord on E (accompanying the torch theme) that moved to an extended F pedal. Now he presents Isolde's ecstatic association of the transfiguration music with Frau Minne's will that it be night in G, allowing that key to dissolve by stages into a recall of the eight measures of E diminished-seventh chord in the earlier solo. At both points, Isolde sings a sustained g″ ("Das Zeichen" in the first instance, "Die Leuchte" in the second) that falls to f″ before the cadence. The parallel between the two solos involves the two appearances of the transfiguration music, in G♭ and G, both of which are directed to the dominant of B♭ in association with Isolde's intuition of the role of night. In the first instance, it is Melot's opening up night for Tristan; in the second Minne's opening it up for Isolde.

The G of the transfiguration music projects both the visionary aspect of Isolde's ecstasy and the passing of that vision over into the extinguishing of the torch. That is, it sounds completely outside the framework of B♭, and is then drawn back into that framework just as was the G♭ of Isolde's earlier solo. Wagner's means of drawing it back is, of course, to have it pass through the pitch G♭ on the way to F, as Isolde's vision of Frau Minne's inner light gives way to the immediacy of night. Once the initial arrival on the dominant of B♭ has been accomplished, Wagner rivets the G/G♭ pitch succession in place by sounding the death motive above the dominant pedal to symbolize the torch's dying out. Transposed to b♭, the initial harmonies of the death motive become G♭⁶ and G, leading to the dominant of b♭. Before the extinguishing of the torch Wagner sounds its theme twice, beginning its long descending line on g‴ above the E diminished seventh chord, then into the F that coincides with Isolde's throwing the torch to the ground. The huge descending chromatic scale in the strings that follows (harmonized by the F diminished seventh chord), leads from f‴ to g♭, to coincide with the entrance of the G♭ chord of the death motive above the pedal FF. And from this point Wagner introduces a much larger descent through the entire orchestra to correspond with the light going out: now five octaves from g♭‴ to FF. The descent articulates the change to the G harmony along the way, then returns to the pitch G♭ before the final convergence on the dominant that initiates the return of the prelude music.

And with the return of the music of the Prelude to the act, we hear the two pitches G♭ and G, in the roles of the minor and major sixth degrees of the scale: the first and second phrases of its new anticipatory theme present the flat sixth as "barrier" to the ascent of the bass from F, while the third skirts the flat sixth to sound the major sixth and continue upward, an analog of the lovers' search for fulfillment. Finally, in the orchestral music that takes over from the music of the prelude, intensifying its preparation for B♭, Wagner develops the anticipatory theme, dropping the day motive, the torch theme, and the desire music, and reiterating the g″ continually until (in measure 529) it sounds as the uppermost pitch of the dominant of B♭; from this point, marked *immer belebter,* Isolde's mounting excitement pushes toward B♭ and the final appearance of the transfiguration music at the point of the lovers' meeting, the overlap between the first and second scenes.

Thus, Wagner ensures that the final return to the dominant of B♭ projects a sense of structural arrival that draws Isolde's G major vision of night into its folds. Isolde's final solo exhibits almost classic qualities of the kind of transition that is set up to bring about the return of the final structural pillar in the design: the music of the prelude in truncated form, built on the dominant of B♭ and merging into a transition creating the expectation of a climactic point of articulation for that key. And yet, Isolde's solo has its own inner design that can hardly be described as a preparation for arrival on F, as it is based on a rapidly changing key succession whose climax, the G major of her "Frau Minne will, es werde Nacht, *dass hell sie dorten leuchte*," does not emerge from the context of B♭. As I mentioned, this solo begins above a pedal A♭ that moves upward by semitones after three measures, in analogy to the chromatic ascent of the desire music ("Die im Busen mir die Glut entfacht; die mir das Herze brennen macht"), then shifts to B major, at which point Wagner brings in the Minne theme in its original form ("die mir als Tag der Seele lacht"). Although the rotating Minne theme again projects the trancelike state of Isolde's mind, this time it is not the point of culmination for her solo. Instead, Wagner turns its B into the dominant of E minor ("Frau Minne will, es werde *Nacht*"), sustaining the e harmony for two measures of darker coloring on the word "Nacht." In terms of traditional dominant preparation, e is the strongest point of tonal arrival in the solo. But Wagner immediately uses it as a springboard to G, bringing in the transfiguration cadence at the pitch level that would correspond to a statement in the latter key ("dass hell sie dorten leuchte"). Isolde's "Tag der Seele" gives way to night and that in turn to Frau Minne's inner light.

This is one of the greatest climaxes of the opera, the point at which the transfiguration music first attains its ecstatic character. Hearing it sung by a great soprano, such as Kirsten Flagstad, is an unforgettable experience. Nevertheless, the G is not only unprepared harmonically, but it gives way almost immediately to a passage of some four measures that settles on a quasi-Phrygian cadence to E ("wo sie dein Licht verscheuchte"). And the E immediately becomes an open e″-e‴ octave that holds for five measures ("Zur Warte du: dort wache treu") before it is absorbed into the abovementioned eight measures of diminished-seventh chord on E ("Die Leuchte, und wär's meines Lebens Licht, lachend sie zu löschen zag' ich nicht"). The latter harmony then shifts to the diminished-seventh chord on F as Isolde throws the torch on the ground. Two measures later the death motive and the torch motive combine over the pedal F to articulate the dominant of b♭, in preparation for the return of music from the prelude to the act.

Because of the shifting tonalities, the transfiguration music, despite its climactic character, does not represent the fulfillment of all that precedes it. The keys (really transposition levels) of A♭ and B, leading to the E minor chord on night, then the emergence of the transfiguration cadence in G from that harmony, anticipate the sequence of desire, night-death, transfiguration that controls the dynamic of the love scene. But there is an important difference: although the emergence of this ecstatic vision fulfills the symbolism behind Wagner's coupling the desire and transfiguration music at earlier points in the scene, there is no real tonal preparation for the sounding of the transfiguration music in G. Objectively, the key of G is hardly present at all; abstracting the harmonies would never lead anyone to imagine that it could figure so prominently in the passage. It is present because it is the correct pitch level to relate to the e of Isolde's "Nacht."

And this is exactly Wagner's point. The vision of transcendence can never be objectively verified. We "hear" the key of G at the climax of Isolde's solo, not because of any tonal preparation, but because it is the correct key for the transfiguration music at this pitch level. The force of the transfiguration music here has nothing to do with the kind of tonal preparation it receives in the *Liebestod*. Instead it arises from two qualities: the first is Wagner's extraordinary attention through this entire sequence of solos to the rising melodic lines of voice and orchestra, which control all the other referential, motivic, and tonal parameters; and the second is the interrelatedness of the leitmotifs, which enables us to supply qualities that are only alluded to here from their more fully developed appearances elsewhere in the opera. In other words, when a leitmotif is solidly defined by its harmonic-tonal content, as the transfiguration music is, the merest hint of that content will often suffice to carry the tonal sense with it. In this case, the undeniable force of a G that is "objectively" fleeting, and that becomes by hindsight part of the return to B♭, highlights the subjectivity of Isolde's vision of night and transcendence.

Wagner's voice leading here and throughout the love scene creates a tremendous sense of forward motion that can, if necessary, reinforce a single key, but that also can bind into a continuity the kinds of rapid key changes that project the ecstasy of sudden surges of discovery or intuition. The stage by stage ascent of Isolde's line in this solo from her initial c″ to the long-held appoggiatura a″ that resolves to the g″ of the transfiguration cadence projects a remarkable sense of mounting excitement for Isolde's intuition that Frau Minne will illumine the night from within. The transfiguration music emerges as the visionary symbol of this subjective light, after which the ever-moving bass and melody lines lead the music toward the above-mentioned "Phrygian" E. Passing downward through f″ to e″ at the end of Isolde's line ("verscheuchte"), the high g″ of the preceding line, on "leuchte," seems to combine in the subsequent phrases with the e″ to converge on Isolde's final pitch f″ at the point at which the F pedal is reached and the torch extinguished. The e of night is converted by stages to the role of leading tone to the dominant of B♭.

Before the point just described, however, nothing in this music suggests that the dominant of B♭ will be its goal, least of all the e harmony that sounds to the word "night." And, climactic as it certainly is, the bursting forth of the transfiguration music is transitional in nature, its G a momentary vision of something beyond the present reality. The return of the dominant of B♭ puts it in perspective, restoring the sense of anticipation that absorbs Isolde after the torch goes out. And yet, despite its steadily increasing intensity, when Tristan arrives and the excitement becomes almost unbearable, the dominant does not resolve to its tonic key at all. Instead, Wagner leads the music to the transfiguration cadence pattern, in B♭, but submerges it once again in the rapid rhythmic motion. The voice-leading is at its most purposeful in getting to that point; but at its peak the transitional character of the transfiguration music skirts any kind of cadence altogether, moving on in rapid tempo until, eventually, the dominant of C takes over for the beginning of the love scene. We are well into the love scene before the momentum of the opening scene subsides. And by that time any expectation of a B♭ cadence has dissipated long before. Isolde's vision of night is overcome by day, the subject of the earlier part of the *Tagesgespräch*. If we diagram the scene as a closed and symmetrical ritornello form, the instrumental prelude to the act has a counterpart in the instrumental music that follows the extinguishing of the torch and leads to the lovers' meeting.[1] But we will miss the point of Wagner's creating such a form: to set in opposition the "visual," symmetrical surface of "day" and the transitional undercurrent (night). Wagner articulates the key of B♭ by means of the dominant pedal throughout the entire scene so as to project Isolde's longing for something that will *not* be fulfilled within the framework of day. Rather, in keeping with Schopenhauer's description of the "chord of the seventh" and its demand for the fundamental chord as an analogy for the need of every tragedy for "an existence of an entirely different kind," Isolde's fixation on night as fulfillment of the excitement and the bliss of physical love is offset toward the end of the scene by an intuition of the metaphoric night that will emerge fully only in the following scene. Her longing for closure in B♭ represents a conception of night that gives way in the love scene to one in which the largest scale of form is transitional rather than closed.

In Isolde's final solo the upward-curving melody line leads to the pitch g″ and the momentary G tonality, then turns downward to e″ (the E cadence), before reinterpreting both the e″ and the g″ in terms of the arrival on F. If we trace the climactic highest tones of Isolde's and Brangaene's melody lines, which often interchange with those of the orchestral line, we find that there is a very purposeful motion toward the high a″ of Isolde's "nun *lass'* mich gehorsam zeigen," the ending of her initial solo of obedience to Frau Minne. At the deceptive cadence that follows both Isolde's and the orchestral line drop an octave, after which the orchestral accompaniment to Brangaene moves up the scale again, reaching a″ once more and suggesting that resolution to b♭″ will be its goal. Brangaene's sudden turn to c, however, involves Wagner's directing the line down through a♭″ to g″ (in the orchestra) for the start of Isolde's final solo. From there the orchestra and Isolde, in combination, lead it toward the a″ of Isolde's "dass *hell* sie dorten leuchte," which, as I have described, moves back down to settle ultimately on f″ as Isolde returns to the dominant of B♭ to extinguish the torch.

Conspicuous by its absence throughout this sequence is the high b♭″ that would lend triumph to Isolde's victory over Brangaene's opposition. As we might imagine, however, the b♭″ *does* arrive, and in very powerful and highly symbolic fashion. With the extinguishing of the torch and the return of music from the prelude to the act as if arising from the depths, Wagner begins a stage-by-stage ascending motion in the orchestral line that may well be the most purposeful such line in the entire opera. From the point at which the return of the prelude music moves into intensified preparation for B♭ (measure 517) Wagner moves the uppermost orchestral line from e″ through f″ (m. 521) to the g″ that, after six measures of reiteration, coincides with the arrival on the dominant of B♭ (m. 529). Extended progressively up the scale to the next octave, it reaches the a♭″/a♭‴ octave as Tristan rushes in, calling "Isolde" with the pitch a♭′. Isolde calls "Tristan" with a♮″ (harmonized with the dominant seventh of B♭), then b♭″ ("Geliebter") as the lovers unite and the music passes over into the transfiguration cadence. This point is the goal of all that Isolde has longed for in the preceding scene. The first three ascending tones of the desire music seem ready to articulate the key of B♭ and the transfiguration music as symbol of Isolde's triumph (ex. 10.6).

At that very moment of ecstasy, however, Isolde's b♭″ enters a measure *before* the c‴–b♭″ appoggiatura of the transfiguration music, as if her impatience to reach that pitch can no longer be held in check. And simultaneously the bass slips down a semitone to E, holding that pitch for two measures before moving to E♭, the correct pitch for the plagal transfiguration cadence. Although the harmony broadens throughout

Example 10.6. Lovers' meeting: beginning of act 2, scene 2

these measures, the extra surge of energy that causes the dominant of F to sound be-neath the orchestra's c''' undermines the ability of the latter pitch to serve as appog-giatura to a B♭ cadence. As a result, the transitional quality that denied resolution of the transfiguration cadence throughout the scene is more pronounced than ever and the rhythmic momentum carries the tonality away from B♭ altogether. The sequen-tial motion leads up a tone until the pitch b''' is reached (in the orchestra) for the be-ginning of the duet that Wagner described as "life overflowing with all the most vio-lent emotions." From this b''' the orchestral line drops suddenly to c', as the tempo abates, from which it builds again step-by-step, but now to settle on the dominant of C major.

With the orchestral b''' Wagner changes to $\frac{2}{4}$ (*sehr lebhaft*). The lovers' short breath-less outcries ("Bist du mein? Hab ich dich wieder?" etc.) lead to the restoration of the original tempo and $\frac{2}{2}$ meter of the act as they unite (on "O Wonne der Seele"). The arrival on C now identifies Isolde's pitch g'' as the one around which this new dominant-centered movement is based. Nevertheless, Isolde here and at one later point in the duet reaches up to the highest tone she sings in the entire opera, c‴, both times leaping up to it (and back down from it) as if to represent it as an isolated ideal pitch. It can be thought of as the culmination of Isolde's earlier high tones, reaching even beyond the b♭″ of the lovers' meeting and confirming that the tonal shift from B♭ to C for the beginning of the love scene represents an intensification of the qualities associated with day. The C major duet brings back the dominant-centered music that anticipated the lovers' meeting, now transposed up a tone and leading into the Minne theme in its most excited form. This is the apex of the lovers' search for *Liebeswonne*, which the Minne theme projects with great vividness. Tristan and Isolde merge into unison ("Ewig, ewig ein!"), accompanied by a powerful climax on the dominant of C, after which the excitement winds down and they begin the exchange that turns into the day/night antithesis of the *Tagesgespräch*. The Minne theme passes over subtly into the torch theme, whose broadened rhythm invites interpretation as the descending chromaticism of the desire music in Tristan's solo "Die Sonne sank, der Tag verging." Out of this, the day motive emerges as the dominant motif of the *Tagesgespräch*.[2]

In this scene, we perceive one of the most revealing instances of the role of transition in *Tristan*. Isolde's ecstatic intuition of Frau Minne's power conveys the idea that transitional music can *itself* represent the attainment of insight, without the need of formal gestures of the kind we usually expect transition to lead toward but not to embody. The G of Isolde's "dass hell sie dorten leuchte" is a point of visionary intuition that comes not as a point of culmination or a new beginning, but in a passage of transition to another key altogether. In this respect, it prefigures the attainment of night in the transition to "O sink hernieder," in which Wagner introduces the next appearance of the transfiguration music in A major, even though the tonal goal of the transition is A♭.

ELEVEN

The Love Scene in Act 2

Transition and Periodicity

O N OCTOBER 12, 1859, soon after the completion of *Tristan*, Wagner wrote to Mathilde Wesendonck the following now-famous lines:

> I recognize now that the characteristic fabric of my music (always of course in the clos-est association with the poetic design), which my friends regard as so new and so sig-nificant, owes its construction above all to the extreme sensitivity which guides me in the direction of mediating and providing an intimate bond between all the different moments of transition that separate the extremes of mood. I should now like to call my most delicate and profound art the art of transition, for the whole fabric of my art is made up of such transitions: all that is abrupt and sudden is now repugnant to me; it is often unavoidable and necessary, but even then it may not occur unless the mood has been clearly prepared in advance, so that the suddenness of the transition appears to come as a matter of course. My greatest masterpiece in the art of the most delicate and gradual transition is without doubt the great scene in the second act of *Tristan und Isolde*. The opening of this scene presents a life overflowing with all the most violent emotions,–its ending the most solemn and heartfelt longing for death. These are the pillars: and now you see, child, how I have joined these pillars together, and how the one of them leads over into the other. This, after all, is the secret of my musical form, which, in its unity and clarity over an expanse that encompasses every detail, I may be bold enough to claim has never before been dreamt of.[1]

It would go beyond the scope of any reasonable length chapter to describe all the ways that the love scene in the second act of *Tristan* exemplifies Wagner's "art of transition." If we accept Wagner's view that transition pervaded the very fabric of his music, then we must recognize that it is not limited to linking relatively stable or closed periodic set pieces to which, by definition, it is subordinate. In describing the "pillars" of the love scene as those of *feeling*, Wagner shifts the emphasis away from the objective signposts of musical structure, usually embodied on this scale by periodic set pieces. And in the processes he called the "motion, shaping and transformation" of the motives, but which apply to other musical parameters as well, he binds relatively open (transitional) and closed (periodic) passages into larger designs in which their boundaries are no longer absolute. The metrical "modulations" described earlier, the preparation for and emergence of A♭ as the key of night, the emergence of the second death motive and its replacing both the first death motive and the day motive, these and other processes articulate the one overarching poetic idea behind the love scene: the change from day to night, both literal and metaphoric. In this design periodicity, which Wagner set forth in *Opera and Drama* as the building block of form, is certainly a vitally important element. But, in setting it in opposition to what he viewed as inner form, associated with night in the 1870 Beethoven essay, Wagner points up the relationship of periodicity and transition as one in which, on the largest scale, the latter takes priority over the former.

Of necessity, much of the musico-poetic design of the love scene has been adumbrated throughout this study. The following discussion will attempt to convey the main points, foremost among which is the increasing depth of night as metaphor for the lovers' coming ever closer to oneness. The background in Gottfried von Strassburg's lovers' cave scene for the ideal of an enclosed "world apart," a place of forgetfulness, of the dream of love, or *Wunschleben*, is evident primarily in the part of the scene from "O sink hernieder" to the end, encompassing the three duets that Alfred Lorenz called the "Nachtgesang" (song of night), the "Sterbelied" (song of death) and the "Liebesekstase" (ecstasy of love).[2] With the transition to a slower tempo, the association of A♭ with night and a higher degree of periodic design (but one that is controlled by a still larger principle of transition), Wagner brings about the lovers' consecration to night and the metaphysical. Preceding it is the most extensive instance of transition-dominated music in Wagner's entire oeuvre, the *Tagesgespräch*. Paradoxically, it presents many signposts of a closed periodic design.

The *Tagesgespräch*

The names that are often associated with the two principal parts of the love scene, especially *Tagesgespräch* and *Nachtgesang* (the former for present purposes taken to include the initial duet and ensuing transition to the *Tagesgespräch* proper, and the latter extended through the duet "O ew'ge Nacht"), encapsulate the poles of Wagner's transitional style: *Gespräch*, meaning dialog or conversation—that is, speech—implies intellectual content, whereas *Gesang*—song—suggests lyricism and feeling. The text of the *Tagesgespräch* has been described, pejoratively at times, as paraphrased Schopenhauer, whereas the night metaphors of the *Nachtgesang* have been linked most often to a poetic source, Novalis's *Hymns to the Night*. Thus the metaphoric *Haupt/Herz* antithesis of act 1 remains in force, stretched out to the dimensions of two segments of more than nine hundred measures in toto, the one exhibiting a primarily transitional character that nevertheless involves features that have been viewed as contributing to tonal closure, and the other introducing extended tonally closed periods along with other large-scale correspondences in what is clearly a tonally open design.

In many respects, the *Tagesgespräch* is like a prelude to the *Nachtgesang*, a recitative preparing the aria that follows. Like a recitative, its musical continuity is dependent on the succession of poetic ideas, without a pronounced musical structure to bind its diverse thematic elements into a single entity. For this reason, it was routinely cut from most performances of *Tristan* until well into the second half of the twentieth century.[3] Nevertheless, its poetic design has a clear sense of purpose and direction behind which we discern the faded outline of conventional formal procedures, an analog of memory. In the *Tagesgespräch*, Tristan and Isolde go back over the events of act 1 and their prior background in Tristan's seeking out Isolde as bride for King Mark, reinterpreting them in terms of Tristan's domination by the values of day and Isolde's seeking night (death) as an escape. Throughout these three hundred–plus measures day dominates the dialog at first. Gradually, however, as Tristan and Isolde reflect on the love-death potion, the qualities of night become increasingly prominent. Isolde recalls her plan of death in act 1, describing it as an attempt to flee the day and draw Tristan into the night with her, bringing the "end of deception." And Tristan, reliving the emotions associated with his coming to understand Isolde's hidden intentions in act 1, proclaims that the love potion, intermingled with the anticipation of death, drove out the day from the picture of Isolde hidden deep in his heart. The expectation of death, in opening up his consciousness of love, enabled him to "see things truly with the 'vision of night.'" Ending the *Tagesgespräch*, Isolde's final solo is a reminder that the arrival at Cornwall overcame Tristan's understanding, casting the lovers back into day. It returns to music recalling Tristan's "Truggeweihtes Glücke" at the end of act 1 as she cries out the lovers' continuing enslavement by day. At this point, the day motive enters in the orchestra, sounding like the deceptive cadence of the desire music and recalling both the beginning of the act and the beginning of the *Tagesgespräch* (ex. 11.1). And to two prominent soundings of the motive Isolde announces that the unbearable torment of the past remains. Tristan's outcry, "O nun waren wir Nachtgeweihte," marks the beginning of a transition to the *Nachtgesang*, completed in "O sink hernieder."

The *Tagesgespräch*, therefore, exhibits many musical correspondences to act 1, although they do not usually involve direct repetition of music from the first act; instead, tonal and motivic recurrences parallel the major dramatic events of that act, their context always altered significantly. When Tristan cries out "Mein Tag war da vollbracht" (There my day was ended), for example, his C minor cadence, deceived by the beginning of the desire music, corresponds to the point where he turned to c immediately before drinking the love potion, after which the desire music had returned (as it now does, along with the death motive, which had preceded it in act 1). Earlier in the *Tagesgespräch*, Wagner makes much out of the alternation of the bass notes A and G♯ (or A♭) in a predominantly enharmonic context; although the music is not directly carried forward from the first act, the text makes clear that the passage corresponds to the alternation of the A♭ and A harmonies of the death motive in act 1. Thus, the process of reinterpretation is ever present, but the musical correspondences always involve much more than the exact recall of music heard before. What Wagner called "the motion, shaping, and transformation" of the motives comes into its own in the *Tagesgespräch*. As a result, the form itself exhibits a very striking element of inner/outer opposition, the former centered on music's transi-

Example 11.1. Act 2, scene 2: ending of the *Tagesgespräch*

tional processes and the latter on what Wagner viewed as the deceptiveness of the conception of musical form that was rooted in the world of appearance, or day.

Tristan: Deception and Day

Although the *Tagesgespräch* is a relatively intellectual attempt to grasp the metaphysical implications of love and death, giving way to a more poetic vision of night in the *Nachtgesang*, even within the *Tagesgespräch* itself we can speak of two parts, nearly equal in length and each comprising five solos, the first part dealing with day and the second with night. The object of the first half is to reveal Tristan's past actions as the result of his domination by day. Tristan's solo "Dem Tage! Dem Tage! Dem tückischen Tage!" has traditionally been taken as the beginning of the *Tagesgespräch*, largely because of its featuring two very striking appearances of the day motive in basically the same form (transposed) that begins the act and that reappears at the end of the *Tagesgespräch*, as cited earlier. "Dem Tage," however, also can be understood as the *Abgesang* of a *Barform* in which the light of the recently extinguished torch is reinterpreted as the minion of a personified day. After the initial duet passes over into the transitional dialogue, the strophes in question establish the metaphoric reinterpretation of day as the subject of what follows. And after "Dem Tage" the next four solos, completing the first half of the *Tagesgespräch*, develop day as a metaphor for Tristan's commitment to worldly values. Its culmination is the extravagant juxtaposition of day and night in Tristan's solo, "Was dich umgliss mit hehrster Pracht."

In the sequence just described, Wagner echoes words and ideas from the preceding solo or solos as the dialogue develops, a device with obvious implications for the unfolding of the leitmotifs, as many have shown. Thus, after "Dem Tage," Tristan's next solo, "Der Tag! Der Tag, der dich umgliss," retains the initial exclamatory character of the preceding two, and introduces variants of the day motive. His next solo—"Was dich umgliss mit hehrster Pracht"—then develops the idea that Isolde's royal "aura" ("Was dich *umgliss*"), drew the response of worldly values such as honor and fame from him. In this, the first really extended solo of the *Tagesgespräch*, Tristan reaches a climactic stage in the understanding of his domination by day. As described earlier, after introducing foreshadowings of the transfiguration music, now associated with day, Tristan juxtaposes B and A♭ as symbols of how the values of day (B) penetrated the innermost recesses of his being (A♭), leading him to bring forth a false picture of Isolde (transition to G). The G major strophic design that follows fulfills a role that is symbolized by the external-sounding G cadence with which it closes. It marks a division within the *Tagesgespräch*, whose first half is concerned exclusively with Tristan's former domination by day.

The first part of the *Tagesgespräch* moves by the stages I have outlined towards the point where, in this eighty-seven measure solo—by far the longest to this point—Wagner presents a complete statement on exactly what the metaphoric day means. For Alfred Lorenz its G represented articulation of the dominant of C, which for him was the tonal center of the complete series of periods that made up the *Tagesgespräch*. And, whereas that interpretation involves an extraordinary amount of dot-connecting, it is meaningful so long as we do not take it as evidence of tonal structure but, rather, as the mere outline of a form that is fundamentally external, the hilt rather than the blade of the sword, to use Wagner's metaphor. The very convergence of the poetic theme of externalizing a picture (*Bild*), and moreover a picture that is *false*, with a pair of strophes of the most hollow kind based on sequences of the day motive, is an expression of opposition between the static conception of form centered on visual metaphors and the true inner form that depends on transition rather than periodicity, sound rather than sight. Isolde's response—"O eitler Tagesknecht!"—sets up the latter kind of form as the basis of the second half of the *Tagesgespräch*.

Tristan's concluding strophes feature the main melodic form of the day motive in the first half of the *Tagesgespräch:* a descending fourth followed by a stepwise rising third. The version of the motive that constitutes its emblematic form, however, utilizes a falling *fifth* rather than fourth, and therefore outlines a triad from the fifth down to the root then up to the third. The one version of the motive encourages endless melodic sequences, whereas the other symbolizes tonal closure. This latter, emblematic form appears in the initial measures of act 2, and in the initial segment of Tristan's "Dem Tage"; but otherwise it never sounds in the first half of the *Tagesgespräch*. In the version of the compositional draft it did not appear at all until Isolde's response to Tristan's "Was dich umgliss." It therefore represented Isolde's version of the motive as opposed to Tristan's.

I have mentioned that the initial solo of the *Tagesgespräch*, Tristan's "Dem Tage! Dem Tage! Dem tückischen Tage," follows two strophically paired solos of Tristan and Isolde as if completing a *Barform*. This is clearer when we consult the version of the compositional draft as well.[4] In the final version there are close parallels between the endings of all three solos, the first of which ends on the dominant of G, whereas the second sets up the same pattern, now in A, but deflects the ending to C instead. The ending of the third, in A♭, resembles that of the first. In the original version, however, Wagner did not modify the ending of the second strophe; instead, its cadence paralleled that of the first a tone higher (i.e., ending on the dominant of A). And the third strophe, Tristan's "Dem Tage," was in B♭ instead of A♭. Because the cadences in all three strophes introduced the Neapolitan harmony before settling on the dominant, the relationship between the second and third solos was closer: the Neapolitan (B♭) of the second strophe returned immediately as the tonic of the third. Then, at the end of the third solo Wagner extended the Neapolitan harmony of its B♭ cadence, notating it at first as C♭, then changing to its enharmonic equivalent, B, and sustaining the latter key for a few measures. The effect was of a rising sequence of keys—G, A, B♭, B—with ties to both the rising third in the melody of the day motive and the ascending chromaticism of the desire music.

Most of all, however, in this original version, the third strophe, Tristan's "Dem Tage," did not begin with the day motive that we know from the final version. And, because Wagner added the day motive to the beginning of the act only at a later stage, there was virtually nothing of that motive before Tristan's "Der Tag der dich umgliss," more than seven hundred measures into the act. At the beginning of "Dem Tage" Wagner introduced a distinctively different motive that he developed in the music that followed. That earlier motive, residues of which remain in "Dem Tage," comprised several reiterations of a single tone (sometimes preceded by a rising sixth) followed by the drop of a semitone or whole tone. In other words, it was derived from the beginning of the desire music by way of the beginning of the torch motive as it appeared in the introduction to the three-strophe grouping as a whole—Tristan's "Das Licht! Das Licht!"—where Wagner reduced its initial chromatic descent to that of a single semitone. In returning to this motive for Tristan's "Dem Tage," Wagner bound the three solos into a continuity that followed from the gradual modifications to the Minne and torch motives. But in replacing both the original day motive and the entire third strophe in the final version he gave far greater importance to the dramatic emergence of the new day motive at the beginning of the third strophe, and hence, to the articulation of a new segment—the *Tagesgespräch*—beginning at that point and paralleling the appearance of the day motive at the beginning of the act. In the final version, Wagner's lessening the strophic character of the sequence of solos (to the point that most commentators have failed to recognize more than the parallel between the first two) led to an *increase* in the structural articulation. Basically, Wagner reinforced the large-scale periodic design at the expense of the smaller, more transitional one.

In the final version the half close in G at the end of the first strophe and full melodic close to C at the end of the second led Lorenz to argue that the *Tagesgespräch* comprised a C major structure. But the fact that the C cadence (alluding to the key in which the scene began) was tacked onto a preexistent form that had nothing to do with C is a telling detail. And Wagner's deceiving it immediately with the A♭+7 chord of the day motive for the beginning of Tristan's "Dem Tage" strophe symbolizes something entirely different: the emergence of A♭ as the key of night.

From its initial A♭ Tristan's solo continues with the same rising chromatic bass line—A♭, A, B♭, B—that had accompanied Isolde's final solo in scene one and that derives, of course, from the desire music (ex. 11.2). In its final version, Tristan's "Dem Tage" is the first sustained appearance of A♭ in the opera. It appears primarily in

Example 11.2. Act 2, scene 2: beginning of the *Tagesgespräch*

sharp notation, however, and even, at one point, with sharp and flat notation simultaneously between voice (flats) and orchestra (sharps). And although such notation is not so unusual in *Tristan* and often reflects simple expediency rather than symbolic content, in this instance it brings out a poetic theme that is not so clearly expressed in the original version of the solo, namely, that beneath Tristan's outcries against day there lies something else that is hidden at this point: longing for night, the theme toward which the *Tagesgespräch* leads. Wagner introduces this theme, solely by musical means, in the initial phrase group of the solo, which describes an upward curve in the bass from A♭ to B by semitones, then descends by step—B–A–G♯–F♯–E♯–E–D♯—to the dominant of A♭. A series of pitches that looks at first like a descending E scale ends up with the tones E♯, E, D♯ (i.e., F, F♭, E♭), which represent the sixth, flat sixth, and dominant of A♭, spelled enharmonically. Wagner uses those last three pitches as the basis of one of the most momentous leitmotif combinations of the love scene, and one that will become increasingly prominent in varied forms until the climax of "O sink hernieder": *harmonic* (rather than simply melodic) combination of the day and desire motives, with the Tristan chord on F followed by the dominant seventh chord on E, that combination now leading, via reinterpretation of the E^7 chord as an augmented-sixth chord, to the dominant of A♭. The A♭ of the third strophe and the appearance of the day motive in its emblematic form foreshadow the eventual absorption of this version of the day motive into the desire music as A♭ becomes associated with night in the latter part of the *Tagesgespräch*. It is established in Isolde's three-strophe grouping, "Getäuscht von ihm, der dich getäuscht," where its replacing the form of the motive that begins with the perfect fourth is associated with what Isolde calls "the end of deception."

Articulation of the dominant of A♭ by means of the augmented-sixth chord on E (F♭) appears three times in Tristan's solo, at the close of each of the three main phrase groups, the second of which already embodies a metaphoric prefiguring of death that derives from Isolde's extinguishing the torch: "Wie du das Licht, o könnt' ich die Leuchte, der Liebe Leiden zu rächen, dem frechen Tage verlöschen" (As you [extinguished] the torch, Oh, if only I could extinguish the light to avenge the sufferings of love to the impudent day). Along with the bass motion from F to F♭ to E♭, it reappears in the transition to "O sink hernieder" and again at the climax of the duet, when the lovers proclaim the subjectivity of the world: "Selbst dann bin ich die Welt." On the word "Welt" the day motive sounds in octaves between flute and oboe in the highest register beginning from the e♭‴ of the flat-notated F Tristan chord and filling in the third from a♭″ to b″ with the rising semitones of the desire music as the harmony changes to the E^7 chord. Basically, it represents the metaphoric change from day to night in terms of the lovers' recognizing the subjectivity of the world of representation (day) and its inseparability from desire—in Schopenhauerian terms the world as will. Tristan's introduction of A♭ in "Dem Tage" marks the beginning of that process.

The relationships just described aid in articulating the shift from day to night as the single great theme of the five hundred measures from Tristan's "Dem Tage" to the solidifying of A♭ as key of night in "O sink hernieder." In Tristan's solo, A♭ is hidden at first by the sharp notation, emerging only momentarily at the end of the strophe. Although its association with night is implied by Tristan's echoing Isolde's reference to death at her extinguishing the torch, it does not emerge in anything close to its metaphoric dimension until "Was dich umgliss." The latter solo highlights everything involved in the day/night antithesis—*Haupt/Herz,* conscious/unconscious, external/internal, open/concealed—mirroring them in every possible musical parameter. Its contours, keys, dynamics, tempo gradations, and, of course, the leitmotifs and other associational aspects, all project the conflicts that divided Tristan in act 1 and that he now relives. Their culmination is the two G major strophes in which Tristan reveals the extent of his domination by day. Its powerful G cadence gives it a reality that Isolde recognizes in her outcry "O eitler Tagesknecht."

Isolde: The "End of Deception"

The first half of the *Tagesgespräch* centers on Tristan and his domination by day, whereas the second arises from Isolde's metaphors of night. Because Tristan, like day, is masculine, while Isolde and night are feminine, Wagner's poetic text articulates a motion in which music (also feminine) gradually takes over the poetry (masculine). Isolde's response to Tristan's eighty-seven measure solo is the second, and only other, extended solo of the *Tagesgespräch* (seventy-eight mm.), a foil to Tristan's "Was dich umgliss" complex. After her initial "O eitler Tagesknecht!" it divides into three clearly distinguishable segments, the first and second comprising a strophic pairing and the third somewhat longer (approximately twenty-five + twenty-three + thirty mm.). The first strophe counters Tristan's G by turning to g and widening the initial interval of the day motive from Tristan's perfect fourth first to a tritone then a perfect fifth. Turning suddenly toward e at the close, it sets up the key of the second strophe, which likewise begins with the perfect-fourth form of the day motive and switches to the perfect-fifth form toward the end. In both strophes, Isolde associates Tristan's version of the day motive with her having been deceived by the same force that caused Tristan's self-deception ("Getäuscht von ihm, der dich getäuscht") and the emergence of the new form with the conflict between the love within her heart and the hatred that arose from Tristan's domination by day: "dort, wo ihn Liebe heiss umfasste, im tiefsten Herzen hell ich hasste!" (there, where love hotly embraced him, in the depths of my heart I hated him) in strophe one, "wenn in des Tages Scheine der treu gehegte Eine der Liebe Blicken schwand, als Feind nur vor mir stand!" (when in the glare of day the glances of love disappeared from the one truly cared for, he stood before me only as an enemy) in strophe two. These texts affirm the derivation of this form of the day motive from the motive of Tristan's heroism.

In her third strophe, Isolde recalls her solution to the conflicts just described: the death potion, the memory of which leads her to new expressions of the relationships of the desire, day and death motives. Now she develops the falling-fifth version of the day motive exclusively, and in association with the key of ab/Ab, in which her solo ends, the opera's first full close in that key.

Das als Verräter	That which revealed you
dich mir wies,	as betrayer to me,
dem Licht des Tages	the light of day

wollt' ich entfliehn,	I wanted to escape,
dorthin, in die Nacht	to draw you with me
dich mit mir ziehn,	off into the night,
wo der Täuschung Ende	where my heart promised me
mein Herz mir verhiess;	the end of deception;
wo des Trug's geahnter	where the feared delusion
Wahn zerrinne;	and lies would disappear;
dort dir zu trinken	there to drink to you
ew'ge Minne,	eternal love,
mit mir dich im Verein	I wanted to consecrate you,
wollt' ich dem Tode weih'n.	in union with me, to death.

The key words in this solo are "der Täuschung Ende," the "end of deception," which Isolde associates with union, death, eternal love, and night. And musical analogs of those qualities dominate the *Tagesgespräch* from this point on. The solos flow into one another with far greater ease than the segmented solos of the first half, whereas the day, death, and desire motives merge increasingly in a context of continual enharmonicism, Wagner's analog of oneness and night.

The process begins with Isolde's lines cited above. Over her initial three phrases Wagner converges a chromatic descent of her uppermost tones—g♯″, g♮″, and f♯″— on the beginning of the desire music—enharmonically notated in Isolde's line as e♯″–e♮″–d♯″—initiated by the rising sixth g♯′ to e♯″. Isolde proclaims the end of deception to these tones, which are accompanied in the bass by the pattern of the Minne theme—G♯–A–A♯–D♯—thereby inviting our hearing this version of the beginning of the desire music in A♭ (although it is notated entirely in sharps). At the close of the phrase, Isolde's melodic d♯″ on "Ende" sounds for a full measure to the dominant of A♭, before slowly falling the fifth to g♯′ to complete the day motive, all the while the harmony shifts to the dominant of B. These gestures perhaps derive from the A♭–B motion in Isolde's hymn to Frau Minne at the end of scene 1. Deceiving the cadence for Isolde's "wo des Trug's geahnter Wahn zerrinne," however, Wagner leads her line chromatically back up to the pitch d♯″, now notated as e♭″, from which he reintroduces the death motive for the first time since Isolde's extinguishing the torch: "*zerrinne; dort dir zu trinken ew'ge Minne, mit mir dich im Verein wollt' ich dem Tode weih'n*" (ex. 11.3).

This passage is a focal point for the tonal character of the remainder of the *Tagesgespräch*. The version of the death motive that appears at this point is no longer centered on C minor, nor does it sound as an independent leitmotif. Instead it is drawn into a fluid harmonic process in which, instead of describing the character of physical death, it is itself reinterpreted in terms of longing for night. Death loses its autonomy, as it were. That process centers on Isolde's belief in union as the "end of deception," which Wagner represents by an enharmonic reworking of the music of Isolde's "wo der Täuschung Ende mein Herz mir verhiess" (notated in sharps) as her "mit mir dich im Verein wollt' ich dem Tode weih'n" (notated in flats). To a long-drawn-out sounding of the day motive Isolde finally completes an a♭ cadence.

In all this, Isolde reconciles the antitheses surrounding A♭ in Tristan's earlier solos as well as the A♭/A antithesis of the death motive. The text makes clear that the enharmonicism is an intensification of Frau Minne's magical weaving power in scene 1:

Example 11.3. Act 2, scene 2: from Isolde's solo on the "end of deception"

"Leben und Tod sind untertan ihr, die sie webt aus Lust und Leid." In scene 1, the enharmonicism was transformational: associated with discrete key change; now it is not. Eternal Minne is death, recalling Gottfried's associating "eweclichez sterben" with the love potion (see chapter 3). Wagner changes from sharp to flat notation within the death motive, at "trinken ew'ge Minne," corresponding to the sharp/flat juxtaposition of the A major chord of the death motive (originally "Haupt") to the f⁶ chord ("todgeweihtes Herz") that brought about the reconciliation.

Whereas Tristan's "Was dich umgliss" had centered on antithesis, ending with the association of two external-sounding periodic strophes with the empty qualities of

Example 11.3. (Continued)

day, Isolde's response begins with two far more complex paired strophes and moves into a representation of union, associated with night. Mostly what enables this passage to achieve its end is Wagner's attention to voice-leading as the means of creating a sense of continuity out of an unusually dense and often microscopically conceived web of shifting tonal and leitmotivic allusions. His centering Isolde's lower-register tones around g♯′/a♭′ and a′ and her upper register around the pitches f″, e″, and e♭″, and his introducing those pitch classes as the basis of the motion of the outermost orchestral voices, merges the beginning tones of the desire music with the initial falling fifth of the day motive and the key of a♭. By allowing the initial falling fifth of the day motive to articulate a melodic cadence to g♯ or a♭ Wagner creates an allegory in sound of desire and day giving way to night.

   With the sharp/flat change of the death motive Isolde's line bonds the two regions in a manner that is very revealing. Her falling fifth from e″ to a′ initiates the melodic pattern of the day motive above the A major chord of the death motive, after which the c″ that coincides with the f⁶ chord initiates a retrograde of that motive, now a semitone lower, ending with the rising fifth from a♭′ to e♭″. In this we have an echo of the associations of those two fifths with the names "Tristan" and "Tantris" in act 1, in which Isolde narrates how Tristan had given a kind of retrograde version of his name to hide his real identity. Tantris, represented by the rising fifth from a♭′, was the man who fell in love with her, whereas the man who returned from Cornwall under the name Tristan to claim her for King Mark, was the knight dominated by worldly values. The falling e″–a′ fifth of Tristan was derived from the beginning of the superficially heroic "Hei, unser Held Tristan" motive.

Whether or not these associational relationships are audible as such is not the main point, which reposes in the way that Wagner uses the kinds of musical relationships just described to bind this and the following sequence of solos into a continuity. Nowhere does Wagner make good his claims for the "inner abstract-self" of the "motion, shaping, and transformation" of the motives more than in passages such as this. The continuity in question is one in which, apart from occasional references to c amid several pockets of A♭ (that is, the keys associated with death in acts 1 and 2), there are virtually no lasting tonal centers. From here to the end of the *Tagesgespräch* Wagner changes key signature frequently, sometimes writing verbal key designations above the solos in the compositional draft (and occasionally inaccurately).[5] His chief concern is not with exact key definition, except for the process of transition that centers on the emergence of A♭. Centering on A♭, E, and C, Wagner's key signatures and key designations identify flat, sharp, and natural tonal regions more than particular keys, except in the case of A♭. E major never appears at all, whereas C is fleeting at best. But Wagner's relating the enharmonic shifting to both the flat/sharp juxtaposition within the first-act death motive and the latent enharmonicism of the desire music—symbols of the lovers' reflection back on the concluding events of act 1—causes the tonal character of this part of the work to suggest the merging of death and desire within the framework of night, the poetic idea that eventually brings forth the new death motive and the A♭ of "O sink hernieder."

With the a♭ cadence of Isolde's solo Wagner changes to sharp notation, beginning Tristan's response on g♯ (in four sharps and headed "E dur" in the compositional draft). Tristan now recalls his realization that the drink of reconciliation Isolde offered him was poison. And from this point until the end of the *Tagesgespräch* one hundred measures later Wagner retains the idea of close enharmonic shifting as the analog of Tristan's acceptance of Isolde's plan of death. The center of the enharmonic wavering is, of course, the pitch class G♯/A♭, which may move upward to A (as in the first phrase of the desire music) or down to G (as in the second phrase). When G♯ alternates with A it is mostly to evoke the sense of desire and day, remembered from act 1; when it alternates with or moves to G (the dominant of c), it is to recall the role of C minor as key of death in act 1. Within this densely leitmotivic and largely atonal span Wagner intermingles recollections of act 1 with anticipations of the point at which the attainment of night and its key, A♭, will finally become complete, in the duet "O sink hernieder." Thus, Tristan's G♯ holds as a pedal tone for most of the first half of his twenty-five-measure solo, alternating briefly with A, as he recounts his initial insight into the meaning of Isolde's talk of atonement, then changes enharmonically to A♭ as he proclaims the dawning of night within his breast as the result of that insight. Along with the change Wagner shifts from melodic variation of the pitches of the desire music to the melodic beginning of "O sink hernieder," a linear

Tristan chord. Nevertheless, the harmony settles on the G♯ Tristan chord, associated with the death motive and the key of c, and moves slowly to the dominant of the latter key as Tristan proclaims that with the drinking of the love-death potion his "day was now finished" ("Mein Tag war da vollbracht"), making a melodic cadence to c.

In numerous such intricate relationships Wagner creates a flow of music in which the enharmonic shifting aligns closely with the opposition of day and night, moving out of and back to the four-flat key signature and its close association with A♭. In Isolde's response to Tristan's c cadence Wagner continues to weave a closely knit web of associational leitmotivic relations, including a still more intimate merging of the desire music with the death motive of the first act. As Tristan extolls the power of the love-death potion, Wagner transposes the desire music up a minor third so that the deceptive cadence—now to A♭ instead of F—sets up the most substantial of the several anticipations of "O sink hernieder" in the *Tagesgespräch,* one in which virtually every harmony is enharmonically related to those of the preceding and following sharp-notated passages. Toward the close of this solo the desire music begins over again, now at pitch and in association with the *Nachtsicht* that Tristan claims came to him through the love-death potion. Moving toward another C minor close, it is deceived by A♭, as Isolde, pointing out that day took its revenge (see the passage cited earlier), moves by major third transposition through E toward C major with continual merging of the deceptive cadence, the day motive, and the Minne theme.

Throughout the music that follows from Isolde's reference to the "end of deception" the pitch e♭″ reappears in the vocal lines continually, drawing the surrounding pitches into its sphere, above all in conjunction with combinations of the day and desire motives. Tristan's final solo returns over and again to the e♭″ until the shift at "Tages täuschenden Schein." After that, however, Isolde's "Doch es rächte sich der verscheuchte Tag" gives stability to e″ rather than e♭″ by sounding it on "Tag" within the major-seventh chord on C and repeatedly thereafter to both that harmony and to the major-seventh chord on F. The latter harmony finally mimics the deceptive cadence of the desire music as Isolde makes the fifth descent from e″ to a′ that ends the *Tagesgespräch.*

The impulse to clarify the design of the love scene by cutting this kind of music was certainly misguided and destructive to Wagner's intentions, as he complained regarding the cuts made to the part of *Tannhäuser* that most exemplified his art of transition. In fact, Wagner's aural symbolism is perfectly clear at all times. The continual enharmonic shifting reinterprets the lovers' memory of the dramatic conflicts leading to the drinking of the love-death potion in terms of their present intuition of a deeper union. Wagner represents Frau Minne's enharmonic weaving of opposites into a reality that is only imperfectly captured by the key signatures and designations—symbols of vision and names—by the alignment of references to day and night with those key signature changes, and even by the very key allusions themselves. I have described the events of the *Tagesgespräch* as a narrative rather than a structure, for the purpose of conveying a sense of how much Wagner invests in the idea of form as transition rather than a visual diagram. Its most striking feature is the emergence of A♭ from the process of continual enharmonic shifting. Nevertheless, gestures such as the return of C in Isolde's final solo prompted Alfred Lorenz to assert that the first half of the love scene was a closed series of periods centered on

C, beginning in C (the first duet), articulating the dominant at the center (the G of Tristan's two strophes in the solo "Was dich umgliss mit hehrster Pracht"), and returning to the C/a relationship at the end. There is, in fact, some truth to this statement. But not of the kind Lorenz intended. Wagner's pejorative remarks on visual metaphors for form—such as symmetry and architectural analogs—make clear that he viewed such conceptions as manifestations of the error behind his sword metaphor: that is, as the worship of music's purely static aspect ("swords without blades") and the failure to grasp its true dynamic nature. Whereas in some instances, such as the "great overture to Leonore," Beethoven had sacrificed the idea and its need for ongoing development to the formal conception, Wagner sets up the *Tagesgespräch* as a mirror of the dominance of the idea over the form.[6] That idea is the emergence of night and the key of A♭ from a background of highly transitional enharmonic relationships that exist within the hollow formal framework of day.

The extensive enharmonicism of the second half of the *Tagesgespräch* is entirely bound up with the A♭/G♯ enharmonicism of the desire music, whose far-reaching implications Wagner realizes in conjunction with the lovers' reinterpretation of the meaning of the love-death potion. Isolde's cadence at "schimmernd dort zu leben" is a symbolic representation of the deceptiveness of the union between desire and day. In response, Tristan's dramatic introduction of the Tristan chord beneath his melodic a♭″ on "O nun waren wir *Nachtgeweihte*" now makes the point that the lovers' conception of night involves a merging of desire and longing for death. From consecration to death, then to the deception of desire and day, consecration to night becomes their goal. The change from the first to the second death motive, at the end of the solo, is its symbol.

Throughout Tristan's solo, Wagner continues the focus on the pitches G♯ and A♭ that ran through the latter part of the *Tagesgespräch*. In Isolde's final solo, G♯ was subordinate to the deceived A minor cadence; in Tristan's "Nachtgeweihte" it changed to A♭. Now Tristan's closing lines—"In des Tages eitlem Wähnen bleibt ihm ein einzig Sehnen,—das Sehnen hin zur heil'gen Nacht, wo urewig, einzig wahr, Liebeswonne ihm lacht" (In the vain delusions of day there remains for him only one longing,— longing for the sacred night, where the only primal, eternal truth, love's bliss, smiles on him)—initiate a sixteen-measure stretch in which the pitch class A♭/G♯ sounds continuously through a series of changing harmonies that encompass the torch motive and the first appearances of the second death motive followed by the beginning of the desire music. The three Tristan chords of the new death motive and the desire music, all of which contain G♯/A♭, symbolize the enharmonic interweaving of the various sharp and flat harmonies as the analog of the night that the lovers long for, while the continually sounding A♭/G♯ mirrors the idea that desire as longing for night reduces to this single pitch, soon to become the key of "O sink hernieder."

In the passage as a whole Wagner leads the desire music into three motives associated with death: the first death motive, the torch motive, and the new death motive. In this process, the torch motive bridges between the first and second death motives. Its diminished-seventh chord harmony binds the broader sequences of harmonies, revealing its background functioning and the tone it shares with the other harmonies and motifs—A♭/G♯—as the analog of the single longing to which desire reduces. Instead of the kind of A♭/G♯ and A alternation of the latter part of the

Tagesgespräch, Wagner emphasizes enharmonic flat/sharp equivalence centered on A♭/G♯, after which the shift from A to A♭ in the transition to "O sink hernieder" vividly projects the poetic meaning behind the entire process: G♯ as longing for night and A♭ as its attainment. With the close association of the new death motive and the desire music Wagner begins a rising line above the dominant of A, closely mimicking one that had sounded over the dominant of A♭ seventeen measures earlier. At its peak, the A♭/G♯ is resolved by the transfiguration music in A, after which it becomes the tonal center of "O sink hernieder." Within the duet, the A/A♭ succession reappears in the transposing sequences of the "Barg im Busen" theme, beginning the second part of the duet and, finally, at the climax of the duet, where the A no longer has independent existence.

Additionally, from the first appearance of the first phrase of the desire music, two measures before "Wer des Todes Nacht liebend erschaut," the bass settles on the pitches F and E; and for twenty measures the only bass notes are F, E, and F♯. E♭ enters in the bass when the second phrase of the desire music shifts to the dominant of A♭, and A♭/G♯ appears after that at the start of the above-mentioned sixteen-measure passage. Wagner keeps the bass tones f♯, f, e, and e♭, in our ears in preparation for the wonderful point in the transition to "O sink hernieder" when the bass f♯ gives way to the entrance of the syncopated rhythm in the bass tones f, f♭, and e♭, the descending chromaticism of the desire music now directed unequivocally toward A♭. As the pitch a′ changes to a♭′ in the melody above these tones, the day motive, sounding like the desire music, aids in articulating, successively, the sounds of the Tristan chord on f, the major seventh chord and the dominant seventh on f♭, in preparation for the arrival on the dominant of A♭. Simultaneously the tempo and meter change to the new much slower framework of the *Nachtgesang*.

In all this, we have a musical allegory of how desire reduces to its primal form for the lovers. The chromatic f♯, f, e, e♭ descent can be interpreted as shift from the sixth to the flat-sixth to the dominant of A then to the dominant of A♭. At the climax of "O sink hernieder" Wagner adds this element to the death motive in the uppermost register—f♯‴, f‴, e‴, e♭‴—as the harmony and voice leading converge on the dominant of A♭. Now the harmony of the desire music, spelled as usual as if it were in A, articulates the flat sixth of A♭ before giving way to the dominant.

Night, Death, Oneness

The character of "O sink hernieder" is bound up with all that I have just described, its A♭ tonality one of the most remarkable points of arrival in the opera. As a whole, it creates the sense not of an A♭ structure that is built up from the articulation of contrast tonal centers and the principle of departure and return—that is, modulation—but of an A♭ that is so all-embracing—self-enclosed—that nothing can challenge its centrality. Tonal structure in this movement is simply the ability of the A♭ tonic key to draw everything that might be potentially contradictory into its folds. Beginning and ending with eighteen measures of A♭ pedal, of which eight comprise the four pairs of chords that Wagner took over from his setting of Mathilde Wesendonk's poem *Träume*, the first of its two sections simply articulates the tonic and

dominant with extended pedal points between which the bass moves entirely by
scalar motion: A♭ (eighteen mm.), scalar descent from a♭ to E♭ (ten mm.), e♭ (two
mm.), A♭ (eight mm.), E♭ (four mm.). There is no motion away from A♭, even
though the one transitional passage introduces many enharmonically notated sharp
harmonies. Above the scalar descent from tonic to dominant in the bass the uppermost orchestral line describes a simple scalar ascent to the tonic, which holds as an
inverted a♭‴ pedal in the violins through the eight measure tonic pedal in the bass
before the half close that ends the section. At the outset the slow-moving dream
chords settle on six-five appoggiaturas over the tonic pedal (ex. 11.4). For the ten-
measure transition, Wagner reintroduces the day motive; and with the return of the
tonic pedal the day motive merges into the six-five appoggiatura pattern, first with
the minor sixth alternating with the dominant, then at the cadence with the major
sixth moving simultaneously at different rates of speed to the dominant. The broad
half close with its f″–e♭″ appoggiatura is one of the most satisfying moments in the
opera, proclaiming the dissolving of the world into night: "heil'ger Dämm'rung
hehres Ahnen löscht des Wähnens Graus *welterlösend aus*" (may noble intimation of
holy twilight dissolve the terror of delusion, *redeeming the world*).

The second segment of the duet might seem, perhaps, to modulate, because it
transposes its successive phrases upward by semitones beginning from A♭ as the
lovers equate their absorption in one another with the dawning of an inner light to
replace the now-dissolved external world. The rising sequences, six measures at first,
shrink to two as the keys allusions turn more and more into upward transposing sequences outlining an ascent from A♭ and A to B♭ and C♭, then C and D♭, the flat-sixth
of each "key" becoming the dominant of the next (ex. 11.5). And with the arrival of
the dominant of D in the bass Wagner reaches up the sixth to f, then f♭, to suggest
the beginning of the desire music. The day motive reappears in the uppermost orchestral lines at the pitch associated throughout the *Tagesgespräch* with Isolde's "end
of deception," the bass passes down through the tonic triad from dominant to tonic,

Example 11.4. Act 2, scene 2: the dream chords of "O sink hernieder" (and the song
"Träume")

Example 11.5. Act 2, scene 2: beginning of the second section of "O sink hernieder"

and beneath the ascending tones of the desire music—ab″, a″, bb″, cb‴—Wagner sounds a series of chromatically rising diminished-seventh chords ("selbst dann bin ich die Welt"). Out of the last of these, on "Welt," the Tristan chord emerges to initiate the events that complete the symbolic confirmation of Ab as key of night (ex. 11.6). The duet ends, as it began, with eighteen measures of Ab pedal, eight of which are the dream chords.

In effect, the second part of "O sink hernieder" is simply a chromatically ascending curve from Ab to the reappearance of the beginning of the desire music as if in A, but of course *not*, because it is immediately absorbed back into Ab. So long as no other key becomes established—which is the case here—we cannot speak of modulation or tonal structure in the usual sense, but simply an articulation, or prolongation, of the tonic. As in the prelude to the opera, the illusion of motion away from the tonic turns back on itself. In "O nun waren wir Nachtgeweihte" the pitch class

Example 11.6. Act 2, scene 2: day and desire combined; from the climax of "O sink hernieder"

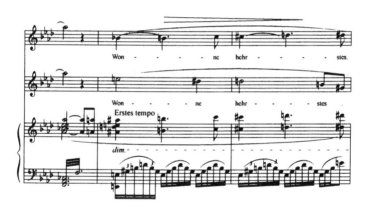

A♭/[G♯], appearing continuously in the diminished-seventh chord, the Tristan chord, the dominant of A and a host of other harmonies, suggests the fleeting nature of existence, wavering and fading along with the momentary tonal centers. In "O sink hernieder" A♭ remains secure because of the absence of any other key; the conflict and drama of the physical world—the motives for key change in Wagner's aesthetics—are no longer present.

"O sink hernieder" can certainly be described as a set piece, its principal motives and pedal points articulating not only the priority of A♭ and E♭, but doing so in phrase units that are nearly always multiples of two (two- four- eight- and eighteen-measure pedals). In this respect, the duet compares with Wagner's most fluid piece, the prelude to *Das Rheingold*, which, despite its poetic subject matter, is built up from units based on multiples of two; in the compositional draft Wagner even used repeat signs to indicate the units. Both "O sink hernieder" and the Prelude to *Das Rheingold* balance their periodic and their transitional aspects for poetic purposes.

In the Prelude, the gradual rhythmic diminution and orchestral expansion create the effect of seamless fluid unfolding, an analog of the emergence of the world from a single point of origin. The underlying regularity of the points of change is perfectly suited to the "multiplying" character of the world itself. "O sink hernieder" suggests the reverse, the narrowing of the lovers' world to the inner dream of love and night.

As is often mentioned, the beginning vocal line of the duet describes the tones of the Tristan chord in a slow ascent. At the end of the phrase, as Tristan reaches the word "Liebe," the first of the dream chords settles on a vertical presentation of the Tristan chord, with one very important difference: the addition of the tone D♭. But that difference renders it into a D♭ dominant harmony whose potential tendency toward G♭ lends a languid character to the beginning of the duet. Although Wagner does not develop the G♭ tendency within the duet, at the end he turns the tonic harmony into the dominant of D♭ (A♭⁷), then, after eight concluding measures in which the lovers drift into an alliterative dreamlike use of language—"Niewiedererwachen's wahnlos holdbewusster Wunsch"—he brings back the dream chords (from the word "Wunsch," an echo of Gottfried's description of the lovers' cave scene as a *Wunschleben*), this time continuing the tendency toward G♭ as the ending of the duet merges into Brangaene's first warning solo.

The poetic idea behind Brangaene's solo, which has been traced in concept to the medieval *aubade*, is a warning of the coming day while it is still night.[7] Wagner uses the day motive as the basis of her melody, augmenting its rhythm so as to suggest a cantus-firmus-like line that floats above the events below, and transposing it by step from its initial d♭" (c♯") through d" and e", to f♯". Tonally, Brangaene's solo is occupied with the gradual emergence of f♯ (g♭) at the same time that it develops several of the melodic components of "O sink hernieder," slowing them down enormously as the quasi-impressionistic harmonies depict her trancelike reflection on the lovers' state of mind. At the end of "O sink hernieder" the dominant of G♭ in the first pair of dream chords prepares the series of increasingly prominent arrivals on the dominant of f♯ in Brangaene's solo, the first of which coincides with the completion of her "Einsam wachend in der Nacht, wem der Traum der Liebe lacht" (Watching alone in the night, on whom the dream of love smiles). At this point, Wagner brings back the "Barg im Busen" melody from "O sink hernieder," following it in turn by a version of the love's peace motive that is closer to its final form than that of the duet. Eventually the day motive dies out and Brangaene's concluding warning takes on a blissful, transcendent character as the "Barg im Busen" line ascends toward a broad articulation of the subdominant with distinct overtones of the transfiguration music. After this dissolves into the sounds of Tristan chords and from there into the final three-measure arrival on the dominant of f♯, we hear the event Wagner has been anticipating: the entrance of the love's peace motive in G♭, articulating the next stage in the lovers' progress toward transcendence, pacification of the will and longing for death.

In describing his intention of "erecting a monument to this most beautiful of dreams" and in referring to the beginning and ending emotions of the love scene as "pillars" Wagner may not have been thinking primarily of metaphors for structure; but, as has long been recognized, in the love scene from "O sink hernieder" on Wagner's groupings of the dialogues and duets create a sense of overall formal design.

We might even sense that, in addition to the metaphoric gate and door that Wagner retained in the text of *Tristan* as printed during his lifetime, something of the architectural analogs that underlie the religion of love in Gottfried von Strassburg's lovers' cave scene operate in Wagner's love scene as well.

Alfred Lorenz was the first to pursue the idea that the part of the love scene from "O sink hernieder" to the transition into "O ew'ge Nacht" could be viewed as a symmetry of two main sections (*Hauptsätze*) framing a central one (*Mittelsatz*). In that view there were two parallel movement sequences, each involving a duet in A♭ ("O sink hernieder" and "So stürben wir," respectively), followed by a warning from Brangaene (called *Wachtgesang* by Lorenz), then by sequences of parallel dialogues in which the roles of the lovers were reversed from the first to the second, Tristan singing what Isolde had before, and vice versa (*Morgenlied*). After these parallel dialogues the correspondences between Lorenz's two *Hauptsätze* do not continue. But Lorenz noted that Wagner had deleted the first fourteen lines of the original transition to the duet "O ew'ge Nacht" (they had been retained in the printed text of the opera), and that the first four of those lines paralleled to some degree the four that followed the parallel dialogue passages in the first *Hauptsatz*. He therefore hypothesized that Wagner had originally intended a symmetrical design that he altered during the composition of the scene when he realized that the *Hauptsätze* were too long in relation to the *Mittelsatz*.[8] The original centerpiece was to have been the lovers' dialogue on the word "and," which, as mentioned in chapter 3, was probably inspired by Gottfried von Strassburg's leaving out the word "and" in the lines "Tristan Isolt, Isolt, Tristan" in his prolog, the beginning of his famous acrostic of the lovers' names. Although Lorenz did not bring out this last point, it is a felicitous one, suggesting that Wagner's reversal of the lovers' roles between the first and second of the near-identical dialogue sequences that follow Brangaene's two warnings were formed in response to Gottfried's use of rhetorical devices such as chiasmus as symbols of the lovers' union. Because the dialogues in question comprised a transposing sequence of parallel units formed from the love's peace motive and the second death motive (three in the first *Hauptsatz*, three in the second), and because the latter motive ran throughout the scene, eventually culminating in the phrase "sehnend verlangter Liebestod," it is distinctly possible that Wagner was inspired not only by Gottfried's lovers' cave scene but by his prolog as well (in which both the omission of "and" and the expression *Liebestod* originated).

In his single-minded search for symmetry, Lorenz claimed that Wagner had reconceived the boundaries of his principal and secondary sections, so that lines of text that were originally paralleled by the deleted transition became part of the *Mittelsatz* rather than the first *Hauptsatz*. In this way Wagner improved the proportions of the three segments, creating a further symmetry involving the afore-mentioned time-signature shifts within the *Mittelsatz* itself (see fig. 11.1). The dialogue on "and" was now to be thought of as the center of the three solos of the *Mittelsatz*, its A♭/D♭ tonality and triple meter preceded and followed by segments in sharp-key regions in quadruple meter, both marked *sehr ruhig*. In support of Lorenz's scheme, it may be pointed out that the beginnings of the two flanking segments of the *Mittelsatz* are built on pedal points on A and E, respectively, their thematic material derived from the beginning and ending of the love's peace motive in straight eighth-note sequences. In ad-

Figure 11.1. Symmetrical diagram of the text of the love scene from "O sink hernieder" through the transition to "O ew'ge Nacht"; based on a diagram in Lorenz, *Das Geheimnis* (p. 181), and expanded to include the full text of the dialogue passages. The enclosed passage was composed by Wagner in the first draft but deleted from the final version. Brackets indicate the major textual and musical correspondences.

Hauptsatz	Mittelsatz	Hauptsatz
"O sink hernieder" (A♭ duet)		"So stürben wir" (A♭ duet)

Hauptsatz	Mittelsatz	Hauptsatz
Brangaene's first warning		Brangaene's second warning
I: Lausch' Geliebter		T: Soll ich lauschen?
T: Laß mich sterben.		I: Laß mich sterben.
I: Neid'sche Wache!		T: Muß ich wachen?
T: Nie erwachen!		I: Nie erwachen!
I: Doch der Tag muß Tristan wecken?		T: Soll der Tag noch Tristan wecken?
T: Laß den Tag dem Tode weichen?		I: Laß den Tag dem Tode weichen!
I: Tag und Tod mit gleichen Streichen sollten uns're Lieb erreichen!		T: Sol der Tod mit seinen Streichen ewig uns den Tag verscheuchen?
T: Uns're Liebe? Tristans Liebe? Dein' und mein' Isoldes Liebe? Welches Todes Streichen Könnte je sie weichen? Stünd' er vor mir der mächt'ge Tod, wie er mir Leib und Leben bedroht. die ich so willig der Liebe lasse, wie wäre seinen Streichen die Liebe selbst zu erreichen? Stürb' ich nun ihr der so gern ich sterbe, wie könnte die Liebe mit mir sterben! Die ewig lebende mit mir enden? Doch, stürbe nie seine Liebe, wie stürbe dann Tristan seiner Liebe?	I: Doch uns're Liebe, heißt sie nicht Tristan und—Isolde? Dies süße Wörtlein: und, was es bindet, der Liebe Bund, wenn Tristan stürb' zerstört' es nicht der Tod? T: Was stürbe dem Tod, als was uns stört, was Tristan wehrt, Isolde immer zu lieben, ewig ihr zu leben? I: Doch dieses Wörtlein: und— wär' es zerstört, wie anders als mit Isoldes eignem Leben wär' Tristan der Tod gegeben?	I: Der uns vereint den ich dir bot, laß' ihm uns weih'n, dem süßen Tod! Mußte er uns das eine Thor, an dem wir standen, verschließen: zu der rechten Thür die uns Minne erkor, hat sie den Weg nun gewiesen. T: Des Tages Dräuen trotzten wir so? I: Seinen Trug ewig zu fliehn. T: Sein dämmernder Schein verscheuchte uns nie? I: Ewig währ uns die Nacht!

dition, the lead-in to "O sink hernieder," to the A♭ beginning of the central solo on the word "and," and to the duet "So stürben wir" all feature the death motive at the same pitch, setting up pedal points on the dominant of A♭ in each instance. Also, culminating the solo on "and," Isolde sings the love's peace motive, the only time it is ever sung, to the words "was es bindet, der Liebe Bund," after which her continuation "wenn Tristan stürb' zerstört' es nicht der Tod?" brings in the poison motive in the bass, dissolving the tonality (and the motive) for the ensuing quadruple-meter segment. These gestures all give considerable symbolic import to the idea of a central dialogue.

Furthermore, had Lorenz consulted the compositional draft he would have found that Wagner's setting of the first four lines of the deleted transition paralleled those of their earlier counterpart to approximately the same degree as did the texts themselves; that is, they were not identical but based on the same material. And the conjunction of the two death motives in that transition had a parallel in the dialogue that followed the first *Hauptsatz*, where the second death motive sounds (twice) to "Welches Todes Streichen könnte je sie weichen?" (Could the blows of death ever weaken it?), followed after one measure by the first death motive "[Stünd' er vor mir der mächt'ge] Tod, wie er mir Leib und Leben bedroht" (If mighty death stood before me, threatening life and limb).

In other words, a considerable case can be made for Lorenz's symmetrical scheme, which unquestionably captures a good deal of what is present. Yet, at the same time, it passes over so much that is vitally important to understanding the love scene that it must virtually be judged erroneous. Correspondences, rhymed parallels, even symmetry are all certainly part of Wagner's means of creating what he called the "clarity over an expanse that encompasses every detail," in the love scene and elsewhere. But they represent no more than a part of what is actually going on, and not the most important part. Wagner could not have deleted most of the original transition to "O ew'ge Nacht" in order to create a more balanced symmetry with the first *Hauptsatz*, for he deleted both textual and musical correspondences that might have clarified the symmetry. And the proportions in the final version are by no means equal. As Lorenz admitted, Brangaene's second warning is a mere eleven measures in relation to the original forty-eight, whereas "O sink hernieder" is nearly twice as long, in timing and in measure numbers, as "So stürben wir." For this reason it must be seriously doubted that the parallels in figure 11.1 constitute the best way of understanding the form of this part of the love scene. "O sink hernieder" is in many respects the culmination of all those points in the *Tagesgespräch* where Wagner anticipates not only the key of A♭ but also the music of the duet. From this standpoint, we might consider that the A♭ duets represent end rather than beginning points; and if this is so, then the idea of symmetry is incidental. In this view, the second *Hauptsatz* was compressed so as to bring out the sense of urgency in the motion toward the final duet, a quality that is further emphasized in the final version by the threefold increase in tempo markings from the transition to the beginning of the duet.

Once again, two viewpoints are possible, the one relying on static correspondences and the other exhibiting a more dynamic, transitional nature. The crux of the matter is the disparity between a visual diagram and the auditory experience, especially since Wagner was unusually sensitive to the difference between the two. In fact, that very sensitivity may reflect his awareness of the tendency toward periodicity and toward reliance on extramusical motivations in his works. Certainly, an important aspect of his development as a composer is his struggle to overcome those qualities that he viewed as external, among which symmetry and periodicity were perhaps the most prominent. The deleted transition to "O ew'ge Nacht" is a case in point; Wagner's original transition was far more dependent on leitmotif processes than the final one, which forms part of a larger motion that reaches back to the dialogue following "So stürben wir" and spans the beginning of the duet.

The main theme of the dialogue that comes between the two duets and warnings, the love's peace motive, provides another instance of the role of periodicity and transition in Wagner's work. The fact that the dialogue eventually deviates from the slow triple meter of the love scene is in large part because of its origins. As Robert Bailey has shown, the love's peace motive was one of the earliest passages that Wagner composed for *Tristan*, passing through several stages of elaboration and revision nearly a year before Wagner began the compositional draft.[9] It originated as a periodic structure in $\frac{4}{4}$ meter, fully qualifying for the epithet "quadratic construction" in that it began with an antecedent/consequent sequence of two two-measure phrases ending on the dominant and the tonic respectively. Associated at that point with the lines "Sink' hernieder Nacht der Liebe, nimm mich auf in deinen Schoss," it represented the sinking of night prosaically by means of the falling third and diminished fifth with which it begins ("hernieder"). And beautiful as the basic melodic idea was, it was severely constricted by the *Tannhäuser*-like multiplication of its two-measure units, not only in the original antecedent/consequent pairing but also in their immediate extension to a further two closing again in the tonic, and then to yet another pair that, although "modulating" upward from G to A♭ and B♭, retained the beginning melodic pattern of the preceding four phrases with little variation. After that the final phrases extended the form as a whole to eighteen rather than the expected sixteen measures, but this did little to alter the quadratic character of the whole.

In the end what survived of this version of the motive was the first four tones of the melody, their rhythm retained but their meter altered from quadruple to triple, some of the harmony and the development of the motive in later phrases, and the ascending semitone transposition pattern of the fifth and sixth phrases, which Wagner adopted in "O sink hernieder" in conjunction with the "Barg im Busen" melody instead. Its original quadruple meter, now syncopated against the bass, completes the equivalent of its original two-measure phrase on the second beat of its third measure. From that point until the beginning of its fifth measure (i.e., the first four-measure phrase) the melodic character dissipates. From the fifth measure, Wagner returns to the beginning of its second phrase, but instead of continuing with a parallel phrase, he reiterates the initial one-measure unit three times (slightly modified) before continuing, again in syncopated rhythm, to the point where the first phrase can start over again in the same key, G♭. As if to compensate for the lack of continuation, on its second presentation Wagner substitutes the second death motive for its second phrase, thereby shutting off the melodic impulse. The love's peace motive itself always leads into a rising, hopeful-sounding line that the death motive turns around with its chromatic descending cadential motion to a dominant-seventh chord. This combination, now comprising four plus three measures, serves as the basis of the threefold ascending-whole-tone transposition pattern that follows, leading to cadences on the dominant-sevenths of F, G, and A.[10]

The pairing of the love's peace motive with the second death motive in these phrases is a metaphor for the interaction of periodicity and transition in the love scene. The aesthetics of beauty, associated by Wagner with periodicity, underlies the character of the love's peace motive and its association with union, whereas its dissolving into the death motive in the dialogue phrases, like its dissolution by the poison motive later in the scene, undermines those qualities. When the poison motive dissolves the tonality of Isolde's reference to the bond of love, Tristan counters with the idea that death can destroy only that which keeps Tristan from loving Isolde eternally; and Isolde responds that with the destruction of the word "and" Tristan could not be given to death unless Isolde died. Referring to themselves in the third person, Tristan and Isolde now view the word "and," the bond symbolized in the love's peace motive, as what separates rather than joins them, in Schopenhauerian terms the bond of phenomenality. The dialogue in question wavers back and forth between flat and sharp regions settling at its close on the dominant of A♭ for the duet "So stürben wir." The wavering is another instance of the separateness of events in the physical world, the word "and" as a form of joining that Tristan rejects. Death, the undermining of such illusions, is the outcome. "So stürben wir" poeticizes the idea that the lovers will die united, nameless but enclosed by love, given solely to each other and living for love alone. The contradictory character of its text conveys the lovers' struggle to grasp the idea of metaphysical oneness in intellectual terms, something that both Schopenhauer and Wagner described as impossible.

In response to Brangaene's first warning, Tristan and Isolde turn more and more to the emotion Wagner described as the goal ("pillar") of the love scene, "the most sincere and heartfelt longing for death." Wagner appends the death motive to the love's peace motive to accompany Tristan's responses to Isolde: "Lass' mich sterben," "Nie erwachen," and "Lass den Tag dem Tode weichen!" And these three phrases, transposing up by successive whole tones, and closing with dominant seventh chords on C, D, and E, completely obliterate the G♭ tonality with which the segment began. After Tristan's "Lass den Tag dem Tode weichen," Isolde's momentary A minor gives way to what will turn out to be a form of E minor for Tristan's extended solo, "Uns're Liebe? Tristans Liebe," the beginning of Lorenz's *Mittelsatz*. Wagner introduces its key signature along with the first change to $\frac{4}{4}$, and he articulates all three principal cadence points in Tristan's solo with half closes in e. The last of these coincides with the return to $\frac{3}{4}$ and it leads immediately to the dominant of A♭ in preparation for Isolde's introduction of the word "and."

At the point just described and again at the end of this dialogue sequence Wagner introduces the death motive to set up the dominant of A♭ (as he had in "O sink hernieder"). These two points mark the principal references to the lovers' deaths before "So stürben wir." At the first one, a half close in e and at the second the dominant of A give way to the dominant of A♭. Common to both points is the reinterpretation of the pitch e″ as f♭″ in preparation for its descent to e♭″. In the earlier solo Wagner underscores the descent by introducing the chromatic descent of the death motive at the pitch level g″, f♯″, f″, e″, following it by the diatonic E minor descent g″, f♯″, e″, d♯″ (which appears at all three E minor half closes in Tristan's solo), before reiterating the death motive at its usual pitch level: f♯″, f″, f♭″, e♭″. In fact, throughout this sequence of solos Wagner centers many of the most prominent voice-leading events around the pitches e″ and e♭″, using the series of transpositions of the phrase that combines the love's peace and death motives to set up the e″ (with the E⁷ chord on "Lass den Tag dem Tode weichen"). The sequence of keys is far less significant than this process, which finally reaches its goal in "So stürben wir." Wagner articulates the arrivals on A♭, not by means of extended tonal preparation or modulation through closely related keys—that is, not with the traditional devices by which tonic arrivals are rendered momentous—but by means of pitches that can be enharmonically reinterpreted—principally e″/d♯″ as f♭″/e♭″—so as to bind the disparate tonal regions into a continuity.

After "So stürben wir" Wagner curtails Brangaene's warning and transposes both it and the repeated dialog passages up a semitone, leading the latter directly into the transition to "O ew'ge Nacht." The shift from A♭ to G as Brangaene's second warning enters, overlapped with the ending of "So stürben wir," changes the pitch e♭″ from the dominant of A♭ to the flat-sixth of G, from which Wagner reintroduces the earlier dialogue sequence a semitone higher than its earlier G♭. Its transposing phrases now end with dominant-seventh chords on C♯, E♭, and F, the last one leading on to B♭ for the transition to "O ew'ge Nacht." Because of the transposition of the second dialogue sequence up a semitone in relation to the first, as well as to the internal whole-tone transposition pattern within each sequence, the death motive transposes to six pitch levels, providing, as mentioned earlier, all twelve Tristan chords, perhaps as an allegory of the permeation of the world—or, at least, the lovers' world apart—by the merging of desire and night that Wagner gives as the primary association for the death motive ("Das Sehnen hin zur heil'gen Nacht").

Within this obviously patterned design, suggesting the allegorical character of Gottfried's cave, however, there are elements whose ultimate trajectory leads outside the enclosed world of night and its association with A♭. The direction of that trajectory is upward, toward the B major of "O ew'ge Nacht." And Wagner provides us with several allegories of that upward motion, the most prominent being the way that the uppermost orchestral and vocal lines continually ascend from the dialogue sequence that follows "So stürben wir" to the A♭/B modulation in "O ew'ge Nacht." The harmony of "So stürben wir" adumbrates the A♭/B shift in the minor third transposition between its first and second phrases—beginning, respectively, in A♭ and C♭—whereas the dominant harmonies that end those phrases—on B♭ and C♯—taken along with the climactic D♯⁶₅ chord of its third phrase ending have the potential to articulate an arpeggiation of the dominant of B. Wagner introduces the B♭ and C♯ as keys in the transition to "O ew'ge Nacht," delaying the potential implication of a dominant arpeggiation until the arrival on F♯ within the duet. In the *Liebestod* his joining the music of "So stürben wir" to the B major music of "O ew'ge Nacht" fulfills this idea (see chapter 15).

Whether or not Lorenz was correct in viewing the two A♭ duets as the beginnings of two *Hauptsätze*, both "O sink hernieder" and "So stürben wir" convey the sense of a rising motion that begins from A♭. In "O sink hernieder" that sense emerges with the rising transpositions of the music associated with the internalizing of light: "Barg im Busen uns sich die Sonne." As the ascending motion continues, Wagner introduces a prefigured form of the love's peace motive, at "Herz an Herz dir, Mund an Mund; eines Atems ein'ger Bund." The sequence as a whole leads to the lovers' insight into the subjectivity of the world, projecting the idea that the inner light of transcendence is bound up with the lovers' increasing sense of oneness. And this idea dictated the rising transpositions of the day motive in Brangaene's first warning as well as the ascending transposition of the combinations of the love's peace and death motives in the two parallel segments and the transposition of the death motive by ascending semitones in the duet "O ew'ge Nacht." This last pattern—culminating in the word "Liebestod"—marks the point where the dream chords of "O sink hernieder" return, along with their A♭ tonality, then pass over into the music of "So stürben wir," now in B.

TWELVE

Tristan's Answer to King Mark

Moral and Philosophical Questions

IN THE EVENTS DESCRIBED at the end of the preceding chapter, what is most palpable to the listener is the tremendous sense of escalation as the final pages of the
love scene take on the character of preparation for a momentous event, the transfiguration music. Beginning with the transition into "O ew'ge Nacht," the tempo
quickens by stages, returning at the beginning of the duet to the $\frac{2}{2}$ *lebhaft mit Steigerung* of the ending of the first act and increasing still further within the duet itself.
Embodied in those gestures, of course, is the mounting ecstasy that forms a counterpart to Isolde's excited state of mind after extinguishing the torch. Capping the first
phrase of the transition, the B♭ transfiguration music is no longer overwhelmed by
the rapid rhythmic motion; nor does it stand apart from the prevailing direction of
the music, as its A major counterpart does in the transition to "O sink hernieder." Instead, the immediate transposition of the entire phrase to C♯ surges into the beginning of the duet, drawing the transfiguration music into the increasing momentum.

   As the voices unite for the initial two phrases, "O eternal night, sweet night! Nobly
sublime night of love" (O ew'ge Nacht, süsse Nacht! Hehr erhab'ne Liebesnacht!),
the death motive, now much broader in rhythm than before, echoes Isolde's move
to C♯ at the end of the transition—her "Ewig währ' uns die Nacht"—intensifying its
original association: longing for night and *Liebeswonne*. Converting the C♯ to a dominant harmony, it transposes immediately up a semitone to lead the resultant D
dominant harmony via a deceptive resolution to e. The impact of these gestures, by
hindsight at least, is to lend a subdominant quality to the e, which holds in the bass
for eight measures as a pedal E above which the first sounds of the dream chords
emerge: "The one whom you embrace, on whom you smile, how could he ever
awaken from you without dismay?" (Wen du umfangen, wem du gelacht, wie wär'
ohne Bangen aus dir er je gewacht?). After that, the duet makes its initial arrival
on the F♯ dominant pedal—"now banish the dismay, noble death" (nun banne das

Bangen, holder Tod)—out of which the final transposition of the death motive emerges as the lovers proclaim their goal: "sehnend verlangter Liebestod!"

What I have just described coincides with a powerful ascending motion of the vocal and orchestral lines towards the g♯‴ of "sehnend verlangter Liebestod," representing the lovers' attempt to lead their vision of transcendence to its fulfillment. Together that phrase and the immediately following reappearance of the dream chords of "O sink hernieder" in their original A♭ (now G♯) tonality—"In deinen Armen, dir geweiht, urheilig Erwarmen" (In your arms, consecrated to you, sacred, primal warmth)—transfer the G♯ to the lower register, where it serves as an eight measure pedal tone before passing through G to its goal, F♯, on "von Erwachen's Not befreit" (freed from the torment of awakening). At this point, the thematic material of "So stürben wir" takes over, in B, as the basis of the duet. And from here on the harmony has but one end: to articulate progressively stronger points of dominant arrival in preparation for the moment of transfiguration. Paralleling Schopenhauer's "path to salvation," the unfolding emotions of the love scene converge in "O ew'ge Nacht," representing the final trancelike state of the lovers' world apart as the entranceway to the world of dreams, eternal oneness, and night from which no awakening can take place. The motion to B major is its symbol.

But the fact that the lovers *do* awaken, that their enraptured state is so easily shattered at its peak by an external event, the arrival of King Mark and his party, is a very disturbing occurrence, calling everything they have attained into question. The musical relationships that bind the desire music, the honor music and the transfiguration music in "O ew'ge Nacht" affirm that in their ecstatic state Tristan and Isolde have come to understand the metaphysical character of desire, its bond with intrinsic honor. The transfiguration cadence emerges securely from the closely interrelated desire and honor music. Nevertheless, its sudden plummet downward through the diminished-seventh chord of the interruption breaks the spell completely. In contrast to the increasingly unified character of the music of the duet, what follows is a series of leitmotif references, entirely separate from one another, plugged in, as it were, for purely associative purposes in a perfect analog of the return of day and the dominance of the visual. The last of these is music carried forward from the solo that began the *Tagesgespräch*, where it accompanied Tristan's complaint against the waking day. Now it underscores Tristan's branding Mark and his party as nothing more than dreams and phantoms: "Tag'sgespenster! Morgenträume! täuschend und wüst!" (Daylight phantoms! Morning dreams! Deceptive and barren!). It is this that most cuts into King Mark. The slow stability of his extended solo and the inversion of the honor motive within its principal theme put the lovers' ecstasy in another perspective altogether.

With Tristan's words Wagner evokes Schopenhauer's dream theories, which distinguish two types of dreaming: the dream of deepest sleep, of which nothing can be remembered, and the "morning dream," which represents a translation of the deep dream into the terms of the waking world—Wagner's day—and, hence, a falsification. Wagner adopted Schopenhauer's dream theories both in *Tristan* and in *Die Meistersinger,* in the latter work treating the morning dream in terms of its value for artistic creativity: the prize song, named the "seelige Morgentraumdeutweise" by Sachs. In *Tristan,* however, the direction is opposite to that of *Die Meistersinger,* as indicated earlier; the goal of dreaming is *denial* of the world—eternal night and for-getfulness—not awakening to the world of day.

Forgetfulness, however, has two sides. As Gottfried describes it, the lovers' with-draw into the cave to forget the stories of tragic love that they read while outside. In-side, love and music-making are the order of the day; the cave is an inner harmony, the intimate communion of love, its physical and spiritual consummation, com-pletely apart from the vision-centered character of Mark's sexual desire for Isolde's beauty, which itself prevents his entrance.[1] For Wagner, forgetfulness is bound up with death from the beginning, as is evident in Tristan's "Vergessen's güt'ger Trank, dich trink ich sonder Wank" before drinking the love-death potion. For those who follow the path of adulterous love, yet wish to retain honor, death is the only escape. In "O sink hernieder" forgetfulness ("gib Vergessen, daß ich lebe") is complete with-drawal from the world of day and consecration to that of night and dreams. "O ew'ge Nacht" is its culmination, reiterating the word "ohne" eight times (before "Wähnen," "Bangen," "Wehen," "Schmachten," "Meiden," "Scheiden," "Nennen" and "Trennen"), at first transposing upward by semitones, then merging the motives of desire and honor as the harmony moves towards increasing reiteration of the domi-nant of B. More and more, the outside world is excluded from the mounting ecstasy, whereas honor and transfiguration become increasingly prominent.

The other perspective on forgetfulness is, of course, that in their isolation Tristan and Isolde withdraw into a world that is fundamentally solipsist, which is what under-lies Tristan's pronouncing Mark and his men mere dreams and phantoms. The lovers' world apart—the dream of love—has become self-centered; no one else matters. Having rejected honor as a manifestation of day in the *Tagesgespräch*, their merging it with desire in "O ew'ge Nacht" raises moral issues that resonate throughout Wag-ner's work as a whole. For, although *Tristan* is the work that is usually left aside when moral questions surrounding Wagner's work are examined—especially his anti-semitism—it is *Tristan* above all that provides the underpinning for the moral stance of the other works. The ahistorical perspective that Wagner felt reached its apex in *Tristan*, in asserting the fundamental oneness of all existence, runs the risk of equating that oneness with the author's own beliefs, to the exclusion of all differ-ence. Tristan's proclaiming honor a dream at the end of act 1 and his describing loy-alty and friendship a delusion (*Wahn*) in the original version of the solo before "O sink hernieder" converge on his reducing Mark and his party to mere morning dreams. Influenced, perhaps, by Gottfried's disquisition on the lovers' honor, and Mark's lack of it (and perhaps also by the critical reception of Gottfried's poem), Wagner reopens the question of honor for the purpose of confronting its extrinsic and intrinsic sides. The mixture of sorrow and reproach in Mark's response—"Mir dies? Dies, Tristan, mir? Wohin nun Treue, da Tristan mich betrog? Wohin nun Ehr' und ächte Art, da aller Ehren Hort, da Tristan sie verlor?" (This to me? This, Tristan, to me? Where now is loyalty, that Tristan has betrayed me? Where now honor and gen-uine chivalry, since the guardian of all honor, Tristan, has lost them?)—culminates in his question regarding the meaning of suffering and life's ultimate purpose. Tris-tan's answer is a focal point for the opera's moral stance.

Tristan's reference to King Mark and his men as "Tag'sgespenster" seems to echo directly a passage from Schopenhauer's essay *On the Basis of Morality*, in which the philosopher juxtaposes "the man who sees his own inner nature, his own true self, in all others, in fact in every living thing" to "the man to whom all others are invariably non-ego, and who in fact ultimately regards only his own person as truly real, looking upon others virtually only as phantoms, attributing to them only a relative existence insofar as they may be a means or an obstacle to his ends."[2] Schopenhauer draws a distinction between the fact that because of the "subjectivity essential to every consciousness, everyone is himself the whole world" and the abolishing of the "barrier between ego and non-ego" through compassion. Although he has proclaimed experience of the former in the "Selbst dann bin ich die Welt" of "O sink hernieder," Tristan has not attained the latter at the end of the love scene. And when we consider the lines Wagner deleted from two points in the compositional draft, it seems clear that in the original conception friendship and loyalty were problems for Tristan, as they appear to have been for Wagner himself as well.[3] In the lines deleted from "O nun waren wir Nachtgeweihte" (see chapter 4) we perceive that for Tristan metaphysical oneness (which in that version Wagner expresses by means of the enharmonic equivalence between the double references to the "tief Geheimnis") renders all else, even friendship, into a manifestation of day, just as Tristan later proclaims by branding King Mark and his party "Morgenträume."

Wagner's doubts about the value of friendship probably derived from Schopenhauer's series of essays "Aphorismen zur Lebensweisheit," in which the philosopher treats of "what a man is," "what a man has," and "what a man represents," a sequence whose direction is from the most internal and metaphysical qualities to the most external and representational.[4] In the last of these essays, Schopenhauer takes up all the qualities of honor, fame, rank, and the like, that Tristan rejects at the beginning of "O nun waren wir Nachtgeweihte" (whose virtual paraphrase of Schopenhauer's language has often been observed). In the second he treats friendship in like manner— as a possession. But in the first he addresses questions of personality and character, referring to his discussion of morality and compassion in the essay *On the Basis of Morality*. Had Wagner followed that lead, encountering passages such as those cited earlier, he might never have included Tristan's dismissal of friendship. Possibly, therefore, he had second thoughts that prompted its deletion at a later time, such as when he deleted the eight lines in which Tristan had characterized Melot as the agent of Minne, without real existence, without setting them to music.

But it is also possible that Wagner originally intended Tristan's including the illusion of friendship among the rejected the attributes of day in "O nun waren wir Nachtgeweihte" to form part of his progressive amendment of Schopenhauer—that is, to present Tristan as only gradually coming to understand the true meaning of night's "deep secret," as his original treatment of *Treu* and *Mitleid* in the prose draft suggests (chapter 4). In that view, Tristan's describing Mark and his men as "Tag'sgespenster" depicts his failure to come to terms with compassion, after which his increasing awareness of Mark's suffering initiates a change. It is supported by Wagner's stage directions, according to which Tristan "slowly sinks his eyes to the ground; as Mark continues, his demeanor expresses increasing grief." Also, as Wagner pointed out to Heinrich Porges, the principal motive of Mark's solo (which, as we know, contains an inversion of the honor motive), encompasses both Mark's good will (*Wohl-*

wollens) and *Tristan's* self-reproach (*Selbstvorwurfs*), the double-sidedness indicating the bond of compassion between them.[5]

Mark's final question culminates and universalizes his anguish: ""Die kein Himmel erlöst, warum mir diese Hölle? Die kein Elend sühnt, warum mir diese Schmach? Den unerforschlich tief geheimnisvollen Grund, wer macht der Welt ihn kund?" ("Since there is no redeeming heaven, why this hell for me? Since no misery brings atonement, why do I have this shame? The undiscoverably deep mysterious cause—who will reveal it to the world?"). His words are sometimes understood simply as his asking Tristan to explain his betrayal, and Tristan's answer as a refusal (presumably motivated by honor) to reveal the secret of the love potion.[6] In this view, the orchestra reveals a truth that would be cumbersome and unpoetic were it to be given in words. Tristan's answer, "O King, that I cannot tell you; and what you ask you can never experience" ("O König, das kann ich dir nicht sagen; und was du frägst, das kannst du nie erfahren"), is accompanied by a reprise of the desire music beginning, for the only time other than the prelude, with the note a rather than a♭. Because Mark's question ended on a, the desire music expresses an element of tonal continuity. Having answered (or failed to answer) Mark, Tristan turns to Isolde and the key of A♭, taking up the seemingly unrelated topic of his impending death in terms of whether Isolde will follow him into the realm of night, his true home. As befits the change of subject, the music is now entirely contrasted in its leitmotifs, meter and key (see ex. 5.4). Lorenz drew a period division at the point of the shift.

But if we allow any truth to Tristan's answer, such an explanation is inadequate, as indeed any careful reading of the poetry would suggest. Mark's question is an existential one, "Why does one suffer to no purpose?" The word "Grund" is a clear indication that he is thinking of a universal explanation for suffering, not merely the motive for Tristan's betrayal. His reference to the "tief geheimnisvollen Grund" of existence inevitably recalls the "tief Geheimnis" of night in "O nun waren wir Nachtgeweihte," the force that rendered friendship a delusion. Tristan's answer links the deep secret with another of Schopenhauer's principal ideas, namely, that in breaking with desire and our own egocentric tendencies we experience compassion, "the great mystery of ethics," "whose grounds cannot be discovered on the path of experience."[7] Tristan's words, "what you are seeking you can never experience," turn on the word "erfahren" (experience), which goes beyond intellectual knowledge. For Mark will, in fact, learn *about* the potion. At the end of the third act, Brangaene discloses that she has explained the secret of the potion to Mark, and Mark reveals with his forgiveness of the lovers (and his musical reprise of the music of Brangaene's consolation) the beneficial working of that knowledge on him.

But Tristan's conception, unlike Brangaene's, is a "philosophical" one. In fact, this segment offers the most concentrated presentation of Wagner's Schopenhauerian metaphysics in the opera, echoing not only a wide range of topics in Schopenhauer's writings but also a considerable number of passages from Wagner's letters and essays. King Mark's framing a question regarding the "tief geheimnisvollen Grund" with the word "Why" is significant (in the prose draft Mark repeats the word several times, ending his solo "Warum, Tristan? Warum mir das?").[8] In *Music of the Future*, written soon after *Tristan*, Wagner refers to the asking of the question "why" as an "in-

eradicable impulse" of the human mind when confronted with an "impressive phenomenon"; arising from "fear of the incomprehensible world," it throws the "perceptual faculties, bound to the laws of causality, into a state of confusion."[9] Wagner
links his own striving for inner rather than outer (causal) motivations in his poetic
texts to the attempt to transcend such questions; that process, as he says, reached its
apex in *Tristan*. Wagner's discussions are indebted, of course, to Schopenhauer, who
emphasizes that all metaphysical knowledge, expressed in the question "Why," is ultimately negative, beyond all experience.[10] In the context of the distinction between
the "ground" (*Grund*) of existence and that of "experience" (*Erfahrung*), Schopenhauer refers to the "ultimate secret of things" as contained in the actual, the "what"
as opposed to the "why" of existence, describing the "secret" as "unfathomable" and
"insoluble," the "content of the phenomenon which cannot be referred to its form,"
that form being equivalent to its external aspect, subject to the principle of sufficient
reason (*Grund*). The "being" or "true essence" of things, however, is "something to
which no ground can ever be assigned."[11] The "ground of being" is metaphysical
(Mark's "tief geheimnisvollen Grund"), whereas the "ground of knowledge," rooted
in the principle of sufficient reason, is phenomenal. The question "why," therefore,
has two forms. Considered in purely phenomenological terms, it can only refer to
causal or scientific explanations, subject to the principle of sufficient reason. As a
question regarding the first cause of existence (which is what Mark intends), it can
have no answer (Tristan's response to Mark). And it deflects humanity from the
deeper truths of existence, which involve the question "what." Mark confuses the
two, but Tristan in his answer affirms that experience, limited to the phenomenal,
can never fathom the ultimate "why." The ground that Mark seeks is, of course, the
Schopenhauerian view of events in the phenomenal world as the outcome of a blind
Will whose tragic effect on the individual only can be negated through the complete
renunciation of desire and denial of the will to live. The sounding of the desire music
in the orchestra does not provide Tristan's answer to the ultimate "why" in Mark's
question; rather, it affirms desire as the "what," that is, the principle behind human
suffering. Tristan's turn to A♭ indicates the solution.

During the composition of *Tristan*, Wagner became intensely interested in such
questions, recording some of his ideas in letters to Mathilde Wesendonck. The letter
of January 19, 1859, written when Wagner had just completed the second act of *Tristan* and was now working on the instrumentation, is of particular interest, for in it
Wagner sets "poetic intuition" in opposition to experience, on which the usual view
of life pivots.[12] According to Wagner, poetic intuition precedes all experience, enabling the poet to represent his prefigurement of "that which is raised above space,
time and causality." A decade later, in the Beethoven essay, Wagner elaborated further
on this idea, explaining the relationship between music and drama as one in which
the drama was "prefigured in those inner musical laws which unconsciously make
themselves valid in the dramatist's mind, just as the laws of causality are unconsciously employed for the apperception of the phenomenal world."[13] He then ac-
corded to Shakespeare a parallel position in the drama to that of Beethoven in music,
referring to the "mysterious ground ["den geheimnisvollen Grund"] of Shakespeare's
inexplicableness." This perhaps unconscious reminiscence of King Mark's question
was equivalent to what Wagner had described in the 1859 letter as "that foreknown

essential Something" that enters the poet's experience as an Idea that shapes the experience, purging his will so that "his aesthetic interest will become a moral one, and to the highest poetic idea will link itself the highest moral consciousness."

The complex of ideas just described underlies Wagner's bringing in the desire music beneath Tristan's answer to Mark, as well as his beginning it, for the only time after the Prelude from the tone a (thus lending it something of the special distinction that belongs to the beginning of the Prelude). Here the desire music signifies the Schopenhauerian concept of desire or Will more fully than anywhere else in the work. And, perceived by Tristan as the "what" rather than the "why" of existence, it is the object of contemplation, detached from will.[14] The negating element in Tristan's answer clearly indicates the necessity of passing beyond desire. Wagner sets Tristan's lines in $\frac{4}{4}$ against the $\frac{6}{8}$ of the desire music. As Tristan turns away from Mark to Isolde, the third phrase of the desire music moves, at the point where the E^7–F deceptive cadence normally appears, from E^7 to an Ab^6_4 chord, bringing in the succession of the love's peace motive followed by the second death motive (a pairing that had appeared six times in this form within the love scene). Tristan now reveals the metric "modulation" that resolves the simultaneous contradiction between his answer to Mark, in $\frac{4}{4}$, and the $\frac{6}{8}$ of the desire music: the hemiola $\frac{6}{4}$ of the love's peace motive passes over into the slow $\frac{3}{4}$ of the death motive, returning to the basic meter of the love scene. And, although Tristan's tritones ("*nicht* sagen"; "*nie* erfahren") express the negative that lies behind sexual desire, the "extra" harmonies that Wagner adds to the endings of the first and second phrases of the desire music—$g\sharp^{\sharp 6}_4$ and b^6_4 chords (see ex. 5.4)—not only restore the pitches that his negatives cancel out—$d\sharp$ and $f\sharp$— they also anticipate the turn to Ab/ab for the love's peace motive and the sequence of three strophes that follow. In the first and second of these strophes Tristan expresses to Isolde that he is about to travel to another land, that of night/death, his true home, and asks whether Isolde will follow, after which Isolde, in a third strophe, expresses her willingness to follow, reintroducing the death motive immediately before completing the Ab that Tristan had left open at the end of his strophes and leading it into a postlude that anticipates the climax of the *Liebestod*. The last of these events moves into deep, enharmonic flats and is broken off, just as the B major of the love scene was broken off earlier and as Isolde's penultimate solo will be broken off in act 3: by the intrusion of the external world, here represented by Melot.

As the death motive passes over into her Ab cadence, Isolde sings "den Weg nun zeig' Isolde," a poetic and musical reminiscence of the original transition to "O ew'ge Nacht." There Wagner had spoken of the gate before which the lovers had stood and that had now had to close, making an association between that gate, derived from Gottfried's lovers' cave scene, and desire. The desire music had moved increasingly into deep sharp regions, only to be enharmonically reinterpreted in terms of Ab as Isolde referred to the "way" to the "right door" shown the lovers by Minne. At that point the love's peace motive had moved, via the combined day-death motive, described earlier, into the transfiguration music. Now, following Isolde's reference to the "way" once more, the beginning of the desire music passes directly into the transfiguration music, in Gb; and as it drifts even further in the flat direction Wagner once again leads toward an enharmonic reinterpretation before breaking off with Melot's intrusion.

Thus, the sequence of desire, night-death, and transfiguration emerges as the only route to the answer sought by Mark. As a whole, this scene progresses from the philosophical *Wahn*, represented by King Mark's question and Tristan's answer, to the visionary or religious *Wahn*, depicted in Isolde's anticipation of the *Liebestod*. Musically, the sequence of events telescopes the course of the opera, summarizing its principal events; that is, it progresses from the beginning of the opera (the desire music), to the middle of act 2 (the A♭/a♭ strophes), and breaks off with the anticipation of music from the ending of the opera. It begins with a representation of desire or Will as the ground of existence and leads through a juxtaposition of the phenomenal and metaphysical spheres (Tristan's two homes), ending with the "way" by which the phenomenal world can be transcended. For Schopenhauer, sexual love, although one of the principal manifestations of compassion, was indissolubly linked to the will-to-life and therefore a delusion (*Wahn*). In both this scene and the original transition to "O ew'ge Nacht," however, Wagner's sequence of motives and keys makes the point that sexual love can lead to denial of the will-to-life, the substance of what he claimed as his amendment of Schopenhauer. Paraphrasing Wagner's 1859 letter, we might say that the Idea that shapes Tristan's experience, purging his will and leading him to highest moral consciousness, is his recognition of desire as enslavement to Will, the "what" of existence, and night-death as the only escape.

In deleting the lines in which Tristan pronounced friendship and loyalty delusions in "O nun waren wir Nachtgeweihte," along with the passage referring to Minne's way in the original transition to "O ew'ge Nacht" and the lines about Minne's control of Melot's actions, Wagner lends greater credence to Tristan's consciousness of his own betrayal as he leads the desire music toward an emphatic D minor cadence: "aus Eifer verriet mich der Freund dem König, den ich verriet!" Instead of asserting Minne's control of events through Melot, Tristan restores King Mark's tonality, as he acknowledges his betrayal. The lines in which Tristan brands Melot as the agent of Minne's way for Tristan had to be deleted if Tristan was to be represented as progressing, through his awakened compassion for Mark, beyond the purely egocentric meaning behind his calling Mark and Melot "Tag'sgespenster" and "Morgenträume." Yet there is no doubt that the segment encompassing Tristan's response to King Mark stands apart from the rest of the scene, its principal key, a♭/A♭, distanced by a tritone from the otherwise magnetic pull of the tonic, d, and signifying on one level a rejection of Mark and his world. The turn to the A♭ music of the love scene—the equivalent of Gottfried's world apart—affirms that its principal insights into the union of desire and night remain valid. The simultaneous sense both of tonal distance and the overcoming of that distance is an expression of the scope of the "weiten Reich der Weltennacht." Nevertheless, it leaves the theme of compassion undeveloped. The return to d and the final peroration of the inverted honor theme (now with subtle musical connections to the day motive with which the act began) confirm that the disparity surrounding the question of the lovers' honor is greater than ever. For further development of that theme we await act 3.

If there is any truth to the foregoing ideas, then in the scene surrounding Tristan's answer to King Mark, arguably the most succinctly Schopenhauerian scene in the opera, Wagner must have intended that the A/A♭ relationship and its dramatic analog, desire giving way to longing for night, form a continuity, not a juxtaposition of disparates (as is emphasized in Lorenz's drawing a period division at the point of the shift to A♭). As analysis of the love scene reveals, the relationship between a/A and A♭ is a running theme whose focal point is the arrival of night in "O sink hernieder," in which Lorenz again diagramed an untenable A/A♭ period division in the middle of a transition-based passage. Like the *Haupt/Herz* succession within the death motive, and the A/A♭ relationship in the love scene, the turn to A♭ following Tristan's answer expresses motion from phenomenality (desire as the "what" of existence) to night, the latter ultimately encompassing the former as well.

In act 3, after Tristan's initial awakening, Wagner returns to this theme (see chapter 14). There, after a long period of near-death unconsciousness, Tristan reiterates his initial response to Mark, "Dass kann ich dir nicht sagen," in association with the impossibility of conveying to Kurvenal where he has been. The passage marks the beginning of Tristan's quest for self-understanding following his return from night to day. Now it merges with the A♭ music of Tristan's other home, night, which passes, via a striking enharmonic shift on the phrase "göttlich ew'ges Urvergessen" (primal forgetfulness, divine and eternal) into the desire music. The sequence, now reversed in relation to that of act 2, is bonded into a continuity by a deep interpretation of forgetfulness, that of night and its musical analogs, transition and the binding of opposites through enharmonic reinterpretation. Wagner's point, expressed in the terms of *Opera and Drama,* is that night is the "generic essence" that binds up the oppositions created by the understanding. In the terms of Wagner's amended Schopenhauerian agenda, the greatest such opposition is that between desire as will-to-life and love as metaphysical ecstasy, leading to denial of the will-to-life. The form of act 3 pivots on this question.

THIRTEEN

Act 3

Musico-poetic Design

For many lovers of *Tristan*, the third act is the richest—the "greatest in
every way," "practically perfect," according to Joseph Kerman—a perception extending back at least as far as Nietzsche's panegyric in *The Birth of Tragedy* (1871).[1] It
is not just because Wagner merges the exigencies of musical and dramatic structure
to an unprecedented degree in this act but also because act 3 completes a palpable
large-scale design for the work in toto. Wagner himself said that act 3 was the "point
of departure for the mood as a whole," a statement confirmed by his 1854 letter to
Liszt, which already looks ahead to the oppositions that attain their point of greatest intensity in act 3. Act 3 pivots around those oppositions: Tristan's curse of the love
potion and his own existence, his relapse into unconsciousness, and his reawakening and clairvoyant vision of Isolde. These events, as mentioned earlier, are centralized within the act.

A measure of symbolic importance can be seen in the fact that with the F cadence
of Tristan's relapse Wagner broke off composition for a month, during which time
he completed the orchestration of the first half of the act and sent it to the publisher
before resuming the composition of the second half.[2] In the solo that follows, Kurvenal's characterization of love as "der Welt holdester *Wahn*," the exact center of the
act in terms of the measure numbers, voices Schopenhauer's view of love as delusion, after which Tristan's reawakening symbolizes the transcendent aspect of love,
anticipating the *Liebestod*. In this light the events in question are a mainstay in Wagner's amendment of Schopenhauer. The f/F–B shift is its primary symbol.

In this sequence, Wagner confronts two versions of the desire music for the only
time in the opera. Before Tristan's relapse the principal version, associated with the
poison of desire, combines with the curse motive. When Tristan reawakens, it is to
the version that derives from the act 1 honor music, completing an arpeggiation of
the F-sharp major triad at its phrase endings. The B major toward which it leads not
only anticipates the transfiguration music; it draws the curse motive, now trans-

formed by the new tonal context, into Tristan's vision. The *Sühnetrank* music, also in B, appears for the first time since act 1. Thus, the love potion is the focus of two views of love, what Wagner called "love as fearful torment" and love as "this most beautiful of dreams."

This process mirrors the dual qualities of negation and transcendence within the desire music. As Tristan reflects on the events that led to the love potion various musical motives reappear, revealing their interrelatedness in terms of the underlying harmonic and intervallic components of the desire music. Within them, Tristan chords turn into diminished-seventh chords, an analog of the negative view of love as *Wahn*. Their culmination is the curse motive itself. After Tristan's relapse, Wagner effects a reversal: Kurvenal's solo moves from the diminished-seventh chord framework to B minor; and in the desire music the rising chromaticism now articulates major rather than minor thirds. The turn to B major reveals that within love there is something more than the delusion and underlying negation of the species will.[3]

In *Music of the Future* (1860), Wagner described his conception of opera in terms of the dominance of "inner psychic motives" over external events, the circumvention of ordinary dramatic causality, symbolized in the question "Why," and the resultant transporting of the listener into a "dreamlike state which soon becomes a clairvoyant vision."[4] As he relates, in *Tristan*, having undergone a period of "questioning" in *Opera and Drama* and his other theoretical writings, he immersed himself in the "depths of the psyche and from this inmost center of the world boldly constructed an external form" in which the "detailed exposition" was of "inner motives" only: "the whole affecting story is the outcome of a soul's inmost need, and it comes to light as reflected from within."[5]

The first half of act 3 depicts the coming to light of that inner need in Tristan. Having denied the possibility of answering the question "Why?" at the end of the preceding act, Tristan reiterates his negative response to Kurvenal—"dass kann ich dir nicht sagen"—after which his reverie on the motives of desire leads him to recognition that "life and death, the import and existence of the external world . . . depend entirely upon inner psychic events." Accompanying this process is Wagner's symbol of Schopenhauer's belief that music provides an Idea or "copy" of the will: the *alte Weise*. Wagner's idea that music was metaphysically prior to the drama (in effect "absolute"), while at the same time conditioned by dramatic-representational exigencies, is mirrored in the interrelatedness of the musical motives, and the revelation of their desire-centered qualities. Wagner's view that they exhibit inner and outer sides is a viable way of describing the situation.

In this light, another Schopenhauerian theme complex is completed in act 3: the progression described by Schopenhauer in his essay "Aphorisms on the wisdom of life" under the headings "What a man is," "What a man has" and "What a man represents," a sequence that becomes increasingly external in character in Schopenhauer's ordering, but that Wagner reverses, in keeping with the fact that the thematic content of *Tristan* centers increasingly on internal questions from the first to the third act. "What a man represents" gives great attention to extrinsic honor. It resonates extensively with *Tristan*, act 1, especially Isolde's narrative and the earlier part of the lovers' confrontation in scene 5. And even after Tristan and Isolde proclaim honor and shame a dream at the end of the act this theme continues, under the rubric day, into the first half of the second act love scene, reaching its climax in Tristan's solo "Was dich umgliss mit hehrster Pracht."

The point that marks the lovers' final rejection of the values embodied in what a man represents comes in "O nun waren wir Nachtgeweihte," which has been recognized as a virtual paraphrase of Schopenhauer, specifying the qualities the philosopher had grouped under the principal subheadings of his essay. In the original version of this solo, Wagner took up the question of loyalty and friendship as well, perhaps influenced by the closing remarks of Schopenhauer's discussion of what a man *has,* where Schopenhauer considers a man's wife and children, then his friends, with some ambivalence as to whether they are "property" or not.[6]

The theme of what a man *has* emerges in full with Tristan's announcing his return "home" in the segment that follows his answer to Mark in act 2. Tristan is speaking metaphorically, of course. The home in question is the "dunkelnächt'ge Land" of night, whose entranceway is death, which Tristan seeks from Melot as the act closes. Isolde responds:

Nun führst du in dein Eigen,	Now lead into your own [land],
dein Erbe mir zu zeigen;	your inheritance to show me;
wie flöh' ich wohl das Land,	how could I flee the land
das alle Welt umspannt?	that encompasses the entire world?
Wo Tristans Haus und Heim,	Wherever Tristan's house and home,
da kehr' Isolde ein:	there Isolde will dwell:

And in act 3 Wagner continues the question of Tristan's home and property by having Kurvenal explain to the barely conscious Tristan that he is now in his true home, Kariol, rather than Cornwall. Wagner projects the distinction between Tristan's two homes by setting Kurvenal's solos in F, in contrast to the f with which the act begins, the dualism of the minor and major modes seeming to signify the opposition of night and day, death and life. To intensify that quality, Wagner begins the act with a new version of the desire music that he associated with the will-to-life via its origins in his setting of Mathilde Wesendonck's poem "Im Treibhaus" (ex. 13.1). The image that dominates Wesendonck's poem is that of tropical plants confined within the artificial world of a greenhouse from which they strive upward toward the light. Influenced by Schopenhauer's discussions of the will-to-life in plants, Wesendonck poeticizes the upward striving of the plants as a futile, deceptive longing that attains only emptiness ("Weit in sehnendem Verlangen breitet ihr die Arme aus, und umschlinget wahnbefangen öder Leere nicht'gen Graus"). And she compares this to the human condition: "although surrounded by light and splendor, our homeland is not here."

The "philosophical" object of the first half of act 3, for which Wagner named "Im Treibhaus" a "study," is to depict the blind will-to-life that permeates all nature as the force that keeps Tristan alive against his conscious willing. The hot, oppressive sunlight of the setting is a visual symbol of the inescapable power of desire and the will over human existence; and the F minor tonality, which holds for the first 160 measures of the act, is an aural symbol of the tragic character of existence. Then, as Tristan awakens to the sound of the *alte Weise*—"the old melody;—why does it wake

Example 13.1. Beginning of act 3

me?"—Wagner makes an enharmonic shift, the d♭′ of "die alte Weise" changing to
c♯′ on "was weckt sie mich," which effects the first shift away from f in the act. Kurvenal's response sets up the F major that contrasts with Tristan's fragmentary utterances for the next 112 measures. In them he itemizes Tristan's property—flocks,
house, court and castle—including even the faithful retainers to whom Tristan con-
signed his property on leaving for Kornwall. The last and most emphatic of Kurvenal's F major cadences completes his joy that Tristan is now in his true home, where
he will finally recover:

Nun bist du daheim,	Now you are at home,
daheim zu Land:	at home in your land:
im ächten Land,	in your true land,
im Heimatland;	in your native land;
auf eig'ner Weid' und Wonne,	among your own fields and joys,
im Schein der alten Sonne,	in the light of your old sun,
darin von Tod und Wunden	where from death and wounds
du selig sollst gesunden.	You shall have a blessed recovery.

We are immediately suspicious at "Schein der alten Sonne," of course, and after
this passage the tonality shifts immediately as Tristan denies Kurvenal's assertion
that he has at last come to his true home: "Do you think that? I know it to be otherwise" (Dünkt dich das? Ich weiss es anders). His denial and the shift toward a♭ as he
recalls the words and music of his answer to King Mark in the preceding act mark
the beginning of his attempt to recapture the memory of the night where he has
been. Tristan's disregard for property is bound up with his reaffirmation of the
"weiten Reich der Weltennacht" rather than Kariol as his true home. In this part of
the act, Tristan recognizes compassion as the basis of Kurvenal's loyalty, responding

in kind to a far greater extent than his compassion for Mark in act 2; and in the ec-stasy that precedes Isolde's arrival later in the act he expresses his understanding in the disposal of his property: "Kurvenal, most loyal of friends! All my property and possessions I entrust to you today" (Kurwenal, treuester Freund! All' mein Hab' und Gut vererb' ich noch heute).[7]

But it is not Tristan's possessions, even of his friends' loyalty, that are foremost in act 3. And it is here that Schopenhauer's "what a man *is*" becomes the central focus. Under that heading, Schopenhauer deals with personality or character, the man in himself as opposed to what he has or represents to others. It is this theme that Wag-ner develops at length in the first half of act 3, in which the setting provided by the medieval legend—Tristan suffering from the wound that will ultimately prove fatal—led him to create the nearest approach to the dynamic of psychoanalysis in all his works: the patient physically passive casting his mind over the events of his life and at-tempting to understand his own character (Wagner calls it his "fate") and its causes. Thus, after recalling that his father had died after his conception and his mother at his birth, Tristan analyzes his own character as fated for tragedy.[8] He then casts his mind back over the more recent events of his relationship with Isolde, viewing them in light of his fate. Because the goal of this entire process is Tristan's curse of the love potion and his own existence, it exhibits more than a psychological function, ulti-mately making the point that even the notion of what a man *is* is subordinate to the forces of desire, metaphysical oneness, and the denial of existence, which is exactly what Schopenhauer had made clear in the introduction to his *Aphorismen*.

And because it is analysis of the meaning of the *alte Weise* that leads Tristan to this insight into his character and fate, Wagner intertwines several Schopenhauerian themes in this part of act 3, each a separate strand of the philosopher's work that de-velops from act to act. Schopenhauer's metaphysics of music is prefigured in the sounds of nature that Wagner had embodied in the sailor's song in act 1 and the hunt music in act 2. In act 3, Wagner presents it in its manifold aspects via the tragic, desire-ridden *alte Weise*, the natural simplicity of the *frohe Weise*, and the inaudibil-ity of the *Weise* that sounds to Isolde's transfiguration. Tristan's death, preceded by his cry "Wie, hör' ich das Licht?" and Isolde's transfiguration, in which her vision of Tristan is transmuted into the subjective sound of the metaphysical "Weise" that em-anates from him, complete the process by which sound exposes the fundamental illusoriness of the world of light.

Although most of this design is pure Schopenhauer, it has origins in the medieval legend as well. Unfortunately, however, we do not have that part of the legend that comprises most of Wagner's third act in a version from Gottfried; and it is difficult to envision how Gottfried would have dealt with it; it has even been suggested that Gottfried might have left his poem incomplete because of his own difficulties with the ending.[9] Nevertheless, what we do have from Gottfried probably stimulated Wagner to center the first half of the act on Tristan's exploration of the role of desire in his life, intensifying that desire because of Isolde's absence, and even emphasizing the role of music in the process of Tristan's self-analysis.

The problem of the final episodes of the Tristan legend centers, of course, on Tris-tan's relationship to "Isolde of the white hands," whom Wagner must originally have intended to introduce into his *Tristan*, because he refers to the black flag that flutters at the end, a detail bound up with her lying to him about the ship on which the real Isolde ("queen Isolde" or "Isolde the Fair") arrives. In the end, Wagner eliminated Isolde of the white hands altogether; and instead of the black flag he has Tristan send Kurvenal to the watch tower where, in answer to Tristan's "Die Flagge? Die Flagge?" he cries out "Der Freude Flagge am Wimpel lustig und hell."[10] Along with the shepherd's *frohe Weise*, this modification of the legend signals the fact that Wagner's transcendent ending has no equivalent in any version of the *Tristan* legend, deriving as it does from Schopenhauer's quasi-religious "path to salvation" through denial of the will-to-life. The parallel between Kurvenal's cry from the watch tower and Brangaene's warning from the tower after "O sink hernieder" is a key to what Wagner presumably intended. For just as Brangaene's warning announces the coming of day, drawing the day motive under the spell of the dream of love, Kurvenal's cry confirms Isolde's arrival as the breakdown of the barrier between day and night, manifested ultimately in Tristan's proclaiming "[O, diese Sonne! Ha, Dieser Tag! Ha, dieser] Wonne sonnigster Tag!" to the second death motive, otherwise associated with longing for night. The further parallels that follow—between Isolde's arrival and Tristan's arrival in act 2 and between Tristan's death and Isolde's extinguishing the torch in the earlier scene—point up the fact that the tragedy of Isolde's arriving too late in the medieval story is for Wagner the apotheosis of what has long been anticipated in his drama as a transfiguring event. In his version, by arriving at the point of Tristan's death Isolde *does* heal Tristan of life, thereby bringing the theme of desire to its completion.

Such an ending was, of course, impossible for Gottfried. What he *does* provide for the part of the poem that corresponds to Wagner's third act is, however, highly interesting and was certainly of influence on Wagner. Gottfried uses the story of Tristan's relationship to Isolde of the white hands to intensify Tristan's inseparability from and longing for the true Isolde. Gottfried describes that longing as a manifestation of his original vision of love as a world apart, joining life and death:

> Note a strange thing here: Tristan was in flight from toil and suffering, and yet he went in search of suffering and toil. He fled Mark and death, and yet sought mortal peril that was death to his heart—absence from Isolde. What was the use of his fleeing death on the one hand and following death on the other? What was the use of his eluding torment in Cornwall, when he bore it on his back, night and day? He saved his life for the sake of the woman, and his life was poisoned with that woman alone. No other living thing was death to his life and soul but his best life, Isolde. Thus he suffered the threat of two deaths.[11]

And Gottfried describes Isolde's death in life in a manner that must have influenced Wagner's conception of the beginning of act 3, in which the language Gottfried assigns to Isolde is transferred to Tristan. Even in English prose translation Gottfried's exploration of the experience of life and death through love has a mysteriously compelling quality:

> Isolde the Fair—Tristan's life and death, his living death—was in pain and torment. That her heart did not break on the day when she followed Tristan and his ship out to

sea with her eyes was because he lived. That he lived helped her to survive. Without him she was powerless either to live or die. Both death and life had poisoned her: she could neither die nor live. . . .

Seeing the sail flying, she said to herself in her heart: " . . . I know that when you flee Isolde, you are leaving your life behind you, since I am indeed your life. Without me you cannot live for one day longer than I can live without you. Our lives and very souls are so interwoven, so utterly enmeshed, the one with the other, that you are taking my life away with you and leaving yours with me. No two lives were ever so intermingled: we hold death and life for each other, since neither can really find life or death unless the other give it. And so poor Isolde is neither alive nor yet quite dead: both ways are denied me."[12]

The influence of such passages on Wagner's *Tristan* is discernable in the dialogue surrounding the word "and" in the love scene—"Doch, dieses Wörtlein: und—wär' es zerstört, wie anders als mit Isolde's eig'nem Leben wär' Tristan der Tod gegeben?"— and in Tristan's knowledge in act 3 that Isolde is still alive because of the desire within him that has called him back from the night.[13] This knowledge emerges in his first real solo, leading him to return to the memory of his awaiting for Isolde to extinguish the torch: "Ach, Isolde, süsse Holde! Wann endlich, wann, ach wann, löschest du die Zünde, dass sie mein Glück mir künde? Das Licht, wann löscht es aus? Wann wird es Ruh' im Haus?" (Ah, Isolde, sweet, noble Isolde! When, finally, when, ah when will you extinguish the flame, that it reveal my happiness to me? The light, when will it go out? When will rest come to the house?) Now, his property relinquished, Tristan himself is the "house" that awaits the night. And after Kurvenal's uncertainty as to whether Isolde is still alive, Tristan cries "Noch losch das Licht nicht aus, noch ward's nicht Nacht im Haus: Isolde lebt und wacht; sie rief mich aus der Nacht" (Still the light did not die out, still it was not night in the house: Isolde lives and awaits; she called me from the night). This theme continues in Tristan's proclaiming his "fate": to be unable to die because of the strength of desire within him. And the climax of that realization—his curse of the love potion and his own existence—involves his recognizing, as Gottfried's lovers do, that his life is death, that desire is a poison within him.

In his exile, Tristan encounters Isolde of the white hands, whose name and beauty bring Isolde the Fair continually into his mind. When Tristan ruminates on the name in a manner that recalls Isolde's turning Tantris and Tristan over in her mind earlier in the story, we are tempted to say, in fact, that for Gottfried the existence of Isolde of the white hands is a device to further intensify Tristan's longing for the true Isolde. Gottfried describes Tristan "assailed by memories of his old sufferings, to which he had been born" and in his mental anguish finding the means to get "free of his desire": "Isolde had robbed Isolde of her Tristan through desire; but now, with desire, Tristan had returned to the love that he was born to. His heart and mind ran entirely on their old sorrow."[14] The intermingling of sorrow and desire for Isolde the Fair enables Tristan to free himself from desire for Isolde of the white hands as if through the recognition of desire's deeper qualities.

This process involved Tristan's embodying his love for the true Isolde in music, composing "love-songs, rondels and courtly little airs" in which he always brought in the refrain

| Isot ma drue, Isot mamie, | Isolde my mistress, Isolde my beloved, |
| en vus ma mort, en vus ma vie! | in you my life, in you my death![15] |

Gottfried cites this refrain twice, explaining that it was the principal deception that led Isolde of the white hands to love for Tristan, causing Tristan in turn to torture himself with desire for both Isoldes, wavering back and forth in a way that reminds us of Mark's wavering doubts in the earlier episodes of the story. Gottfried's remarkable ability to prolong conflict by suspending its resolution indefinitely—in Tristan's case the conflict of desire—must have influenced Wagner in his attempt to depict the endlessly unfulfilled desire described by Schopenhauer as the poison that prevents Tristan's death.

Gottfried's poem breaks off with Tristan in the midst of such conflicts. But, despite his eliminating all references to Isolde of the white hands, in the first half of act 3 Wagner developed certain of Gottfried's themes, above all Tristan's death-in-life and its relationship to the lovers' union through desire despite their physical separation. Tristan not only recognizes desire for Isolde as the reason he has not been able to die, but also he associates a particular musical tune—the *alte Weise*—with desire for Isolde as well as with his own sorrowful fate (the meaning of the name Tristan) as the result of desire. Beyond these desire-centered themes there is little in Gottfried that directly corresponds to Wagner's third act. But Gottfried's treatment of Isolde of the white hands as virtually the product of Tristan's desire, a kind of substitute or false Isolde, echoes in Wagner's device of having Tristan experience two visions of Isolde's arrival to heal him from life—the first one false and the second one true, the first dominated by desire and the second resulting from Tristan's curse of the love potion and his rebirth to music associated with the transformation of desire. The one vision of Isolde is the product of desire, pure and simple, and the other a love that ultimately transcends desire.

Cycles of Desire

In centering more than three quarters of his third act on Tristan alone, his struggle against desire, his search for self-identity through the exploration of what Wagner called "psychic motives," Wagner wove together many running themes of the work into what is perhaps his most impressive achievement: the stages by which Tristan comes to terms with his own existence and its meaning. The vehicle Wagner developed for this voyage of self-discovery is what has been described as a series of cycles, usually two; Joseph Kerman describes it as a "double cycle" of recollection, curse, relapse, anticipation, a pattern that has its origins in Alfred Lorenz's division of the act as a whole into three main parts forming a huge Barform, of which Tristan's cycles (the first one extending back to the beginning of the act) are the two Stollen.[16] Kerman's cycles are more circumspect than Lorenz's but far too general in outline for our purposes. And Lorenz's unfortunately suffer not only from the familiar pitfalls of his quest for periodic substructures and parallel correspondences, but also from his division of each of the cycles into quasi-symphonic "movements," following patterns emphasized by earlier authors and tracing back, ultimately, to Nietzsche's remarks in *The Birth of Tragedy*.[17] Lorenz's scheme, in fact, does not account for Tristan's awakening and vision of Isolde at the center of the act, other than to draw an entirely untenable musical correspondence to Tristan's awakening earlier in the act. In addition, for his third division Lorenz lapsed back into one of his more routine schemes, interpreting it as an arch form (*Bogen*) comprising two main sections—Isolde's lament over Tristan's death and Mark's lament over the tragic events in general—that surround a middle section, the conflagration between Kurvenal's and Mark's men and Kurvenal's death. Within the form of the act as a whole the *Liebestod* became the coda of an *Abgesang*.

Although Lorenz's scheme is untenable on any number of counts, it is important to recognize that the idea of cycles is essential to the completion of Wagner's Schopenhauerian agenda. In this respect, act 3 doubles back to what Wagner described in his program notes for the prelude: "all phases of the vain struggle against inner ardor, until this, sinking back powerless upon itself, seems to be extinguished in death." These words perfectly describe Tristan's relapse and the events leading to it, while his reawakening mirrors Wagner's description of the concert ending as a "glimpse into the attainment of highest rapture." The act 3 cycles are expanded renewals of the cycle of desire described in the prelude, with the difference that what could not be satisfactorily completed in the prelude—even in the version with the concert ending—now is.

Wagner's symbol of that completion is the tritone shift at the center of the act and over its course, the pivot between Tristan's struggle with "love as fearful torment" and love as "this most beautiful of dreams." The idea of love as delusion—"der Welt holdester Wahn"—which comes between the two, must have been in Wagner's mind from the beginning, for it appears in the prose draft, in Tristan's first cycle, where Tristan cries out, "Ach! Isolde selbst wird mir ein Wahn!"

In the first cycle Tristan awakens gradually to the *alte Weise*, experiences the return and intensification of desire, curses the day and sinks back at the end of his first solo. In a second solo (following Kurvenal's explanation that he has sent for Isolde: a genuine Barform whose three units are based on the three phrases of the desire music), he experiences an excited vision of Isolde's arrival that turns out to be false, since it is dominated by desire. In the second cycle the *alte Weise* returns to accompany Tristan's "analysis" of the role of desire and tragedy in his life, the intensification leads to his curse of the love potion and his own existence, and the relapse is into unconsciousness. Then, following another solo of Kurvenal (his pronouncing love a delusion), Tristan reawakens to the desire music with another vision of Isolde. This time the vision is the product of Tristan's renewed contact with night. It passes over into the anticipatory phase, Tristan's cry "Das Schiff? Säh'st du's noch nicht?" paralleling that at the end of the first cycle. Here the *frohe Weise* enters. It is logical, therefore, to view this as a *third* cycle, in which Tristan's renewed longing to see Isolde is bound up with his anticipation of struggle with her, which he compares to his battle with Morold; this third stage is struggle against the delusion of love. This time after an extended period of anticipation Isolde does arrive. In this cycle Tristan has no curse; instead, the process of intensification culminates in the most dissonant music of the entire opera, Tristan's final rejection of his life. His third relapse is his death.

Over the course of the three cycles the degree of dissonance increases as well as the magnitude of the subsequent relapse. Each relapse is followed by the return of desire, although, paradoxically, Tristan's third relapse (his death) is accompanied by the desire music, its character reversed in its dynamic, as described earlier, so as to close Tristan's cycles. At this point Isolde's cycle begins, embodying her own struggle against desire in the solo she sings in response to Tristan's death. It contains no curse, but it reaches a point of maximum intensity towards the end as Isolde, resistant to Tristan's death, cries for him to awaken. This is resolved in her vision of Tristan's reawakening once more, which coincides with her own relapse. Her own reawakening, which is stretched out over time, its motives fragmented and set apart from the surrounding events, as Tristan's initial reawakening was, leads to the *Liebestod*, which takes her vision of Tristan's reawakening to the metaphysical—that is, his transfiguration—as its starting point, and ends with Isolde's final relapse into unconsciousness. Now the relapse and the ecstatic vision are united ("unbewusst, höchste Lust").

All four cycles involve music: it is the *alte Weise* that brings Tristan back to consciousness, initiating his questioning, then drops out for the first cycle; the tune reappears for the beginning of the second cycle, but is replaced by the *frohe Weise* in the third; in Isolde's cycle Wagner specifies in the prose draft the sounding of an "alte Liebesweise" for the part of his text that corresponds to the *Liebestod*; in the poetic text of the *Liebestod* Isolde refers to a *Weise* that only she can hear. The cycles, in fact, all begin with the return of desire in some form and all contain points of great intensification, relapses and visions. The basic idea is that of unconsciousness versus consciousness (awakening) in constant alternation. Consciousness is associated with desire, unconsciousness with metaphysical intuition and eventually the overcoming of desire.

The idea of cycles, then, is a flexible one, not a fixed formal scheme involving immutable parallels. Ultimately, the convergence of the elements in Isolde's cycle breaks them down, affirming that the transitional character of form takes precedence over the schematic. The cycles are symbols of the former, not the latter. The main idea is that Wagner returns to what he had set forth in the program notes for the prelude to the opera regarding the continual recurrence of desire, its intensification to the point of dissatisfaction and longing for transcendence, followed by relapse and new beginning. In the prelude the point of maximum intensity is the apparent motion toward e♭, which turns out to lapse back to a. At the central pivot of act 3, completing Tristan's second cycle, the equivalent is the motion toward f, which then moves in Kurvenal's solo to b and in Tristan's reawakening to B (equivalent to the A of the concert ending). Now the version of the desire music that precedes Tristan's relapse is the original one, combined with Tristan's curse, while the one that accompanies his reawakening is an extension of the tritone-shifted first phrase that appeared at the climax of the prelude. The completion of the version of desire that was associated in the prelude with the lovers' search for the breach into night is the turning point in the act.

In the Prelude, each of the three main themes has its own tension/relapse pattern (see chapter 6); so do the main sections of the prelude as a whole. In this design the *Sühnetrank* music and its E major (dominant) tonality suggest the ideal of love, while the glance music and its D minor (subdominant) is associated with the relapse element. The glance music combines with the desire music at the climax because of its metaphysical association with compassion—seeing "night," as it were, in another person's eyes. It precipitates the enharmonic collapse. In act 3, after Tristan's reawakening, the reappearance of the *Sühnetrank* music is associated with his vision of atonement and the ideal of love; much later, the glance music reappears to accompany Tristan's death, his final relapse.

From the point of his reawakening to that of his death Wagner reverses the tonal relationships that arise from the desire music. That is, the a–C/c–e motion in the desire music (articulated by their dominants), then that from the subdominant (d) of the glance music to the dominant (E) of the *Sühnetrank* music, now becomes a motion from the B of Tristan's reawakening to E for the main body of his vision, then to C for the music dominated by the *frohe Weise*, turning to c as Isolde arrives, then giving way to a for the desire music. The desire music, now reversed in its dynamic associations, passes over into the glance music, which accompanies Tristan's death to the same Tristan chord that had precipitated the motion toward eb at the climax of the prelude. Tristan's third cycle deals with his struggle against the idea of love itself, embodied in Isolde. His death and Isolde's transfiguration complete the process by which Wagner attempts to define love as both desire (which dies symbolically with Tristan) and something beyond desire.

In what I have outlined the F/B antithesis of act 3 can be considered Wagner's means of fulfilling all that underlies the apparent tritone shift in the prelude to the opera and the dual qualities in the desire and honor music. The diminished-seventh chord harmonies in the music that precedes Tristan's relapse complete Tristan's "analysis" of desire, whereas the turn to B brings out its other, visionary side. In this light, the Tristan chord can be said to bridge between the diminished-seventh chord on F and the key of B, an expansion of its tendency towards the dominant in the desire music. Or, conversely, the f/B relationship can be considered to arise from the Tristan chord, whose lower third relates to f and its upper third to B, its three lowest pitches describing a diminished triad on F and the three uppermost pitches an ab triad. In what precedes Tristan's reawakening desire "regresses" to a pure negative analogous to the Tristan chord turning back into the diminished-seventh chord; with his reawakening it "progresses" to a metaphysical vision, associated with B. This is the principal means by which Wagner carried out his amendment of Schopenhauer, allowing love a determining role in the process of denial of the will-to-life and transfiguration.

Tristan's first cycle involves two extended solos, the first ending in Ab and the second on the dominant of Ab. Although the cycle as a whole features several alternations between the realms of day and night, the various recurrences of Ab, either as a key or a prominent climactic sonority, define it as the goal of Tristan's search for night, mixing memory and desire in his mind. The first solo of his second cycle, however, culminates in a full close in f/F, after which the second arises from the desire music, now transformed so as to lead to the transfiguration music in B. The Ab/B relationship of the love scene remains important in terms of the relationship of Tristan's two visions and the respective appearances of the transfiguration music in each cycle. But it is the replacing of Ab by f, symbolizing the negation of existence—and

completing the pattern that underlies the keys of death in the three acts: c–A♭–f—
that enables the tritone transformation of Tristan's metaphysical rebirth.

Isolde's cycle is a direct response to Tristan's, fulfilling Wagner's ideas regarding
the "redeeming" of male by female, poetry by music, and the like; poetically, the dramatic meaning is the fulfillment of Tristan's longing to expire, as he says, *in* Isolde.
That is, his transfiguration takes place within Isolde's cycle, her vision of his ascent
to night. At the beginning of act 3 Tristan returns from unconsciousness to consciousness, a process that is echoed at the center of the act and completed in his death, after
which Isolde lapses into unconsciousness, returns to consciousness and cycles back
to unconsciousness. At the beginning, Tristan's return to counciousness is the outcome of the will-to-life within him. In the opening theme of the act, taken over from
"Im Treibhaus," the Tristan chord on G functions as iv^{+6} (i.e., b♭$^{+6}$) in a plagal cadence
to f whose heaviness, especially in its threefold repetition, suggests the inevitability
of the pull towards death, against which the will-to-life is feeble. On the third repetition of this motive its rising line continues upward more than two octaves in a
tonally open (dominant) pattern that Wagner associates in the song with the futility
of the plants' struggle for life— "Weit in sehnendem Verlangen breitet ihr die Arme
aus, und umschlinget wahnbefangen *öder Leere nicht'gen Graus*"—and in *Tristan* with
the empty sea as symbol of Tristan's hope: "Öd' und leer das Meer!"[18] At the end, the
waves of metaphysical sound that engulf Isolde comprise, perhaps, the largest scale
of reversal in the opera, completing the underlying meaning of the ocean/land setting of the first act. And in this light it is interesting to note that the initial measures
of the third act and the transfiguration cadence of the ending can be viewed, poetically,
as inversions of one another: the pattern of the latter is also a plagal cadence featuring an added-sixth chord, but now in major and shifted at the tritone: E^{+6}–B. The
diatonic rising forth from the supertonic (the added sixth of the chord) to the dominant (g to c′) in the "Im Treibhaus" theme becomes in the transfiguration music a
diatonic falling fifth from the supertonic/added-sixth to the dominant (c♯‴ to f♯‴).
The poetic association of the f cadence and its "open" continuation is, of course, the
will-to-life resisting death in Tristan, whereas that of the B cadence, articulating closure rather than openness, is Isolde's denial of the will-to-life.

FOURTEEN

Love as Fearful Torment

Tristan's First Solo

In *Tristan,* form rooted in musical and dramatic correspondences mirrors the representational aspect of the drama, but as such it often seems imposed or external, demanding that it be understood in relation to "deeper," purely musical processes of the kind that Wagner described as transitional and developmental. In act 3, Tristan's cycles—his quest for self-understanding—are the embodiment of the latter. In keeping with Wagner's Schopenhauerian agenda, they are occupied with the role of desire in his life.

From the point of his awakening (m. 159) until his first extended solo (mm. 277–440) Tristan speaks in nothing more than the most fragmented utterances, often sounding to little more than a Tristan chord or related harmony. He now sings a solo of just over 160 measures long, featuring more than a dozen different leitmotifs, most of which contain multiple references within them. The overall impression is of his newly returned consciousness assailed by memories associated with the inevitable return of desire, their as yet not fully understood point of unity.

Tristan's solo is occupied with his attempt to recapture the past, in particular the night that is now lost to him. He begins on the pitch ab, its initial context merely that of denying Kurvenal's optimistic F tonality. Tristan now reiterates to Kurvenal his negative response to King Mark in act 2: "das kann ich dir nicht sagen," on which Wagner introduces music from "Im Treibhaus" corresponding to Wesendonck's imagery of the sun longing to escape the day, whose contradictions parallel Tristan's present condition.[1] In the bass the four ascending tones of the theme that begins the act (a diatonic version of desire, associated with the will-to-life) transpose downward by step, mirroring Tristan's attempt to describe his former "awakening" in the realm of night. Unable to remember anything of that realm, Tristan reiterates the words just cited twice more, on completion of which the bass melody itself turns downward to describe the fifth descent in a♭, the first secure point of tonal arrival in the solo. Tristan's first "memory" corresponds to the beginning of his initial strophe on his other home, night, at the end of act 2, now associated with where he has been.

In Tristan's first solo A♭/a♭ is the closest equivalent to a tonic key, recurring several times, while in the second, which is not at all in A♭, it returns at the climax, ending on the dominant. In attempting to recapture the night, Tristan returns to memories of Isolde. A♭ is the symbol of his search, but it is not yet "deep" enough, as its centering on memory mixed with desire keeps him alive against his will. The f that Tristan skirts in his denial of Kurvenal's F is the symbol of the deeper meaning of desire, as will-to-life. Only when he confronts it, in his second cycle, is the "transcendental change" possible.

At first the closest Tristan can come is the a♭ music of night at the end of act 2. But now it *precedes* the desire music, the latter leading through the quintessential motive of longing for night—the second death motive—and on, ultimately, to the day motive, as Tristan realizes that Isolde is still alive, that desire prevents his attaining the rest he seeks. On a large scale, the parade of leitmotifs in this solo is guided by the conflict between Tristan's desire for Isolde and his hatred of the returning day. The direction is backward chronologically: from his response to Mark, to the love scene and, at the climax of the solo, to the day motive, just as it sounded at the beginning of the *Tagesgespräch*. Wagner then introduces the softly changing harmonies that had followed the day motive at the beginning of the second act. This passes over into the torch motive and that in turn into a version of the combined desire-transfiguration music in A♭, as in the prelude to act 2.

Thus, Tristan returns in his memory to his waiting for Isolde to extinguish the torch, a metaphoric foreshadowing of his present condition and an anticipation of his death. Wagner's setting Tristan's curse of day at the same pitch as the beginning of the *Tagesgespräch*—beginning with an A♭$^{+7}$ chord—and his ending the solo with an A♭ version of the desire and transfiguration music link up three points in act 2 that were concerned with establishing the associational role of A♭: the point of its first emergence in the opera, that of its first appearance in the love scene, and the point where it sounded unequivocally as the key of night, in "O sink hernieder."

Tristan's solo comprises a fivefold alternation between three segments in the four-flat tonal region associated primarily with A♭/a♭ and two contrast regions, the first introducing the desire music at its usual pitch, a, and the second beginning from a juxtaposition of f and F. Each of the former segments culminates in an expression of the association between night and death, for which Tristan longs; and each is followed by a tonal shift of a transformational character associated with the return of desire and day. The transformations, however, do not articulate such great shifts as their notation might suggest. The harmonies before and after the key signature changes are often very closely related; and, in keeping with the fact that Tristan is suspended between night and day, the recurrences of A♭, although easily recognizable, are generally fleeting and incapable on their own of binding the solos into overarching tonal forms. Instead, Wagner's primary organizational device is the ascent of Tristan's upper register tones in a curve from a♭ to a♭' whose apex is the curse of day, after which it falls off gradually to the end, returning to a♭. The orchestral melody line amplifies the curve, reaching a♭''' for Tristan's "Verfluchter Tag! Wächst du *ewig* meiner Pein?" (Accursed day! Will you forever awaken my pain?), then winding down three octaves to merge with Tristan's ab. This curve takes precedence over key relationships. The intimations of tonal form, a symbol of Tristan's longing for the rest that eludes him, are not fulfilled.

As the solo unfolds Wagner draws on devices he had used in the first scenes of *Das Rheingold* to mirror the emergence of the primal consciousness of the Rhine maidens and, eventually, the more purpose-oriented natures of Alberich and Wotan: *Stabreime*—here involving the letter "w"—to reflect Tristan's struggle to remember the night.

Dünkt dich das?	Do you think so?
Ich *weiss* es anders,	I know it to be otherwise,
doch kann ich's dir nicht sagen.	yet I cannot tell it to you.
Wo ich er*w*acht'—	Where I awoke,
weilt' ich nicht;	I did not remain;
doch, *wo* ich *w*eilte,	yet, where I did remain,
das kann ich dir nicht sagen.	that I cannot tell you.
Die Sonne sah ich nicht,	The sun I did not see,
noch sah' ich Land und Leute:	nor did I see land or people:
doch, *w*as ich sah,	yet, what I saw,
das kann ich dir nicht sagen.	that I cannot tell you.
Ich *w*ar,	I was
*w*o ich von je ge*w*esen,	where I have always been,
*w*ohin auf je ich geh':	where I ever go:
im *w*eiten Reich der *W*eltennacht.	in the wide realm of universal night.
Nur ein *W*issen dort uns eigen:	Only one knowledge is ours there:
göttlich e*w*'ges Urvergessen!	divine forgetfulness, eternal and primal!
*W*ie sch*w*and mir seine Ahnung?	How did its intuition disappear from me?

Tristan's solo is organized at first around his three utterances of "das kann ich dir nicht sagen," the second and third of which enclose a string of "s" sounds associated primarily with the world of vision: "sagen," "Sonne" and "sah." In contrast, the "w" sounds are associated with Tristan's attempt to convey where he has been, from his initial contradiction of Kurveval ("Ich weiss es anders") to the grouping that leads to his second denial: "Wo ich erwacht'—weilt' ich nicht; doch wo ich weilte." After his third denial, this quality increases suddenly—"Ich war, wo ich von je gewesen, wohin auf je ich geh': im weiten Reich der Weltennacht"—returning with "nur ein Wissen dort uns eigen" to its starting point, the impossibility of any knowledge of night. The softening of the "w" to "v" on "Urvergessen" is, along with its harmony, mysteriously, and paradoxically, revelatory; and after "Wie schwand mir seine Ahnung" we hear very little of the "w" *Stabreime*.

At first, Tristan's negative utterances all remain close to his initial ab. Gradually, however, his uppermost pitches rise in pitch until, after the arrival on Ab for "Ich war, wo ich von je gewesen," he reaches the db'/db octave above the dominant of Ab on the word "Weltennacht" (universal night). Within this span—emphasizing the pitches ab, a, bb, cb', db'—Wagner introduces db' twice ("wo *ich weilte*" and "Ich war, wo ich von je *gewesen*"). The point is not that it sound fresh on its symbolic association with "Weltennacht." Just the opposite: its preparation is of the essence. The bass E♭ of "Weltennacht" holds as a seven-measure pedal as if in preparation for Tristan's further recall of night—"Nur ein Wissen dort uns eigen"—but with his description of that knowledge—"göttlich ew'ges Urvergessen!"—his ascent through the a♭ scale reaches d♮' instead of e♭'. The D major (E♭♭) chord on "Urvergessen" marks the first point of transformation in the solo, canceling out the memory of the d♭' of "Weltennacht" and the key of a♭, then, as it changes to minor, bringing in the desire music: "Wie schwand mir seine Ahnung?" (ex. 14.1).

Just before the a♭ tonality dissolves altogether we hear the first hint in the act of the day motive, impelling the line "göttlich ew'ges Urvergessen" to the transformation that erases Tristan's memory of the night. Wagner embeds it within a harmonic context that derives from the desire music. The next segment makes the association between desire and day musically explicit, leading Tristan's line upward through a rising chromatic scale that, finally, brings the day motive into the open. At that point the motive sounds first to the same E♭$^{+7}$ chord as on its initial appearance in the

Example 14.1. Act 3, scene 1: from Tristan's first extended solo

opera (now on the word "trügend"), then transposes up by semitones—so as to begin from [d″], e♭″, f♭″ and finally f″—while the harmony increasingly takes on the character of the dominant of A♭. At its peak, the rhythm broadens and the f″–e♭″ appoggiatura of the day motive sets up a melodic cadence to a♭ to coincide with Tristan's realization that Isolde is still alive: "Was einzig mir geblieben, ein heiss inbrünstig Lieben, aus Todes-Wonne-Grauen jagt's mich, das Licht zu schauen, das trügend hell und golden noch dir, *Isolden, scheint!*" (What alone remains to me, a fervent burning love, from the dreadful rapture of death drives me to look upon the light that, deceptively bright and golden, still shines on you, Isolde"). And as he bewails this realization—"Isolde noch im Reich der Sonne! Im Tagesschimmer noch Isolde!" (Isolde still in the realm of the sun! Isolde still in the shimmering daylight!)—the day motive settles on a♭, as in the *Tagesgespräch.*

Throughout this passage we hear not merely the associational character of the motives and key allusions, but the establishing of the next in the ascending series of Tristan's highest pitches, e♭′. The third phrase of the desire music had ushered in the shift from the d″ of "Urvergessen" to d♯″, even sounding e″ as appoggiatura to the d♯″. With the rising chromatic line Wagner finally establishes e♭″ as the dominant of A♭, pushing upwards through f♭″ to the f″ appoggiatura tone. After that, e♭″ remains secure within the day motive (on "Tagesschimmer").

Wagner now leads Tristan's memory back to music heard only once before in the opera: the opening scene of act 1, in which Brangaene had described Isolde's condition on leaving Ireland for Cornwall: "von der Heimat scheidend kalt und stumm, bleich und schweigend auf der Fahrt; ohne Nahrung, ohne Schlaf" (departing from your home cold and dumb, pale and silent on the journey; without nourishment, without sleep). Because this music contains the glance motive within it and because Tristan also refers to his longing to *see* Isolde—"Welches Sehnen! Welches Bangen! Sie zu sehen, welch' Verlangen!" (Such a longing! Such a torment! To see her, such yearning!)—it evokes a buried memory of Isolde's suffering appearance.

In act 1, this music had transposed up by a series of whole tones. Wagner now transposes it once, using it to shift the most prominent pitch in Tristan's solo from e♭″ to f″ ("Sie zu sehen, welch' Verlangen"). And to complete the process he brings in the first death motive, now in f—"Krachend hört' ich hinter mir schon des Todes Tor sich schliessen" (Crashing behind me I already heard the door of death close)—leading it into the second point of transformation in the solo as Tristan cries out "weit nun steht es wieder offen" (now it stands wide open again) to a melodic cadence on f′. Tristan's memories have returned to Isolde's state of mind during the ocean voyage.

With the shift from "schliessen" to "offen" the harmony shifts from the four-flat to the one-flat tonal region, a♭ changing to g♯ in preparation for a′, on which Wagner now reintroduces the day motive: "der Sonne Strahlen sprengt' es auf" (the sun's rays sprung it open). Tristan realizes that the night is irrevocably lost: "mit hell erschloss'nen Augen muss ich der Nacht enttauchen" (with clear open eyes I must emerge from the night). The first contrast segment had introduced the day motive and its major-seventh chord in association with Tristan's returning desire; in this one Wagner follows the sound of the day motive by four measures of parallel augmented triads, centered by that on F in preparation for completion of motion upward to the third, a′, of F major, in which Wagner brings in the "love's peace" motive, now in quadruple meter and marked *belebt*.

Tristan's juxtaposing the keys of f and F is a reminder of his two homes from the first part of the act. The night is now closed to him and the day open once more. The augmented triads signal his coming under the grip of his present desire for Isolde. Instead of its original restful character, the love's peace motive now projects a sense of urgency, mirroring the move away from the a♭/f of night and into the sphere of vision and desire: "sie zu suchen, sie zu sehen; sie zu finden, in der einzig zu vergehen, zu entschwinden Tristan ist vergönt" (to seek her, to see her; to find her, in her alone to expire, to lose himself Tristan is granted). Betraying the merging of sexual desire with death, Tristan's line outlines a curve upward from b to g′ ("einzig") then downward to b♭, the g′ anticipating the next in the rising series of pitches in his solo.

Beneath Tristan's b♭, the orchestra changes to sharp notation, beginning the most intense part of his solo from a♯ and leading to the curse of day:

Weh! Nun wächst	Woe! Now dawns
bleich und bang,	pale and fearful,
mir des Tages	the day's
wilder Drang;	wild ungency;
grell und täuschend	dazzling and deceptive
sein Gestirn	its countenance
weckt zu Trug	wakes my brain
und Wahn mir das Hirn!	to deceit and delusion!
Verfluchter Tag,	Accursed day,
mit deinem Schein!	with your glare!
Wachst du ewig	Will you forever awaken
meiner Pein?	my pain?

This segment comprises the ascent of a curve whose apex, the curse of day, leads Tristan's uppermost register to g′ (above the A♭+7 chord of the day motive), then pushes upward, on "ewig," to the highest pitch of the solo, a♭′ (ex. 14.2). As if to underscore the force of day, the former association of the "w" *Stabreime* with night is now completely turned around ("Weh," "wächst," "wilder Drang," "weckt," "Wahn," and, finally, "ewig"). Intensifying the conflict of yearning (ascending chromaticism) and suffering (descending chromaticism) within the desire music, the passage begins from another variant of the theme of "Im Treibhaus." In the song, its text describes the futile longing and upward striving of the greenhouse plants. Wagner now associates it with the dawning of day for Tristan, using it to set up a dominant-thirteenth chord on D♯. Tristan now sings "Tages wilder Drang" to the tones d♯′, d♯, b, a♯, a, that is, to the beginning tones of the desire music, now shifted at the tritone. And after holding the bass D♯ for three and a half measures, Wagner outlines the same pattern, more slowly, in the bass. The goal of the chromatic descent is now the bass of the A♭+7 chord of the curse of day. What is most striking, however, is that from the uppermost tones of the dominant-thirteenth chord Wagner introduces another series of parallel augmented triads, now more than thirty in all, which sweep upward through a chromatic scale of more than two octaves, leading directly into the curse of day.

Example 14.2. Act 3, scene 1: climax of Tristan's first extended solo; curse of day

Accompanied by the contrary motion between the bass and the parallel augmented triads, which continue upward toward the high g‴ of the orchestra and the g′ of the curse, Tristan's words—"grell und täuschend sein Gestirn weckt zu Trug und Wahn mir das Hirn!"—are revealing, especially his reaching g′ on the word "Hirn." When Wagner introduces purely physiological terms—"brain" in this case and "skull" in Tristan's "Was dich umgliss" from the first half of the *Tagesgespräch*—it is to intensify the oppressiveness of day beyond anything that might be reduced to mere "poetic" language. Tristan experiences the link between desire and day— Schopenhauer's process of representation—as an intensely painful but inescapable physiological fact.

With the curse of day the bass completes its motion from D♯ through the chromatically filled-in tones of the g♯/a♭ triad to the bass of the A♭⁺⁷ chord. The motion is not a *tonal* one in the ordinary sense, however. Although the D♯ retains something of its dominant character, the A♭⁺⁷ chord does not represent the key of A♭. After two iterations of the day motive, the d♭⁶₄ chord on "ewig" provides the pitches A♭ and a♭‴

Example 14.2. (Continued)

in the outermost voices, while Tristan reaches his highest tone, a♭'. The a♭' holds for more than a measure, after which chromatic motion of the inner voices enables the chord that is Wagner's goal, the diminished-seventh chord on B/F, which Tristan arpeggiates as his line plummets downward from a♭'. This point is simultaneously the apex and the turning point to the final descent to a♭ at the end of the solo.

Tristan's strength now wanes, and along with it the intensity of his desire. He now seeks only rest:

Verfluchter Tag,	Accursed day,
mit deinem Schein!	with your glare!
Wachst du ewig	Will you forever awaken
meiner Pein?	my pain?
Brennt sie ewig'	Will it burn forever,
diese Leuchte,	this light,
die selbst nachts	which even in the night
von ihr mich scheuchte?	keeps me from her?

Ach, Isolde,	Ah, Isolde,
süße Holde!	sweet and noble!
Wann, endlich,	when, finally,
wann, ach wann	when, ah when
löschest du die Zünde,	will you extinguish the signal,
daß sie mein Glück mir künde?	to announce my happiness?
Das Licht—wann löscht es aus?	The light—when will it go out?
Wann wird es Ruh' im Haus?	When will rest come to the house?

The succession of motifs from the prelude to act 2 now settles on transposing series of diminished-seventh chords, especially those bounded by the bass motion between D and F, with that on F as its primary focal point. Wagner uses the torch motive to establish an F pedal above which the other diminished-seventh harmonies sound, leading it into the desire music, its Tristan chords now replaced by diminished sevenths. Following three iterations harmonized by the diminished seventh on e (above the F pedal) it shifts to the diminished seventh on F, alternating that with the E^7 chord (notated, of course, as F$\flat^7$) for an additional three. This Wagner leads to the dominant of A$\flat$ (completing the F, F$\flat$, E$\flat$, descent of the desire music in the bass), for the entrance of the transfiguration music in basically the same form that appeared in the transition to "O sink hernieder" (there in A). Simultaneously, Tristan's line works its way chromatically downward by stages from the a$\flat'$ of "ewig" to the a$\flat$/e$\flat'$ of his "wann löscht es aus?" The orchestral line has made an even more dramatic descent from the f″ of the torch motive to the d$\flat'$, d′, e$\flat'$ of the desire music as it leads into the transfiguration music. The transfiguration music curves upward to the b$\flat'$/a$\flat'$ appoggiatura of its plagal cadence pattern, which does not cadence of course, but continues to weave its way down an octave eventually to reach unison with Tristan's final a$\flat$.

The solo as a whole suggests the hope that a point of attainment (or stability analogous to a tonal arrival) will arise from the floating tonal relationships, ending the tension associated with day and desire. Although Tristan's relapse is back to tonality, what controls the dynamic of the solo is not the key of A$\flat$, but the melodic curve, which, as is so often the case in *Tristan,* is only distantly related to the tonal centers. The *kind* of A$\flat$ tonality that Wagner defines in this solo as the goal of Tristan's reawakened memory is not the same as that which arrives in "O sink hernieder" as the lovers give themselves over to night. Instead, it more closely resembles the A$\flat$ of the latter part of the *Tagesgespräch,* emerging briefly and disappearing again before becoming established as a concrete reality (albeit only briefly). In this solo Wagner evokes quasi-functional tonal devices but divests them of their tonal potential. The usual harmonic signposts of tonal form exist for the purpose of reinforcing the motion from one pitch to another not the reverse. The increasing emergence of major-seventh chords and augmented triads underscores the external character of the motion toward Tristan's curse, after which the reversion to diminished-seventh chords conveys the loss of strength that causes his sinking back exhausted. The microcosm is one of individual harmonies, now invested with distinct associative properties that usurp their traditional functional characters; the macrocosm is the purposeful ascent/descent motion of Tristan's line.

In this solo, Wagner makes the point that the security of the vision of night has been lost. The final A♭ is Tristan's attempt to hold onto that vision; but the ease with which the desire music reenters, erasing it altogether, is a very telling point. Wagner spells the final pitch of Tristan's solo, a♭, as g♯ in the orchestra, using it to bring in the beginning of the desire music for Kurvenal's response, returning Tristan to the eternal starting point and a second phase in his struggle.

Tristan's Second Solo

Kurvenal's solo immediately takes us out of the realm of Tristan's metaphysical searching and back into the world of conventional values. An unmistakable barform, in G, its two *Stollen* begin with the first and second phrases of the desire music, respectively, whereas the first half of the *Abgesang* makes explicit connections between Isolde's first act narrative and her second act Frau Minne music, as well as between both those themes and the desire music. After that, Kurvenal returns to the version of the desire music that had begun each of his two *Stollen,* harmonizing it first with the fifth descent from c♯ to F♯ in the bass (i.e., the dominant of B: F♯⁷), then transposing it up a fourth to the dominant of e. This extension of the sharp motion within the third phrase of the desire music accompanies his announcing that he has sent to Cornwall for Isolde the "physician," completing his recollections of Isolde's healing Tristan of Morold's wound in the first half of the *Abgesang:* "Die beste Ärztin bald ich fand; nach Kornwall hab' ich ausgesandt: ein treuer Mann wohl über's Meer bringt dir Isolden her" (I soon found the best physician; I sent to Cornwall: a trusted man certainly brings Isolde across the sea here to you). After that the solo turns back toward G in which it ends.

That this solo articulates a conventional tonal framework while at the same time invoking ideas that extend beyond its limits is because, through his compassion, Kurvenal identifies with Tristan's desire and suffering, none of which he experiences himself. The effect on Tristan is immediate, and in response he sings a solo that begins with two strophes based on the variant of the desire music introduced by Kurvenal at "Die beste Ärztin." That he enters *fortissimo,* reverting to the $\frac{2}{2}$ meter and *sehr lebhaft* tempo of the second act at this point, is telling. Before the end of the first *Stollen,* Wagner brings out a connection of his rhythm to the music that led to the lovers' meeting in act 2. Tristan now reexperiences what Wagner called "life overflowing with the most violent emotions." Nevertheless, he recognizes loyalty and compassion in Kurvenal's identification with his needs, leading his second strophe into another theme from "Im Treibhaus," where it is associated with the poet's sympathy for the suffering plants. The chromatically descending nature of that theme opens up the first real departure from tonalities related to G for the remainder of Tristan's solo. The theme itself, however, belongs in the slow $\frac{4}{4}$ meter of the song and the beginning of act 3, not the fast $\frac{2}{2}$ that has taken over Tristan altogether at this point. And this difference prepares for the ending of Tristan's solo. After recalling Kurvenal's loyalty Tristan slows the tempo, returning to G and to the slow $\frac{4}{4}$ meter momentarily to rivet the theme of compassion in our minds: "mit leidest du, wenn ich leide: nur was ich leide, das kannst du nicht leiden!" (you suffer along with my suffering: only what I suffer, that you can never suffer!). But, in fact, all sense of a definite tonal center has long gone; and what follows is no longer related to compassion but to desire, pure and simple. In *Tristan* Wagner nods in the direction of knowledge through compassion—the "durch Mitleid wissend" of *Parsifal*—but it is nowhere near compelling enough to overcome the force of desire. Wagner shifts back to the fast $\frac{2}{2}$ for the rest of the solo.

The turning point is Tristan's proclaiming that although Kurvenal identifies with Tristan's suffering, he cannot experience *what* Tristan suffers, an idea borrowed from Schopenhauer.[2] As Tristan expands on that "what," identifying it with burning desire, Wagner brings back the second death motive, transposing it up the scale and contracting it as he does, then leading it into the "compassion" motive from "Im Treibhaus," which likewise transposes upward a full octave scale. Behind these sequences lies the controlling pitch g' of Tristan's line, duplicated of course in the upper octaves of the orchestra. Out of the G of Kurvenal's strophes and the closely related strophic pairing that begin Tristan's solo Wagner identifies G as the principal recurrent tonal element, beginning the compassion motive from a bright-sounding G at key points and leading Tristan's line toward g' within each of the three last segments of his solo. For the final segment, however, Wagner brings back the "dream chords" of "O sink hernieder" at their usual pitch, A♭, but totally transformed in character by the fast tempo and *crescendi*. Despite the return to A♭, Tristan sings the g' almost as an obsessively recurrent pitch throughout the entire passage, seemingly pushing up toward a♭', but ending finally on g' as he cries out to Kurvenal for news of Isolde's ship: "Kurwenal! Siehst du es nicht?" (Kuvenal! Don't you see it?).

Thus, three themes normally associated with the metaphysical night have been compelled to support Tristan's burning desire, forced completely out of their intrinsic characters by the return of the rapid $\frac{2}{2}$ tempo, the continually ascending lines and Tristan's obsessive reiteration of the pitch g'. Tristan's g', associated with his curse of day in the preceding solo, becomes the leading tone of A♭ at the climactic endpoint of this one, but there is nowhere for it to go; Tristan's vision cannot be fulfilled, for, despite his earlier curse of day, it no longer has anything to do with night. What will lead him back is the metaphysical character of music, embodied in the *alte Weise*.

The *Alte Weise*

In the final measures of his solo Tristan sings "Siehst du es nicht" twice, the first time ending on g♭' and the second on g'. The g' coincides with the point where the violins, having swept upward in a sudden crescendo, reach a *fortissimo* b♭"/b♭'" octave, extending the dominant of A♭ after the other instruments have dropped out. Tristan's anticipation is at its peak, but there is no longer any support from below; and beneath the violins the *alte Weise* reenters in the original tempo and meter after an absence of 467 measures (ex. 14.3).

Wagner begins the return of the melody with measures 29 through 37 of its forty-two measures, the part of the solo that is most explicitly concerned with alternation of the pitches g♭' and g'. The English horn sounds almost exactly the same passage from the *alte Weise* that it had on its last previous appearance, in measures 146–61,

Example 14.3. Act 3, scene 1: climax of Tristan's second solo, with reentrance of the *alte Weise*

where it began three measures earlier than here. There it followed the shepherd's response to Kurvenal's query regarding Isolde's ship: "Öd' und leer das Meer!" (Barren and empty the sea!). Now, beginning from g♭', it contradicts the g' that climaxes Tristan's vision; and at the end of its first phrase Kurvenal answers Tristan's query regarding the ship by leading the g♭ to an f cadence: "Noch ist kein Schiff zu sehn!" (Still there is no ship to see!). At the earlier point, the tune had then returned to the beginning, to which Tristan had awakened—"Die alte Weise;—was weckt sie mich?"—turning the music toward F. In bringing it back from almost exactly the same point but this time supplying an f cadence, then beginning it over in f, Wagner articulates the beginning of a second stage (cycle), depicting Tristan's abandoning his former resistance to the meaning of the melody. Instead of turning away—outward—from the *alte Weise* and its f tonality, instead of searching for A♭, Tristan turns inward, reaching back into the past, long before his relationship with Isolde.

In its sequences the *alte Weise* creates the sense of almost continual downward motion. g♭' is the symbol of that motion, replacing the upward tendency of Tristan's g' toward a♭' by a downward tendency towards f. Tristan's first three phrases—

"*Muss ich dich* so verstehn,/*du alte* ernste Weise,/mit deiner *Klage* Klang?"—associate the g♭' with an element of tragic necessity within the tune, inviting its interpretation in terms of Schopenhauer's view of music as "copy of the will." Because in that view understanding music is tantamount to penetrating the meaning of the world, its essential nothingness, Wagner strips the f of the *alte Weise* of its tonal character long before Tristan's f/F cadence. The stages of Tristan's self-understanding, represented by his reflection on the associational qualities of the *alte Weise*, are mirrored by Wagner not only in the tonal and motivic characteristics of the melody itself but also—in the second part of Tristan's solo, when he internalizes the melody—in the processes by which he relates the *alte Weise* to several of the principal motives of the opera, above all those representing day and desire.[3]

In Schopenhauerian terms, the goal of Tristan's self-analysis through music is to transcend desire through recognition of the conflict of the Will with itself as the primary cause of human suffering, and thereby to overcome the perpetuation of the world of representation as the battlefield of that conflict, centered on desire. The *alte Weise* is constructed so as to embody the conflict of the Will with itself in terms of its leitmotif references and its chromatic tonal character. The alternation of the pitches g♭' and g'—that is, the opposition between the tritone and the perfect-fifth division of the c'/c" octave—serves as one of its primary symbols. The *frohe Weise*, by contrast, is purely diatonic, featuring only six pitches in toto and dividing the g'–g" octave at c'. Containing nothing in the way of motivic elements, it represents, as mentioned earlier, a stage that is closer to the primal state of innocence at which natural music emerges from the metaphysical night, as in the Prelude to *Das Rheingold*. The final stage, of course, is silence.

In contrast to the diatonic simplicity of the *frohe Weise*, the *alte Weise* is made up of a complex array of references to the motives of day and desire. In this it compares with the sailor's song that begins act 1. But there is an important difference: whereas the sailor's song had differentiated its chromatic and diatonic phrases from each other, setting up an opposition between the physical goal of the ship and the goal of Isolde's inner brooding, the *alte Weise* merges the two in ways that, as Wagner reveals in Tristan's self-analysis, reveal desire and day as two sides of the same coin. The second phrase of the melody makes that clear: its initial four tones—g', f', e♭', b♭'—outlining an E♭ triad, are easily recognizable as the tones of the day motive in retrograde; but, in treating the motive immediately in sequence, Wagner contracts the whole tones of the diatonic third descent to semitones—e♭', d', d♭', a♭'—then expands the rising fifth to a rising minor sixth—d♭', c', b, g'—revealing by degrees a hidden relationship between the retrograde of the day motive and the retrograde inversion of the beginning of the desire music. The chromatically descending semitone patterns of the melody—especially the g♭', f', e' that saturate the music preceding both Tristan's awakening and his self-analysis—inevitably invoke the desire music, whereas other elements, such as the falling minor sixth (d♭"–f'), remind us of the inverted forms of the initial rising sixth of that music that appear very early in the prelude (the glance, *Sühnetrank*, and poison motives). In this way the *alte Weise* seems almost to analyze itself; but in fact it is more accurate to say that Wagner has constructed it so as to provide continual reminders of the desire music, whose elements are shuffled in ways that draw us into the analytic process. Even without such analysis we will feel that hidden relationships are present. And in relation to the need for self-understanding that draws Tristan into associational analysis of the tune, we readily perceive the analogy Wagner sets up: between fragmentary memories of early life—Tristan's reaching back to all he knows of the circumstances of his conception and birth in relation to the deaths of his parents—and the inner musical relationships between the *alte Weise* and the desire music.

Tristan has two names, Tantris and Tristan, as Isolde narrates in act 1, the former a deception adopted by Tristan to cover his identity as Morold's slayer so that he could benefit from Isolde's healing abilities. Tantris was the name by which Isolde knew the patient in her inner chamber, the "sorrowful man" with whom she fell in love, whom she healed, then spared, after recognizing him as Morold's slayer. On his return to Ireland to claim Isolde as bride for King Mark, however, the name Tristan became associated with the knight whose enslavement to worldly values was expressed in Kurvenal's "Hei, unser Held Tristan."

In her narrative Isolde associates the names Tantris and Tristan with the rising and falling fifth respectively, making the connection of the latter to the beginning of Kurvenal's heroic theme and, eventually to the day motive as well. For that reason, perhaps, Wagner begins the *alte Weise* with the rising fifth; then, after a phrase in which he links the rising fifth to the retrograde of the day motive, he returns to the opening phrase, extending it and leading it into a phrase that begins with the exact inversion of its first seven notes. The *alte Weise* utilizes inversion, retrograde, and retrograde inversion in addition to the alternation between the tritone and perfect fifth, perhaps to convey the unity behind Tristan's hidden and manifest identities. And by shuffling the motivic and intervallic elements of the desire music throughout the tune Wagner lends it an evocative rather than systematic character. In Schopenhauer's metaphysics of music harmony is music's deepest, most internal, quality; so although the *alte Weise* originally sounds unaccompanied on the English horn, Wagner increasingly reveals its harmonic basis as that of the desire music and its diminished-seventh chord background, finally having the motifs of desire, the curse, the *alte Weise* and day dissolve into the diminished-seventh chord immediately before Tristan's final F cadence.

Tristan's Third Solo

Part 1: The Alte Weise on the English Horn
(mm. 626–727)

The first solo of Tristan's second cycle extends from the entrance of the *alte Weise* in measure 626 to Tristan's f cadence and collapse in measure 840 following his curse of the love potion and his own existence. The reentrance of the *alte Weise* now impels Tristan's memory back beyond the earliest events recollected in his first cycle; and from there it leads him forward to the point at which he recognizes his present circumstances as rooted in the distant past. Within the 215 measures of his solo, therefore, there is an obvious division into two parts. The first (mm. 626–727) centers on Tristan's recollection of his learning in childhood of his parents' deaths, his questioning the meaning of that knowledge for his fate and his attempt to provide an answer to that question. The second (mm. 728–840) begins with Tristan's memory of his relationship to Isolde from the point of his first journeying to Ireland to seek her healing powers up to the love potion, then continues with the impact and meaning of the potion itself, culminating in the curse and lapse into unconsciousness. The first of these segments coincides with the sounding of the *alte Weise* by the English horn on stage—that is from the shepherd himself—whereas the second sounds the tune only in fragmented form (nearly always just its first four tones) within the orchestra without English horn. The former segment features only limited leitmotif combinations, for the purpose of making clear the union of desire and day within the tune. The second features many leitmotif combinations culminating in a new motive for Tristan's realization and curse. Owing to the magnetic pull of the *alte Weise*, the first segment is in some sense "in" F minor, and entirely in the four-flat key signature, whereas the second moves away from both the key of f and its key signature, returning to four flats for twenty-six measures toward the end, to coincide with Tristan's realization that he brewed the potion himself, then canceling the key signature for the final nine measures, culminating in Tristan's f/F cadence. Nothing of the second segment is in f/F however, so both the return of the key signature and the f/F cadence are primarily symbolic.

This solo describes a two-stage progression in Tristan's understanding of his fate, the first leading to his question, "zu welchem Loos erkoren, ich damals wohl geboren? Zu welchem Loos?" (chosen for what fate was I then born? For what fate?) and the two "answers" that follow: "Die alte Weise sagt mir's wieder: mich sehnen und sterben!" (The *alte Weise* says to me once more: to desire and die!) and "Nein! Ach nein! So heisst sie nicht! Sehnen! Sehnen! Im Sterben mich zu sehnen, vor Sehnsucht nicht zu sterben!" (No! Ah no! That's not what it is! Longing! Longing! In death longing, for longing *not* to die!). Directly following the second of these passages Wagner introduces the first phrase of the *alte Weise*, the last time that any of the melody sounds on the English horn (mm. 713–18). With Tristan's next phrase, "Die nie erstirbt, sehnend nun ruft um Sterbens Ruh' sie der fernen Ärztin zu" (That which never dies out now calls yearningly to the distant physician for the rest of death), Wagner assigns the continuation of the *alte Weise* to oboe and clarinet, which reaches a cadence to F in measure 727.[4] These details suggest a new beginning, and from this point on the music of the *alte Weise*—limited for the most part to its first four tones—sounds in the orchestra in combination with one or more other motives. The second part of Tristan's solo concentrates on its relationship to an array of other themes, as Tristan reinterprets his relationship with Isolde in terms of the message of the tune: that he was fated for sorrowful desire and longing for death. What Wagner called the "wonderful concord of two themes"—the beginning of the *alte Weise* and the theme of Isolde's narrative, beginning in measure 727—initiates the latter process.

As mentioned earlier, not only does Wagner begin Tristan's solo from the return of the *alte Weise* on the pitch g♭″, but he has Kurvenal enter on g♭, then cadence to f for "Noch ist kein Schiff zu sehn!" The *alte Weise* starts over from the beginning at that point, and Tristan's initial three phrases either begin on g♭′ and move to f′ ("Muss ich dich so versteh'n" and "du alte ernste Weise") or the reverse ("mit deiner Klage Klang"). All the while the accompaniment descends gradually from the b♭″/b♭‴

octave of Tristan's "Kurvenal! Siehst du es nicht?" to the bass C. Focus on g♭ as a symbol of the downward turning, tragic character of the tune, continues throughout this entire phase of the solo, especially at points of arrival on the dominant, C, where g♭ and g usually alternate, g♭ always taking precedence. Thus the dominant harmony usually has the pitch content of the augmented-sixth chord (c, e, g♭, b♭) but sounds like a dominant, the g♭ lending it a quasi-Phrygian tendency downward to f. The first segment where the *alte Weise* drops out for any length of time (mm. 670–89) begins from such a cadence, on which Tristan, beginning again from g♭ as he relates his father's death, makes a kind of modulation to g♭ as he recalls his mother's. At this point, the *alte Weise* itself begins on g♭ instead of f in the orchestra. The continual chromaticism leads it back, of course, and as Tristan questions his fate ("zu welchem Loos?"), the g♭/g wavering returns, leading to a dominant cadence in which g♭ again replaces g. At this point Wagner conflates measures 10–15 of the *alte Weise* (where the tune starts over a second time) with its ending (mm. 38–42), using it to accompany Tristan's first answer—"Die alte Weise sagt mir's wieder: mich sehnen und sterben." Now we hear the closest equivalent of a final cadence in the solo, Tristan's falling fifth to f sounding above the dominant, directly before the *alte Weise* comes to a close for the only time other than its unaccompanied presentation early in the act.

Tristan realizes, however, that for him the meaning of the tune is more than the cycle of yearning and death; and to underscore that fact Wagner deceives the cadence with the day motive for Tristan's second answer regarding his fate. The second answer is the climax of the first half of the solo, his realization that desire prevents him from dying. On the word "nicht" ("Nein! Ach Nein! So heisst sie nicht!") he pushes his line upwards from the f″ of "sehnen und sterben" (the only point where the final phrase of the *alte Weise* sounds in his solo), to g♭″, then to g″ and a♭″ (twice) on "Sehnen" and "Sehnsucht," to its highest tone, a″ ("vor Sehnsucht *nicht*"), holding it for six beats before dropping suddenly on "zu sterben." It is here that the *initial* four measures of the *alte Weise* return, marking the shift to a new stage in Tristan's quest for self-understanding. As Tristan sings "die nie erstirbt, sehnend nun ruft um Sterbens Ruh'," its melody passes into the orchestra, sounding the retrograde inversion of the beginning of the desire music in sequence. Desire for Isolde, which had called Tristan from the night now calls Isolde to heal him. Tristan sings the G♭ arpeggio on "Sterbens Ruh'" and a quasi-cadential F arpeggio on "[der fernen] Ärztin zu."

Part Two: Tristan's Recollection, Curse, and Relapse
(mm. 727–840)

This is the only time in Tristan's solo where the *alte Weise* reaches an F/f harmony, all other comparable points leading the dominant into some form of deceptive cadence. Tristan's F[6] chord begins a new phase, bringing in the theme of Isolde's narrative to parallel Tristan's insight that desire necessitates Isolde's coming to heal him. As Tristan now understands it, the goal of that healing, "Sterbens Ruh'," was denied him by Isolde twice prior to his wounding by Melot. Tristan returns first to the memory of his drifting to Ireland in a skiff after his battle with Morold in search of healing from Isolde: "Sterbend lag ich stumm im Kahn, der Wunde Gift dem Herzen nah'" (Dying I lay dumb in the skiff, the poison of the wound close to the heart). But

Isolde, after healing his wound, had torn it open again with the sword ("Die Wunde, die sie heilend schloss, riss mit dem Schwert sie wieder los"). What Tristan remembers, however, did not happen literally; Isolde did not use the sword, she dropped it, as Tristan now describes, "das Schwert dann aber liess sie sinken." This is no slip of either Wagner's or Tristan's memory. Isolde's tearing the wound open with the sword was accomplished *by* her dropping the sword—that is, by *not* killing Tristan. The wound that was torn open was the wound of desire. Tristan conflates Isolde's sparing his life in Ireland with her refusal to kill him with the sword on board the ship to Cornwall.[5] Instead, as Tristan narrates, she gave him the poison drink with which he hoped to recover—that is, to die—only to find that its "searing magic" kept him from dying: "den Gifttrank gab sie mir zu trinken: wie ich da hoffte ganz zu genesen, da ward der sehrendste Zauber erlesen: dass nie ich sollte sterben, mich ew'ger Qual vererben!" (The poison drink she gave me to drink: although then I hoped to recover completely, instead the most searing magic was chosen: so that I should never die but inherit eternal torment!). Tristan's thoughts center on the potion as symbol of the inescapable torment of desire. With his realization that he brewed it himself comes the understanding that the "poison" is inseparable from the events of his life:

Den furchtbaren Trank	The fearful drink
der der Qual mich vertraut,	which gave me such torment,
ich selbst—ich selbst,	I myself—I myself,
ich hab' ihn gebraut!	I brewed it!
Aus Vaters Not	From my father's torment
und Mutterweh,	and my mother's woe,
aus Liebestränen	from the tears of love
eh und je—	then and forever—
aus Lachen und Weinen,	from laughter and weeping,
Wonnen und Wunden	joys and wounds
hab' ich des Trankes	there the drink's
Gifte gefunden!	poison I found!

What follows, therefore, is his curse of the potion and his own existence:

Den ich gebraut,	That which I brewed,
der mir geflossen,	which flowed through me,
den wonneschlürfend	which, gulping down bliss
je ich genossen—	I always enjoyed—
verflucht sei, furchtbarer Trank!	be accursed, terrifying drink!
Verflucht, wer dich gebraut!	Accursed he who brewed you!

Musically, this part of Tristan's solo is occupied, as I have said, with revealing desire as the common bond among several of the principal motives of the drama, including the *alte Weise* and the motive of Tristan's curse, as well as with revealing the diminished-seventh chord that bonds the keys of f and B as the harmony behind the desire music itself. Whereas the first part of the solo is anchored around f by the *alte Weise*, this part is not at all concerned with tonal form in the usual sense. The cadence to f/F with which it closes is not in any sense the tonic key, not even a recurrent tonality in this part of the solo, such as A♭, however weakly expressed, is in Tristan's first cycle.

Yet Wagner is certainly concerned with *pitch* relationships; and, as usual, he draws on the traditional harmonies of tonal music to aid in their articulation, but without invoking their functions on anything more than the most local level. The predominant quality is that of denial, which means that we hear the tonal potential of the musical gestures to the degree that we recognize the denial of their fulfillment as such. At the same time, those gestures open up the possibility of another way of hearing, one in which the quality of negation, as it is associated with a philosophical "truth," the nothingness of the world, attains, however paradoxically, a positive value in the process of self-understanding and, ultimately, transcendence.

As we might expect, the pitch relationships in question involve F, on which the solo will end, and F♯/G♭, the pitch that Wagner directs toward F in the *alte Weise*, and emphasizes in the first half of Tristan's solo, but that also—as the dominant of B— will determine the arpeggiation pattern of the desire music as it accompanies Tristan's reawakening to his clairvoyant vision of Isolde. The segment of Tristan's solo that Wagner calls the "sick man's voyage"—drawing a parallel between Tristan's seeking physical healing in Ireland and his present voyage in search of metaphysical healing—picks up from the point at which the g♭ of the *alte Weise* finally moves to F; and from that F (the above-mentioned F^6 chord) Wagner brings back the theme of Isolde's narrative as it accompanied her recounting the episode of the sword. Ingeniously combining the narrative theme with the day motive and as many as two excerpts from the *alte Weise* (and implying that the *alte Weise* was the music that Tristan played as he drifted to Ireland in search of healing), Wagner leads Tristan's memory of Isolde's dropping the sword to a highly symbolic f♯ cadence that is "deceived" by the poison motive in the bass (m. 754). And from this point on Wagner unfolds the process of motivic reinterpretation that leads to Tristan's curse and relapse. When Tristan and Isolde reflected back on the events of act 1 in the *Tagesgespräch*, the tonal goal was A♭, the key of night-death, out of which the B of "O ew'ge Nacht" ultimately arose. Now it is F, out of which the B of Tristan's reawakening and vision of transcendence will emerge.

The process just introduced involves the most systematic exploration of pitch relationships surrounding the desire music in the entire opera. It centers on the F diminished seventh chord as the background harmony for the Tristan chord and the desire music, and it emphasizes shifting between the single pitch that differentiates the two harmonies. This would be d/d♯ in the F Tristan chord, of course, but Wagner focuses instead on the f/f♯ shift that belongs to the second phrase of the desire music and that was so important in the third phrase, and in the honor music. In this he sets up the shift from the f cadence of Tristan's relapse to the F♯ dominant harmony of his rebirth. After Tristan's f♯ cadence, Wagner uses motion between the pitches F♯ and F to link the poison motive with the second death motive and that in turn with the reappearance of the first two phrases of the desire music in combination with the beginning of the "alte Weise." Wagner even modifies the interval from the third to the fourth tone of the *alte Weise* from a whole tone to a semitone in order to bring this out; it leads, eventually, to the beginning of the curse motive. Throughout the entire sequence the diminished-seventh chord on F bonds the above-mentioned themes. As Tristan narrates how his hope that the poisoned drink would bring recovery (i.e., death) was thwarted by desire—"den Gifttrank gab sie mir zu trinken: wie ich da hoffte ganz zu genesen"—Wagner settles on the F diminished-seventh chord, leading it into the death motive and that in turn into the desire music in combination with the beginning tones of the *alte Weise.* He then leads the Tristan chord of the desire music not into the usual E^7 chord but into the diminished-seventh chord as the poetic text explains how Tristan's hopes for recovery became the endless torment of desire.

From this point on Tristan explores his experience of desire in terms of the impact of the potion. Wagner's primary device is tritone relationships arising from the F diminished-seventh chord. Returning in memory to the moments immediately following the drinking of the potion, Tristan brings back music that has not been heard since that point, developing its implications far more fully than on its first appearance and using its harmonic content and interval structure both to further clarify what we have just heard and to prepare the curse motive to come. The music in question had followed the second phrase of the desire music, where it introduced an alternation of the diminished-seventh chord and the Tristan chords on F and B by means of a melodic pattern that exchanged the pitches D and Eb (the F diminished-seventh and Tristan chords) then Ab and A (the B diminished-seventh and Tristan chords) in different registers. In other words, two tritone-related Tristan chords had changed back and forth with the same diminished-seventh chord. Now Wagner brings back this music, using it to reveal the derivation of the full range of four Tristan chords from the diminished-seventh chord. First the F Tristan chord emerges from the diminished seventh and returns to it via the d–eb shifting of the motive, then the same process takes place with the B Tristan chord. Wagner keeps this process of alternation going for four measures before transposing it so as to reveal the same relationship between the D and G♯ Tristan chords and the diminished seventh, likewise for four measures (ex. 14.4).

If we compare this passage with the first three appearances of the curse motive in the orchestra directly following Tristan's "ich selbst, ich hab' ihn gebraut," we find that the initial intervals (and pitches) of all three appearances of the curse motive derive directly from the passage just described: first eb‴–d‴–f″, then a″–ab″–b′, and finally c‴–b″–d″. The curse motive, too, articulates the shift from Tristan chords on F, B and D to the same diminished-seventh chord. And immediately after that it combines with the desire music so as to articulate the sequence of Tristan chord followed by diminished-seventh chord then dominant-seventh chord, the entire process revealing the diminished-seventh chord as the background harmony for the desire music.

Wagner next introduces a fourfold sequence in which each of the four Tristan chords on G♯, B, D, and F moves to a major seventh chord (on G, Bb, Db, and E, respectively), the last of these bringing back the combination of the beginning of the *alte Weise* with the day motive. Tristan's growing understanding is mirrored in the revelation of relationships involving the primary four-tone chords of the opera. Finally, to prepare for his curse, Wagner returns to the theme from "Im Treibhaus" that he had used to set up Tristan's earlier curse of day. Now he transposes it so that in-

Example 14.4. Act 3, scene 1: tritone-related transpositions of the Tristan chord in Tristan's second cycle.

stead of settling on the dominant of A♭ it leads three times to the dominant of B. As in the earlier passage, Tristan refers to his brain (*Hirn*), accompanied by an ascending sequence of augmented triads: "O dieser Sonne sengender Strahl, wie brennt mir das Hirn seine glühende Qual!" (Oh the scorching ray of the sun, how its glowing torment burns my brain!). The entire sequence from Tristan's remembering Isolde's dropping the sword to this point has dealt once again, but now in vastly more systematic fashion, with the emergence of Tristan chords, major-seventh chords, and augmented triads from the diminished seventh chord. Now Wagner develops harmonic relationships arising from the *alte Weise* that feature tritone-related dominant sevenths.

As the sequence of parallel augmented triads sweeps upward above the pedal F♯ in the bass (as it had above the pedal D♯ of the first cycle), Wagner leads Tristan's line upward toward f♯', at that point ("Qual") changing the bass F♯, which still retains a sense of the dominant of B, to G♭. And with that change he brings in the sound of the dominant seventh of F in the uppermost register of the orchestra (minus G, of course). Here in one stroke whatever tonal sense we possess is shifted at the tritone, from B to F, although not an ordinary F, nor even one that prepares for Tristan's f/F cadence to come. To rivet the F in our consciousness Wagner uses the G♭ to bring back the melody of the *alte Weise* in the bass from the point he had chosen for its return at the beginning of Tristan's second cycle (itself a reference back to the sounding of the *alte Weise* at the point of Tristan's awakening). And he inverts (or retrogrades) its chromatic g♭, f, e descent in horn and oboe with the chromatic ascent of the desire music—e', f', f♯', g'—transposed so as to indicate the key of F. Tristan's line centers on the descending semitone from the flat sixth to the dominant (d♭–c) almost exclusively. Finally, Wagner brings in the initial four tones of the *alte Weise* in the piccolo and first violins, beginning from c" (i.e., c", g", b♭", a"). And as the b♭" moves to a", we hear the Tristan chord change to the diminished-seventh chord again. Throughout the passage Tristan touches g' three times in preparation for the entrance of the curse motive from that pitch and the final ascent of his upper register tones to the a" of the curse itself.

The tritone B/F relationship that Wagner invokes in the passage just described can be related, of course, to the F/B relationship of Tristan's curse-relapse and his reawakening. But, although it anticipates that relationship, it is no more causally determining of it—in terms of the musical continuity—than Isolde's A♭/B succession in her "Frau Minne" solo in act 2, scene 1, is determining of the same succession of keys in her *Liebestod*. Wagner is not preparing an event that will seem to be the direct outcome of what has preceded it, but on reinforcing the suspended tonality that is heard throughout the opera in conjunction with desire. The tritone relationship derives from the desire music; and its quintessential manifestation is the climax of the Prelude, in which the enharmonicism is far more apparent (audibly transformational) than here. In this passage the tritone relationship is a part of a larger motion that can hardly be described as tonal, at least in the sense of articulating a single key. The semitone motion in the *alte Weise*, the bass, and Tristan's lines is the key feature in pushing the music up a tone, so that the alternation of d" and e♭", reiterated for several measures, eventually leads into an e♭⁶₄ chord ("Den furchtbaren *Trank*") as Tristan's line reaches the tone g♭' (enharmonic equivalent of his f♯' on "Qual"). Here Wagner brings back the four-flat key signature, although it is purely a symbolic gesture.

The goal of the passage is Tristan's realization that he brewed the potion himself— "Ich selbst hab' ihn gebraut"—at which he reaches g' for the first appearance of the curse motive. It is in no sense a point of tonal arrival in the usual sense. When we examine the harmonic motion, we find that the harmonies are determined by the necessity of supporting individual *pitches*, by the motivic exigencies and the chromatic voice leading, *not* by long-range tonal considerations. The music that follows will reveal the "atonal" side of the desire music; even the unresolved dominant-seventh chords of its individual phrases are now replaced by diminished-seventh chords.

After its initial sounding, Wagner presents the curse motive in a sequence derived from the diminished-seventh chord background of the desire music: the three phrases begin from e♭‴, a″ and c‴, respectively (Tristan chords on F, B, and A♭), duplicating the pitch, harmony, and interval structure of Wagner's development of the theme that sounded following the drinking of the potion in act 1. It leads almost directly into a combination of the curse motive and the desire music in which the three phrases transpose upward in the exact pattern of the desire music—Tristan chords on F, G♯, and D—the curse motive beginning from e♭‴, f♯‴, and a‴. At the end of the third phrase Tristan finally reaches the pitch a′ ("Verflucht"). His curse of the potion—"Verflucht sei, furchtbarer *Trank*"—introduces the F Tristan chord along with the desire music, the beginning of the *alte Weise* and the curse motive. The curse motive effects the change from d♯ to d (F Tristan chord to diminished seventh) and the *alte Weise* sounds the f♯‴–f‴ shift (G♯ Tristan chord to diminished seventh) immediately afterward. Wagner holds the diminished-seventh chord for an extra measure in which he sounds the day motive, now outlining the g♯′, d′, f′ triad. Tristan's f/F cadence, which now follows, using the G Tristan chord from the beginning of the act to underline the flat sixth degree, completes the goal of the entire solo, "Verflucht, wer dich gebraut" (ex. 14.5).

Example 14.5. Act 3, scene 1: Tristan's curse and relapse.

Example 14.5. (Continued)

In the process just described Wagner develops the latent negating tendency within the desire music to its fullest point. Its goal, which he described as his amendment of Schopenhauer, is the coming to consciousness of the species Will (love as fearful torment) within Tristan. The interlocking tritones and latent enharmonicism of the diminished-seventh chord are a quintessential harmonic analog of the quality of negation. Although the tendency toward atonality that results may be invoked as a symbol of denial within a predominantly tonal context, when it exists as the product of other means of musical organization and coherence, such as voice-leading and motivic processes, it loses its pejorative associations. Wagner does not take that final step. The reduction of the harmony of Tristan's curse to the diminished-seventh chord is, therefore, not the final stage in his metaphysical understanding. But it is the final one insofar as *intellectual* understanding is concerned. Having come to realization of the "nothingness of the world," Tristan can go no further with the philosophical or intellectual *Wahn*. With his "rebirth," therefore, there is a reemergence of tonality via the transformation of the desire music so as to arpeggiate the dominant of B.

That process begins at the point at which Kurvenal pronounces love "der Welt holdester Wahn." The first eight measures of Kurvenal's solo continue the harmonic relationships of Tristan's solo. Both Kurvenal and the orchestra enter on b above the bare f of Tristan's cadence. As Kurvenal, distraught, cries out in horror—"Mein Herre! Tristan! Schrecklicher Zauber! O Minnetrug! O Liebeszwang!"—the orchestra carries the curse motive rapidly upward in sequence, its initial tones outlining the pitches of the diminished seventh, then the Tristan chord at its peak: b, d′, f′, ab′ (the diminished seventh), then b′, d″, f″, a″ (the Tristan chord). At the peak the orchestra returns to the curse motive in its basic form, beginning first from the B Tristan chord ("O Minnetrug") then the D Tristan chord ("O Liebeszwang"), each time leading the Tristan chord back into the diminished seventh. With "Der Welt holdester Wahn," however, Wagner brings in a B major dominant harmony (B$^4_2$), assigning Kurvenal the d♯′ on "holdester" and changing the key signature to two sharps on "Wahn." Replacing the eb′ on which the next entrance of the curse motive would enter, Kurvenal's d♯′ heralds a momentous change. On "Wahn" Kurvenal sings the curse motive himself for the first time, beginning not from a Tristan chord but from the diminished-seventh chord. And it does not become increasingly "atonal" but just the reverse: its final pitch brings in the Tristan chord that functions as the supertonic of b. And the measures that follow move toward Kurvenal's B minor cadence: "Hier liegt er nun, der wonnige Mann, der wie Keiner geliebt und geminnt. Nun seht, was von ihm sie Dankes gewann, was je Minne sich gewinnt!" (Here he lies now, the happy man, loved and desired as no other. Now see what thanks she got from him, what Minne ever attains!). In his final measures Kurvenal sounds the curse motive in a tonal sequence by which it loses a great deal of its negating force. The approach to the final cadence introduces the rising chromaticism of the desire music in the orchestra, beginning from g♯ above the dominant (F♯) pedal and passing through a to the leading tone (a♯) within the dominant-seventh chord, after which Kurvenal's line leads to its cadential tone, b. Once again the tritone enters in the bass beneath the voice, but this time, although notated as F, it is in reality E♯, the beginning of the desire music in its transformed tonal form (see ex. 15.1).

FIFTEEN

The Road to Salvation

Tristan's Awakening and Clairvoyant Vision

The tritone that sounds as Tristan sinks unconscious to F and the orchestra and Kurvenal enter on B is an expression of the purely negating view of existence. When Kurvenal, having pronounced love a delusion, cadences in B minor—"Behold what thanks love has won from him, what love ever wins"—Wagner brings in the F beneath his cadential b, then the Tristan chord, an octave below its usual pitch and in its darkest coloring, as if to evoke only the negative side of his words, not their ironic truth. Revealing that truth is the central theme of the opera from this point on, as expressed in the title of this chapter, taken from the final sections of Schopenhauer's treatise and echoed by Wagner in his description of his amendment.

While Kurvenal sings, the Tristan chord repeats in a softly pulsating, syncopated rhythm, sounding some forty times before the initial melody tone moves and the harmony changes, settling on a $B\flat^9$ chord, the beginning of the transformed version of the desire music. The F$\sharp$ triadic arpeggiation pattern that unfolds throughout its three phrases derives from the act one honor music; but now the rising melodic lines of all three units outline major instead of minor thirds (ex. 15.1).

This change had appeared at the climax of the prelude (for the first phrase only); but there it was immediately offset by the interaction of the melody with the glance motive, whose emphasis on the minor third reinforced the sound of the tritone and diminished seventh chord, contradicting any impulse toward the major key. At the drinking of the love potion Wagner limited the harmony to the *minor* dominant ninth chord and the glance motive. At both points, therefore, the phrase went no further in the direction of transformation; and the enharmonic relapse back to the starting point sealed off any hopes of the lovers finding the "breach" into night. And although the honor music introduced the arpeggiation of the F$\sharp$ triad over its three phrases, the melody remained locked into the minor-third transpositions of the

266

Example 15.1. Act 3, scene 1: Tristan's reawakening to the transformed version of the desire music

Example 15.1. (Continued)

diminished-seventh chord. So did the first two phrases of the version of the desire music that Wagner introduced in the deleted transition to "O ew'ge Nacht." The only exception was the duet "So stürben wir," where, despite the minor-third arpeggiation in the melody, Wagner lent the rising major third a quasi-transcendental character on the B♭ and C♯ cadences of its first two phrases. The F♯ arpeggiation pattern, however, remained an unfulfilled potential that would emerge only in the *Liebestod*.

On Tristan's awakening the change to the major third links up the first and second phrases with what was already present in the third. The sense of a break with the pitch framework of the diminished-seventh chord is present from the beginning. Now the dominant ninth chords of the first and second phrase endings contain Tristan chords from the original sphere within them, their meaning altered by the new bass tones. Wagner had treated the Tristan chord as an incomplete dominant-ninth chord and even, with the addition of the extra tone, as a full dominant-ninth chord at several points in the love scene. The first of the dream chords of "O sink hernieder" is an instance, leading the ending of the duet to pass over into the f♯ tonality of Brangaene's warning. Another is the melodic high point of "So stürben wir," where it forms a key element in the abovementioned "potential" toward the dominant of

B. And for the original modulation from A♭ to B in "O ew'ge Nacht" Wagner had introduced the Tristan chord as a deceptive resolution of the dominant (E♭) harmony, then reinterpreted the chord in sharps—that is, as the incomplete dominant ninth of F♯, now with the bass tone functioning as E♯—to set up the shift to B (see ex. 4.6).

What I have just described is an important part of the background for the transformed version of the desire music around which act 3 pivots. As the Tristan chord enters beneath Kurvenal's melodic cadence to b, it functions, at least momentarily, as the incomplete dominant ninth (of the dominant, F♯) again. Wagner does not notate it as such (the bass tuba plays the pitch F beneath the sharp-notated pitches of the trombones); but the piano scores of Bülow, Klindworth and Kleinmichel all spell the initial Tristan chord with E♯ instead of F in the bass, thereby anticipating the eventual motion toward B from the start. The e♯ appears explicitly very soon after that in the b–e♯ tritone ending Kurvenal's line "Bist du nun tot? *Lebst du noch?*" When the final line of Kurvenal's solo cadences with a half close in F♯, directly before phrase three of the desire music, its final tones, f♯–e♯, highlight the change of the F into an E♯ leading tone to F♯. In the unfolding of the desire music as Tristan gradually revives, the difference between E♯ and F is a factor of the same kind of wavering that I have indicated in the original version of the desire music and that Wagner emphasizes in Tristan's answer to Mark. As the third phrase passes over into an adumbration of the transfiguration music, we know that the hold of the F and the diminished-seventh chord framework has been overcome.

Because the B♭ dominant ninth harmony of the first phrase does not immediately suggest F♯ or B, this version of the desire music conveys a greater sense of transformation than on any previous appearance, in any form. This is owing primarily to the perfect-fifth relationship between the dominant harmonies of the second and third phrases, in which the dominant of the third phrase (F♯) is anticipated by *its* dominant (C♯) in the second. Wagner reinforces this quality with additional details in the harmony and vocal lines. And over the course of the three phrases the bass tones of the dominant sevenths—B♭, C♯ and F♯—hold for increasingly long spans (approximately two, six, and ten measures, respectively). F♯ becomes the symbol of the transcendent quality in the desire music.

Once we understand the significance of the turning point, many other details can be seen to mirror the sense of antithesis and transformation. Thus, the pitch F♯, identifying the key of B as its goal, can be viewed as reversing the tendency of the G♭ of the *alte Weise* toward f. In this light, the f♯–e♯ appoggiatura of Kurvenal's "Das Schiff? Gewiss, es naht noch heut'; es kann nicht lang' mehr säumen!" (The ship? Certainly it will come today; it can't last much longer!") reverses the tonal character of his g♭–f at "Noch ist kein Schiff zu sehn" (Still no ship to see), the beginning of Tristan's sorrowful meditation on the meaning of the *alte Weise* and its F minor tonality. After Tristan's awakening, the curse motive, formerly associated with the "regression" of Tristan chords into diminished-seventh chords, is transformed by the turn to B major; for its last appearance Wagner turns its chromatic descending element around, leading it, too, upward so as to articulate the e♯″–f♯″ appoggiatura as it settles on a B major harmony. Most of all, the return of the *Sühnetrank* music makes the point that the drink of atonement is the antidote to the conception of the love potion that Tristan curses before his relapse. Already in the first act cadences to f♯ (the dominant of b) were associated with the opposition of the sword and the drink of atonement, especially in Isolde's "Nun laß uns Sühne trinken." And in his second cycle Tristan had returned to the memory of all that as he cadenced to f♯, the beginning of his reinterpretation of a sequence of motives in terms of the f♯/f alternation between the Tristan chord and the diminished seventh chord. Whereas Tristan's curse of the love potion was associated with the semitone motion from g♭ to f in the *alte Weise*, his recall of the "drink of reconciliation" is associated with the motion from e♯″ to f♯″ in the third phrase of the desire music. Thus, Wagner fulfills the implications of the motion to the dominant within the desire music, its association with the E major of the *Sühnetrank* motive in the prelude, and with the b/f♯ tonality of the first half of act 1, scene 5.

In the Prelude, the E major of the *Sühnetrank* music never became securely established, an allegory, as I have suggested (chapter 6), of the failure of the lovers' vision of ideal union to determine the form (which moves toward e♭ instead). The E of Tristan's clairvoyant vision, however, is remarkably secure, one of the contributing factors to Lorenz's viewing it as a manifestation of the tonic key of the opera, depicting the Idea of love in the Schopenhauerian-Platonic sense. Although Wagner introduces a hint of F that turns the E into the dominant of A at its only internal subdivision, the second part simply returns after a dozen measures from A to E in which it remains. Wagner bases the solo primarily on the love's peace motive, linking it particularly to the appearance of that motive in the act 2 solo in which Isolde introduces the meaning of the word "and," combining it with the orchestral counter melody that sounds when Isolde sings the love's peace motive itself at "was es bindet, der Liebe Bund." The "bond of love" is what enables Tristan to experience his clairvoyant vision of Isolde; physical distance no longer matters. This solo, therefore, must be understood as an expression of metaphysical unity through love. At the same time, it evokes the dream of love in a musical detail that Wagner introduces in its second half. There he reshapes the love's peace motive, widening the interval of its leap upward so as to reach the tone, a″, which has held in the violins since the beginning of the motive. As it descends the violins lead the a″ into a g♯″/f♯″ appoggiatura that resolves into a sustained diminished-seventh chord, duplicating the pattern of the second of the dream chords of "O sink hernieder" (transposed). Wagner reinforces the connection by introducing the syncopated rhythm of that duet for the two measures of diminished-seventh chord harmony. Coinciding with Tristan's "Sie lächelt mir Trost und süsse Ruh'" (She smiles with consolation and sweet rest for me), this detail evokes the idea of the dream of love again. Its quintessential expression comes with Tristan's "Ach, Isolde! Isolde! Wie schön bist du" (Ah, Isolde! Isolde! How beautiful you are), Tristan's lingering with the appoggiatura-laden B major dominant harmony lending the whole an indescribably nostalgic character. There is nothing, however, of the quality that accompanied the diminished-seventh chord in the music that led to Tristan's curse; now the diminished-seventh chords, prolonged for two full measures each time, suggest a dissolving but not a negating quality.

The mechanism by which Wagner sets up the E major beginning of the solo, with its four horns providing the romantic aura of the dream of love, is the circle-of-fifths motion from within the transformed version of the desire music—the C♯ of the second phrase, even with hints of *its* dominant, passing into the F♯ of the third phrase, then the B major adumbration of the transfiguration music, the transformed curse motive, and the drink of atonement music. The last of these passes through g♯ on the way to E, so that the E is invested with a romantic flat-sixth character as it begins. On a larger scale, however, the falling-fifth, falling-third motion does not end here. As I have suggested earlier, the E gives way to a transition to C for the entrance of the *frohe Weise*. The C (presented with its dominant in the bass) centers a stretch of nearly three hundred measures that come to an end only as Isolde arrives and the tonality passes over into a for the desire music and Tristan's death. The E, C, and a tonalities reverse the arpeggiation pattern of the beginning of the opera, completing the cycle of desire by moving from the romantic ideal of love, through love as nature and the physical, thwarted by Tristan's death, as desire returns to its metaphysical origins.

The *Frohe Weise* and Tristan's Death

At the end of his vision, Tristan's "Wie schön bist du" luxuriates in the sound of the dominant seventh for two measures before moving into the theme that will sound more than twenty times in the bass over the next three hundred measures (including eight times in inversion): the "Barg im Busen" theme of "O sink hernieder." This motive symbolizes, as Wagner said, the "Tristanesque night"—that is, the light that comes solely from within. In the love scene Brangaene had taken up this theme in her first warning, intermingling the idea of the subjectivity of light from "O sink hernieder" with her warning of the coming day. Now, the motive is instrumental in preparing for the turn to C and the entrance of the *frohe Weise*. At the latter point Tristan cries out "Das Schiff? Säh'st du's noch nicht?" an echo of his cry to Kurvenal at the end of the first cycle. And the pitch g′ is the goal of his lines once more, now in preparation for its functioning as the dominant of C for most of the next three hundred measures. During that span its arising from the depths beneath the *frohe Weise* suggests night as the depth that encompasses day as well.

Throughout the more than 150 measures from the entrance of the *frohe Weise* to the beginning of scene 2, Wagner sounds only the *frohe Weise*, the "Barg im Busen" melody and the motive of Tristan's "Ach, Isolde" from his vision. These measures are concerned with anticipation of the arrival and landing of Isolde's ship. Their continually returning to the dominant of C sets up the expectation of her arrival with the same device (transposed) that Wagner had used to depict Isolde's awaiting Tristan's arrival in the transition to the love scene in act 2. The C major duet that began the love scene was clearly a return to day, or as Wagner expressed it "life overflowing with all the most violent emotions." Now the emotions are violent once again, and the day is no longer threatening. In the prose draft Wagner added the marginal note "Preis des Tages! der Sonne—nur einmal leben—endlich leben—!" (Praise of the day! Of the Sun—just once life—finally life!).[1]

Scene 2, defined by Kurvenal's hastening to help Isolde from the ship, symbolically coincides with Tristan's reversing the meaning of day—"O diese Sonne! Ha! Dieser Tag! Ha, dieser Wonne sonnigster Tag!" (O this sun! Ah! This day! Ah, this blessed, sunniest of days)—his phrase culminating in the second death motive. The jubilant Minne theme from the beginning of the love scene sounds once more. And Wagner reinforces the meaning by bringing back another motive not heard since the first act: the A major version of the desire music that I have called A″ in chapter 6. In the prelude its optimistic surface gives way to the move toward e♭ at the climax. And when the music of the prelude returns after the drinking of the love potion this music reappears, again on the dominant of A major, but this time preceded by the dominant of E as well. Its text—"Sehnender Minne schwellendes Blühen, schmachtender Liebe seliges Glühen!" (Swelling bloom of yearning love, blessed glow of languishing love)—identifies it as an expression of the surge of ecstasy that overcomes the lovers. In act 3, Wagner presents it in D♭—a function of C—combining it with the "Barg im Busen" theme, and leading them both into the music that climaxes Tristan's ecstasy, the "love's peace" motive, now in C major and in a quasi-ostinato $\frac{5}{4}$ meter. To this music, which includes several presentations of the "Ach, Isolde" motive, Tristan stands up, rips off his bandages, and staggers forward to meet Isolde, comparing the moment to his battle with Morold:

Tristan, der Held,	Tristan the hero,
in jubelnder Kraft,	in jubilant strength
hat sich vom Tod	has snatched himself
emporgerafft.	away from death.
Mit blutender Wunde	With bleeding wounds
bekämft' ich einst Morolden:	I once battled Morold:
mit blutender Wunde	with bleeding wounds
erjag' ich mir heut' Isolden!	today I will conquer Isolde!
Heia, mein Blut!	Hah, my blood!
Lustig nun fliesse!	Flow now in joy!
Die mir die Wunde	She who forever
ewig schliesse,	closes my wounds,
sie naht wie ein Held,	she comes like a hero,
sie naht mir zum Heil!	she comes for my salvation!
Vergeh' die Welt	Let the world pass away
meiner jauchzenden eil'!	to my rejoicing haste!

Apart from the leitmotif recollections and combinations, this entire passage is characterized by two musical qualities. The first is its drawing all secondary tonal and harmonic events (such as the D♭ of the "sehnender Minne" music from act 1) into the perspective of the dominant of C, introduced by the *frohe Weise* but reaching its climax in the ecstatic $\frac{5}{4}$ version of the "love's peace" motive. And the second is the movement of the rhythm and meter toward the return of the slow $\frac{6}{8}$ of the prelude for the six measures of the glance music that culminate in Tristan's death. In the 150 measures during which we hear either the *frohe Weise* itself or orchestral passages based on it, the dominant of C returns constantly, but C never once sounds itself in the bass. The point where it finally does, Kurvenal's announcing the arrival of Isolde's ship—"Im Hafen der Kiel! *Isolde*" (the keel is in the harbor! Isolde!)—marks also the first shift of meter in those 150 measures, from the rapid $\frac{3}{4}$ to $\frac{2}{2}$, that is, to the basic meter and tempo of the first half of the second act. The tonality does not settle on C at this point, however, and with scene two the metric character changes again, simultaneously with the sudden reappearance of the string of motives described earlier. Now the music shifts frequently and rapidly between $\frac{3}{4}$ and $\frac{4}{4}$ until the $\frac{5}{4}$ of the love's peace motive takes over. Then, at the end of the lines cited earlier, Wagner shifts the meter progressively from $\frac{5}{4}$ to $\frac{4}{4}$, $\frac{3}{4}$ and $\frac{2}{4}$, indicating simultaneously an *accelerando*. The goal is the rapid $\frac{2}{2}$ again; and it arrives exactly at the point where the G dominant pedal finally moves to c'. Throughout this passage the love's peace motive dissolves into figuration that becomes more and more like the beginning of the torch motive. With the arrival on c' Wagner dissolves the harmony as well, into ten measures of the C diminished-seventh chord above which the torch motive reenters. The passage parallels the eight measures of diminished-seventh chord that led to Isolde's extinguishing the torch in act 2.

I have described how the C diminished-seventh chord passes into the dominant of C once more at the end of Tristan's "Wie, hör' ich das Licht? Die Leuchte, ha! Die Leuchte verlischt. Zu ihr! Zu ihr!" To the reappearance of the music of Isolde's extinguishing the torch—the "torch" motive and the death motive, now transposed to c—Wagner adds, as I mentioned, the "Barg im Busen" melody, now in the uppermost voice, its Ab/A transposition pattern from "O sink hernieder" merged with the Ab/A harmonies of the death motive (see ex. 7.3).Wagner sets the motive in $\frac{3}{2}$ within the basic $\frac{2}{2}$ time signature, at the same time crossing its rising line with the descent of the $\frac{2}{2}$ torch motive. The no-longer-metaphoric extinguishing of life and light gives way to the rise of an inner light, the fulfillment of Frau Minne's work, whose music reappears as the enharmonic transition from c to a. The desire music, however, remains in $\frac{2}{2}$ in the winds even though the strings change their time signature to $\frac{3}{2}$ at the entrance of the Tristan chord. The first change comes at the entrance of the Tristan chord of phrase three, at which point the cellos changes from $\frac{3}{2}$ to $\frac{6}{4}$. After two measures the $\frac{6}{4}$ meter spreads to the violas as well and after two more measures to the second violins. One by one the winds drop out until, finally, only a single oboe is left in $\frac{4}{4}$ to play the alternating e#" and f#" as the melody leads into the deceptive cadence. For the cadence Wagner arpeggiates the F major chord for two measures in the harp, the first measure with six quarter notes (thus $\frac{6}{4}$) and the second with four. As the b" (held for two and a half measures) resolves to a" in the oboe line, the cellos, now muted, enter with the glance music, beginning of course from the a on which they had played this motive in the prelude, the a with which the prelude and the opera began. The meter finally reaches the original slow $\frac{6}{8}$.

Isolde's Cycle

If Tristan's death is in some sense a resolution, what follows from here to the beginning of the *Liebestod* opens up a rift between the physical and metaphysical perspectives on existence. Isolde now enters a world that is more truly apart from that of the other characters than at any other point in the drama. It begins with the first of her two solos, depicting her struggle against Tristan's death and her own desire and ends with her conversion to night. And, indeed, all that surrounds that process and its completion in the *Liebestod* can be described as another cycle, Isolde's two solos corresponding in several ways to the two solos of each of Tristan's first two cycles.

Isolde's lament over Tristan's corpse can justly be called her own conversion in that it deals with her overcoming the worldly elements in her dream of love. At the end she collapses unconscious on Tristan's body and during the scene that follows, dominated by external events, she reawakens, as Tristan had done, with increasing metaphysical insight. During her revival, set apart from the other events on stage, Brangaene gives her perspective on the love potion, as Kurvenal had given his on Minne during Tristan's reawakening. And finally, with the *Liebestod*, Isolde experiences her own clairvoyant vision of Tristan, as Tristan had of her. Isolde's vision centers on metaphysical sound, as Tristan's had arisen from the internalized *alte Weise*; it ends with a nostalgic echo of desire as Tristan's had with the romantic idealized vision of love.

Isolde's first words—"Ich bin's, ich bin's, süssester Freund! Auf, noch einmal hör' meinen Ruf! Isolde ruft; Isolde kam, mit Tristan treu zu sterben!" (It's I, it's I, sweetest friend! Up, hear my call once more! Isolde calls; Isolde came to die faithfully with Tristan)—recall Tristan's insight earlier in the act that it was Isolde, still in the realm of day, who had called him from the night. They provide us with the means to understand her struggle against her own worldly inclinations, her resistance to his death, including even her hopes of the lovers' marriage. In this, Wagner seems to allude to Schopenhauer's discussion of marriage as the institutionalizing of the species Will in the essay that prompted Wagner's amendment.

The primary motive of the solo—"Isolde ruft; Isolde kam, mit Tristan treu zu sterben"—begins with an introductory series of alternating diminished-seventh and Tristan chords before settling on the dominant of g, which holds for two measures. It then moves downward from e♭″ through the tones of the dominant of g ("treu zu") and back upward through the D Tristan chord (including the bass d), on "sterben," to end on the dominant of d♭ with the motive that combines the honor motive with the cadence of the first death motive (ex. 15.2). The tritone shift from g (the predominant tonality of the solo) to d♭ is one that Wagner develops throughout the solo, whose motion between tritone-related tonal regions depicts the conflicts between Isolde's longing to have died with Tristan, the resistance, regret, and reproach associated with that longing, and her intuition of the metaphysical night, with which the solo ends. The first of these emotional spheres is associated with the physical fact of Tristan's death, the principal motif and its g tonality returning at approximately the midpoint and the end of the solo, whereas the second is associated with the sounding of music from the *Liebestod* in flat keys that are enharmonically related to B. The tritone shift in Isolde's motive is therefore the primary agency and symbol of the tonal shifting, its shape suggesting the dualism of death and rebirth, the later culminating in the honor/death motive.

Isolde's struggle is with her desire and its goal, the "einzige, ewigkurze, letzte Weltenglück" (single, eternally short, last worldly happiness) that in dying Tristan has denied her. Wagner leads the phrase to D minor, as if to affirm a conventional tonal design. But as she refers to healing Tristan's wounds—"Die Wunde? Wo? Lass' sie mich heilen!"—the music turns towards the beginning of "So stürben wir," now on F and shifting at the tritone as it continues to C♭ (B), even sounding the transfiguration cadence briefly in that key as Isolde speaks of sharing the night with Tristan. And it continues on into the music from "O ew'ge Nacht" where the lovers' deny

Example 15.2. Act 3, scene 2: excerpt from the beginning of Isolde's first solo

their individual identities, before circling back to g for Isolde's further regret and re-sponse to Tristan's death: "Gebrochen der Blick! Still das Herz! Nicht eines Atems flücht'ges Weh'n!" (His glance broken! His heart still! Not a fleeting breath!).

To indicate the conflict, Wagner transposes Isolde's theme at the tritone in over-lapping presentations beginning in g and d♭ and therefore leading back to g. Isolde now reveals the extent to which desire has motivated her journey to heal Tristan: "Muss sie nun jammernd vor dir steh'n, die sich wonnig dir zu vermählen mutig kam über's Meer?" (Must she now stand before you in sorrow, she who came across the sea blissfully to marry you?). On the key words, "wonnig dir zu vermählen," Wag-ner harmonizes what is otherwise a two-measure anticipation of a triadic theme from the *Liebestod* with the Tristan chord, a wrong note, signaling that Isolde's vi-sion of the lovers' deaths has been intermingled not just with desire but desire of a conventional kind.

Isolde's "wonnig dir zu vermählen" connects up with a detail that comes later in the act: King Mark's relating that upon hearing of the cause of Tristan and Isolde's love—the magic potion—he put out to sea in order to sanction their marriage: "Dem holden Mann *dich zu vermählen*, mit vollen Segeln flog ich dir nach." Mark has been told the story of the potion by Brangaene, as his music reveals; and Brangaene, as *her* reference to what she calls the "secret" of the potion brings out, has under-stood its magic in the purely physical terms of her first-act consolation. Isolde's ref-erence to marriage implies that she, too, had harbored such thoughts; it leads with an enharmonic shift from her deep flats to the dominant of g and the return once again of the main theme of the solo. Now, shorn of its honor/death appendage, it transposes up by whole tones, sounding four times in all to accompany Isolde's final resistance—"Zu spät! Trotziger Mann! Strafst du mich so mit härtestem Bann? Ganz ohne Huld meiner Leidensschuld? Nicht meine Klagen darf ich dir sagen?" (Too late! Stubborn man! Why sentence me with the hardest of all punishment? The debt of my suffering completely without grace? Not even to be able to tell you my complaints?). But, as Isolde cries for one last response from Tristan—"Nur einmal— ach! Nur einmal noch!" (Just once—alas! Just once more!)—it returns to its starting point. And Wagner leads it once more enharmonically into the beginning of the *Liebestod*, transposed at the fifth (Db); to this music Isolde "hears" Tristan awaken: "Horch! Er wacht! Geliebter! [the original final word, "Nacht," deleted as we know]." Of the tritone-related tonalities of the solo Db rather than g is the entranceway to night. The music of the *Liebestod* starts over again as Isolde sinks unconscious on Tristan's body, this time tracing the tritone from Cb to F (rather than F to Cb as before) and breaking off on F for the shift of perspective from night to day for the events on stage. Now its transpositions are downward rather than upward (as noted in chapter 4, transposition one more degree would lead it to the starting pitch of the *Liebestod*, from which it ascends); and its dynamic level, instead of increasing, decreases from *pp* to *ppp*, as Isolde sinks unconscious onto Tristan's corpse. Her reawakening will reverse the pattern, leading from F to Ab and from there to B (the *Liebestod*).

Isolde's sinking unconscious marks the shift to scene three, most of which Wagner notates in the one-flat key signature as if it were the outcome of Isolde's F. The one-flat key signature holds until King Mark's final solo, whose a/Eb shift, carried over from Brangaene's consolation, prepares for the Ab beginning of the *Liebestod*. Most of the 160 measures during which it holds involve the most physically active segment of the opera, the conflagration between Tristan's men, led by Kurvenal, and Mark's. We cannot say that this music is in F, however, although at a few symbolic points—notably Kurvenal's confronting King Mark and later his lying down beside Tristan to die—Wagner introduces a few measures of F. Rather, it is dominated by the recurrence of leitmotifs from act 3: an excerpt from the *alte Weise* (from the segment of the tune that preceded Tristan's awakening and that led, as we know, to F), two motifs associated with Kurvenal and his relationship to Tristan, and the motif of Isolde's solo (now associated with death in general). The motivic processes often involve transposition patterns suggesting tonal motion without confirming any central key. The F serves as a symbolic framework for a string of events that represent, like Kurvenal's F in the first half of the act, the conventional world of day. This music is a foil to the *Liebestod*, as the music leading to Tristan's curse was to the B of his reawakening.

The final appearance of F marks the turning point to Isolde's reawakening. It is prepared for by the solo of King Mark that follows Kurvenal's death. The fighting ended, Mark comments on the tragedy—"tot denn Alles! Alles tot!"—leading the motive of Isolde's earlier solo into that of his own solo in act 2. At the end of that solo he had ended on a for his question regarding the "tief geheimnisvollen Grund" of existence, which Tristan, accompanied by the desire music, had proclaimed unanswerable. Now he turns the emotions of the earlier scene around, his grief at Tristan's final "betrayal"—that is, his death—intermingled with feelings of Tristan's honor and loyalty. He closes with an A minor cadence that is deceived by the reappearance of the motif that ended Isolde's solo, and at the same pitch, F. For Isolde that F is the beginning of a transition to A♭ for the beginning of the *Liebestod*, her conversion to the metaphysical. For Brangaene, who sees the first signs of Isolde's reawakening, however, it signifies just the opposite, prompting her to an "explanation" of the desire music in purely pragmatic terms. From here on the split between the metaphysical and dramatic-representational perspectives is absolute.

In her diary for the year 1879, Cosima Wagner relates of this passage that for Wagner the "loveliest moment" in the ending of Tristan was "when the theme enters three times with muted horns and violins, as Isolde's only response to the sympathy of the others."[2] The first and second of those appearances of the theme—in F and G♭, respectively—precede and follow Brangaene's telling Isolde of her having explained the secret of the potion to King Mark, on which Mark's final solo sets up its third appearance, in G. The beginning of the *Liebestod* takes the theme up the final step, to A♭. The first three times it enters as a deceptive cadence, first in F to Mark's a, then in G♭ to Brangaene's b♭ and finally, in G to Mark's b. For the *Liebestod*, however, Wagner sets it up with a slow dominant-tonic progression.

Behind these and a host of other allegorical details in the music that leads to the *Liebestod* is the central theme of Isolde's inhabiting a world apart from the others and their concerns. As Brangaene sees Isolde reawaken—"Sie wacht, sie lebt! Isolde! hör' mich, vernimm' meine Sühne!" (She wakes, she lives! Isolde! Hear me, accept my atonement!)—she leads Isolde's F theme, which has just arrived on A♭, toward an f cadence whose melodic a♭′ in her line becomes the initial g♯′ of the desire music: "Des Trankes Geheimnis entdeckt' ich dem König" (The secret of the potion I revealed to the king). Brangaene's is the last three-phrase presentation of the desire music in the opera, and the third version to sound in the second half of Act Three. Tristan's reawakening had introduced the transcendent version of the desire music, arpeggiating the F♯ major triad, his death had returned to the primary form, arpeggiating the e minor triad. Brangaene's version is closely related to Isolde's diminished-seventh chord version in act 1, scene 2. Because it is the only one to introduce all four Tristan chords and dominant-seventh chords in the transposition pattern of the diminished-seventh chord, it can be said to disclose the "secret" behind the desire music that Brangaene described as "her work" in act 2: her foiling Isolde's plan of suicide by substituting the potions of love and death. Brangaene now leads its third phrase toward a cadence in b♭ as she narrates King Mark's setting out to give Isolde to Tristan. King Mark forgives Tristan and Isolde because they intended to commit suicide rather than adultery and were forced into the latter by the magic of the potion.

Brangaene's version is square and matter-of-factish, not at all mysterious like the version she had introduced when bringing forth the magic potions for the first time in act 1. Brangaene sings the first two phrases in the minor-third pattern—"Des Trankes Geheimnis / entdeckt' ich dem König"—modifying the third so as to present the remaining two Tristan chords in the diminished-seventh chord sequence before the remaining two dominant sevenths (ex. 15.3). The third phrase is, of course, the one that makes all the difference in the character of the desire music, the one that breaks the pattern of the preceding two and determines their meaning. Because of its

Example 15.3. Act 3, scene 2: Brangaene narrates her explanation of the secret of the potion to the desire music

adhering to the minor-third relationships, Brangaene's version of the desire music does not progress to B⁷, much less the F♯ of Tristan's awakening. Instead, it takes the F of Isolde's theme, reinterprets its minor third, a♭', as g♯ in the lower octave, then continues upward, outlining an octave ascent to a♭'' before curving back down to her cadential b♭'. On the third phrase her line emphasizes f'', the only pitch common to both Tristan chords (B and D) and both dominant-seventh chords of her version of that phrase (B♭ and D♭), the harmony converting Isolde's F into the dominant of b♭.

In deceiving Brangaene's cadence by the G♭ version of Isolde's theme Wagner picks up on the minor-third motion in the theme itself, which enables him to have King Mark return to the a of his earlier cadence. In this key he brings back the ending of the third strophe of Brangaene's consolation, heard for the first time since act 1. At the corresponding point Brangaene had asserted the power of the love potion to produce love between Isolde and her husband-to-be. And Mark, knowing this, brings back the tritone shifting within that music to effect a reinterpretation of Brangaene's b♭ as the dominant of E♭. Mark's understanding, his forgiveness of the lovers, and willingness that they be married, are entirely the result of Brangaene's "explanation"; and at the point of change from a to the dominant of E♭ he introduces the fourth Tristan chord from the diminished-seventh cycle, that on B, just as Brangaene had in her consolation and her explanation.

Mark's turn to E♭ suggests a causal connection to the A♭ beginning of the *Liebestod*. But in the intervening measures Wagner interrupts the sense of continuity between the two points, as he does in the music that comes between Isolde's two solos in general. Signposts of continuity are present throughout the final scene in devices such as the progressive transposition of thematic elements and circle-of-fifths patterns. But, because of the many interruptions, their efficacy in bringing about the final outcome is, if anything, called into question rather than affirmed. The *real* continuity is that between the ending of Isolde's first solo and the beginning of the *Liebestod*, and they are nearly two hundred measures apart. In the *Liebestod*, however, Wagner has the opera's most brilliant expression of continuity and transition up his sleeve.

Isolde's Transfiguration

If, in naming the "A-flat major of *Tristan*" the key to his music, Wagner was referring to the *Liebestod*, then he must have been thinking particularly of its initial twelve measures, basically the music of the A♭ duet "So stürben wir," slightly adjusted at the end so as to lead to B major, key of the remaining sixty-eight measures of the solo.[3] In the love scene, the music of "So stürben wir" had first circled back to its starting point, A♭, then, on its immediate repetition, moved on to G. Calling it "the A♭ major of *Tristan*," therefore, seems a little strange; yet it appears that Wagner did so, as Cosima in her diaries refers to Liszt's playing the "A♭ major of *Tristan*," apparently referring to his piano arrangement of the *Liebestod*.

I think it quite possible, in fact, that Wagner did refer to the *Liebestod* this way, meaning thereby to allude to the fact that, poetically, this movement depicts what Schopenhauer called the "transcendental change," the Will (desire or love) appearing "freely and without hindrance, in order that it can *recognize or know* its own inner nature in this phenomenon." The point of Wagner's amendment of Schopenhauer was that sexual love could lead to that knowledge, a view that broke with Schopenhauer. Thus, the text of "So stürben wir" describes a contradictory situation: the lovers, as they proclaim, will be united after death, given completely to one another and living for love alone, but without names: "So stürben wir um ungetrennt, ewig einig, ohne End', ohn' Erwachen, ohn' Erbangen, namenlos in Lieb' umfangen, ganz uns selbst gegeben, der Liebe nur zu leben!" (Then we would die without separation, eternally united, without end, without awakening, without fearing, nameless, surrounded by love, completely given to each other, living for love alone). But, as Bryan Magee remarks, insofar as the "uns selbst" of this movement refers to anything other than a completely undifferentiated union "with everything and everybody else, including all the other characters in the opera," this and related passages in *Tristan* pose an "unresolved problem" in terms of Schopenhauer's ideas. The problem, in fact, is what Wagner viewed as his amendment of Schopenhauer, the notion that "sexual love is also a way in which the will can be led to self-awareness and self-denial."[4]

In this light, the shift from A♭ to B is a tonal equivalent of what Wagner described as "the Buddhist theory of creation—a breath clouds the clear expanse of heaven." The breath of desire reaches out to the infinite, the "highest *Ātman*" or world-self of the Upanishads, as cited by Schopenhauer when he, too, grappled with the paradox of music's seeming to "exalt our minds and speak of worlds different from and better than ours," even while it "nevertheless flatters only the will-to-live, since it depicts the true nature of the will, gives it a glowing account of its success, and at the end expresses its satisfaction and contentment" (see chapter 3). The paradox is that the Will's knowing itself in Isolde, her final experience of desire, is equivalent to her ecstatically sinking into oneness with the world-self and ultimately unconsciousness.[5]

In poetic terms, the "A♭ major" of the *Liebestod* is the ground out of which the vision of transcendence arises; in more pragmatic terms, it is a key that contains within it the elements of a different one, B. In this respect it is the perfect embodiment of Wagner's art of transition. It retains the diminished-seventh chord transposition pattern of the melody of the honor music and the negating version of the desire music, but instead of projecting a conflict between that element and the tonal character of the movement, it introduces tonal qualities suggestive of transcendence. One of Wagner's greatest inspirations was to embed the rising major third in the theme of the movement in such a way that in the melody of the first phrase the chromatic descent from a♭′ to g♭′ is followed by the stepwise diatonic ascent from g♭′ to b♭′. The initial rising fourth and chromatic descent cause the theme to resemble the beginning of the desire music, while the diatonically rising major third suggests a transformation of the chromatic ascent that leads the melody upward to the starting tone of the next phrase. Wagner's harmonization of the rising third initiates the most prophetic event within the movement: the tonal motion that leads eventually to the emergence of B major.

In the initial twelve measures of the *Liebestod* harmonies and melodic gestures associated at first with A♭ are reinterpreted at the end in terms of B (ex. 15.4). This is particularly true of the harmony that emerges in the first phrase as the major triad on the minor third degree of the scale, C♭, enharmonic equivalent of B. In the first phrase Wagner uses the C♭ harmony to suggest modulation to the dominant by treating it as the harmony a semitone above the dominant of E♭: A♭⁶₄–E♭⁷–C♭–[a♭⁶]–B♭. Although the first phrase ends with a half close on the dominant of the dominant, beneath the rising major third of the melody the C♭ chord sets up a Phrygian cadence pattern—♭VI–iv⁶–V (in E♭)—a cadence of romantic transcendent character, and one that hints at interpretation not merely as a half close on the dominant of E♭ but also as a cadence on the third-scale degree of the "system"—in this case as III of G♭. The impact is to reinforce the inner logic of the transposition from the first phrase to the second, to hint that motion toward F♯ as the dominant of B is their goal.

In the beginning of the *Liebestod*, but not of "So stürben wir," the vocal line of the cadential B♭ chord reaches down to the pitch f′, so that it functions as a melodic leading-tone to the initial f♯′ of the next phrase (enharmonically g♭′). The effect is to increase the sense that the B⁶₄ chord on which the second phrase begins is prepared within the first, that, in returning to begin on the C♭ chord of the first phrase, the

Example 15.4. Act 3, scene 2: beginning of Isolde's *Liebestod*

second transforms what originally sounded like an anomalous event—the major triad on the minor-third degree of a major key—into the basis for continuation. The second phrase transposes the first at the minor third, beginning now with the C♭ chord, enharmonically notated as B, and ends once again on the dominant of the dominant: B$^{6}_{4}$–F♯^{7}–D–[b^{6}]- C♯. With the beginning of the third phrase, now four measures instead of two, the continuing pattern of rising minor-third transposition simply involves the tonic and dominant harmonies of D and F for two measures. Once it reaches the upper octave of its starting point in A♭, Wagner continues to the supertonic, b♭^{7}, and reintroduces the C♭ harmony again, this time to shift toward G♭. The cadence once again is to a D♭ harmony, as was that of the preceding phrase, but now it is a first-inversion dominant-seventh chord (D♭$^{6}_{5}$) in which an appoggiatura e♭' resolves to d♭'. This is, of course, the pattern of the first pair of dream chords from "O sink hernieder," in which the Tristan chord of the initial melody of the duet emerges as a vertical harmony. In the *Liebestod* the phrase mirrors in microcosm the gradual shift from A♭ to G♭ between "O sink hernieder" and the ending of Brangaene's warning, a motion in which the Tristan chord, interpreted as the dominant of G♭, instigates a tonal (circle-of-fifths) progression that culminates in the entrance of the "love's peace motive" in G♭. The C♯ of the second phrase ending has been converted into a dominant function, as the first of the dream chords was to the dominant of F♯/G♭ in Brangaene's first warning (and as the Tristan chord in both the original modulation to B in "O ew'ge Nacht" and the C♯ of the second phrase of the desire music was for Tristan's awakening).

"So stürben wir" introduces considerable emphasis on the arpeggiation pattern that is shared by the first *two* phrases of the honor music and the music of Tristan's reawakening: dominant chords on B♭ and C♯ as the cadential harmonies of its first two phrases. In addition, the cadence of its third phrase is an intensified form of the dominant seventh chord on C♯ (D♭$^{6}_{5}$). Wagner, however, does not pick up on the dominant potential of that gesture but instead suspends it by returning to a B♭ dominant harmony (B♭$^{4}_{3}$) for the cadence of phrase four. All four phrases to this point have ended with dominant harmonies on either B♭ or D♭. The fifth and final phrase simply returns to begin on the A♭$^{6}_{4}$ harmony with which the solo began. In the initial strophe of "So stürben wir" Wagner ties together the preceding events in terms of A♭ by passing through the harmony of the flat sixth (F♭) to C♭, and from there to the dominant, E♭^{7}. The melody of the return to A♭ is that of the diatonic major third from c♭" to e♭". The effect is that despite its transcendent-sounding harmonies, almost exclusively major, the movement nevertheless circles back to the starting point.[6]

In joining the music of "So stürben wir" to the B major music of "O ew'ge Nacht," Wagner reveals qualities in the duet that he presumably foresaw but did not fulfill in the love scene, above all its potential to lead to the dominant of B. The key events are already present in "So stürben wir": motion from B (C♭) to the dominant of its dominant in phrase two and, much more telling, the progression from C♭ to the dominant of G♭ at the cadence of phrase three.

The vocal line of the *Liebestod* reinforces this motion. The first two phrases describe an ascent from a♭' to c♯" (d♭"). Within the next two measures Wagner, instead of duplicating the rising sequence of the orchestral melody in the voice, leads the line back down toward a♭'. This circling back to the starting point perfectly matches

Isolde's awareness of her physical surroundings: "seht ihr's Freunde? Säh't ihr's nicht?" (Do you see it, friends? Do you not see it?). With the remainder of the phrase—"Immer lichter wie erleuchtet" (ever lighter as if shining)—however, her vision of Tristan leads the initial rising fourth from eb′ to ab′ upward in the fourth from ab′ to db″, completing the phrase with the further ascent from eb″ to ab″, and placing the Cb harmony of the first two phrases in the context of motion toward the dominant of Gb/F♯. Tonally, the climactic character of the Db♮§ chord on "erleuchtet" confirms the tonal role of the C♯ ending of the second phrase, representing the dominant of Gb as a powerful point of arrival.

Because the *Liebestod* depicts Isolde's passage to a new state, change of key is essential to its meaning. At the same time, the change must appear as prepared as possible within the old key. This is the essence of Wagner's "art of transition." But as the Ab is as much minor as major, it might well seem that little or no preparation is necessary: because ab or g♯ is the relative minor of B it should move to the latter key with perfect ease. Nothing could be further from the truth. Wagner, as we have seen, takes great pains to lend the modulation a transcendent character, the quality that the romantic composers associated particularly with cadences in which the final (relatively sharp) major chord was preceded by a (relatively flat) minor harmony, such as in the Phrygian cadence and the plagal cadence in which the minor subdominant harmony precedes the major tonic. In both cadences the minor harmony is a foil to the otherworldly bliss of the major, whose character is all the more emphasized when the melody rises a major third to settle on the third of the final major chord.

The final cadence of *Tristan* is of the second type: its plagal cadence with the minor subdominant moving to the major tonic arises from the plagal transfiguration cadence—E (with added sixth c♯‴) to B—changing the subdominant to minor as Isolde sings the word "unbewusst." This not only enabled Wagner to convey the ecstasy of unconsciousness ("unbewusst, höchste Lust") on the B major chord, but also inspired him to bring back the first phrase of the desire music at the cadence, its E^7 chord changed to the minor subdominant (e) of B, and thereby stripped of the quality that most suggests desire (the tritone relationship between the dissonant minor seventh and the "leading-tone" major third). The desire music is absorbed into the perspective of B entirely, the f of the Tristan chord simply rendered into a downward leading-tone function to the e of the minor subdominant.

Wagner associated the rising semitones of the desire music, as we know, with the idea of creation and need for continuance—the process of representation itself. In linking an echo of the desire music with the plagal cadence to B, therefore, he managed to convey the idea that desire had been transcended, absorbed into something greater. At the same time, in continuing the fourth tone of the chromatic ascent, b′, up through c♯″ to the third, d♯′, of the final chord, Wagner represented that event as a blissful one. The diatonic rising major third replaces the chromatic rising minor third, legitimating the d♯″ of the Tristan chord for the last time, while in parallel with it the rising third from d♯‴ to f♯‴ in the uppermost orchestral voices confirms the final victory of F♯ over F. And nothing could confirm that Wagner conceived of the rising major third—the interval that replaces the minor third on the third phrase of the desire music and on all three phrases of that music when Tristan reawakens at the middle of the act—as his final symbol of transcendence more than the fact that

284   The Tragic and the Ecstatic

he has the English horn stop with the b' so that it does not continue into the final chord. The dropping-out of the English horn, whose sound is associated closely with the desire music throughout the opera, the instrument that plays the *alte Weise* and the *frohe Weise*, makes the point that metaphysical meaning is equivalent to the *absence* rather than the presence of something, the "end of all dreams."

At the point of the Ab/B shift Wagner adumbrates the ending of the *Liebestod* by the simple expedient of reinterpreting the Fb chord (formerly the flat sixth of Ab) as the subdominant of B and changing it immediately to the minor subdominant. Using these two chords to harmonize the major third b–c♯'–d♯', Wagner anticipates in microcosm the chief harmonic events in the final page of the *Liebestod*. The arrival of F♯ in the bass—the first in a series of four structural arrivals on that tone in the *Liebestod*—completes the tendency of the D♮⁶ chord on "erleuchtet." At that point Isolde had sung the pitches ab"–cb". Now she sings ab"–ab'–cb" at the point of the modulation, picking up on the enharmonic equivalent of cb" (b") as the horn and bassoon complete the b–c♯'–d♯' third.

From this point on the main sequence of ideas in the *Liebestod* centers on four points of arrival on the dominant (F♯) in the bass, symbolizing the stages of Isolde's transfiguration. The first, begins a segment whose beginning—"Seht ihr's nicht?"—and ending—"Seht! Fühlt und seht ihr's nicht?"—make clear Isolde's seeing what the others cannot. The latter phrase, leading back to the dominant pedal, combines the motifs of desire and honor. The second segment, beginning "Höre ich nur diese Weise," introduces the shift from visual to auditory metaphors; as it moves toward the third point of arrival on F♯, it again combines the desire and honor motives—"in mich dringet, auf ich schwinget, hold erhallend um mich klinget"—leading them into the transfiguration cadence as the bass reaches the dominant. Three still-rapid iterations of that cadence (without as yet the root-position tonic chord) initiate the final bass motion toward the fourth arrival on F♯, a dominant pedal of six measures that finally leads to the completion of the transfiguration cadence to the root-position B major chord. The metaphors now are all of the metaphysical *Wellen* that Isolde feels surrounding her and to which she succumbs in the most famous cadence in the whole of music.

Much ink has been spilled over the years on Wagner's reserving resolution of the dominant-seventh chord throughout the opera for this ending. Certainly, of the principal places in the opera where extended dominant pedals appear in connection with anticipation of the lovers' union, physical or metaphysical—in addition to the *Liebestod*, act 2, scene 1, "O ew'ge Nacht" and the stretch from the *frohe Weise* to Isolde's arrival in act 3—this one is unique, not only for its completion of the cadence but also for its drawing out the cadence in a representation of the bliss of dying, the vision of night. That quality was an inspiration to countless composers who, in their own versions, pointed to its deepest meaning: nostalgia for the end of romanticism, "this most beautiful of dreams."

Appendix: Transcriptions from the Compositional Draft of Act 2, Scene 2

THE FOLLOWING TRANSCRIPTIONS from Wagner's compositional draft (see the facsimiles of the corresponding pages in figs. A1–5) were made at Bayreuth from Wagner's autograph sketches, which, as is well known, were written in pencil and later inked over by Mathilde Wesendonck. Besides the difficulties in deciphering Wagner's rapid hand, his changes of mind, excisions and revisions, and the like, Wesendonck's inking-over makes the task of transcription often formidably difficult. Wesendonck frequently misinterpreted the pitches and rhythms, sometimes even placing the note head on the opposite end of the stem from the correct one. Working from the original sometimes enables one to discern the original pencil markings, but more often does not. Were we to read the individual notes as they *appear*, the result would often be nonsense. This situation has occurred in certain of the transcriptions made by Ulrich Bartels in the second part of his study of the second- and third-act sketches. In the original transition to "O sink hernieder," for example, Wagner considered presenting the transfiguration music successively in A♭ and C♭, writing the latter on a separate staff. Bartels, apparently not grasping that fact, and copying the sketch as it appeared, presents the d♭" appoggiatura tone of the line as f", against the f♭ of the bass. Similarly, as the desire music enters for Tristan's answer to Mark later in the act, Bartels transcribes the e–g♯ third of the E dominant-seventh chord of the first phrase as f♯–d♮'. There are other mistranscriptions of a similar kind. Clearly, copying the sketches as they look is grossly misleading. It is frequently necessary to make decisions based on knowledge of the opera as a whole and in detail, rather than to follow Mathilde Wesendonck's conjectures. Wagner's style, however, enables us to transcribe difficult passages with some confidence, because there are few places in the opera that do not refer, usually both musically and textually, to other places. Of the two transcriptions given here the first presents relatively few difficulties, and errors can be corrected readily. In the second, Wagner himself had difficulty at several points, in one case recording that fact in the Venice Diary (as described in chapter 4).

Figure A.1.

Figure A.2.

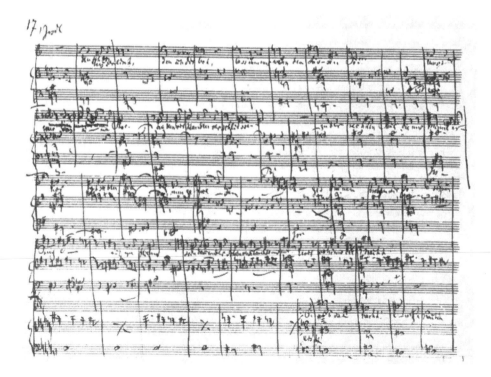

Figure A.3.

Figure A.4.

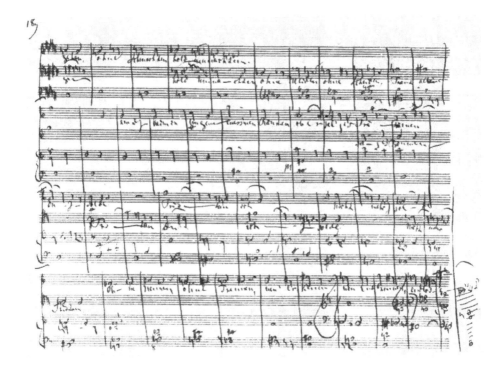

Figure A.5.

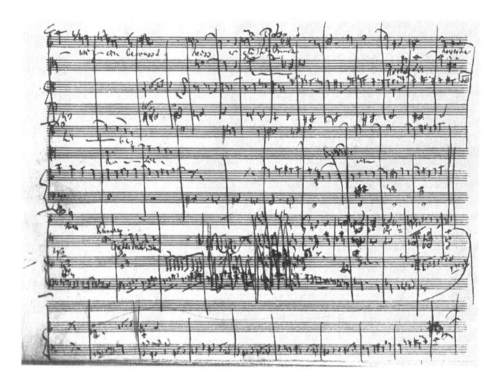

His original intention, of bringing in the glance music at three points, is documented, in the first two cases, by considering the melody and bass line independently of the harmonies sketched on the middle staff. Those harmonies (with extra bar lines in the second instance) represent his final solution, to introduce the "dream chords" of "O sink hernieder" instead. We therefore have two solutions whose appearance of simultaneity is misleading, and rendered vastly more impenetrable by Mathilde Wesendonck's inking. Given time and study such passages often yield up their meaning, whereas rapid transcription following the appearance of the inked-over draft inevitably leads to many errors.

I have of necessity corrected impossible pitches in cases where Wagner's intention seemed clear. In other cases I have had to reproduce Mathilde Wesendonck's inkings, knowing that they cannot be completely correct. Mostly, however, Wagner's intentions are clear in terms of the leitmotifs and musical references, if the exact details of the harmony are not always so.

The Original Transition to "O ew'ge Nacht"

As discussed in chapter 3, this passage (ex. A1) contains fourteen lines of text that Wagner retained in the printed text of *Tristan* and set to music in the compositional draft, but deleted from the final version of the opera.

Example A.1.

Example A.1. (Continued)

Example A.1. (Continued)

Excerpt from the Original Version of "O ew'ge Nacht"

The beginning of this passage (ex. A2) follows directly from the ending of the preceding transcription; I have separated them here because they are discussed at different points in the text. Example A2 illustrates the original appearances of the glance music in the duet (deleted from the final version) and extends several measures beyond the original modulation from G♯ (A♭) to B.

Example A.2.

Example A.2. (Continued)

Example A.2. (Continued)

Excerpt from the Original Version of "O ew'ge Nacht"

This (ex. A3) is the approach to the climax of the duet according to the version of the compositional draft. It shows the reappearance of the glance music at its original pitch, as in the Prelude to the opera, notated here in $\frac{2}{4}$ instead of $\frac{6}{8}$ against the $\frac{4}{4}$ of the rest of the movement.

Example A.3.

Example A.3. (Continued)

Notes

Introduction

1. See Stewart Spencer, trans., and Barry Millington, ed., *Selected Letters of Richard Wagner* (New York: Norton, 1987), pp. 323–24. On the possibility that Wagner first encountered Schopenhauer's work in 1852 (without, however, reading it at that time) see Edouard Sans, *Richard Wagner et la pensée Schopenhauerienne* (Paris: Klinksieck, 1969), pp. 17–21. The most recent study of the influence of Schopenhauer on Wagner is Bryan Magee, *Wagner and Philosophy* (London: Allen Lane, 2000), pp. 126–227.

2. Richard Wagner, *My Life*, trans. Andrew Gray, ed. Mary Whittall (Cambridge: Cambridge University Press, 1983), p. 510.

3. W. T. H. Jackson, "Tristan the Artist in Gottfried's Poem," *PMLA* 71 (1962): 364–72.

4. Wagner, *My Life*, p. 511. In his autobiography, Wagner does not specify the date of this draft. A closely related description appears, however, under the year 1855 in *The Diary of Richard Wagner: The Brown Book: 1865–1882*, trans. George Bird, ed. Joachim Bergfeld (Cambridge: Cambridge University Press, 1980), p. 105. There we read "Tristan conceived in more definite form: Act III point of departure of mood for whole. (with weaving in of Grail-seeking Parzival)."

5. Spencer and Millington, *Selected Letters*, p. 366.

6. See "Music of the Future" (1860), in Robert L. Jacobs, trans., *Three Wagner Essays* (London: Eulenburg Books, 1979), pp. 33–35.

7. Schopenhauer, *The World as Will and Representation* (henceforth *WWR*), trans. E. F. J. Payne, two vols. (New York: Dover, 1969), vol. 1, pp. 3–4.

8. Martin Gregor-Dellin and Dietrich Mack, eds., Geoffrey Skelton, trans., *Cosima Wagner's Diaries* (New York: Harcourt Brace Jovanovich, 1977–78), vol. 2, pp. 855, 861.

9. Carl Dahlhaus, *Between Romanticism and Modernism*, trans. Mary Whittall (Berkeley: University of California Press, 1980), pp. 1–39.

10. Recognition that Wagner's love scene paralleled Gottfried's lovers' cave scene extends as least as far back as Franz Carl Friedrich Müller's 1865 book, *Tristan und Isolde nach Sage und Dichtung: Ein Skizzenbild. Zur Einführung in das Drama Richard Wagner's* (Munich: Christian Kaiser, 1865), p. 142.

11. Wagner, *Beethoven* (1870), trans. William Ashton Ellis (*Richard Wagner's Prose Works*, 2nd ed. (London: Kegan Paul, Trench, Trübner, 1895–99), vol. 5 (1896), pp. 107–13.

12. Schopenhauer, *WWR*, 2, p. 538.

13. "The Sorrows and Grandeur of Richard Wagner" (1933), in Thomas Mann, *Pro and Contra Wagner*, trans. Allan Blunden (London: Faber and Faber, 1985), p. 126.

14. Denis de Rougement, *Love in the Western World*, trans. Montgomery Belgion, rev. and augmented edition (Princeton: Princeton University Press, 1985), pp. 230–31.

15. William Ashton Ellis, ed. and trans., *Richard Wagner to Mathilde Wesendonck*, 2nd ed. (New York: Vienna House, 1972), pp. 75–76.

16. Ibid., p. 76. See also *Richard Wagner: Sämtliche Briefe*, vol. 10, ed. Andreas Mielke. Leipzig: Breitkopf & Härtel, 2000, p. 208.

17. Robert Bailey, "The Genesis of 'Tristan und Isolde'" (unpub. Ph.D. diss., Princeton University, 1968); Ulrich Barthels, *Studien zu Wagners Tristan und Isolde anhand der Kompositionsskizze des zweiten und dritten Aktes*. Three parts: 1 (text), 2 (transcriptions), 3 (facsimiles) (Cologne: Studio, Verlag Schewe, 1995).

18. Carl Dahlhaus, *The Idea of Absolute Music*, trans. Roger Lustig (Chicago: University of Chicago Press, 1989).

19. Edward Lockspeiser, *Debussy: His Life and Mind*, 4th ed. (New York: McGraw-Hill, 1972), pp. 204–5.

1. The Path to Schopenhauer

1. Wagner, *My Life*, pp. 429–30; see also p. 509.

2. Carl Dahlhaus, *The Idea of Absolute Music*, p. 18.

3. Walter Benjamin, *The Origin of German Tragic Drama*, trans. John Osborne (London: New Left Books, 1977), p. 159.

4. Novalis's philosophical writings occupy two large volumes of his collected works (see note 6). Schlegel's philosophical writings are even more voluminous; see note 26 for full citation of his *Transcendentalphilosophie*. Hölderlin did not write as extensively on philosophy as Novalis and Schlegel, but his critique of Fichte is very highly regarded (see, for example, Andrew Bowie, *Aesthetics and Subjectivity: From Kant to Nietzsche* [Manchester, Manchester University Press, 1990], pp. 67–72). For Schleiermacher's aesthetic writings, see note 8. On Wagner's discussion of Schiller's relationship to Kant, see *Beethoven*, trans. Ashton Ellis, pp. 64–65).

5. See John Neubauer, *The Emancipation of Music from Language* (New Haven: Yale University Press, 1986), pp. 193–210. Bowie, *Aesthetics and Subjectivity*, pp. 176–205.

6. Novalis, *Schriften*, ed. Richard Samuel (Stuttgart: W. Kohlhammer Verlag, 1960), vol. 2 (*Das philosophische Werk* I), pp. 533–36 (on "poësie," including statements such as "Das Poém des Verstands ist Philosophie," "Poësie [ist] der Schlüssel der Philosophie, ihr Zweck und ihre Bedeutung," "Die transcendentale Poësie ist aus Philosophie und Poësie gemischt"), 568 (on "absolute Poësie"), 573–74 (on the *a priori* character of music and painting); vol. 3 (*Das philosophische Werk* II), pp. 573 ("language is for philosophy as it is for music and painting: not the right medium of representation"), 685 ("eigentliche Musik"), 691 ("wahre Musik"), and so on.

7. See Andrew Bowie, "German idealism and the arts," in *The Cambridge Companion to German Idealism*, ed. Karl Ameriks (Cambridge: Cambridge University Press, 2000), pp. 239–57.

8. Friedrich Daniel Ernst Schleiermacher, *Ästhetik (1819/25): Über den Begriff der Kunst (1831/32)*, ed. Thomas Lahnerer (Hamburg: Felix Meiner Verlag, 1984), pp. 47–48; idem, *Hermeneutics and Criticism and Other Writings*, ed. and trans. Andrew Bowie (Cambridge: Cambridge University Press, 1998).

9. Oskar Walzel, *German Romanticism*, trans. Alma Elise Lussky (New York: Capricorn Books, 1966), p. 28.

10. F. W. J. Schelling, *System of Transcendental Idealism*, trans. Peter Heath (Charlottesville: University of Virginia Press, 1978), pp. 217–18. *Idem.*, *The Philosophy of Art*, ed. and trans. Douglas W. Stott (Minneapolis: University of Minnesota Press, 1989), p. xxxiv. This treatise, given as lectures in 1801 and 1804, was published only after Schelling's death in 1854.

11. Schelling, *System of Transcendental Idealism*, pp. 222–24.

12. See Peter Heath, introduction to Schelling, *System of Transcendental Idealism*, p. xxxix.

13. Schelling, *System of Transcendental Idealism*, pp. 231, 221–22.

14. Hegel's terms have little or nothing to do with the way we understand "classical" and "romantic" today; as he sets them forth in the introduction to his *Aesthetics* (pp. 75–81; source cited in note 16), symbolic art is the art of the ancient East, classical art that of classical antiquity and romantic art that of the Christian Era. They represent "the three relations of the Idea to its shape in the sphere of art, . . . the striving for, the attainment, and the transcendence of the Ideal as the true Idea of beauty" (p. 81).

15. William Desmond, *Art and the Absolute: A Study of Hegel's Aesthetics* (Albany: State University of New York Press, 1986), p. 44.

16. *Hegel's Aesthetics: Lectures on Fine Art*, trans. T. M. Knox. Two vols. (Oxford: Oxford University Press, 1975), vol. 1, p. 101; Desmond, *Art and the Absolute*, pp. xiv–xv.

17. Dahlhaus, *The Idea of Absolute Music*, pp. 58–77. Karl Kropfinger, *Wagner and Beethoven*, trans. Peter Palmer (Cambridge: Cambridge University Press, 1991), pp. 14–67.

18. See Robert Jacobs and Geoffrey Skelton, ed. and trans., *Wagner writes from Paris . . . Stories, Essays and Articles by the Young Composer* (London: George Allen & Unwin Ltd., 1973), p. 180.

19. Ibid., p. 186. It may be mentioned that Suzanne Langer (*Philosophy in a New Key*, 3rd ed. [Cambridge, Mass.: Harvard University Press, 1957], pp. 221–22) cites Wagner's remarks as the "most explicit rendering" of the principle that she calls "the most persistent, plausible, and interesting doctrine of meaning in music."

20. Schopenhauer, *WWR*, 1, p. 261.

21. Jacobs and Skelton, *Wagner Writes from Paris*, p. 183.

22. Schopenhauer, *WWR*, 1, p. 263; 2, p. 449.

23. Schopenhauer, *WWR*, 1, p. 262; 2, pp. 452–55. Wagner, *Opera and Drama,* trans., William Ashton Ellis. 2nd ed. (London: K. Paul, Trench, Trübner, 1900), pp. 42–57, 103–4, 280, 284–86, 295.

24. Dahlhaus, *The Idea of Absolute Music*, pp. 30, 32.

25. These characteristics of Mozart's and Beethoven's music derive in large part from E. T. A. Hoffmann. See *E. T. A. Hoffmann's Musical Writings: Kreisleriana, The Poet and the Composer, Music Criticism*, ed., David Charlton, trans. Martyn Clarke (Cambridge: Cambridge University Press, 1989), pp. 106 (Mozart), 98, 251, 302, 318, and so on.

26. Jacobs and Skelton, *Wagner writes from Paris*, pp. 180, 184–85. In his *Transcendentalphilosophie* of 1800–01, Friedrich Schlegel defines the philosophical term "Konsequenz" as "die Einheit, die auf einen Zweck geht, und mit Stätigkeit ihn zu erreichen sucht" (see Friedrich Schlegel, *Transcendentalphilosophie*, ed. Michael Elsässer [Hamburg: Felix Meiner Verlag, 1991], p. 81).

27. Jacobs and Skelton, *Wagner Writes from Paris*, pp. 185–87.

28. Klaus Kropfinger (*Wagner and Beethoven*, p. 124), in maintaining that in "A Happy Evening," Wagner "excludes the 'philosophical idea' as an irrelevance," does not account for the positive treatment of the obviously related "philosophical consequence" [or "consistency"] set forth in the preceding paragraph of Wagner's story, nor for the fact that, although there is initial apparent disagreement between the two friends of Wagner's story, the narrator

denies that he intended his "philosophical idea" as the exaggerated form of program music that his friend supplies; in the end, the two friends reach a complete agreement regarding music's ideal nature. What is denied is not the "philosophical idea" but the implication that it involves a preconceived descriptive program that the music then follows.

29. The idea that art exhibits absolute and empirical sides was characteristic of some romantic aesthetics. Schelling, for example, articulated it in an 1802 letter to August Wilhelm Schlegel cited by Douglas W. Stott in his introduction to Schelling's *The Philosophy of Art* (p. xxvii). Schelling speaks of "higher forms" of art that he juxtaposes to the empirical side of art: "Just as there are real or empirical things, there is also real or empirical art—and such art is the concern of *theory.*" And "just as there are intellectual things, things *in and for themselves,* however, there is also *art in and for itself,* of which empirical art is merely this appearance in the phenomenal world." On Hegel, see Desmond, *Art and the Absolute,* pp. 1–13.

30. R. W. Griepenkerl, *Das Musikfest oder die Beethovener,* second edition, (Braunschweig: Eduard Leibrock Verlag, 1841), pp. 110–11, vi. Griepenkerl uses the word "Durchbruch" in the figurative sense given by the Grimm brothers in their dictionary as "der eintritt einer entschiedneren, innigeren gesinnung, bezeugung, ansicht, besonders einer religiösen." See Jacob and Wilhelm Grimm, *Deutsches Wörterbuch,* 33 vols. Reprint ed. (Munich: Deutsche Taschenbuch Verlag, 1999), vol. 2 (1860), p. 1595.

31. Griepenkerl, pp. xii–xiv.

32. Ibid., pp. 32, 62, 58.

33. Griepenkerl, pp. 256–57: "Vergessen hatte er das heilige Werk unter seinen Händen, vergessen den heiligen Ort. Hinausgehoben in jene Sphäre des Geistes, wo Religion nicht als in den Schranken des Individuums erkannt wird, sondern dahinaus, wo sich Religion als höchste Bestimmung der absoluten Idee selber in den Erscheinungen der Weltgeschichte offenbart—dahin gelangt trat der Spieler aus den Formen einseitiger Kirchenmusik heraus, und suchte aus dem Zusammen aller Erscheinungen, schon um der Gegensätze willen, die Idee überwältigender, überzeugender hervorzurufen. Ein Verfahren der Kunst, dessen letzter Gewinn Religion ist in höchster Bedeutung des Wortes. Wohl werden kommende Zeiten nicht viel Oratorien im älteren Sinne mehr hervorbringen, wohl aber Oratorien im neueren Sinne, das ist, *redende* Denkmäler grosser Völkerzustände, in denen endlich einmal die welthistorischen Resultate der Christensonne hervortreten, nicht die bis zum Ekel überall vorgeschobenen Blut- und Marterszenen. Für jede Kunst, auch für die Malerei, sind diese Zustände vorüber."

34. G. W. F. Hegel, *The Encyclopaedia Logic,* trans. T. F. Geraets, W. A. Suchting, and H. S. Harris (Indianapolis: Hackett Publishing Company, 1991), p. 94.

35. On Wagner's use of the term "Durchbruch" see p. 143. The association of the "Durchbruch" idea to Mahler is mainly the work of Theodor Adorno (*Mahler: A Musical Physiognomy,* trans. Edmund Jephcott [Chicago: University of Chicago Press, 1992], pp. 3–17). See L. J. Rather, *Reading Wagner* (Baton Rouge: Louisiana State University Press, 1990), p. 169.

36. *E. T. A. Hoffmann's Musical Writings,* pp. 188–209.

37. Ibid., pp. 195–97. In order to compress his meaning, I have slightly reordered Hoffmann's discussion.

38. "Music of the Future" (1860), in Robert L. Jacobs, trans., *Three Wagner Essays* (London: Eulenburg Books, 1979) pp. 34–35.

39. Charles Osborne, ed., *Richard Wagner: Stories and Essays* (New York: The Library Press, 1973), p. 75.

40. In the words of culture historian, William Everdell, "smoothness, in fact, was one of the ruling metaphors of the age. Nineteenth-century minds disagreed about almost everything except how much they disliked hard edges. Between one thing and another, whether on the

canvas of an academic painter or in the natural and social worlds, there was always a *sfumato*, a transition. Marx, Hegel, and Darwin agreed that change was, if not regular, at least smooth. The tidal wave of dialectic, the *Aufhebung* (elevation) of Being, the evolutionary origin of a species, was a spectacular show, but it was neither catastrophic nor unpredictable. It was more like the forbiddingly complex but entirely harmonic development of a Brahms symphony." See Everdell, *The First Moderns* (Chicago: University of Chicago Press, 1997), pp. 9–10.

41. See Paul Guyer, "Absolute idealism and the rejection of Kantian dualism," in Karl Ameriks, ed., *The Cambridge Companion to German Idealism*, p. 39.

42. See *Richard Wagner's Gesammelte Schriften*, 14 vols., ed. Julius Kapp (Leipzig: Hesse & Becker, n.d.), vol. 9, pp. 118–27. W. Ashton Ellis, trans., *Richard Wagner's Prose Works*, Vol. 7, pp. 247–55.

43. Wilhelm Heinrich Wackenroder and Ludwig Tieck, *Phantasien über die Kunst* [1799, ed. Wolfgang Nehring [Stuttgart, Philipp Reclam jun., 1973], pp. 77–87.

44. The excerpt from Tieck, which has never been precisely identified, resembles passages in Wackenroder's and Tieck's *Phantasien über die Kunst*, especially the essays "Das eigentümliche innere Wesen der Tonkunst und die Seelenlehre der heutigen Instrumentalmusik" and "Die Töne" und "Symphonien" (see the source cited in the preceding note, pp. 81, 82, 83, 101, 109). Also *E. T. A. Hoffmann's Musical Writings*, p. 238.

45. Griepenkerl characterized the passage in similar terms (p. 118): "die Nacht des Chaos theilend, bis dahin—ja bis dahin, wo er in D schloss—malte sein Spiel des grossen Menschenganzen ungeheure Arbeit, zu brechen, was Form is, los aller kettenlastenden Endlichkeit zusammenzustiessen mit dem unsichtbaren, allversöhnenden Unendlichen—Und das war gut."

46. *Richard Wagner's Prose Works*, vol. 1 ("The Artwork of the Future" [1849]), pp. 123, 126–28, 130–31, 190–91.

47. See *Opera and Drama*, pp. 217, 337–38. On transition, see later, pp. 194–95.

48. Wilhelm Heinrich Wackenroder's *Confessions and Fantasies*, trans., Mary Hurst Schubert (University Park: Pennsylvania State University Press, 1971), p. 194.

49. In addition, some of the language of Isolde's *Liebestod* (and its overall conception) resembles the transfiguration of the naked saint in the Wackenroder story cited later (chapter 2, p. 43).

50. Nietzsche held this view regarding *Tristan*. See note 62.

51. *My Life*, pp. 430–31. At one point, Wagner admits "what really induced me to attach so much importance to Feuerbach was his conclusion, . . . that the best philosophy is to have no philosophy at all, a theory whereby the study of it, which had hitherto deterred me, became immeasurably easier for me." Wagner praises Feuerbach's "lyrical style" and the "appealing circumstantiality" with which Feuerbach treated the "absorbing questions" of philosophy that Wagner had otherwise largely encountered through the "poetic animadversions on the subject which are to be found here and there in the works of our great writers." Wagner was attracted to the "tragic implications" of Feuerbach's *Thoughts on Death and Immortality*, finding it "elevating and consoling to be assured that the sole authentic immortality adheres only to sublime deeds and inspired works of art." In other words, Wagner's interest in Feuerbach was wholly artistic.

52. See Marx W. Wartofsky, *Feuerbach* (Cambridge: Cambridge University Press, 1977), pp. 196–204; also Van A. Harvey, *Feuerbach and the Interpretation of Religion* (Cambridge: Cambridge University Press, 1995), pp. 33–48.

53. Feuerbach, *Principles of the Philosophy of the Future* (1843), trans. Manfred Vogal (Indianapolis: Hackett Publishing Company, 1986), pp. 51–55.

54. See Feuerbach, *Principles of the Philosophy of the Future*, p. 68. Also Wartofsky, *Feuerbach*, p. 286.

55. Wartofsky, *Feuerbach*, p. 284.

56. See *WWR*, 1, pp. 26, 273, 483–84, 521; 2, pp. 43, 82, 185, 351, 644.

57. Wartofsky, *Feuerbach*, p. 286. A typical instance of the Feuerbach element in Wagner's view of the leitmotif (not, of course, designated as such) is his remark (in *Opera and Drama*) on the motives of foreboding and recollection that "even thought is aroused by the emotion, and must necessarily flow back into emotion; for *a thought is the bond between an absent* [i.e., past or future] *and a present emotion, each struggling for enouncement* [Wagner's italics]." See William Ashton Ellis, *Richard Wagner's Prose Works*, vol. 2 (1893), p. 327. Wagner's entire discussion of gestures and motives is permeated by Feuerbach's reduction of thought to feeling. For Wagner's post-Schopenhauer "theory" of the leitmotiv see later, pp. 134–37.

58. "Music of the Future," p. 33. See also Wagner, *My Life*, pp. 508–10.

59. On the influence of Feuerbach on Wagner, see S. Rawidowicz, *Ludwig Feuerbachs Philosophie: Ursprung und Schicksal* (Berlin: Reuther & Richard, 1931), pp. 388–410; Bryan Magee, *Wagner and Philosophy*, pp. 48–68.

60. We may remember that Griepenkerl (see p. 24) had used the expression "Kunstabsolutismus des Individuums" with very similar associations to Wagner's pejorative use of the term "absolute".

61. Thus, as Dahlhaus points out *(The Idea of Absolute Music)*, "the polemic against the term absolute music . . . must not obscure Wagner's latent affinity for the idea of absolute music" (p. 26). His adherence to the idea of absolute music even as he polemicized against it in Feuerbachian language, meant that his writings were sometimes contradictory on the subject. He praises "absolute harmony," for example, "in language indistinguishable from the metaphysical excesses of Tieck, Wackenroder, and E. T. Hoffmann, excesses that clash with the tone of Feuerbachian anthropology" (p. 23). The association between "absolute harmony" and Wagner's ocean simile linked "absolute harmony" to the infinite depths that constituted the true source of music.

62. Ultimately, however, it was not Wagner but Nietzsche who united the romantic and Schopenhauerian ideas of "absolute music" with the term that was first used by Wagner. As Dahlhaus says, "the idea of absolute music that E. T. A. Hoffmann had experienced in Beethoven's Fifth Symphony—related to Wackenroder and Tieck's metaphysics of instrumental music—was revealed to Nietzsche in Wagner's *Tristan*: the idea that music attains its metaphysical destiny in the very process of distancing itself ever further from empirical circumstances—from functions, words, plots, and finally even from humanly palpable feelings and affections . . . in Nietzsche's aesthetic Wagner's *Tristan* is absolute music." See *The Idea of Absolute Music*, pp. 33–34. It might be added that the ending of *Tristan*—in which Isolde proclaims the sounding of a metaphysical *Weise* that only she can hear—distances itself even from sound, perhaps what Wagner had in mind when he spoke of *Tristan* and the "great art of sounding silence."

63. Wagner outlines both his fascination and his growing disaffection with Feuerbach in *My Life*, pp. 430–31.

2. *Tristan and Schopenhauer*

1. Letter to August Röckel of August 23, 1856, in Spencer and Millington, *Selected Letters*, pp. 357–58.

2. Among Wagner's various remarks to that effect are, for example, his statements that the "A-flat major" of *Tristan* was the key to his music as a whole and that he had "done nothing new" since *Tristan* (see *Cosima Wagner's Diaries*, Vol. 2, pp. 283, 286).

3. *WWR*, 1, p. 3. Schopenhauer reiterates this dictum elsewhere, sometimes citing the Upanishads as his source; see, for example, *WWR*, 1, p. 281.

4. Wagner described *Träume,* the origin of the "dream chords" of "O sink hernieder," as the source from which the night scene of *Tristan* sprang (Ashton Ellis, *Richard Wagner to Mathilde Wesendonck,* p. 283).

5. See Schopenhauer, *Parerga and Paralipomena* (henceforth *PP*), trans. E. F. J. Payne, two vols. (New York: Oxford, 1974), vol. 1, pp. 239–41, 263–64, 272–73. Wagner takes up the two kinds of dreams in the 1864 essay "On State and Religion," but his fullest statement on this theme can be found in his 1870 essay, *Beethoven* where he extends the metaphors of night and day to all-encompassing aesthetic qualities.

6. "Music of the Future," pp. 34–35.

7. "Music of the Future," p. 34. Wagner's various statements on the artist as clairvoyant follow soon after the composition of *Tristan* and culminate in the 1870 Beethoven essay, Wagner's fullest presentation of his Schopenhauer-derived aesthetics (see pp. 28–31, 43, 67). The passage cited echoes many points in Schopenhauer's writings (see, for example, *WWR*, 1, pp. 69–83, *PP*, 1, pp. 223–309). Wackenroder, too, spoke pejoratively of the "why" as the search for purpose, origins and concepts that stood in opposition to the "beauty and spirituality" of things themselves (Wackenroder/Tieck, *Phantasien über die Kunst,* p. 81). A letter from Wagner to Mathilde Wesendonck of January 1859 (Spencer and Millington, *Selected Letters,* pp. 441–43) meditates on the role of clairvoyance in artistic creation in a manner that resembles the poetic subject matter of *Tristan.*

8. "Music of the Future," p. 35. On Wagner's condensing Gottfried's *Tristan* to three love scenes, see *Cosima Wagner's Diaries,* vol. 1, p. 322. See also Spencer and Millington, *Selected Letters of Richard Wagner,* pp. 460 (on the *Parzifal* poem) and 458 (on *Tristan*).

9. Novalis (*Schriften,* vol. 2, pp. 573–74) took a similar view of the outer and inner (or a priori) character of music.

10. George Bernard Shaw, *The Perfect Wagnerite* (New York: Dover, 1967); Robert Donington, *Wagner's 'Ring' and its Symbols* (London: Faber and Faber, 1963).

11. On Novalis and other romantic antecedents of Wagner's night/day metaphor see Arthur Prüfer, "Novalis Hymnen an die Nacht in ihren Beziehungen zu Wagners Tristan und Isolde," in *Richard Wagner-Jahrbuch,* 1 (1906), pp. 290–304; Thomas Mann, "The Sorrows and Grandeur," pp. 124–26. See also Dieter Borchmeyer, "The World in a Dying Light: *Tristan und Isolde* and the Myth of Night," in Borchmeyer, *Richard Wagner: Theory and Theatre,* trans. Stewart Spencer (Oxford: Clarendon Press, 1991), pp. 326–67. In *WWR*, 2, p. 185, Schopenhauer uses the metaphor of a torch, as Wagner does in Act Two, to express the limits of human understanding in comparison with the "depth of night" that symbolizes the metaphysical noumenon. He uses "night" in this way at other points in his treatise (see *WWR*, 1, pp. 280–81, 366–67, for example). He also placed the following lines from Goethe at the head of his essay "On Spirit-seeing and everything connected therewith": "Und laß dir rathen, habe/Die Sonne nicht zu lieb und nicht die Sterne./Komm, folge mir ins dunkle Reich hinab!" (see *Arthur Schopenhauer: Sämtliche Werke,* vol. 5. *Parerga und Paralipomena* 1, ed. Arthur Hübscher [Wiesbaden: Brockhaus, 1966], p. 239). See the following chapter for the influence of Hermann Kurtz's translation of Gottfried's poem on Wagner's night/day metaphors.

12. "Music of the Future," pp. 28–29, 34–35, 39.

13. *WWR*, 1, pp. 106–7.

14. See, among many instances of Schopenhauer's anti-Hegelian view of history, *WWR*, 2, p. 443.

15. See, for example, William J. Mitchell, "The *Tristan* Prelude: Techniques and Structure," in *The Music Forum,* vol. 1, ed. William J. Mitchell and Felix Salzer (New York, 1967), pp. 163–203.

16. *WWR*, 1, pp. 252–53.

17. Ibid., p. 253.

18. *Cosima Wagner's Diaries*, 2, pp. 855, 861. Joseph Kerman's remark that "*Tristan und Isolde* is not a tragedy. Wagner never intended it to be. It is a religious drama" is erroneous in its implying a contradiction between tragedy and religious drama. For Wagner and Schopenhauer tragedy was rooted in the hero's coming through suffering to perceive the illusory nature of existence, a knowledge that produced in him a state of resignation and exaltation, the latter arising from the quasi-religious intuition of a world beyond. Attaining that condition enabled him to deny the will-to-life. Joseph Kerman, *Opera as Drama*. New and rev. ed. (Berkeley: University of California Press, 1988), pp. 159–60.

19. Jacobs, *Three Wagner Essays*, p. 13.

20. *WWR*, 2, pp. 435–36.

21. *WWR*, 1, p. 257.

22. Carl Dahlhaus, *Between Romanticism and Modernism*, pp. 19–39.

23. Ibid., p. 35. Dahlhaus remarks that the 1857 essay on Liszt represented a "turning point," after which Wagner dropped the term (absolute music) "probably to avoid using it with a positive, instead of negative, emphasis." Wagner does, in fact, use the term "absolute music" after the 1850s, but only sporadically. In his later years Wagner adopted an explicitly positive view of absolute music, associating it with Bach (see Borchmeyer, *Richard Wagner: Theory and Theatre*, p. 121).

24. Wagner, *Beethoven*, pp. 106–7.

25. See Edmund Burke, *A Philosophical Enquiry into the Origin of our Ideas of the Sublime and Beautiful*, ed. with intro., notes, James T. Boulton (London: Routledge & Kegan Paul, 1958. Reprint ed. Notre Dame, Indiana: University of Notre Dame Press, 1968); Immanuel Kant, *Observations on the Feeling of the Beautiful and Sublime* (1764), trans. John T. Goldthwait (Berkeley: University of California Press, 1960); *Idem., The Critique of Judgment*, trans. J. H. Bernard (London: Macmillan, 1892. reprint edition, Amherst, N.Y.: Prometheus Books, 2000).

26. Burke, *A Philosophical Enquiry*, pp. 80, 124, 143–49; Kant, *Observations*, p. 47.

27. *WWR*, 1, pp. 199, 203.

28. *WWR*, 1, p. 207.

29. Ibid., p. 205.

30. See Burke, *A Philosophical Enquiry*, pp. 57–58, 71, 136, 160, 176; Kant, *Observations*, p. 47; *Idem, The Critique of Judgment*, p. 137. On Schopenhauer's linking death, astonishment and the impulse to metaphysics, see later, p. 40.

31. Kant, *Critique of Judgment*, pp. 132–47.

32. *WWR*, 1, pp. 532, 203–9.

33. Wagner, *Beethoven*, p. 34. It may be mentioned that Hegel (in his Introduction to his *Aesthetics*, p. 4) makes the following remark: "The beautiful [*Schöne*] has its being in pure appearance [*Schein*]." And, as T. M. Knox points out (p. 4, n. 1), he is following Kant (*Critique of Judgment*, part 1) in this definition of beauty. Schopenhauer makes a similar association between *Schönheit* and the English "to show," emphasizing their visual qualities (see "On the Metaphysics of the Beautiful and Aesthetics" in *PP*, 2, p. 424). In his notes for the Beethoven essay Wagner makes clear the connection to Hanslick. See Bergfield/Bird, *The Brown Book*, pp. 176–77.

34. *The Brown Book*, p. 177.

35. See *The Thirteen Principal Upanishads*, translated by Robert Ernest Hume. 2nd ed., rev. (Delhi: Oxford University Press, 1989), p. 43.

36. Ibid., pp. 23–36, 437–38.

37. *WWR*, 1, p. 196.

38. Wackenroder/Tieck, *Phantasien über die Kunst*, pp. 59–63.

39. *WWR*, 1, pp. 267 (see also pp. 232, 411). Raphael's painting of St. Cecilia became with Wackenroder, presumably Schopenhauer's source, a symbol of the transcendent character of music. Wagner refers to Raphael in the same terms in *Beethoven* (1870), and *Religion and Art* (1880).

40. Wagner's analogy between Beethoven's conception of form and the "transparency" that transmits inner light is derived (along with several other conceptions in Wagner's essay, such as clairvoyance, *actio in distans* and the "dream organ") from Schopenhauer's essay "On Spirit Seeing and Everything Connected Therewith" (*PP*, 1, pp. 225–309).

41. Ibid., p. 274.

42. Ibid., pp. 307–8.

43. *WWR*, 1, pp. 374, 398.

44. In the prose draft Tristan's curse is "Verfluchte Liebe, lass mich loß!" (see Dieter Borchmeyer, ed., *Richard Wagner Dichtungen und Schriften*, vol. 4, p. 101).

45. Already in early 1854 Wagner wrote to August Röckel regarding *Das Rheingold:* "I have once again realized how much of the work's meaning (given the nature of my poetic intent) is only made clear by the music: I can now no longer bear to look at the poem without music . . . it has become a close knit unity: there is scarcely a bar in the orchestra which does not develop out of preceding motifs." Spencer and Millington, *Selected Letters*, p. 310.

46. The change in Wagner's view toward the finale of the Beethoven Ninth Symphony can be found in a letter to Liszt of 1855 (see Spencer and Millington, *Selected Letters*, p. 343); it echoes at various points of Wagner's 1870 essay on Beethoven (see pp. 86–98, 119–20). Nietzsche, *The Birth of Tragedy and the Case of Wagner*, trans. Walter Kaufmann (New York: Random House, 1967), pp. 7, 8, 17–18.

47. William Ashton Ellis, *Richard Wagner's Prose Works*, 1, p. 331.

48. See the letter to Jakob Sulzer of May 1855 in Spencer and Millington, *Selected Letters*, pp. 338–39. In *Die Meistersinger* Wagner embodied the idea of an optimistic surface beneath which lies the tragic meaning of existence in the combination of Sachs's cheerful cobbler's song with the *Wahn* motive, both in act 2 and in act 3. In both places Eva senses the tragic undercurrent. And in the act 3 scene her response brings out a chromatic theme with decided affinities to the desire music of *Tristan*, which Sachs then introduces explicitly as he voices the necessity of his renunciation of Eva. The larger meaning of all this, of course, is that for Wagner behind the optimistic diatonic world of *Die Meistersinger* lies the chromatic Schopenhauerian background of *Tristan*.

49. On forgetfulness (*vergezzen*) in Gottfried, see W. T. H. Jackson (*The Anatomy of Love: The Tristan of Gottfried von Strassburg* [New York: Columbia University Press, 1971], p. 128).

50. Gottfried's "lieben tot" does not mean what Wagner's *Liebestod* does, of course. The favored German translation is "glücklicher Tod." Hatto (*op. cit.*, p. 42) translates it as "dear death," and W. T. H. Jackson (*The Anatomy of Love*, p. 54) as "loving death." Volker Mertens (*op. cit.*, p. 255) points out that "the idea of the *Liebestod* or love-death is already hinted at by Gottfried in Tristan's reference to 'êweclîchez sterben,' or 'eternal death,' in contrast to eternal life and as a consequence of the love potion." In Mertens's view, "in order to portray love's absolutist claims, Gottfried used a means of expression offered him by the one thing that, in the medieval world, could lay claim to absolute status—namely religion."

51. In light of Paul Bekker's and Robert Bailey's arguments against the title *Liebestod* for Isolde's final solo, it may be mentioned that in a diary entry for September 16, 1882, Cosima Wagner describes Wagner himself using the title *Liebestod* for Isolde's transfiguration. See Paul Bekker, *Richard Wagner: His Life in His Work*, trans. M. M. Bozman (New York: W. W. Norton & Co. Inc., 1931), pp. 302–3; Wagner, *Prelude and Transfiguration from Tristan and*

Isolde, ed. Robert Bailey (New York: W.W. Norton & Company, 1985), pp. 41–43; *Cosima Wagner's Diaries*, 1, p. 532; 2, p. 910.

52. See William Ashton Ellis, *Richard Wagner's Prose Works*, 3, pp. 236–54.

53. Thus, Richard Strauss remarked that with the final measure of *Tristan* Wagner "closed the door on Romanticism." See Borchmeyer, *Richard Wagner: Theory and Theatre*, p. 367.

3. Minne

1. See, for example, Denis de Rougement, *Love in the West*, pp. 227–31; August Closs, ed., *Gottfried von Strassburg: Tristan und Isolt*, (Oxford: Basil Blackwell, 1974), p. xlvii; Peter Wapnewski, *Der Traurige Gott; Richard Wagner in seinen Helden*, 2nd ed. (Munich: C. H. Beck, 1980), pp. 45–85.

2. See Mertens, "Wagner's Middle Ages," pp. 254–59. Curt von Westernhagen, *Richard Wagners Dresdener Bibliothek: 1842–1849* (Wiesbaden: Brockhaus, 1967). Wagner owned editions in middle high German edited by Friedrich H. von der Hagen (1823) and Hans F. Massmann (1843), as well as a translation into modern German with an extensive introduction by Hermann Kurtz (1847). The standard modern edition is Friedrich Ranke, ed., *Gottfried von Strassburg. Tristan und Isold.* (Berlin: 1930) I have used the fifteenth edition (Zürich: Weidmann, 1978). Gottfried's poem of around 1210 is incomplete, breaking off at the point at which Tristan is involved with Isolde of the White Hands. Two completions from the end of the thirteenth century—one by Ulrich von Türheim and the other by Heinrich von Freiberg—were well known however. The Massmann edition of Gottfried's poem included Türheim's ending and the von der Hagen edition both Türheim's and Freiberg's. Wagner also acquired the translation of Karl Simrock (1855) at some point, perhaps after the completion of *Tristan*. I find no evidence, however, that it influenced the poetry of *Tristan*.

3. See Rosemary Picozzi, *A History of Tristan Scholarship* (Berne: Hervert Lang & Co. Ltd., 1971), pp. 79–92. See also Peter Wapnewski, *Tristan der Held Richard Wagners* (Berlin: Severin und Siedler, 1981), pp. 64–68.

4. See A. T. Hatto, ed. and trans., *Gottfried von Strassburg: Tristan*, pp. 19–20, 248. All translations in this book are from this edition. On the conflict of honor and *Minne* in Gottfried see Wapnewski, *Tristan der Held Richard Wagners*, pp. 76–95.

5. Wolfram von Eschenbach, *Parzival*, trans. A. T. Hatto (Hammondsworth: Penguin Books, 1980), pp. 15–16.

6. Picozzi, *A History of Tristan Scholarship*, pp. 79–97.

7. Ibid., pp. 19–21, 88–92.

8. This and all subsequent citations from Gottfried are taken from the edition by Friedrich Ranke cited in note 2.

9. See Wapnewski, *Tristan der Held Richard Wagners*, pp. 102–6.

10. Hatto, Introduction to *Gottfried von Strassburg Tristan*, pp. 13–18.

11. Gottfried von Strassburg, *Tristan und Isold*, ed. Friedrich Ranke, p. 1, lines 55–66.

12. Hatto, *op. cit.*, p. 16.

13. See chapter 7, "The First Death Motive."

14. Gottfried shows awareness of this opposition at two points in his poem. The first is the literary "excursus" he supplies in place of Tristan's investiture. There, stimulated by the visual splendor of Tristan's garments and their allegorical interpretation, Gottfried launches into a famous critical appraisal of contemporary poets. And, as W. T. H. Jackson points out (*The Anatomy of Love*, p. 50), "in this passage of literary criticism it is made clear that Gottfried regards Hartmann von Aue, Bligger von Steinach, and to a large extent Heinrich von Veldecke as visual poets, and there is a strong presumption that he regards the writing of the romance in general as an exercise in visual imagery, superficial descriptions, and external appearances.

The inner being is revealed rather by sound and the organized impact of music." See also Jackson, "Tristan the Artist in Gottfried's Poem." Even more significantly, Gottfried's associating music with the idyllic harmony of the lovers in the *Minnegrotte* episode emphasizes both its "internal" aspect (when they want to forget the outside world and the stories of tragic lovers as told in literary works Tristan and Isolde retire into the cave for the more intimate communion of music) and its serving as a metaphor for love making (on the latter quality see Ruth Goldschmidt Kunzer, *The Tristan of Gottfried von Strassburg: An Ironic Perspective* [Berkeley: University of California Press, 1973], p. 167).

15. On the influence of Gottfried's use of chiasmus on the poetry of *Tristan*, see Arthur Groos, "Appropriation in Wagner's *Tristan* Libretto," in Arthur Groos and Roger Parker, eds., *Reading Opera* (Princeton: Princeton University Press, 1983), pp. 19–24.

16. On the sacramental character of this sequence, see Albrecht Schöne, "Zu Gottfrieds 'Tristan'-Prolog," *Deutsche Vierteljahrsschrift für Literaturwissenschaft und Geistesgeschichte* 29 (1955), pp. 447–74. Reprinted in Wolf (ed.), *Gottfried von Strassburg*, pp. 147–81; see pp. 174–81.

17. Interest in Gottfried's acrostic is at least as old as von der Hagen's edition of 1823 (*Einleitung*, p. vii), in which the author uncovers part of the meaning and points out the connection between the T and I initials of the acrostic and the T and I that Isolde carves on the pieces of bark that float down the brook as a signal for Tristan in the love scene know as the "Assignation by the Brook." See Hendrik Scholte, "Gottfrieds von Straßburg Initialenspiel," in *Beiträge zur Geschichte der deutschen Sprache und Literatur* 65 (1942), pp. 280–302 (reprinted in Alois Wolf, ed., *Gottfried von Strassburg. Wege der Forschung*, 320 [Darmstadt: Wissenschaftliche Buchgesellschaft, 1973], pp. 74–96; Jean Fourquet, "Das Kryptogramm des 'Tristan' und der Aufbau des Epos" (1963) in idem, pp. 362–70. For a view of Gottfried's acrostic in which the initials of the dedicate, of Gottfried himself and of the lovers (in the form TRISTAN and ISOLDEN) would run through the complete poem see Christoph Huber, *Gottfried von Straßburg: Tristan* (Berlin: Erich Schmidt, 2000), p. 38.

18. As Denis de Rougement points out (*Love in the Western World*, p. 135, n. 2), lines such as "Tristan und Isot, ir und ich . . . niwan ein Tristan und ein Isot" (18,352–57) from Gottfried's poem served as the source of lines such as Wagner's "nicht mehr Tristan . . . nicht mehr Isolde" in the love scene.

19. Gottfried's omission of the word "and" in the lines just cited has been interpreted by literary scholars, along with the chiasmus, as a device representing *Liebeseinheit*. See, for example, Albrecht Schöne, "Zu Gottfrieds 'Tristan'-Prolog," pp. 168–69. On the symmetrical construction of Gottfried's lovers' cave scene, see Rainer Gruenter, "Bauformen der Waldleben-Episode in Gotfrids Tristan und Isold," in *Gestaltprobleme der Dichtung. Günther Müller zu seinem 65. Geburtstag am 15. Dezember 1955*, ed. R. Alewyn et al. (Bonn, 1957), pp. 21–48. On Wagner's parallel dialogues see chapter 11, pp. 214–16.

20. See Jackson, *The Anatomy of Love*, pp. 92, 95, 141.

21. Ibid., pp. 180–88. See also Ruth Goldschmidt Kunzer, *op. cit.*, p. 176.

22. This understanding of Gottfried's *Minnegrotte* scene is indebted to Friedrich Ranke's groundbreaking article, "Die Allegorie der Minnegrotte in Gottfrieds Tristan" [1925], reprinted in Wolf, ed., *Gottfried von Strassburg*, pp. 1–24.

23. August Closs so describes it in the introduction to his edition of Gottfried's *Tristan* (p. xxxiv); and Ruth Goldschmidt Kunzer characterizes it as an "erotic dreamland" (*op. cit.*, p. 177). Friedrich Ranke ("Die Allegorie der Minnegrotte in Gottfrieds Tristan," p. 19) speaks of the lovers' cave scene as the "Traum Gottfrieds von wahrer Liebe." Gottfried himself uses the term *Wunschleben*, which perhaps underlies the line "Liebeheiligstes *Leben*, Niewiedererwachens wahnlos holdbewusster *Wunsch*" from "O sink hernieder." See Herbert Kolb, "Der Minne Hus: Zur Allegorie der Minnegrotte in Gottfrieds Tristan" (*Euphorion* 56 [1962], pp. 229–47; reprinted in Wolf, ed., *Gottfried von Strassburg*, pp. 305–33), p. 305.

24. Dieter Borchmeyer, ed., *Richard Wagner Dichtungen und Schriften*, vol. 4, p. 93.

25. Ashton Ellis, *Richard Wagner to Mathilde Wesendonck*, pp. 74–76, 78, 80. See chapter 4, pp. 75–77.

26. The theme of Minne's "way" is one that literary scholars have found in Gottfried's lovers' cave scene. Thus, Friedrich Ranke ("Die Allegorie der Minnegrotte in Gottfrieds Tristan," pp. 7–8) describes the difficult "way" to Minne as an extension of the hidden wilderness location of the cave. Albrecht Schöne ("Zu Gottfrieds 'Tristan'-Prolog," p. 165) describes Minne as the "Mittel und Weg zum *summum bonum*," that is, to "Minnetranszendenz."

27. Spencer and Millington, *Selected Letters*, p. 308.

28. *National Archiv der Richard-Wagner-Stiftung*, Bayreuth. Ms. A III h5, p. 48.

29. Hatto, *Gottfried von Strassburg: Tristan*, pp. 201–2.

4. Honor

1. Hatto, p. 265.

2. Ibid., p. 265.

3. Ibid., p. 266.

4. This distinction is drawn by Gottfried Weber (*Gottfried von Strassburg: Tristan: Text, Nacherzählung, Wort- und Begriffserklärungen* [Darmstadt, 1967], pp. 833–34), who makes clear that honor in Gottfried's world took basically the form of external honor, equivalent to reputation. See also George F. Jones, *Honor in German Literature* (Chapel Hill: University of North Carolina Press, 1959), pp. 6, 190.

5. The beginning of the prelude in the version from this source, the so-called New York Public Library Worksheet (NYPL: JOB 73–92; see *WWV*, p. 435), is transcribed in Bailey, *Prelude and Transfiguration*, p. 131. In this version, the first two phrases begin with tritones rather than sixths.

6. The deceptive cadence on Tristan's "O truggeweihtes Glücke" introduces the major seventh chord to underscore the quality of deception that Wagner associates with the day motive, which does not enter until the opening measures of the second act.

7. See later, pp. 192–93. It also returns to C at the end, reintroducing the day motive repeatedly at the pitch of Tristan's "O truggeweihtes Glücke," making the connection between the two places musically explicit.

8. See chapter 3, note 25.

9. In a letter to Heinrich Porges Wagner named Mark's motif that of his *Wohlwollens*, claiming that it contained the motif of Tristan's "self reproach" (*Selbstentwurf*) within it; the latter was, presumably, the melodic descent that follows the inversion of the honor motive. Heinrich Porges, *Tristan und Isolde*, ed. Hans von Wolzogen (Leipzig: Breitkopf & Härtel, 1906), p. 39.

10. *PP*, 1, p. 362.

11. "Aphorisms on the Wisdom of Life" (*PP*, 1, pp. 323–403).

12. In *WWR*, 2, pp. 601–2, Schopenhauer remarks: "On this metaphysical identity of the will as thing-in-itself rest in general three phenomena, in spite of the infinite multiplicity of its appearances, and these three can be brought under the common concept of *sympathy:* (1) *sympathy or compassion,* . . ; (2) *sexual love,* . . ; (3) *magic,* . . . . Accordingly, *sympathy* is to be defined as the empirical appearance of the will's metaphysical identity, through the physical multiplicity of its phenomena." In this light the desire music is connected not just to sexual love but to "sympathy" in this broader sense. Hence its entrance at the beginning of Tristan's answer to King Mark's question. In the first and second acts "magic" is associated with the love potion and with Frau Minne, both times invoking the desire music.

13. Letter to Liszt of January 23–24, 1858 (Spencer and Millington, *Selected Letters of Richard Wagner*, pp. 375–76). Wagner finished the first act of *Tristan* on December 31, 1857,

and he wrote to Liszt on January 1, 1858, informing him of that fact and adding that his reading was "at present confined to Calderón" (see Francis Hueffer, trans., *Correspondence of Wagner and Liszt*, 2nd ed. rev. W. Ashton Ellis. 2 vols. [New York: Charles Scribner's Sons, 1897], vol. 2, p. 217).

14. Peter Wapnewski makes the point that the influence of Calderón on Wagner was by way of Schopenhauer (*Tristan der Held Richard Wagners*, p. 92).

15. In this light another of Wagner's letters, written to Mathilde Wesendonck during the composition of *Tristan* (April 7, 1858), offers a perspective on the ending of *Tristan* as Wagner's ideal "completion" of Gottfried's poem in Schopenhauerian terms. In this, the famous letter whose interception by Wagner's wife Minna caused Wagner to withdraw to Venice, Wagner complains about the ending of Goethe's *Faust* as an "external" apotheosis, an avoidance of "the great compassion" that comes only from within, through "active participation [*Mitleid*] in the world's suffering," so that the individual (a "saint") "becomes the world," the only source of salvation. Wagner obviously felt that his own ending (not yet written) would achieve that in which Goethe's failed: the "absorption of the individual by the world." See John Burk, ed., *Letters of Richard Wagner: The Burrell Collection* (New York: Macmillan, 1950); also Arthur Groos, "Appropriation in the *Tristan* Libretto," pp. 29–33.

16. It is worth noting, however, that even in the orchestral draft of the transition to "O ew'ge Nacht," Wagner was still toying with the idea of making an A flat/B modulation as the lead-in to the duet, for he wrote in the margin "oder As dur?" and below it "und H dur?" (Or A flat major? And B major?)

17. See H. B. Wilson, "*Senen* and *triuwe*: Gottfried's unfinished *Tristan*," in Adrian Stevens and Roy Wisbey, eds., *Gottfried von Strassburg and the Medieval Tristan Legend* (London: D. S. Brewer and The Institute of Germanic Studies, 1990), pp. 247–56.

18. Ibid., p. 249.

19. Max Wehrle, "Der Tristan Gottfrieds von Strassburg," in *Trivium* 4 (1946), pp. 81–117. Reprinted in Alois Wolf, ed., *Gottfried von Strassburg*, pp. 97–134; see pp. 104, 120, 127.

20. This detail confirms the textual connection pointed out by Peter Wapnewski between the two places (*Tristan der Held Richard Wagners*, p. 95).

21. See Borchmeyer, *Richard Wagner: Schriften und Dichtungen*, vol. 4, p. 101.

22. See Borchmeyer, *Richard Wagner: Schriften und Dichtungen*, vol. 4, p. 101.

5. The Desire Music

1. Letter to Mathilde Wesendonck of March 3, 1860 (Spencer and Millington, *Selected Letters of Richard Wagner*, p. 486). Thomas Mann, "The Sorrows and Grandeur of Richard Wagner," pp. 126–27.

2. *WWR*, 2, pp. 601–2.

3. For a summary of this tendency, see David W. Bernstein, "Symmetry and Symmetrical Inversion in Turn-of-the-Century Theory and Practice," in Christopher Hatch and David W. Bernstein, eds., *Music Theory and the Exploration of the Past* (Chicago: University of Chicago Press, 1993), pp. 377–407.

4. For the sequence of theorists who give a prominent place to symmetry, see Bernstein, "Symmetry," pp. 381–99. On the "metaphysical" aspect of Hauptmann's dualism, see the translator's preface and introductory essay written by W. E. Heathcote to the English edition of Hauptmann's treatise (*The Nature of Harmony and Metre*, trans. and ed. W. E. Heathcote [London: S. Sonnenschein, 1888; 2nd ed., 1893], pp. vii–viii and xv–xxxiii). Reprint Da Capo Press (New York, 1991).

5. See Bernstein, pp. 393–94.

6. Ibid., pp. 391–92.

7. See William Mitchell, *op. cit.*; Benjamin Boretz, "Meta-variations, Part IV: Analytical Fallout (I)," *Perspectives of New Music*, Fall–Winter 1972: pp. 164–201.

8. William J. Mitchell (ibid., pp. 178–80) uses it to confirm his interpretation of the role of the diminished chord in the prelude. In that version Wagner used the rising major sixth (or diminished seventh) for the third phrase.

9. I have outlined this process in *Monteverdi's Tonal Language* (New York: Schirmer Books, 1992), pp. 22–49.

10. See pp. 286–95, especially p. 294.

11. In the first scene of *Tristan* Wagner transposes several passages, most notably the first phrase of the desire music, by cycles of whole tones, a representation of Isolde's mounting anger.

12. Alfred Lorenz, for example, points out this quality (*Das Geheimnis der Form bei Richard Wagner*, II: *Der Musikalische Aufbau von Richard Wagners "Tristan und Isolde"* [Berlin, 1926], p. 20), characterizing the e♭ as an "illusion" (*Schein*).

13. See George Perle, *The Operas of Alban Berg, Volume Two: Lulu* (Berkeley: University of California Press, 1985). And *Lulu* bears the unmistakable influence of *Tristan*, especially in the music associated with Alwa, the composer's persona, whom Berg explicitly related to Tristan in his sketches and whose "chromatic set" begins with the rising chromatic tones of the desire music. In addition, as has been discovered by Silvio Josè dos Santos (unpublished Ph. D. dissertation, "Alban Berg's *Lulu* and the Representation of Desire," Brandeis University, 2003), Berg originally included the first phrase of the *Tristan* desire music at the climax of the first phase of the duet between Lulu and Alwa, at the point at which Alwa declares his love for Lulu.

14. See p. 436. The Wagner-Archiv in Bayreuth possesses a facsimile of the document in question (A III h 11 (1)) along with an explanatory page concerning the history of the sheet written by Gertrude Strobel; the original is in possession of the Österreichische Nationalbibliothek, Vienna.

15. Louis Schlösser, "Ein Besuch bei Richard Wagner in Paris," *Allgemeine Musik-Zeitung*, XII. Jahrgang, No. 21 (May 22, 1885), pp. 191–92.

16. Because the white-note scale on D follows the same interval pattern ascending and descending, the white-note scale pairs whose starting pitches are equidistant from D—for example, C and E, B and F, A and G—similarly invert each other.

17. *Hanslick's Music Criticisms*, trans. and ed. Henry Pleasants (New York: Dover Publications, 1950), p. 38.

18. Spencer and Millington, *Selected Letters of Richard Wagner*, pp. 132–35.

19. Hanslick's remark is cited in Bailey, *Prelude and Transfiguration*, p. 39. In his *Harmonielehre* (1911), Schönberg refers to Hanslick as "our Viennese professor who found *Tristan* dull because so many diminished seventh chords occur in it"; Schönberg found Hanslick's view "nonsensical," commenting that "in *Tristan* there are not all that many diminished seventh chords." The context of Schönberg's remarks, the lack of variety in purely whole-tone music, indicates that he considered Hanslick's failure to understand *Tristan* owing to his recognizing the symmetrical qualities of the diminished-seventh chord but not the ways by which Wagner offsets them—that is, the role of the Tristan chord in relation to the diminished seventh chord. See Arnold Schönberg, *Theory of Harmony*, trans. Roy E. Carter (Berkeley: University of California Press, 1978), p. 394. It might be mentioned, also, that Alban Berg in a letter to his wife of June 2, 1907, referred to the Tristan chord as an "altered diminished seventh" (see Alban Berg, *Letters to his Wife*, trans. Bernard Grun [New York: St. Martin's Press, 1971], pp. 24–25).

20. For a summary of the principal interpretations of the Tristan chord, see Martin Vogel, *Der Tristan-Akkord und die Krise der modernen Harmonie-Lehre*, vol. 2 of *Orpheus-Schriftenreihe zu Grundfragen der Musik* (Düsseldorf: Gesellschaft zur Förderung der systematischen

Musikwissenschaft, 1962). For the multiple-key view, see, for example, Karl Mayrberger, "The Harmonic Style of Richard Wagner, Elucidated with Respect to the Leitmotifs of 'Tristan and Isolde'" (1881), in Ian Bent, ed., *Music Analysis in the Nineteenth Century*, Volume One (Cambridge: Cambridge University Press, 1994) p. 228. Berlioz ("The Richard Wagner Concerts") was apparently the first to interpret the long-held dissonances in the prelude as appoggiaturas.

21. And in the compositional draft Wagner, instead of bringing back the first phrase of the desire music, reintroduced the diminished-seventh chord as the penultimate harmony of the opera, sustaining it and leading it into the B major chord in a manner that is reminiscent of the third phrase of the desire music: the uppermost orchestral line moves upward by semitones from d‴ to the final f♯‴, the shift from e♮‴ to f♯‴ coinciding with the change of harmony from the diminished-seventh chord to the B major chord. See the transcription in Bailey, *Prelude and Transfiguration*, pp. 107–12.

22. Schopenhauer takes up the metaphysical meaning of the glance in *WWR*, 2, pp. 237–39. See later, pp. 147–48 for discussion of Schopenhauer's remarks in the context of the glance motive.

23. See chapter 6 for citations from Wagner's program notes to the Prelude.

24. The German expression for "deceptive cadence," *Trugschluss*, fits with the great emphasis on *Trug* and *Täuschung* (both meaning lie or deception) in the part of the love scene known as the *Tagesgespräch*, where the incidence of deceptive cadences, enharmonic changes and other "deceiving" devices is greatest in the opera (the analog of the illusoriness of "day").

6. The Prelude

1. Cited from Bailey, *Prelude and Transfiguration*, p. 48.

2. The concert ending has been published in Bailey, *Prelude and Transfiguration*, pp. 70–75.

3. Bailey, *Prelude and Transfiguration*, pp. 47–48. Bailey's is a "modified" version of Ashton Ellis's translation (*Richard Wagner's Prose Works*, vol. 8 (London, 1899), pp. 366–67. For the German original, see vol. 9 of *Richard Wagner's Gesammelte Schriften*, ed. Julius Kapp, pp. 61–62.

4. This version of the prelude, a fair copy, is preserved as MS A III h7 at the *Nationalarchiv der Richard-Wagner-Stiftung*, Bayreuth.

5. *WWR*, 2, pp. 238–39.

6. Ibid., pp. 536, 548–49, 559–60.

7. *Richard Wagner: Theory and Theatre*, p. 344.

8. See John Burk, ed., *Letters of Richard Wagner: The Burrell Collection*, pp. 370–71.

9. See chapter 2, note 11. For other possible poetic sources for the torch, see Borchmeyer, *Richard Wagner: Theory and Theatre*, pp. 349–50.

10. *WWR*, 2, pp. 548–49.

11. In Gottfried Tristan is healed from Morold's poisoned wound by Isolde's mother on his first visit to Ireland (the episode known as "Tantris"), while the episode of the "Splinter" takes place during his second visit ("The Wooing Expedition"); in Wagner's version, told in Isolde's narrative, Isolde made the discovery of the splinter on his first stay in Ireland when she herself healed him from Morold's wound.

12. Hatto, p. 173. The lines from Gottfried that might have influenced Wagner are the following: "si blickte im dicke tougen/an die hende und under d'ougen" (She secretly glanced often at his hands and in his eyes). See lines 9,995–96.

13. Ibid., p. 174: "Her heart was turned, her eye impelled to where his equipment lay. I have no idea how she could do such a thing, but she took up the sword in her hands."

14. Ibid., p. 176.

15. Borchmeyer, *Richard Wagner: Theory and Theatre*, p. 342.

16. See *Cosima Wagner's Diaries*, 1, p. 698 (November 17, 1873).

17. See lines 16, 815–18.

18. See the discussion of tempo and meter in act 2 on pp. 180–82.

19. Interestingly, this detail is not to be found in any of the endings of Gottfried's poem that Wagner knew. It is, however, the way that Tristan dies in the *Tristan* of Gottfried's source, Thomas of Brittany (in which Tristan speaks Isolde's name three times before dying; Isolde, however, is not present) and presumably, therefore, would have been retained by Gottfried had he completed his poem. Thomas's poem had not been rediscovered when Wagner wrote *Tristan*.

20. The only other appearance of the *Sühnetrank* motive in the opera confirms this. It sounds in Isolde's penultimate solo, sung over the dead Tristan, accompanying her cry that she had come to die united with Tristan.

21. Wagner makes clear that this motive is a variant of the desire music not only by leading it directly into the glance music and the deceptive cadence in measures 40–44 but also by substituting it for the third phrase of the desire music in measures 89–92 and by transposing it at the minor third according to the pitch levels of the first two phrases of the desire music in the orchestral passage that follows soon after Tristan's "Seligste Frau!" toward the end of act 1.

22. In a recent study of the prelude ("Circular Form in the *Tristan* Prelude," in *Journal of the American Musicological Society*, vol. 53, no. 1 [Spring 2000], pp. 69–103), Robert Morgan points out that the boundary points of the many "units" that make up the prelude (i.e., the desire, glance and *Sühnetrank* motives in their various permutations) articulate a pattern of rotating thirds, E/G♯, F/A, D/F, and A/C♯ until the shift to c at the end. Morgan is not describing a sequence of "keys," of course, although there is considerable correspondence between his thirds and the dominant (E), tonic (a/A) and subdominant (d) levels of the *Sühnetrank*, desire, and glance units. In my view, Morgan's third cycle fulfills the role of connecting the three basic themes (including at some points their extensions) and their associated tonal regions; it does not itself represent an underlying structural principle, which is more the property of the themes and tonal regions themselves.

23. In addition there is a substantial contrast in sonority at this point (m. 94), in that the trombones, which had entered first at the end of measure 66, as well as the bass tuba and kettledrums (which had entered first in m. 74) drop out in measures 83–85. Wagner's many expressive markings in the concert ending (*morendo, expressivo, sehr zart, sehr ruhig, dolcissimo, sehr weich*), and the light *pizzicato* bass, soft dynamics, divided cellos, bowed tremolos in the strings, and the like, all create an orchestral atmosphere worthy of Debussy's later prelude. Presumably Wagner intended the break with the prevailing rhythmic character of the movement as an allegory of the "metaphysical" priority of harmony over rhythm. See pp. 180–82, for further discussion of the rhythmic-metric and tempo aspects of *Tristan* and their poetic symbolisms.

7. Tragedy and Dramatic Structure

1. *WWR*, 2, p. 628.

2. *WWR*, 2, p. 433.

3. *WWR*, 2, p. 456.

4. William Ashton Ellis, ed. and trans., *Richard to Minna Wagner*, vol. 2 (London: H. Grevel & Company, 1909), p. 537.

5. The scale in question comprises the pitches g, c′, d′, e′, f′, and g′. It may be mentioned that in the published score of *Siegfried* Wagner added the following note (which was repeated in the score of *Die Götterdämmerung*): "Instead of the English horn, which is too weak for the desired effects, the composer has had an 'alto oboe' constructed, which he would like to have permanently substituted for the English horn in his score (see Richard Wagner, *Siegfried* [New York: Dover Publications, 1983]). In the second act of *Siegfried* Wagner calls on the English

horn to play the music for the natural instrument made of wood that Siegfried makes to imitate the woodbird—that is, to come to a closer understanding of nature. The second act of *Siegfried,* the last part of the Ring to be set to music before Wagner turned to *Tristan,* features two natural instruments, the other one being Siegfried's horn. And the diatonic music they play is juxtaposed to Fafner's numerous tritones, an opposition that reappears in the *alte Weise* of *Tristan,* act 3, and that underlies the emphasis on the perfect fifth in the *frohe Weise.*

6. That the natural horn could not play the pitches demanded in *Tristan* mirrors Schopenhauer's remark (*WWR,* 1, p. 266) that a "perfectly harmonious system of tones is impossible not only physically but even arithmetically." Schopenhauer viewed this as a mirroring of the will's "inner contradiction" with itself. It may be mentioned that similar religious perceptions of the impossibility of perfect temperament go back much earlier in time and probably influenced Schopenhauer. See, for example, Andreas Werckmeister, *Musicae mathematicae hodegus curiousus* (Frankfurt and Leipzig: Calvisi, 1687), pp. 141–54.

7. See chapter 9 for a fuller discussion of the scene as a whole.

8. *WWR,* 2, p. 634.

9. Wagner, *Beethoven,* pp. 40–41.

10. Ibid., pp. 31–35.

11. *Beethoven,* pp. 117–20.

12. In another song from the *Wesendonck Lieder,* "Schmerzen," Mathilde Wesendonck takes up another Schopenhauer-derived image: that of the analogy between the setting sun and death, the rising sun and rebirth. See *WWR,* 1, pp. 280–81. Again, the cyclic theme is paramount; and again, the song shifts from its c, B♭, A♭, tonal region to C major at the end, now to coincide with the poet's thanking "nature" for bringing the pain that alone can lead to bliss. "Schmerzen" is pervaded by the sound of the major-seventh chord, associated in *Tristan* with the day motive.

13. See *WWR,* 1, pp. 185, 196; 2, pp. 477, 481. On Wackenroder, see chapter 2, p. 43. The "Ixion wheel of appearances" was an idea from Schopenhauer that influenced Mahler in the design of his third symphony, whose adagio Mahler likened to the cessation of the wheel (see Natalie Bauer-Lechner, *Recollections of Gustav Mahler,* trans. Dika Newlin, ed. and ann. Peter Franklin [Cambridge: Cambridge University Press, 1980], pp. 67, 203–4).

14. The conception of nature as "holy" was one that Wagner disagreed with. While composing the second act of *Tristan,* he wrote to Mathilde Wesendonck: "I had a strong mind to rechristen the "heil'ge Natur"—the thought is right, but not the expression: Nature is nowhere holy, saving where she revokes and denies herself." See Ellis, *Richard Wagner to Mathilde Wesendonck,* pp. 58–59.

8. The Two Death Motives

1. *WWR,* 2, p. 448.

2. See chapter 2, p. 38.

3. *WWR,* 2, p. 449.

4. Similarly, as Carl Dahlhaus remarks, in Schoenberg's aesthetics "the idea which assumes concrete form in a work such as the Chamber Symphony is thus realized less in the musical shapes that make up the surface than in the tissue of relationships which, hidden beneath, connect the ideas with one another." "Schoenberg's aesthetic theology," in Carl Dahlhaus, *Schoenberg and the New Music,* trans. Derrick Puffett and Alfred Clayton (Cambridge: Cambridge University Press, 1987), p. 81.

5. "On Franz Liszt's Symphonic Poems," p. 242.

6. *WWR,* 2, pp. 160–61. On the association of astonishment and the sublime, see earlier, p. 40.

7. Schopenhauer, *WWR*, 1, p. 26; 2, pp. 43, 82, 185, 351.

8. *WWR*, 2, pp. 237–39.

9. Nevertheless, many musicians have attempted to account for it in terms of functional tonality. Karl Mayrberger (see pp. 238–39 of the source cited in chapter 5, note 20), for example, respells it as a B♭♭ chord, calling it a modulation to D♭ minor, whereas Schönberg ("Brahms the Progressive" in *Style and Idea*, ed., Leonard Stein trans. Leo Black [Berkeley: University of California Press, 1975], p. 403) describes it as the Neapolitan harmony of A♭. Although such "explanations" bring out the idea that Wagner's C minor half close overcomes the "distant" character of the A major chord, in my view in eliminating the idea of antithesis they cover up more than revealing Wagner's intention.

10. These relationships are well known. See, for example, Bailey, *Prelude and Transfiguration*, pp. 138–39.

11. William Ashton Ellis, trans., *Richard Wagner's Prose Works*, 2, p. 287.

12. Periodicity was recognized as a recurrent feature of the Wagner leitmotifs by Schönberg, who viewed it as a weakness in comparison with the principle of developing variation. Schönberg, "Criteria for the Evaluation of Music," in *Style and Idea*, pp. 129–30. In Wagner's terms, however, the fact that many of the leitmotifs exhibit periodic designs in dialogue with other harmonic and motivic qualities means that such motives mirror "the character of all phenomena of the world [their periodicity and associational qualities], according to their most inner abstract-self [their harmonic and intervallic interrelatedness with the other motives]."

13. See chapter 10, pp. 185–91.

14. See the source cited in chapter 4, note 8.

15. For transcriptions of Wagner's sketches for this melody, see Robert Bailey, "The Method of Composition," in Peter Burbidge and Richard Sutton, eds., *The Wagner Companion* (New York: Cambridge University Press, 1979), pp. 308–15.

16. See Carl Dahlhaus, "Wagner's 'Kunst des Überganges: Der Zwiegesang in 'Tristan und Isolde'," in Dahlhaus, *Vom Musikdrama zur Literaturoper* (Munich/Mainz: Schott/Piper, 1989), pp. 159–60.

9. Musico-poetic Design in Act 1

1. In the final lines of the prose draft, Wagner describes "fragrant blooms of ecstasy that ascend, swelling to an ocean of fragrant waves, a melody that rushes ever-higher—Isolde expires from bliss, throws herself into the ocean, to drown, to forget." See Borchmeyer, *Richard Wagner Dichtungen und Schriften*, vol. 4, p. 103.

2. Lorenz, *Das Geheimnis*, vol. 2 (*Tristan*), pp. 71–72.

3. See Ashton Ellis, trans., *Richard Wagner's Prose Works*, 1 (1895), pp. 110–12.

4. Ibid., pp. 112, 115.

5. *Opera and Drama*, pp. 198, 211–12, 216–18, 224–25, 230–33, 249–50, 310–12.

6. *Opera and Drama*, pp. 42, 45, 82, 88.

7. Ibid., pp. 115–16. In "The Artwork of the Future" (*Richard Wagner's Prose Works*, 1, pp. 121–22), Wagner allies infinite melody to freedom from periodicity. A decade later in *Music of the Future*, after expressing his derision for "rhythmic melody" and "periodic structure," Wagner describes Bach as having brought about the union of melody and harmony in which "the lyrical impulse of the rhythmic melody seems to surge through an ocean of harmonic waves" (Jacobs, *Three Wagner Essays*, pp. 25–26). Later in the same essay Wagner returns to the ocean metaphor to convey the universal musicopoetic source that remains in "constant touch with the firm ground of a dramatic action." The poet recedes into the background so that the musician can bring the "great Unsaid to sounding life, and the unmistak-

able form of his resounding silence is *endless melody*" (*Ibid.*, p. 40). For a fuller treatment of the subject, see Kropfinger, *Wagner and Beethoven*, pp. 100–14; Dahlhaus, *Between Romanticism and Modernism*, pp. 52–64.

8. Bailey, "The Genesis of 'Tristan und Isolde'," pp. 151–52.

9. Bailey's argument that the curse is set apart by virtue of the fact that, unlike the narrative proper, it is addressed to Tristan, rather than Brangaene and therefore represents present emotion rather than recall of the past is only half true. In the remainder of the narrative Isolde makes similar outbursts of present emotion that, although not addressed directly to Tristan, are not part of the story she is recounting for Brangaene. Those passages link up musically with the curse. In this solo, Isolde relives the cause of her present emotion which surfaces completely at the end. It is probably true that no scene of recollection in Wagner's mature works is really narrative in nature, at least to the extent that narration can be separated from present emotion.

10. The other appearance of the death motive coincides with Isolde's words, "[Wir sind am Ziel: in kurzer] Frist steh'n wir vor König Marke" (a full close to c), immediately following which Isolde shifts to C to mock Tristan with a parody of what he might say to King Mark on arrival in Cornwall.

11. Matthew Brown, "Isolde's Narrative: From *Hauptmotiv* to Tonal Model," in Carolyn Abbate and Roger Parker, eds., *Analyzing Opera: Verdi and Wagner* (Berkeley: University of California Press, 1989), pp. 180–201.

10. Night and Minne

1. In this light Antony Newcomb's characterization of the opening scene of act 2 as a "ritornello ritornato" describes only that aspect of its form that Wagner intended to represent the day—that is, the periodic design that serves as the "surface" of a form that is, in fact, "subversive" in nature. To the extent that Wagner might have been influenced by ritornello designs in Bach, as Newcomb suggests, that influence is merely that of Wagner's conception of the pitfalls of eighteenth-century periodic forms in general. In fact, the form has nothing whatever to do with Bach, and its periodic qualities—what Wagner would have called "quadratic construction"—exist for their own denial, a quality that is palpable within the musical form itself, and all the more so when we take the poetic text into account. See Newcomb, "Ritornello Ritornato: a Variety of Wagnerian Refrain Form," in Carolyn Abbate and Roger Parker, eds., *Analyzing Opera* (Berkeley: University of California Press, 1989), pp. 202–21.

2. See Dahlhaus, "Wagner's Kunst des Übergangs," pp. 153–61.

11. The Love Scene in Act 2

1. Spencer and Millington, *Selected Letters*, pp. 474–75.

2. Lorenz, *Tristan*, pp. 111, 118, 123.

3. The earliest instance of this cut that is known to me was made by Gustav Mahler at the Vienna opera. Mahler's score of *Tristan*, presently housed in the archive of the Vienna opera, indicates a cut beginning with the "deceptive" cadence—G[7]–A♭—that overlaps the ending of Isolde's "bot ich dem Tage *Trutz*" and the beginning of Tristan's "*Dem Tage! Dem Tage! Dem tückischen Tage*" (the beginning of the *Tagesgespräch*, m. 682), and ending with another such cadence, at Tristan's "wahr es zu sehen tauge" (m. 1003). I am grateful to Katarina Marković Stokes for this information.

4. The passage is reproduced in facsimile and transcribed in Bartels, *Studien zu Wagners Tristan und Isolde anhand der Kompositionsskizze des zweiten und dritten Aktes*, part 2, pp. 39–41; part 3, fol. 8.

5. After indicating G for the concluding strophes of Tristan's "Was dich umgliss" Wagner writes E, A♭, E, A♭, A♭, and C at various points in the second half of the *Tagesgespräch*.

6. "On Franz Liszt's Symphonic Poems," p. 245.

7. See Borchmeyer, *Richard Wagner: Theory and Theatre*, pp. 328–29.

8. Lorenz, *Tristan*, p. 122.

9. Bailey, "The Method of Composition," in Peter Burbidge and Richard Sutton, eds., *The Wagner Companion* (New York: Cambridge University Press, 1979), p. 308.

10. We are not dealing with exact transpositions, however, as the harmony is altered each time.

12. Tristan's Answer to King Mark

1. See Jackson, *The Anatomy of Love*, pp. 127–32.

2. Schopenhauer, *On the Basis of Morality*, trans. E. F. J. Payne (Providence: Berghahn Books, 1995), pp. 210–12.

3. A passage in the Venice Diary (October 3, 1858) makes this clear: "with Schopenhauer, I begin to doubt the possibility of any genuine friendship, to rank as utter fable what is dubbed so . . . " (Ellis, *Richard Wagner to Mathilde Wesendonck*, p. 52).

4. *PP*, 1, pp. 323–403.

5. See chapter 4, note 9.

6. See, for example, Calvin S. Brown, *Music and Literature*, pp. 98–99.

7. *On the Basis of Morality*, pp. 212, 166.

8. Borchmeyer, *Richard Wagner Dichtungen und Schriften*, vol. 4, p. 97.

9. Jacobs, *Three Wagner Essays*, pp. 28–29, 34–35, 39.

10. Schopenhauer, *WWR*, 1, pp. 69ff.

11. Schopenhauer, *On The Four-fold Root of the Principle of Sufficient Reason*, trans. E. F. J. Payne (La Salle, Ill.: Open Court, 1974), pp. 5–6, 11, 212; *WWR*, 1, pp. 69–83, 124–25, 178–81, 273–74, 483; 2, pp. 72, 180–82, 318, 530, 579, 641.

12. Ellis, *Richard Wagner to Mathilde Wesendonck*, pp. 95–98.

13. Wagner, *Beethoven*, trans. Albert J. Parsons (Boston: Lee & Shepard, 1872), p. 107.

14. Schopenhauer, *WWR*, 1, pp. 178–81.

13. Act 3: Musico-poetic Design

1. Kerman, *Opera as Drama*, pp. 208, 196. Nietzsche, *The Birth of Tragedy*, pp. 126–28 (section 21).

2. On the compositional draft Wagner placed the dates of his breaking off—May 16 (1859)—and resuming composition (June 19) at the point at which Tristan collapses to the f/F cadence. On May 1, Wagner had already begun the orchestral sketches to the act and within a few days after that the full score. On May 30, he wrote Mathilde Wesendonck that he was busy with the "working out" (*Ausarbeitung*) of the first half of the act, and on June 17 he wrote that he had sent "the first manuscript of the third act" to Härtels in Leipzig (see Ashton Ellis, *Richard Wagner to Mathilde Wesendonck*, pp. 139, 146).

3. In *WWR*, 1, pp. 398–402, Schopenhauer explains that "the will itself cannot be abolished by anything except *knowledge*. Therefore the only path to salvation is that the will should appear freely and without hindrance, in order that it can *recognize or know* its own inner nature in this phenomenon. Only in consequence of this knowledge can the will abolish itself, and thus end the suffering that is inseparable from its phenomenon." Wagner's divergence from Schopenhauer centers on his belief that sexual love could lead to the knowl-

edge that would enable what Schopenhauer, earlier in the same passage, calls the "transcendental change."

4. "Music of the Future," p. 34.

5. Ibid., pp. 34–35.

6. Schopenhauer, *PP* 1, p. 352.

7. In a letter to Mathilde Wesendonck written during the composition of act 3 Wagner describes Kurvenal's "Auf eig'ner Weid' und Wonne im Schein der alten Sonne, darin von Tod und Wunden—du selig sollst gesunden," as "very harrowing—especially as it makes no impression at all upon Tristan, but passes o'er him like a hollow sound. There's immense tragedy in it! Overwhelming!" (Ellis, *Richard Wagner to Mathilde Wesendonck*, p. 119).

8. In act 1, scene 5, Isolde had taunted Tristan with allusions to the death motive, one of which, at "dein Loos nun selber magst du dir sagen," triggered Tristan's understanding of her hidden meaning (as described in chapter 7). There, as in act 3, Tristan's intuition of his "fate" was the beginning of his looking inward.

9. Wapnewski, *Der Traurige Gott*, p. 59.

10. Ibid., p. 62, n. 31.

11. Hatto, p. 284.

12. Ibid., pp. 284–85.

13. As Peter Wapnewski points out (*Der Traurige Gott*, p. 75), Isolde's use of the third person in her speech is carried over by Wagner into the love scene as one of the poetic devices (abandonment of the "ich" as symbol of personal identity) that culminate in the expressions of oneness in "O ew'ge Nacht."

14. Hatto, p. 293.

15. Ibid., p. 293.

16. Lorenz, *Tristan*, pp. 168–72; Kerman, *Opera as Drama*, pp. 165–68.

17. Nietzsche, *The Birth of Tragedy*, section 21.

18. This is exactly the way that Schopenhauer describes the will-to-life (*WWR*, 2, pp. 357–60).

14. Love as Fearful Torment

1. Wesendonck took the sun allegory, contradictions and all, from Schopenhauer, see *WWR*, 1, pp. 280–81.

2. Tristan's reference to *Mitleid* corresponds to Schopenhauer's refuting the idea that in compassion "we put ourselves in the position of the sufferer, and have the idea that we are suffering *his* pains in our person. This is by no means the case; on the contrary, at every moment we remain clearly conscious that *he* is the sufferer, not *we;* and it is precisely in *his* person, not in ours, that we feel the suffering, to our grief and sorrow. We suffer *with* him and hence *in* him; we feel his pain as *his,* and do not imagine that it is ours." Schopenhauer, *On the Basis of Morality*, p. 147.

3. Interestingly, among the psychoanalytic writings from the Freud circle in Vienna is a book on this very subject by Theodor Reik, *The Haunting Melody: Psychoanalytic Experiences in Life and Music* (New York: Grove Press, 1953), written after Reik's emigration to the United States. Reik uses psychoanalytical procedures to explore why a particular musical composition (usually represented by a tune) comes to embody psychological significance. His method is rooted in musical associations rather than musical analysis, which Reik felt unequipped to carry out. But Reik thought that musical analysis should also be an important part of the process. And Tristan's "method," although necessarily rooted in associations surrounding the "alte Weise," involves a dimension of musical analysis that is embodied in the leitmotif procedures and is, of course, left to the musical analyst to describe.

4. In a letter to Mathilde Wesendonck, Wagner described this passage as a transition: "As 8 days since I could get no further with the actual composition (at the transition, in fact, from "vor Sehnsucht nicht zu sterben" to the sick man's voyage), I had then let it be, and taken up instead the working-out of the commencement, . . . now I'm perfectly happy: the transition has succeeded beyond belief, with a quite wonderful concord of two themes." Ellis, *Richard Wagner to Mathilde Wesendonck*, p. 130.

5. Isolde's dropping the sword was very closely bound up with the glance of love that passed between the lovers at that point, as Wagner makes clear at several points in Isolde's narrative and in act 1, scene 5.

15. The Road to Salvation

1. Borchmeyer, *Richard Wagner: Dichtungen und Schriften*, vol. 4, p. 103.

2. *Cosima Wagner's Diaries*, 2, p. 277.

3. Wagner had, in fact, introduced music very like that of "So stürben wir"—or at least like the pattern of its third, fourth, and fifth measures—in the so-called Unschuld motif of *Lohengrin*, where it also appears in A♭. In *Lohengrin*, however, it is simply a motif that transposes by successive minor thirds, outlining the pattern of the diminished-seventh chord A♭, C♭ [B], D, F, before returning to its starting point. The only deviations are major-minor shifting in the triads (to facilitate progression to the next transposition level) and slight harmonic elaboration of both the initial motion *from* A♭ and the concluding motion back from F *to* A♭.

4. Magee, *The Philosophy of Schopenhauer* (New York: Oxford University Press, 1983), pp. 393–94.

5. As is often pointed out, the melody of Isolde's "ertrinken, versinken" is the same (transposed) as that of Tristan's "Urvergessen," earlier in the act, which he describes as the only "knowledge" possessed by the inhabitants of night, a paradoxical statement matched by perhaps the most mysterious enharmonic relationship in the opera.

6. Under the title "Wagner conducts Wagner," the Italian label *Grammofono 2000* (*Fono Enterprise*, Como, 1997) has issued what purports to be a cylinder recording from around 1880 possibly conducted by Wagner himself. The four-minute excerpt in question presents a combination of "So stürben wir" and the B major segment of "O ew'ge Nacht" that begins in measure nine of "So stürben wir" (m. 1385 of act 2), at the point at which Tristan sings "ohn' Erwachen." It then continues on into the duet version of the movement, including Brangaene's G major second warning. At the point where the G major cadence occurs (m. 1433), however, it reinterprets the G as the flat sixth of B, jumping from there to a recomposed version of the measures that precede the modulation to B in "O ew'ge Nacht" (1529). It then continues on until measure 1612 of the duet before breaking off. The excerpt is not a purely orchestral arrangement, and even Brangaene's few measures of G are sung. This arrangement demonstrates the flexibility and variability of "So stürben wir." If it indeed derives from Wagner, it may reflect his experimenting with alternate ways of introducing the *Liebestod* or with a shortened version of the love scene. Because the excerpt lacks its beginning and ending, it might well have been conceived as part of a longer span.

Bibliography

Abbate, Carolyn, and Roger Parker, eds. *Analyzing Opera: Verdi and Wagner.* Berkeley: University of California Press, 1989.

Abrams, M. H. *The Mirror and the Lamp.* New York: Oxford University Press, 1953.

Adorno, Theodore. *Mahler: A Musical Physiognomy.* Trans. Edmund Jephcott. Chicago: University of Chicago Press, 1992.

———. *Prisms.* Trans. Samuel and Shierry Weber. Cambridge, Mass.: MIT Press, 1982.

Bailey, Robert. *Richard Wagner: Prelude and Transfiguration from Tristan and Isolde.* New York: W.W. Norton, 1985.

———. "The Genesis of 'Tristan and Isolde' and a Study of Wagner's Sketches and Drafts for the First Act." Ph.D. diss., Princeton, 1968.

———. "The Method of Composition." In *The Wagner Companion,* ed. Peter Burbidge and Richard Sutton. New York: Cambridge University Press, 1979.

Bartels, Ulrich. *Studien zu Wagners Tristan und Isolde anhand der Kompositionsskizze des zweiten und dritten Aktes.* 3 vols. In *Musik und Musikanschauung im 19. Jahrhundert: Studien und Quellen,* ed. Detlef Altenburg. Köln: Studio, Verlag Schewe, 1991.

Barzun, Jacques. *Darwin, Marx, Wagner.* Revised 2nd. edition. Garden City, N.Y,: Doubleday, 1958.

Bauer-Lechner, Natalie. *Recollections of Gustav Mahler.* Trans. Dika Newlin, ed. and annotated by Peter Franklin. Cambridge: Cambridge University Press, 1980.

Bekker, Paul. *Richard Wagner: His Life in His Work.* Trans. M. M. Bozmen New York: W.W. Norton, 1931.

Benjamin, Walter. *The Origin of German Tragic Drama.* Trans. John Osborne. London: New Left Books, 1977.

Berg, Alban. *Letters to his Wife.* Trans. Bernard Grun. New York: St. Martin's Press, 1971.

Bernstein, David W. "Symmetry and Symmetrical Inversion in Turn-of-the-Century Theory and Practice." In *Music Theory and the Exploration of the Past,* ed. Christopher Hatch and David W. Bernstein. Chicago: University of Chicago Press, 1993.

Boretz, Benjamin. "Meta-variations, Part IV: Analytical Fallout (I)." *Perspectives of New Music* 11 (Fall/Winter 1972): 164–201.

Borchmeyer, Dieter, ed. *Richard Wagner: Dichtungen und Schriften.* 10 vols. Frankfurt am Main: Insel Verlag, 1983.

———. *Richard Wagner: Theory and Theatre.* Trans. Stewart Spencer. Oxford: Clarendon Press, 1991.

Bowie, Andrew. *Aesthetics and Subjectivity: From Kant to Nietzsche.* Manchester: Manchester University Press, 1990.

———. "German Idealism and the Arts." In *The Cambridge Companion to German Idealism* ed. Karl Ameriks. Cambridge: Cambridge University Press, 2000.

Brown, Calvin S. *Music and Literature: A Comparison of the Arts.* Hanover, N.H.: University Press of New England, 1987.

Brown, Matthew. "Isolde's Narrative: From *Hauptmotiv* to Tonal Model." In *Analyzing Opera: Verdi and Wagner,* ed. Carolyn Abbate and Roger Parker. Berkeley: University of California Press, 1989.

Burk, John, ed. *Letters of Richard Wagner: The Burrell Collection.* New York: Macmillan, 1950.

Burke, Edmund. *A Philosophical Enquiry into the Origin of Our Ideas of the Sublime and Beautiful.* Ed. James T. Boulton. London: Routledge & Kegan Paul, 1958. Reprint edition, Notre Dame, Indiana: University of Notre Dame Press, 1968.

Chafe, Eric. *Analyzing Bach Cantatas.* New York: Oxford University Press, 2000.

———. *Monteverdi's Tonal Language.* New York: Schirmer Books, 1992.

———. *Tonal Allegory in the Vocal Music of J. S. Bach.* Berkeley: University of California Press, 1991.

Charlton, David, ed. *E. T. A. Hoffmann's Musical Writings: Kreisleriana, The Poet and the Composer, Music Criticism.* Trans. Martyn Clarke. Cambridge: Cambridge University Press, 1989.

Closs, August, ed. *Tristan und Ísolt: A Poem by Gottfried von Strassburg.* Oxford: Basil Blackwell, 1974.

Dahlhaus, Carl. *Between Romanticism and Modernism: Four Studies in Music of the Later Nineteenth Century.* Trans. Mary Whithall. Berkeley: University of California Press, 1980.

———. *The Idea of Absolute Music.* Trans. Roger Lustig. Chicago: University of Chicago Press, 1989.

———. *Klassische und romantische Musikästhetik.* Laaber: Laaber-Verlag, 1988.

———. *Richard Wagner's Music Dramas,* Trans. Mary Whittall. Cambridge: Cambridge University Press.

———. *Schoenberg and the New Music.* Trans. Derrick Puffett and Alfred Clayton. Cambridge: Cambridge University Press, 1987.

———. *Wagners Konzeption des musikalischen Dramas.* Gustave Bosse Verlag: Regensburg, 1971.

———. "Wagner's 'Kunst des Übergangs: Der Zwiegesang in 'Tristan und Isolde.'" In *Vom Musikdrama zur Literaturoper.* Munich: Schott; Mainz: Piper, 1989.

Darcy, Warren. *Wagner's Das Rheingold.* New York: Oxford University Press, 1993.

Deathridge, John, et al. *Wagner Werk-Verzeichnis.* Mainz: Schott, 1986.

Desmond, William. *Art and the Absolute: A Study of Hegel's Aesthetics.* Albany: State University of New York Press, 1986.

Donington, Robert. *Wagner's "Ring" and Its Symbols.* London: Faber and Faber, 1963.

Ellis, William Ashton, trans. *Richard Wagner's Prose Works.* 8 vols. 1895–99. Reprint, Lincoln: University of Nebraska Press, 1995.

Everdell, William. *The First Moderns.* Chicago: University of Chicago Press, 1997.

Feuerbach, Ludwig. *Principles of the Philosophy of the Future* (1843). Trans. Manfred Vogel. Indianapolis: Hackett, 1986.

Fourquet, Jean. "Das Kryptogramm des 'Tristan' und der Aufbau des Epos." In *Gottfried von*

Strassburg: Wege der Forschung; ed. Alois Wolf. Darmstadt: Wissenschaftliche Buchgesellschaft, 1973.

Glass, Frank W. *The Fertilizing Seed: Wagner's Concept of the Poetic Intent.* Ann Arbor: UMI Research Press, 1983.

Gottfried von Strassburg. *Tristan.* Ed. and trans. A. T. Hatto. Harmondsworth: Penguin Books, 1967.

Gottfried von Strassburg. *Tristan und Isold.* Ed. Friedrich Ranke. 15th edition. Zürich: Weidmann, 1978.

Grey, Thomas. *Wagner's Musical Prose.* Berkeley: University of California Press, 1995.

Griepenkerl, R. W. *Das Musifest, oder die Beethovener.* 2nd edition. Braunschweig: Eduard Leibrock Verlag, 1841.

Grimm, Jacob, and Wilhelm Grimm. *Deutsches Wörterbuch.* 33 vols. Leipzig: S. Hirsel, 1922. Reprint, Munich: Deutsche Taschenbuch Verlag, 1999.

Groos, Arthur, and Roger Parker. "Appropriation in Wagner's *Tristan* Libretto." In *Reading Opera,* ed. Arthur Groos and Roger Parker. Princeton: Princeton University Press, 1983.

Guyer, Paul. "Absolute Idealism and the Rejection of Kantian Dualism." In *The Cambridge Companion to German Idealism,* ed. Karl Ameriks. Cambridge: Cambridge University Press, 2000.

Hagen, Friedrich H. von der. *Gottfried von Strassburg Werke aus den beßten Handschriften mit Einleitung und Wörterbuch.* 2 vols. Breslau: Josef Marx, 1823.

Harvey, Van A. *Feuerbach and the Interpretation of Religion.* Cambridge: Cambridge University Press, 1995.

Hauptmann, Moritz. *The Nature of Harmony and Metre* (1853). Trans. and ed. W. E. Heathcote (London, 1893). Reprint edition, New York: Da Capo Press, 1991.

Hegel, Georg Wilhelm Friedrich. *Aesthetics: Lectures on Fine Arts.* Trans. T. M. Knox. Oxford: Oxford University Press, 1975.

———. *The Encyclopaedia Logic.* Trans. T. F. Geraets, W. A. Suchting, and H. S. Harris. Indianapolis: Hackett, 1991.

Hoffmann, E. T. A. *E. T. A. Hoffmann's Musical Writings: Kreisleriana, The Poet and the Composer, Music Criticism.* Ed. David Charlton, trans. Martyn Clarke. Cambridge: Cambridge University Press, 1989.

Huber, Christoph. *Gottfried von Strassburg: Tristan.* Berlin: Erich Schmidt, 2000.

Hueffer, Francis, trans. *Correspondence of Wagner and Liszt.* 2nd. edition revised by W. Ashton Ellis. 2 vols. New York: Charles Scribner's Sons, 1897.

Jacobs, Robert, and Geoffrey Skelton, ed. and trans. *Wagner Writes from Paris . . . Stories, Essays and Articles by the Young Composer.* London: George Allen & Unwin, 1973.

Jackson, W. T. H. *The Anatomy of Love: The* Tristan *of Gottfried von Strassburg.* New York: Columbia University Press, 1971.

———. "Tristan the Artist in Gottfried's Poem." *PMLA* 71 (1962), pp. 364–72.

Jones, George F. *Honor in German Literature.* Chapel Hill: University of North Carolina Press, 1959.

Kant, Immanuel. *The Critique of Judgement.* Trans. J. H. Bernard. London: Macmillan, 1892. Reprint. Amherst, N.Y.: Prometheus Books, 2000.

———. *Observations on the Feeling of the Beautiful and Sublime* (1784). Trans. John T. Goldthwait. Berkeley: University of California Press, 1960.

Kerman, Joseph. *Opera as Drama.* New and revised edition. Berkeley: University of California Press, 1988.

Kolb, Herbert. "Der Minne Hus: Zur Allegorie der Minnegrotte in Gottfrieds Tristan." *Euphorion* 56 (1962): 229–47. Reprinted in *Gottfried von Straßburg: Wege der Forschung.* ed., Alois Wolf. Darmstadt: Wissenschaftliche Buchgesellschaft, 1973.

Kropfinger, Karl. *Wagner and Beethoven*. Trans. Peter Palmer. Cambridge: Cambridge University Press, 1991.

Kunzer, Ruth Goldschmidt. *The Tristan of Gottfried von Strassburg: An Ironic Perspective*. Berkeley: University of California Press, 1973.

Kurth, Ernst. *Romantische Harmonik und ihre Krise in Wagner's "Tristan und Isolde."* Reprint ed. Hildesheim: Georg Olms, 1968.

Kurtz, Hermann, trans. *Tristan und Isolde. Gedicht von Gottfried von Straßburg*. 2nd ed. Stuttgart: J.G. Cotta'schen Buchhandlung, 1847.

Langer, Suzanne. *Philosophy in a New Key*. Cambridge, Mass.: Harvard University Press, 1957.

Lockspeiser, Edward. *Debussy: His Life and Mind*. 4th ed. New York: McGraw-Hill, 1972.

Lorenz, Alfred Ottokar. *Das Geheimnis der Form bei Richard Wagner*. Vol. 2, *Der Musikalische Aufbau von Richard Wagners "Tristan und Isolde."* Berlin: M. Hesse, 1924.

Magee, Bryan. *The Philosophy of Schopenhauer*. Oxford: Clarendon Press, 1983.

———. *Wagner and Philosophy*. London: Allen Lane, 2000.

Mahler-Werfel, Alma. *Diaries: 1898–1902*. Trans. Antony Beaumont. Ithaca: Cornell University Press, 1999.

Mann, Thomas. *Pro and Contra Wagner*. Trans. Allan Blunden. London: Faber and Faber, 1985.

Massmann, Hans F. *Tristan und Isolt von Gottfried von Strassburg. Dichtungen des deutschen Mittelalters, vol. 2*. Leipzig: G.J. Göschen'sche Verlagshandlung, 1843.

Mayer, Hans. "Tristans Schweigen." In *Richard Wagner: Tristan und Isolde*, ed. Attila Csampai and Dietmar Holland. Reinbeck bei Hamburg: Rowohlt Taschenbuch Verlag, 1983.

Mayrberger, Karl. "The Harmonic Style of Richard Wagner, Elucidated with Respect to the Leitmotifs of 'Tristan and Isolde'" (1881). In *Music Analysis in the Nineteenth Century*, ed. Ian Bent. Vol. 1. Cambridge: Cambridge University Press, 1994.

Mertens, Volker. "Wagner's Middle Ages." In *Wagner Handbook*, ed. Ulrich Mueller and Peter Wapenewski, trans. John Deathridge. Cambridge, Mass.: Harvard University Press, 1992.

Mitchell, William J. "The *Tristan* Prelude: Techniques and Structure." *Music Forum* 1 (1967): 163–203.

Morgan, Robert. "Circular Form in the *Tristan* Prelude." *Journal of the American Musicological Society* 53, no.1 (Spring 2000): 69–103.

———. "Dissonant Prolongation: Theoretical and Compositional Precedents." *Journal of Music Theory* 20, no. 1 (Spring 1976): 49–91.

Müller, Carl Friedrich. *Tristan und Isolde nach Sage und Dichtung. Ein Skizzenbild. Zur Einführung in das Drama Richard Wagner's*. Munich: Christian Kaiser, 1865.

Müller, Ulrich and Peter Wapnewski, eds. *The Wagner Companion*. Trans. John Deathridge. Cambridge, Mass.: Harvard University Press, 1992.

Neubauer, John. *The Emancipation of Music from Language*. New Haven: Yale University Press, 1986.

Newcombe, Anthony. "*Ritornello Ritornato*: A Variety of Wagnerian Refrain Form." In *Analyzing Opera*, ed. Carolyn Abbate and Roger Parker. Berkeley: University of California Press, 1989.

———. "The Birth of Music out of the Spirit of Drama: An Essay on Wagnerian Formal Analysis." *19th Century Music* 5, no. 1 (Summer 1981): 36–66.

Nietzsche, Friedrich. *The Birth of Tragedy and the Case of Wagner*. Trans. Walter Kaufmann. New York: Random House, 1967.

———. "Richard Wagner in Bayreuth" (1876). In *Untimely Meditations*, trans. R. J. Hollingdale. Cambridge: Cambridge University Press, 1983.

Novalis (Friedrich von Hardenburg). *Schriften*. 4 vols. Ed. Richard Samuel. Stuttgurt: W. Kohlhammer Verlag, 1960.

Perle, George. *The Operas of Alban Berg. Volume Two: Lulu.* Berkeley: University of California Press, 1985.

Picozzi, Rosemary. *A History of Tristan Scholarship.* Berne: Hervert, 1971.

Pleasants, Henry, trans. and ed. *Hanslick's Music Criticisms.* New York: Dover, 1950.

Porges, Heinrich. *Tristan und Isolde.* Ed. Hans von Wolzogen. Leipzig: Breitkopf & Härtel, 1906.

Prüfer, Arthur. "Novalis Hymnen an die Nacht in ihrer Beziehungen zu Wagners Tristan und Isolde." *Richard Wagner-Jahrbuch* 1 (1906): 290–304.

———. "Über die Entwicklung des Wahnbegriffs von Herder bis Wagner." *Richard Wagner Jahrbuch* 2 (1907): 290–304.

Ranke, Friedrich, ed. *Gottfried von Straßburg. Tristan und Isolde,* 15th ed. Zürich: Weidmann, 1978.

———. "Die Allegorie der Minnegrotte in Gottfrieds Tristan" (1925). Reprinted in *Gottfried von Straßburg: Wege der Forschung,* ed. Alois Wolf. Darmstadt: Wissenschaftliche Buchgesellschaft, 1973.

Rather, L. J. *The Dream of Self-destruction.* Baton Rouge: Louisiana State University Press, 1979.

———. *Reading Wagner: A Study in the History of Ideas.* Baton Rouge: Louisiana State University Press, 1990.

Rawidowicz, Simon. *Ludwig Feuerbachs Philosophie: Ursprung und Schicksal.* Berlin: Reuther & Richard, 1931.

Reik, Theodor. *The Haunting Melody: Psychoanalytic Experiences in Life and Music.* New York: Grove Press, 1953.

Rougement, Denis de. *Love in the Western World.* Trans. Montgomery Belgion. Princeton: Princeton University Press, 1983.

Sans, Edouard. *Richard Wagner et la pensée Schopenhauerienne.* Paris: Klinksieck, 1969.

Schelling, F. W. J. *The Philosophy of Art.* Ed. and trans. Peter Heath. Charlottesville: University of Virginia Press, 1978.

———. *System of Transcendental Idealism.* Trans. Peter Heath. Charlottesville: University of Virginia Press, 1978.

Schlegel, Friedrich. *Transcendentalphilosophie.* Ed. Michael Elsässer. Hamburg: Felix Meiner Verlag, 1991.

Schleiermacher, Friedrich Daniel Ernst. *Äesthetik (1819/25); Über den Begriff der Kunst (1831/32).* Ed. Thomas Lahnerer. Hamburg: Felix Meiner Verlag, 1984.

———. *Hermeneutics and Criticism and Other Writings.* Ed. and trans. Andrew Bowie. Cambridge: Cambridge University Press, 1998.

Schlösser, Louis. "Ein Besuch bei Richard Wagner in Paris." *Allgemeine Musik-Zeitung* 12, no. 21 (May 22, 1885): 191–92.

Scholte, Hendrik. "Gottfrieds von Straßburg Initialenspiel." *Beiträge zur Geschichte der deutschen Sprache und Literatur* 65 (1942): 280–302. Reprinted in *Gottfried von Straßburg. Wege der Forschung* 320, ed. Alois Wolf. Darmstadt: Wissenschaftliche Buchgesellschaft, 1973.

Schönberg, Arnold. "Brahms the Progressive." In *Style and Idea,* ed. Leonard Stein, trans. Leo Black. Berkeley: University of California Press, 1975.

———. "Criteria for the Evaluation of Music." In *Style and Idea,* ed. Leonard Stein, trans. Leo Black. Berkeley: University of California Press, 1975.

———. *Harmonielehre.* Vienna: Universal-Edition, 1911.

———. *Structural Functions of Harmony,* revised edition. Ed. Leonard Stein. New York: Norton, 1969.

———. *Theory of Harmony.* Trans. Roy E. Carter. Berkeley: University of California Press, 1978.

Schöne, Albrecht. "Zu Gottfrieds 'Tristan'-Prolog." *Deutsche Viertelhandsschrift für Literaturwissenschaft und Geistesgeschichte* 29 (1955): 447–74. Reprinted in *Gottfried von Straßburg: Wege der Forschung* 320, ed. Alois Wolf. Darmstadt: Wissenschaftliche Buchgesselschaft, 1973.

Schopenhauer, Arthur. *Der Briefwechsel mit Goethe und andere Dokumente zur Farbenlehre.* Ed. Ludger Lütkehaus. Zürich: Haffmans, 1992.

———. *The Four-fold Root of the Principle of Sufficient Reason.* Trans. E. F. J. Payne. LaSalle, Ill.: Open Court, 1974.

———. *On the Basis of Morality.* Trans. E. F. J. Payne. Providence: Berghahn Books, 1995.

———. *Parerga and Paralipomena.* Trans. E. F. J. Payne. Oxford: Oxford University Press, 1974.

———. *Arthur Schopenhauer: Sämtliche Werke. Vol. 5, Parerga und Paralipomena I.* Ed. Arthur Hübscher. Wiesbaden: Brockhaus, 1996.

———. *The Word as Will and Representation.* Trans. E. F. J. Payne. New York: Dover, 1969.

Scruton, Roger. *Death-Devoted Heart: Sex and the Sacred in Wagner's Tristan and Isolde.* New York: Oxford University Press, 2004.

Shaw, George Bernard. *The Perfect Wagnerite.* New York: Dover, 1967.

Simrock, Karl, trans. *Tristan und Isolde von Gottfried von Strassburg.* Leipzig: Brockhaus, 1855.

———. *Die Quellen des Shakspeare in Novellen, Märchen und Sagen, mit sagensgeschichtlichen Nachweisungen,* Bonn: A. Marcus, 1870.

Spencer, Stewart, and Barry Millington, trans. and ed. *Selected Letters of Richard Wagner.* New York: W.W. Norton, 1987.

Stevens, Adrian, and Roy Wisbey, eds. *Gottfried von Strassburg and the Medieval Tristan Legend.* Cambridge: D. S. Brewer and London: The Institute of Germanic Studies, 1990.

Stravinsky, Igor. *Poetics of Music.* Translated by Arthur Knodel and Ingolf Dahl. New York: Vintage Books, 1956.

Tax, Petrus W. "Wounds and Healings: Aspects of Salvation and Tragic Love in Gottfried's *Tristan.*" In *Gottfried von Strassburg and the Medieval Tristan Legend,* ed. Adrian Stevens and Roy Wisbey, 223–34. Cambridge: D.S. Brewer and London: The Institute of Germanic Studies, 1990.

Urmoneit, Sebastian. "Untersuchungen zu den beiden 'Todesmotiven' aus *Tristan und Isolde.*" *Musik-Konzepte* 57/58 (November 1987): 104–17.

Vogel, Martin. *Orpheus-Schriftenreihe zu Grundfragen der Musik. Vol. 2, Der Tristan-Akkord und die Krise der modernen Harmonie-Lehre.* Düsseldorf: Gesellschaft zur Förderung der systematischen Musikwissenschaft, 1962.

Wackenroder, Wilhelm Heinrich, and Ludwig Tieck. *Confessions and Fantasies.* Trans. Mary Hurst Schubert. University Park: Pennsylvania State University Press, 1971.

———. *Phantasien über die Kunst* (1799). Ed. Wolfgang Nehring. Stuttgart: Philipp Reclam, 1973.

Wagner, Cosima. *Cosima Wagner's Diaries.* Ed. Martin Gregor-Dellin and Dietrich Mack, trans. Geoffrey Skelton. New York: Harcourt Jovanovich, 1980.

Wagner, Richard. *Beethoven* (1870). Trans. Albert Parsons. Boston: Lee & Shepard, 1872.

———. *The Diary of Richard Wagner: The Brown Book: 1865–1882.* Trans. George Bird, ed. Joachim Bergfeld. Cambridge: Cambridge University Press, 1980.

———. *Gesammelte Schriften.* Ed. Julius Kapp. 14 vols. Leipzig: Hesse & Becker, 1914.

———. "Music of the Future." In *Three Wagner Essays.* Trans. Robert L. Jacobs. London: Eulenburg Books, 1979.

———. *My Life.* Trans. Andrew Gray. Ed. Mary Whittall. Cambridge: Cambridge University Press, 1983.

———. *Prelude and Transfiguration from* Tristan and Isolde. Ed. Robert Bailey New York: W.W. Norton, 1985.

———. *Richard Wagner's Prose Works*. Trans. William Ashton Ellis. 8 vols. 1895–99. Reprint, Lincoln: University of Nebraska Press, 1995.

———. *Richard Wagner an Mathilde Wesendonck: Tagebuchblatter und Briefe, 1853-1871*. Vol. 3. Ed. Wolfgang Krebs. Frankfurter Zeitschrift für Musikwissenschaft, 2000.

———. *Stories and Essays*. Ed. Charles Osborne. London: Owen, 1973.

———. *Three Wagner Essays*. Trans. Robert L. Jacobs. London: Eulenburg Books, 1979.

Walzel, Oskar. *German Romanticism*. Trans. Alma Elise Lussky. New York: Capricorn Books, 1966.

Wapnewski, Peter. *Der Traurige Gott: Richard Wagner in seinen Helden*. 2nd ed. Munich: C.H. Beck, 1980.

———. *Tristan der Held Richard Wagners*. Berlin: Severin und Siedler, 1981.

Wartofsky, Marx W. *Feuerbach*. Cambridge: Cambridge University Press, 1977.

Weber, Gottfried. *Gottfried von Strassburg: Tristan: Text, Nacherzählung, Wort- und Begriffs-erklärungen*. Darmstadt: Wissenschaftliche Buchgesellschaft, 1967.

Wehrle, Max. "Der Tristan Gottfrieds von Strassburg." *Trivium* 4 (1946): 81–117.

Werckmeister, Andreas. *Musicae mathematicae hodegus curiosus oder, Richtiger musicalischer Weg-weiser*. Franckfurt: T. P. Calvisius, 1696.

Westernhagen, Curt von. *Richard Wagners Dresdener Bibliothek: 1842–1849*. Wiesbaden: Brockhaus, 1966.

Wilson, H. B. "*Senen* und *triuwe*: Gottfried's unfinished *Tristan*." In *Gottfried von Strassburg and the Medieval Tristan Legend,* ed. Adrian Stevens and Roy Wisbey. Cambridge: D. S. Brewer and London: The Institute of Germanic Studies, 1990.

Wolfram von Eschenbach. *Parzival*. Trans. A. T. Hatto. Hammondsworth: Penguin Books, 1980.

Index

328   Index

Printed in the United States
135378LV00002B/99/P

2614390R00185

Printed in Great Britain
by Amazon.co.uk, Ltd.,
Marston Gate.